Routledge Revivals

The Therapeutic Community

First published in 1980, *The Therapeutic Community* surveys and discusses international developments and deficiencies in the therapeutic community field during the two decades since 1959, with the intention of providing a stimulus for change. It is based on the direct experience of Richmond Fellowship and draws on that experience amongst others to clarify therapeutic community philosophies and practice.

The intention of the Mental Health Act 1959 (UK) and of similar legislation elsewhere was not simply to rescue people from institutions but to initiate new and more effective forms of help. The book explores nature of the problems at that time, the recommended measures, the available resources, what was actually provided, and what impact was made on the problem. More specifically, it considers therapeutic community within government thinking and policy-making, and the consequent developments from these policies.

The contributions focus on the role of therapeutic community and represent the views and experience of those closely involved in this field, both professional and governmental, as well as helping to identify the particular contribution which the therapeutic community was able to make, in order to promote its full-scale development as part of mental health services.

The Therapeutic Community

Outside the Hospital

Edited by Elly Jansen

Routledge
Taylor & Francis Group

First published in 1980
by Croom Helm Ltd

This edition first published in 2026 by Routledge
4 Park Square, Milton Park, Abingdon, Oxon, OX14 4RN

and by Routledge
605 Third Avenue, New York, NY 10158

Routledge is an imprint of the Taylor & Francis Group, an informa business

Publisher's Note
The publisher has gone to great lengths to ensure the quality of this reprint but points out that some imperfections in the original copies may be apparent.

Disclaimer
The publisher has made every effort to trace copyright holders and welcomes correspondence from those they have been unable to contact.

For Product Safety Concerns and Information please contact our EU representative GPSR@taylorandfrancis.com. Taylor & Francis Verlag GmbH, Kaufingerstraße 24, 80331 München, Germany

A Library of Congress record exists under LCCN: 80514482

ISBN: 978-1-041-43885-4 (hbk)
ISBN: 978-1-042-03531-1 (ebk)
ISBN: 978-1-041-43891-5 (pbk)

Book DOI 10.4324/9781042035311

The Therapeutic Community

OUTSIDE THE HOSPITAL

Edited by ELLY JANSEN

CROOM HELM LONDON

Croom Helm Ltd, 2-10 St John's Road, London SW11

British Library Cataloguing in Publication Data

The therapeutic community.
1. Therapeutic community – Addresses, essays, lectures
I. Jansen, Elly II. Richmond Fellowship
362.2'0425 RC489.T67

ISBN 0-85664-967-8
ISBN 0-7099-0359-6 Pbk

Printed in Great Britain by
Biddles Ltd, Guildford, Surrey

CONTENTS

PREFACE

This book is the product of disquiet; it is presented with the intention of providing a stimulus for change.

The Richmond Fellowship was engendered in England in 1959, in the climate of the new policies formulated in the Mental Health Act; the subsequent development both of the Fellowship, and of government action for mental health, have proceeded side by side – and sometimes in step! In the same period a similar evolution of thinking and policy has taken place in other industrialised countries, in the context of slowly changing attitudes towards the mentally disturbed. In the words of the Royal Commission which preceded the British legislation: 'Patients should not be retained as hospital in-patients when they have reached the stage at which they could return home, if they had reasonably good homes to go to.' The experiences, thinking and ideals which lie behind this modest statement have been fully documented in many publications, and are referred to in several of the chapters contained in this book. It is important however to note that the statement did not represent simply a humane response to the negative effects of institutionalisation. It was also an attempt to initiate new and more effective forms of help, in the light of the then newly emerging views on the nature of mental illness (the debate on which is still very far from being resolved). As a result of the developments in social psychiatry and group therapy following the Second World War, not only the medical approach but also the psychodynamic approach to individual pathology was being questioned: the person was coming to be viewed as a participant in a social context, engaged in a continual process of relating and adapting. It was recognised that progress could be influenced by the design of a therapeutic environment, and that 'environment' primarily consists of other people.

The two decades since 1959 have therefore been a period of re-thinking and of opportunity, but also of great uncertainty and more recently of harsh financial constraints which have greatly modified government intentions. The implications for an innovative voluntary organisation correspond precisely with those political realities: opportunity, uncertainty and financial hardship. For the Richmond Fellowship, relations with government, and the ongoing debate on allocation of resources, have always been a fact of life – not inappropriately, perhaps, for an organisation which concerns itself with issues of relationships. At times the input involved has seemed excessive; to quote the Red Queen in *Alice Through the Looking Glass*,

> here . . . it takes all the running you can do, to stay in the same place. If you want to get somewhere else, you must run at least twice as fast as that!

But the effort has borne fruit, in the amassing of a detailed first-hand knowledge of the problems of transforming policy into practice; this the Fellowship has been glad to share and to use for the advancement of the therapeutic community movement in the wider international context.

The more generally recognised task of the therapeutic community is to foster 'therapeutic' relationships which will enable mentally disturbed people to become more whole, and to live a maximally independent, rewarding and contented life. As a form of help the therapeutic community demands great commitment and an unusual combination of personal qualities and expertise amongst staff; in addition, it has to operate in a society which still has many reservations about its basic tenets. A criticism which is often levelled at 'alternative' modes of social interaction is that they cannot be transferred from the community to the 'normal' world; Rapoport,[1] for instance, comments that the open expression of negative feeling is prognostic of good adjustment to the treatment unit, but of poor adjustment after leaving. If this stricture is merited it has grave consequences for the future of the therapeutic community, which aims to provide, as well as 'therapy', a transition to maximally independent life. In the experience of the Richmond Fellowship, however, the therapeutic community in the non-medical setting is able to face just this challenge: that is, it can enable the resident to become more open in his relations with others, and concurrently to acquire social competence and sensitivity, so that he is assisted in integration with society. It has also been found that the therapeutic community, in interaction with the neighbourhood, is capable not only of receiving but also of offering benefits, in the form of facilitating a better understanding of and communication with others.

If the therapeutic community sets out to become such a model, the leadership of staff will be essential in determining its success or failure. Techniques of communication and interaction are developed as a tool for staff, and are essential in order that staff may develop competence and confidence. Primary emphasis however must be placed on the qualities which enable staff to respect, validate and cherish residents (and colleagues) as whole people and to create a therapeutic community which reflects this. The non-medical milieu is no doubt helpful in avoiding the labelling process which depersonalises the 'patient'; ultimately, however, a personal attitude is required which perceives and is concerned for the whole person. The ability to value others, and at the same time to relate honestly, is not a therapeutic tool only, but can be transferred into the ordinary social context where it rightfully belongs and indeed occasionally flourishes. Greater awareness within society of the factors leading to wholeness or to personal and social dysfunctioning needs to be fostered if there is to be a reversal of the 'state of bankruptcy' prevailing in industrialised countries, not only regarding financial resources to combat emotional disorder, but also their corollary: personal and emotional resources. Could it be that the 'lack of concern', so universally portrayed, has less to do with stigma, fear, indifference or miserliness than with people's sense of their own deprivation and need for rescue?

My own heart let me more have pity on; let
Me live to my sad self hereafter kind,
Charitable; not live this tormented mind
With this tormented mind tormenting yet.
I cast for comfort I can no more get
By groping round my comfortless, than blind
Eyes in their dark can day or thirst can find
Thirst's all-in-all in all a world of wet.
(Gerard Manley Hopkins, 'Carrion Comfort')

Whilst the background of this book is human suffering, its aim is to address the issues in practical terms. It is based on the direct experience of the Richmond Fellowship, and hence draws extensively on that experience in an attempt to clarify therapeutic community philosophies and practice. However, the book has wider terms of reference than the experiences of one organisation, and some comments on its form and purpose may here be in order.

It has already been stated that the intention of the Mental Health Act 1959 was not simply to rescue people from institutions, but to initiate new and more effective forms of help. It is therefore relevant for the purpose of this book to ask, what was the nature of the problem at that time, what measures were recommended, what resources were made available, what has actually been provided, and what impact has been made on the problem? More specifically, what place has the therapeutic community established in government thinking and policy-making, and what developments have taken place as a result of, and sometimes despite, those policies?

It is felt that the discussion of these issues will provide a relevant context for the papers, most of which were first presented at the International Conferences convened by the Richmond Fellowship in 1973, 1975 and 1976. They focus on the role of the therapeutic community, and represent the views and experience of those closely involved in this field, both professional and governmental. The purpose of the conferences was to enable those engaged in the work to extend their knowledge of developments and methods, to share ideas and clarify problems, and also to identify the particular contribution which the therapeutic community is able to make, in order to promote its full-scale development as part of mental health services. It is hoped that this book will fulfil the same purpose for a wider audience.

Note

1. R.N. Rapoport, *Community as Doctor* (Tavistock Publications, London, 1960).

ACKNOWLEDGEMENTS

The editor acknowledges with gratitude the valuable participation of George Whitehouse in the research for this book; also the considerable assistance with drafting and editing given by Alison Terrington. Thanks are also due to Tony Moore for his contribution to the section on legislation in England and Wales, and to Diana Birkett and Ryder Whalley for their contribution.

Dr Robert Gosling read and commented on the manuscript and his help was much appreciated. Valuable co-operation was received from the staff of St Charles House and Amadeus House and from residents and ex-residents of the Richmond Fellowship. Paula Bateson undertook the major task of typing and retyping manuscript; her professional competence was invaluable.

Gratitude is due to the German Marshall Memorial Fund who sponsored a survey of government approaches to deinstitutionalisation of the mentally ill and the provision of community alternatives in industrialised countries. Without the generous award given by the Fund for this purpose much of the material for this book could not have been obtained. The Gatsby Charitable Foundation also gave financial assistance for travel in connection with the survey, which was a necessary preliminary for Richmond Fellowship developments ahead. The Council of the Fellowship have ever given moral support and provided financial aid necessary to give birth to this book.

INTRODUCTION

It is not within the scope or purpose of this book to give more than a cursory account of historical developments, although Chapters 1, 2 and 19 contain references. The history of mental health care in Britain has been covered extensively by other writers: see, for instance, *A History of the Mental Health Services* by Kathleen Jones. A comprehensive survey of the present situation in the United States is contained in the report to Congress by the Comptroller General of the United States, published January 1977 and entitled 'Returning the Mentally Disabled to the Community: Government Needs to do More.'

The following brief comments are intended simply to draw attention to the antecedents of the present-day situation.

The large mental hospitals established in the late eighteenth and nineteenth centuries are the inheritance on which current dilemmas are focused. Bricks and mortar are, however, not only physical obstacles to innovation, but are also the outward and visible sign of long-standing and deeply felt attitudes towards the care of the mentally disturbed, and towards theories of mental disturbance. The 'single lunatic' chained beneath the stairs in the family home aroused as much fear and inhumanity as did the lunatics herded into the asylum.

The status of psychiatry has reflected the ambivalence towards enlightened care of the disturbed. Although medically qualified, the superintendents of asylums were seen largely as managers, and were not able to progress to consultant status. The first nationally qualifying training in psychiatry was not introduced until 1911, when three universities established courses leading to the Diploma of Psychological Medicine. (The General Nursing Council set up its course leading to the Mental Nursing Certificate in 1921.) Up to the late nineteenth century the clinical treatments available were limited largely to blood-letting and purging; those doctors who were not content with primitive physical treatments and custodial duties turned to social measures. 1796 saw the establishment of the York Retreat, under the leadership of the Quaker, William Tuke. Tuke introduced the abolition of mechanical restraints and employed the 'moral', or humane, treatment advocated and practiced by Pinel. This philosophy was shortly to be carried to the United States, despite the prevailing problems in trans-atlantic communication, and a number of small hospitals were founded there on the same basis. In 1841 Dorothea Dix started a national campaign in the States to provide widespread hospital facilities for the mentally ill, who were at that time inappropriately treated by imprisonment; and in 1845 she extended her campaign to England and Scotland.

For some decades, the asylum population remained small enough for the medical officers to exercise a direct personal influence on the management of their patients, and this was by no means confined to their clinical role: the setting was favourable to one of the elements of the therapeutic community, face-to-face encounter. The tradition of social therapy was able to continue into the mid-nineteenth century, despite the growth of the asylum population: Dr D.F. Tyerman, who took up his post in 1852 as one of the medical officers of Colney Hatch Asylum (now Friern Hospital), was a keen cricketer and provided a pitch in the hospital grounds where the patients were encouraged to play with bat, hard ball and stumps: in good English tradition, he attributed the recovery of a suicidal patient to delight in the game.[1]

During the second half of the nineteenth century, however, historical developments were to divorce medical staff from their closer personal involvement with the daily routine of their patients. Institutional care was seen as the most humane and appropriate form of care; but the establishment of new asylums did not keep pace with the escalation in the numbers of the hospital population. Colney Hatch, established in 1851 to take 1,250 patients, was gradually enlarged to take 2,000, and by 1937 it housed nearly 2,700.[2] Lancaster Asylum was established in 1816 to take 170 patients, and had reached 600 by 1852. Hanwell, established to take 1,000 patients, saw an increase to nearly twice that number by 1877. The total number of patients in asylums in England and Wales rose from 7,140 in 1850 to 74,004 in 1900 (representing a rise of over 500 per cent relative to the population increase); the average number of patients per asylum for those years rose from 297 to 961.[3]

The need to control large numbers of patients with insufficient staff, allied to the development of medical technology and the need of psychiatry for recognition as a clinical discipline, contributed to reliance on physical treatment as the primary tool of psychiatry, to the neglect of social and psychological measures. In addition, as Kathleen Jones has pointed out, the Lunacy Act of 1890 promoted the custodial role of the asylums by its legalistic framework. 'Asylums could only take certified patients; and patients could not be certified until the illness had reached a stage where it was obvious to a lay authority – the J.P. (Justice of the Peace). This made it impossible for the asylums to deal with early diagnosis and the treatment of most mild or acute cases. Their work thus became largely custodial.' For decades the treatment of psychosis and of neurosis was therefore to be split, the former taking place under compulsion, in large institutions, and the latter in the completely different milieu of the analyst's consulting room. Cross-fertilisation of ideas and experience arising from treatment of the different diagnostic groups was consequently severely restricted until after 1930, when it again became possible to admit patients on a voluntary basis (the Mental Treatment Act 1930).

Historical developments, in addition, exacerbated the belief that physical distance was to be preserved between the mentally disturbed and the general population. At one period, to be sure, the care of the insane was allied to the care of the poor and was contained within the parish. When separate provision began to be made, this was as often as not a part of general medical facilities in towns. 'The earliest asylums, as the lunatic hospitals and private madhouses before them, were built in towns, and were small: and when they soon began to move further out this was in response to the by now fashionable belief in the value of good fresh air.'[4] Yet the result of this isolation was to increase the fears and phantasies attaching to the insane, and to reinforce the suspicion that segregation was necessary. Enlightened medical officers encouraged links with the community by means of visits home, open days and excursions into the neighbourhood; but irrational fears eroded these individual initiatives, and the battle to overcome resistance to care in the community is still being fought today.

It was during the Second World War that changes were initiated which were increasingly felt to be necessary. New methods were fostered through the recognition, initially in the Forces, that psychopathology was related to stressful environments, deficient group leadership and low morale, and that so-called sick people could be helped to look at and change their behaviour. The positive value of the social milieu was indicated, and a new avenue of enquiry opened up, through which the depersonalising social systems of hospitals were in some cases altered to become one of the tools of therapy. The philosophy and methods of social psychiatry began to be developed by Dr Tom Main at Northfield Mental Hospital and Dr Maxwell Jones at Belmont; concurrently W.R. Bion and Dr S.H. Foulkes were prominent in exploring group methods of psychoanalysis. Developments in Britain were studied by visitors from the States and introduced there – notably by Karl Menninger and his colleagues.

The concept of the 'therapeutic community' began to be defined. In 1946 Dr Main became Director of the Cassel Hospital in Richmond, Surrey, and in 1947 the experiment at Belmont (later Henderson Hospital) attracted administrative support so that its survival was assured. Ten years later Dr Dennis Martin at Claybury was able to extend methods developed in a relatively self-contained neurosis unit to the whole hospital, albeit with initial difficulties: 'The first reaction was one of very considerable hostility and the rapid spread of phantasies of various kinds. Fears that the patients would soon be running the hospital, and that nurses would lose all respect and authority, were fairly widespread . . . This mixture of anxiety and hostility persisted for months and died out gradually'.[5] Analytical theories of individual development, stagnation and regression, applied by these pioneers, were generally meeting with increasing acceptance, both within the field of psychiatric expertise and amongst others concerned with helping disturbed people.

The Community Care Movement and Central Government

Developments in psychiatric theory have over the last three decades offered support to a community-based rather than institutional model of care for the mentally disturbed; a model which has been congruent also with the growth in grass-roots participation in local and national affairs. In the field of mental health, as in other areas of need formerly served by institutions, governments, particularly in the United States and the United Kingdom, have been able to utilise private initiatives and social trends in order to review and alter legislation. In 1955 the US Congress established the Joint Commission on Mental Illness and Health with a mandate to study mental illness and to make recommendations for a national mental health programme. In the UK, in 1954, the Royal Commission on the Law relating to Mental Illness and Mental Deficiency had been set up 'to inquire as regards England and Wales into the existing law governing . . . persons who are or are alleged to be suffering from mental illness or mental defect . . . to consider . . . the extent to which it is now or should be made, statutorily possible for such persons to be treated, as voluntary patients, without certification; and to make recommendations'. The recommendations, when they appeared in 1957, were as much concerned with returning the patient to the community as with hospital reform: 'In relation to almost all forms of mental disorder, there is increasing medical emphasis on forms of treatment and training and social services which can be given without bringing patients into hospital as in-patients, or which make it possible to discharge them from hospital sooner than was usual in the past . . . For those who cannot live with their own relatives it is considered more appropriate to provide residential homes in towns and villages, with as many as possible of the residents working in normal employment and the others having suitable occupation either in the homes or hostels themselves, or in some form of sheltered employment or occupation centres'.[6] The Mental Health Act 1959 empowered local authorities to make residential provision, and the power was converted into a statutory duty through the Health Services and Public Health Act 1968, and later consolidated in the National Health Service Act 1977.

In the States the Report of the Joint Commission was published in 1960. As in the UK, its main recommendation was that mental health care should be provided within the community. The recommendation was to be implemented by setting up regional centres with a maximum of 1,000 beds, and emergency psychiatric services which were also to be community-based. A broad range of rehabilitative services was envisaged, covering prevention, treatment and after-care. The programme was to be established through massive federal funding, and would comply with standards set and maintained at federal level. (For a more detailed account see Chapter 19.) The report led in 1963 to the Community Mental Health Centers Act.

The stage was set both in the UK and the States for a major reorientation in mental health care; the reality has been a major reduction in the mental hospital population, unaccompanied by a corresponding increase in community resources.

Notes

1. R. Hunter and I. MacAlpine, *Psychiatry for the Poor: 1851 Colney Hatch Asylum – Friern Hospital, 1973* (Dawsons, London, 1974).
2. Ibid.
3. K. Jones, *A History of the Mental Health Services* (Routledge and Kegan Paul, London, 1972), p. 337.
4. P. Allderidge, 'Hospitals, Madhouses and Asylums: Cycles in the Care of the Insane', *British Journal of Psychiatry* (April 1979).
5. D.V. Martin, 'Problems in Developing a Community Approach to Mental Hospital Treatment', *British Journal of Psychiatric Social Work*, vol. 5, no. 2 (1959).
6. Report of the Royal Commission on the Law relating to Mental Illness and Mental Deficiency 1957, HMSO, Cmd. 169, para. 601.

Part One

THEORY AND MODELS OF THE THERAPEUTIC COMMUNITY

Who shall decide when doctors disagree?

Alexander Pope, Moral Essays

EDITOR'S DISCUSSION

The failure of legislation and government directives is attributable to two major weaknesses: *first, that governments have been insufficiently detailed and specific in their proposals, and second, that they have failed to enable and enforce implementation*. The first problem is discussed here; the second is the central issue of Part Three.

Antecedents of the Therapeutic Community

The failure of governments to issue sufficiently detailed plans is not surprising, when it is considered that experience of working with the mentally disturbed derives almost exclusively from the medical environment: seen in terms of a *health problem*, there have been few precedents for mental disturbance to be addressed in the community. The *residential facility* suffers similarly from a lack of suitable models. Historically, most of our experience in providing residential care has been garnered from institutions with a largely custodial function: asylums, prisons, children's and old people's homes. All of the existing models exemplify situations in which the resident has little freedom to choose, either to join or to leave; nor is his participation usually such as to further his own individuality and creativity. What are we doing, planning yet more establishments which may foster conformity to institutional norms?

However, when mental disturbance is viewed in terms of *problems in relationships*, it becomes apparent that there are indeed precedents for the non-medical therapeutic community. Shoenberg (Chapter 2) refers to the long history of communities, religious, political and psychological, which have attempted to provide solutions to human problems. In every context, the healing factor has been the ideal of brotherly love, or caring through relationship. A contemporary manifestation of the caring community is the commune, evolved in an era which is sensitive to the emotional and economic vulnerability of the individual, and in a climate of renewed interest in communal activity as a means of revitalising society. The commune movement has demonstrated that groups can exist which do not bear the stigma of compulsory membership or of authoritarian management.

Nor have the professional carers themselves been entirely blind to the therapeutic potential of community care and humanitarian values. As was stated previously, enlightened doctors have always pursued the aim of reintegration of the patient into society. In addition, a few projects have struggled to keep the torch burning in an unpromising climate of opinion, the best known perhaps being the Mental After Care Association. This organisation was set up in the UK in 1879 by the chaplain of Colney Hatch Asylum to provide residential aftercare and assistance to individuals. At that time a therapeutic community approach had not been introduced, and the population catered for was mainly chronic schizophrenic; the residential facilities reflected this, and were largely benevolently 'management' orientated. It was not until the Second World War that the contribution of voluntary agencies working in the community began to be accorded greater recognition, resulting in 1946 in the amalgamation of three of the major British organisations into the National Association of Mental Health. Traditional ways of thinking about mental disturbance began to be called in question, until by the time of the Mental Health Act 1959, 'the accumulating knowledge of the social sciences, particularly of sociology, began to permeate a sphere which had been inexorably and exclusively medical for over a century'.[1] The problem was to transform theoretical frameworks into workable models and to provide means of implementation; and here little help was forthcoming, particularly in the field of residential care. 'There was a good deal of confusion – partly because there was no central guidance and partly because different authorities saw hostels as being the panacea for their own particular problems . . . A number of authorities became somewhat disillusioned with hostels when their first hopes of rapid turnover or limited costs were dashed. Good hostels did not turn out to be a cheap form of care.'[2]

The Richmond Fellowship Project

In this climate of nebulous expectations, confusion and lack of guidance, it was possible for a private individual to take initiatives which were unthinkable for formalised authorities. A number of accounts have been given of the origins of the Richmond Fellowship (see Chapter 25); what can never be adequately conveyed is the temerity of launching, in isolation, a non-medical therapeutic community, on an experimental egalitarian basis, in a rented house in the heart of a genteel residential suburb. The project survived and prospered but survival was frequently in doubt during the first months. The problems encountered were of two kinds: problems of legitimisation by the authorities and subsequent recognition and support; and problems of formulating a new model of care which was not based on a psychiatric premiss (whilst recognising the proper role of psychiatry in treatment).

The issue of legitimisation was raised as soon as the embryo community increased to more than two members. Since no similar scheme existed, the responsible local authority saw it as falling within the category of 'Hostels for the Mentally Disordered' and thereby as Part III Accommodation. They required that the 'home' be registered under the National Assistance Act 1948 as amended by the recently passed Mental Health Act 1959. The requirement was successfully contested on the grounds that ex-psychiatric patients had the same civil rights as other citizens and were at liberty to choose their own accommodation.

It was necessary to establish the right to operate without restrictions, in order to establish the project on the innovative lines envisaged, and without the funds to make structural alterations which might be required for multiple use. The freedom from restrictions was, however, of limited usefulness, as in time official recognition and support were needed to pass from the stage of a pilot venture to a full-scale organisation. Within the first year, therefore, when the community was seen to be workable, it became necessary to seek local authority support for a second house; this was registered as a 'hostel for the mentally disordered' without unwelcome restrictions (apart from the terminology of the registration). The scheme became established as a charity, with an accompanying 50 per cent capital grant from the relevant local authority for a further house.

Internal issues stemmed from the basic orientation which was crucial to the success of the project. It was felt essential to begin, not from 'the psychiatric angle' – that is, with assumptions of disability and helplessness – but from its opposite pole, normality. Daily experience could then be expected to elucidate to what extent a community structure and roles would need to evolve in order to meet personal and community needs. Discharged psychiatric patients needing accommodation and companionship were contacted through an advertisement placed on the notice board of two local mental hospitals. On enquiry, applicants found a young Dutch 'landlady' who was sympathetic and yet held certain expectations of their ability to function. Eleven applicants were initially accepted, ranging in age from

15 to 86, and including an unmarried mother with a two-year-old child. They were invited to share the house on an egalitarian basis, contributing their share of the rent and housework.

It transpired that support and understanding were acceptable to the new residents, whereas expectations were not! Issues which arose were not those of sickness but those of the spurious appeal to sickness as a means of evading the more demanding aspects of life: getting up in the morning, contributing to household tasks, seeking work. A determined attempt was made by residents to transfer the hospital ethos into the community and to sustain the sick role. It became apparent that a staff role existed, as distinct from peer relationships, and that the skills of this role were different from the traditional medical ones. It was essential to believe in the ability of residents to move in the direction of autonomy, to motivate them in this direction and to counter the manipulative behaviour which served to resist progress.

Similar expectations had begun to infiltrate mental hospitals, influenced by the pioneering experimental units. In the medical setting, however, they were of necessity of limited application, since ultimately appeal could be made to medical authority and to the greater validity of the clinical judgement as against the 'patient's' point of view. Responsibility for decisions affecting the patient's health rested in the last resort with the consultant psychiatrist, and constraints for a patient's behaviour could be found in drugs or the padded cell.
For the hospital inmate the primary role is that of 'patient', no matter on what basis the hospital is managed or in what form 'treatment' is administered. The significance of the innovative project in Richmond, Surrey, in 1959, was that it exposed the concept of the therapeutic community to an environment in which it was free of contamination from the medical ethos, and wide open to the standards and values of the immediate environment. This, however, did not mean that conformity was sought at the expense of the resolution of inner or interpersonal conflicts. Rather, the exploration of problems was undertaken in a reality context, and in terms of wider human values and concern than those enshrined in medical or societal dogmas.

The impact of the small community was not confined to its staff and residents. The neighbourhood was introduced to the concept of communal living for people who were lonely or unequal to the demands of society, and very soon the community attracted people needing to share their problems, as well as people who considered it a 'worthy cause'. It is through such ventures that it becomes apparent how few people have access to a confidant in times of need, or to an accepting milieu. From within the small neighbourhood regular visitors emerged: the lonely housewife whose children were growing beyond her control; the divorced woman who had resorted to shoplifting; the father who felt overburdened by his family responsibilities.

The model set by the Richmond house and subsequent houses began to make an impact in some quarters, although implemented partially and with caution. Ambivalence towards new concepts is illustrated by the following extract from an address given in 1967, in which fear of transgressing professional boundaries is in conflict with the desire to provide a therapeutic community milieu.

> We thought it would be a good idea to start weekly group meetings between residents, residential staff and a social worker, in order to foster greater communication between residents and staff, and to improve relationships within the hostel. The staff disliked this idea at first, but now feel that the meetings are really valuable . . .
>
> Many of the residents are seen each week and given intensive casework support. The residential staff and the social workers work as a team, *with the residential staff concentrating on the day-to-day functioning and difficulties of the residents, and the caseworker concentrating on the emotional and relationship problems.* A flexible approach is needed, however, and the roles of residential staff and social worker sometimes merge.[3]

The reservations displayed in the above address are now largely overcome. However, although the basic tenets of the therapeutic community have gradually become widely accepted, implementation presents a challenge which has not yet been met on a larger scale. There seems to have been a failure of courage in applying the concept to the mentally disturbed, and a reluctance to give up the protection and control which attaches to medical concepts and medical settings. The revival of the therapeutic community has taken place in hospitals and has been curiously reluctant to leave them, although not in itself a medical discipline. Attempts at truly community-based therapeutic communities have therefore had to take a further step towards the unknown – or rather, towards a neglected resource: the ability of mankind to exercise universal human skills and qualities in caring for others.

Principles and Theory

Drawing on the disciplines of social psychiatry and group psychoanalysis, as well as on fundamental humanitarian ideals, the therapeutic community is based on a number of principles, some of which present paradoxes which are part of either the charm or the exasperation of the work, depending on one's point of view.

What are the usual components of the therapeutic community?

- agreement to join after the fullest possible exploration of the issues
- for an agreed purpose which is shared by the other members
- the purpose being to obtain help with psychological difficulties
- within a structure specially designed to illuminate personal problems, by involving people directly in community living and encouraging face-to-face encounter
- with the aim of eventually leaving the community
- in order to live as a viable member of society.

The features which enable a community to fulfil its therapeutic aims have defied close definition; however, some consensus has evolved on the governing principles. Robert N. Rapoport formulated a set of beliefs which he felt tended to unify all forms of the therapeutic community (with reference to the hospital setting):[4]

- the total social organisation in which the patient is involved – and not only the relationship with the doctor – is seen as affecting the therapeutic outcome
- the social organisation is not regarded as a routinized background to treatment, but as a vital force, useful for creating a milieu that will maximise therapeutic effects
- the core element in such an institutional context is the provision of opportunities for patients to take an active part in the affairs of the institution ('democratization')
- *all* relationships within the hospital are regarded as potentially therapeutic
- the 'emotional climate' of the institution is accorded significance, and warmth and acceptance are in general regarded as helpful
- a high value is placed on communication *per se*, for its morale-building and therapeutic effect on staff as well as patients.

Similar operating principles have been articulated by Hoffman (see Chapter 3), who finds the following elements both important and common to all therapeutic communities (again with reference to the hospital setting):

- awareness and sensitivity of the community to its own 'value system'

- 'open communication'
- participatory decision-making
- overlapping of staff roles
- the integration of treatment and rehabilitation
- administrative support for this method.

The test of the principles and methods is the response of the patient-resident. Morris Schwartz has proposed that the therapeutic community should offer the following benefits:[5]

- provide the patient with experiences that will minimise his distortions of reality
- facilitate his realistic and meaningful communicative exchange with others
- facilitate his participation with others so that he derives greater satisfaction and security therefrom
- reduce his anxiety and increase his comfort
- increase his self-esteem
- provide him with insight into the causes and manifestations of his mental illness
- mobilize his initiative and motivate him to realise more fully his potentialities for creativity and productivity.

The various accounts in this section illustrate the operation of therapeutic communities on the above principles and also divergences from them. A range of approaches is described which relate to some extent to the philosophy of the founders, and to some extent to the characteristics of the group for which they cater. Kingsley Hall aimed particularly to help those experiencing psychosis; Phoenix House aims to help drug abusers, and Overing Apartments to help a mixed diagnostic group, some of whom are characterised by antisocial behaviour. Spring Lake Ranch and the Richmond Fellowship accept a wide range of applicants, although within the Fellowship differentiated care is also provided for certain groups: disturbed adolescents, families in distress, alcoholics, drug addicts and longer-term schizophrenics. The needs of such distinct groups to some extent shape the mode of helping and the structure and programme of the communities.

Applications of Theory

Theoretical considerations form the basis for the above-mentioned programmes. However, perhaps because the community-based therapeutic community operates in a social rather than clinical setting and employs a variety of skills and approaches, the theoretical base tends to be obscured and is rarely articulated. It may also be that there is a resistance to acknowledging the role of theory, since staff tend to esteem highly the uniqueness of the individual, spontaneity in relationships and the minimising of role barriers. It is not sufficiently recognised that theorising is an ongoing process which does not militate against spontaneity and change.

Freudian theory has become the cornerstone of psychological understanding as applied within most personal therapeutic systems, including the therapeutic community. Salient concepts have proved to be the significance of indirect and non-verbal communications and the operation of ego defences against anxiety aroused by unacceptable feelings. Such insights have always been available to perceptive observers of human behaviour. The contribution of psychoanalysis has been to clarify and adduce clinical evidence for these insights, and to create a coherent system which enables them to be systematically and widely applied.

The Richmond Fellowship, whilst eclectic in approach, bases its view of individual development mainly on Freudian and post-Freudian theory; thus, residents in one-to-one counselling are able in some measure to satisfy, and also to explore, their need for a parental figure, whilst receiving encouragement to relate on a peer basis and to extend their range of relationships within and outside the community. Ability to confront painful issues is variable and requires a sensitive approach to the individual; many psychotic residents, for example, can tolerate only the most cautious approaches to interpretation. Nevertheless, the understanding counsellor may enable the psychotic person, to some degree, to reconcile conflicts and achieve equilibrium.

Concurrently with individual issues, collective communications are striving for attention. Within the community, movements and attitudes are constantly arising which may not be true of each individual (and which may indeed be repudiated by some) but which characterise the collective and anonymously generated behaviour and mood of the community: for example, excitement, antagonism, apathy. In attempting to understand these group phenomena and relate them to individual behaviour, it has been found helpful to draw on the theories originally developed by W.R. Bion, and collated in his book *Experiences in Groups*. Bion discerned the tendency of members to seek cohesion by disowning individual differences and 'agreeing' (at an unconscious level) to act on any one of three assumptions which may exist within a group. The 'basic assumptions' (identified by Bion as dependency, pairing and fight/flight) may or may not further the ostensible, or 'work' task for which the group is formed. Even when the basic assumption is, as it were, tugging the group in the opposite direction, it is not *per se* a negative phenomenon; it *exists*, in the same way as individual emotions or defence mechanisms exist, as an irrational force which is to be reckoned with.

Staff, therefore, need to develop a heightened awareness of the 'assumptions' which are operating in a community in order that they may harness them, if possible, to further the aim of the therapeutic community: to address the disturbance of residents, and explore avenues leading to adjustment. At times, however, the emotional basis of the group may not accord with constructive activity. For instance, the assumption that staff are available in order to provide solutions ('dependency') will militate against the group arriving at a decision on such aspects of community life as, for example, acceptable levels of noise in the house late at night or the need for backsliders to participate in the washing-up rota. It appears that groups often find it hard to come to decisions which may involve discriminating between members, and making critical judgements; in such a situation the group may revert to a basic assumption which provides a comfortable, unifying feeling, leaving the staff to voice criticism or dissent. If the community becomes sufficiently uncomfortable with staff leadership, it may alternatively produce a rival, possibly a sick leader, who will lead the group astray – perhaps towards flight into madness. These phenomena, when they occur, need to be clarified first amongst staff, and then with residents.

There is no fundamental incompatibility between attending to the needs of the group and of the individual, although there may at times be conflicting *demands*. As Bion has pointed out, the individual always exists in a group context, even though that group may reject him or exist only in phantasy; and one of the aims (perhaps the primary aim) of living in a therapeutic community is that the individual may learn how to integrate with, develop in, and derive satisfaction from contributing to his group. The challenge is to achieve these aims, despite the inherent frustrations. Bion holds that the task of establishing contact with the emotional life of the group is as difficult for the adult as the relationship with the breast appears to be for the infant, and that the failure to meet the demands of this task is revealed in the regression of the individual (or of the group). Nevertheless, the task must be pursued, since on it depend essential developmental processes: separation from the parent-figure, and identity formation, both of which are needed in order that the individual may acquire the capacity for social functioning and intimacy at an adult level. *Although membership of a group is not always in the interests of the individual, it is in the individual's interests to learn this, and to learn also that frustrations are accompanied by opportunities for maturation.*

Of the various developmental approaches employed as the basis for therapeutic communities, a few receive specific comment in this book. The psycho-education programme (Chapter 10) guides the child/adolescent, who is referred by reason of delinquency or behaviour disorder, through a sequence based particularly on the developmental theories of Erikson and Piaget; account is taken of the total development of the child, physical, cognitive and affective. The programme thus consists of experiences and tasks of increasing complexity, which are matched to the child's developmental processes and which ensure that the necessary level of competence is achieved before the following stage is attempted.

The stages in the programme, as described by Gauthier, are acclimatisation; control; productivity; and personality, in which the young person begins to exercise his new skills towards the goal of self-direction. The painstaking process of re-education and the method of utilising every possible life-experience to this end are illustrated by Jeannine Guindon.[6] She gives the example of a seventeen-year-old delinquent boy, who is at the stage of his third week of the entry phase, *acclimatisation.* The activity is football practice. The boy makes one mistake but continues to practise the technique he has been taught, and he is successful in the ensuing games. At the end of the practice period he feels satisfied with his performance. He says to the educator, referring to the opposing team: 'We have got the better of them, haven't we? We should start another game right away. I'm sure we would beat them again.' He is satisfied that because he did 'exactly as he was told', the environment responded predictably, except in the first game.

Guindon comments that progress is achieved in this example through the actualisation of five ego strengths, and that similar processes are in operation throughout the re-education programme.

First, the adolescent *learns to test his environment*, as he finds it responsive, in a predictable manner, to his efforts.

Secondly, he *acquires self-confidence*, through a rewarding participation in activities.

Thirdly, the experience of success through applying a learned experience of tactics enables the adolescent to *distinguish cause and effect*, and to identify his own role in events.

Fourth, physical participation, requiring co-ordination and self-discipline, helps to *build a favourable body-image*, and thus to increase self-confidence.

Fifth, the adolescent learns, through successful application of strategies, to *respect a disciplined and logical approach to tasks*. He is thus enabled to operate effectively within acceptable social norms.

A primary factor, essential in securing the adolescent's involvement and motivation, is the participation and interest of the educator.

In summary, the experience of successful outcome, repeated in many contexts and on many occasions, establishes the confidence and ability of the adolescent in his interaction with the world: 'In making use of the techniques learned in a constant fashion, the young man will live experiences where he feels successful, thus gaining confidence in himself when confronted with this activity, and so he will feel secure and confident while participating in football practices. If such experiences are repeated often enough, they may convey a "secure apperception" of this type of activity, and if this is also repeated in other segments of reality (i.e. other activities) he will gradually acquire a "secure apperception" of the external world: in this case, the micro-society represented by the treatment centre, which brings him appropriate stimulus-nutriment needed in his life program.'[7]

The child's, or adolescent's, co-operation is engaged at the beginning through building on his strengths and by accepting him at the level of his functioning. Encouragement to attempt more complex tasks, and to assume responsibilities, depends on strong bonding with staff, and especially with one member of staff who establishes a one-to-one relationship. Learning can take place through identification with this parent-figure, through whom healthy social behaviour and aspirations are internalised. Until this is achieved, the child is not exposed to freedoms and responsibilities which he is not equipped to handle; the staff and community structure set his boundaries, which he gradually comes to adopt.

Phoenix House (see Chapter 6) postulates that its residents, all drug addicts, are functioning at an infantile and delinquent level, and therefore the Phoenix communities have been organised to fulfil coercive, and sometimes punitive, super-ego functions. This approach is, however, currently undergoing rethinking and modification, in favour of greater attention to individual needs and the diminished use of sanctions, whilst retaining some sense of ritual.[8] The manipulative potential of residents is felt to be too powerful to allow of individual staff/resident counselling, and therefore bonding to the group is encouraged. It is felt that identification with the group, with its non-drug culture, will enable residents to abandon the drug scene and develop other aspirations in life.

Kingsley Hall (see Chapter 5), in common with the therapeutic community movement, accepted the validity of the psychotic state in terms of the individual's early experience, but took a further step in placing a positive, therapeutic value on the psychotic experience. In accordance with R.D. Laing's tenet that the schizophrenic needs to journey into and through his madness, unrestricted regression was encouraged, to the developmental level at which, according to Klein,[9] splitting and the consequent paranoid/schizoid defences originated. As an experiment the community attracted considerable interest, which is now being expressed in the exploration of the value of regression for 'normal' individuals.

As a model of a community and of a treatment method for schizophrenics, Kingsley Hall has proved of debatable value. Its emphasis was clearly not on transition into society, or on social adjustment, and its capacity for being replicated is probably limited by practical considerations and by doubts as to its social value. In addition, doubts have been raised as to the therapeutic value of the absence of boundaries, which for disintegrated people may have the effect of intensifying their terror. There is a radical division, therefore, between the Laingian therapists and between more eclectic philosophies such as that of the Richmond Fellowship, where it is felt that for the schizophrenic there is therapeutic value in building on existing ego-strengths, and in according him the opportunity of exercising the adult aspects of his personality.

There is also fundamental divergence of views on causation of the schizophrenic 'condition'. The existential psychotherapists categorically define it as a functional coping mechanism, which is developed in response to specific family patterns; they therefore exclude other postulates, although the evidence for family pathology is not conclusive or specific. The position regarding family studies has been concisely stated by Clare: 'To date, there has not been a single well-controlled study that demonstrates any substantial difference between the family relationships of schizophrenics and those of non-schizophrenics from similar backgrounds.'[10] In most studies, such patterns of communication as have been identified as pathological, 'far from being specific to schizophrenic families are in fact commonplace and found in many families'.[11]

It is regrettable that in their zeal to identify family pathology (with which a correlation may indeed exist), the exponents of this theory have tended to overstate and to caricature, as in the film, *Family Life*. Parents are portrayed as insensitive, smothering, distorting; they are shown as basically unable to acknowledge negative feelings, to which the 'patient' nevertheless reacts, and by reason of which he is then invalidated as 'mad'. The theorists profess not to impute blame but in such portrayals both blame and ridicule are invited. R.D. Laing, when speaking of the family's socialising functions, says: 'Adapt to what? To society? To a world gone mad? The family's function is to repress Eros: to induce a false consciousness of security: to deny death by avoiding life: to cut off transcendence: to believe in God, not to experience the void; to create, in short, one-dimensional man: to promote respect, conformity or to con children out of play: to induce a fear of failure: to promote a respect for work: to promote a respect for "respectability".'[12]

As Clare comments:

> The bosom of the family is seen to nourish all that is twisted and pathological in the human condition – the child molester, the mass murderer, the baby-batterer, the sadistic torturer; all these, the family's critics remind us, emerge from the sanctity of the home.
>
> In view of the family's track record in such matters, it is not surprising that some students of family relationships argue that it is in this area that the key to the development of schizophrenia is to be found. Schizophrenia is seen as a response, an intelligible and inevitable response by the child, to overwhelming interpersonal and social stresses, the main source of which is located in the parents.[13]

Clare concludes his discussion by restating the position adopted by Jules Henry,[14] that 'current formulations represent the necessary preliminary steps to discovering further and possibly vital information concerning the aetiology of emotional suffering in general'.[15] It is observable that 'schizophrenia' can develop in stable, well-functioning families. *It may also be that specific family problems in some cases lead to its development.* Accusatory attitudes have, however, led to resistance to this avenue of enquiry amongst family support groups, with a backlash of reliance on physical treatments and the search for purely organic aetiology. The American Schizophrenia Foundation, for instance, which was formed mainly to enable families of patients to offer one another enlightened support, prefers to explain schizophrenia in terms of biological deficiency and holds that, for many, a cure has been found in nutritional or medical formulae. The National Schizophrenia Fellowship (UK) expresses its views as follows: 'Schizophrenia is an affliction and not a disgrace . . . it is not a product of delinquent parenthood . . . it can in great measure be contained, if not quite mastered, by medical treatment, tolerance and understanding, compassionate care and support.'[16]

In view of the charges laid against families, the emergence of a defensive element in support groups is entirely understandable. This can, however, militate against communication with the 'dis-eased' member, and against the identification of possibly unhelpful interactions in the family. It may be conjectured that a relatively higher number of parents of schizophrenics might be found to correspond with the traits and patterns identified above; certainly the obverse, that is, an understanding, friendly, but dispassionate milieu, has been found to be favourable in reducing schizophrenic symptoms and maximising functioning. In addition, it is a common human experience that certain relationships are conducive to freedom and joy, and tend to channel energies into life-enhancing activities; conversely, attitudes or relationships may be so tortuous that a breakdown of some kind is almost inevitable for any member of the family apart from the most robust or insensitive. *Whatever the cause, the fact that a family has a casualty demands a willingness to examine all aspects of the problem, including family relationships.* In doing so, families need to be helped to come to terms with their pain, resentment and fear, in order to discover what changes may be needed to establish rapprochement with the disturbed member, and with one another.

Aspects of the Therapeutic Community

A wide variety of programmes and practice is clearly included within the term 'therapeutic community', *but common principles dictate that the therapeutic community, whatever its context, should provide a communal living experience which encourages open communication, and promotes intrapsychic and social adjustment, to the maximum capacity of the individual.* The theoretical framework and the philosophy of the organisation, interacting with the characteristics of the resident and staff groups, combine to produce variations in structure and practice. Despite differences, however, there is sufficient common ground to enable general comments to be made on some salient issues.

Dependence or Autonomy?

In establishing a therapeutic community, immediately there is a potentially anti-therapeutic component. A degree of dependence is invited and the question arises, will it result in conformity and stagnation, as is typical of the institution, or can a transference of dependency needs on to the community be used to release the individual's potential for maturation?

In order to achieve the latter, most communities have found it necessary to take positive measures involving expectations, limits and constraints. Common elements in ensuring that the community exerts a positive effect are (i) *explanation to the applicant of the community's goals and programme*, so as to establish that he/she is broadly in agreement before taking up residence. This is a process which may have to be very much modified in the case of some applicants: for instance, the out-of-touch psychotic and the drop-out adolescent. Some applicants may not apply of their own volition: for instance, offenders against the law; and this may significantly alter the chances of a successful outcome. In a study of the Phoenix House programme for drug addicts in New York, for instance, it was found that ability to remain in the programme for a substantial period, or for the whole period, was significantly related to the voluntary or compulsory nature of the resident's entry: on follow-up two years after entering, 40 per cent of the 'voluntary' men were still in the programme, as against 27 per cent of those who were convicted of drug offences and referred through the legal system.[17]

Having attempted to enrol motivated residents, the community offers (ii) *a programme which is planned in order to engage and retain the involvement of residents.* Resident participation is commonly sought in planning the house programme, in selecting new residents and helping them to adjust to the community and in forming links with the neighbourhood.

The impact of the house programme is reinforced by (iii) *the community's culture, norms and values, which exert pressure on members to adhere to the programme and to encourage others to do so.*

The Phoenix House model, in particular, relies for its effectiveness on group cohesion and determination to adopt a new, constructive way of life; therefore, negative, subversive talk is strongly discouraged. The ability of residents to place their trust in the community, and to adopt its values, requires that (iv) *the environment be reliable and congruent with its declared aims and practice.* The staff have a particular responsibility to see that all members are treated equitably, and that the programme is consistently implemented. This may be harder to demonstrate, the more flexible the community. Finally, (v) *reviews of progress*, which regularly restate and perhaps reformulate the goals, have a place in most communities and assist staff as well as residents to bear in mind the transitional nature of membership of the community.

Measures oriented towards autonomy and separation do of course need to be balanced by a timespan which is sufficient to enable the resident to become secure; and this varies greatly with the type of disturbance and the age-group of the residents, and with the philosophy of the community. Phoenix House programme, dealing with drug addicts mostly in their 20s, has found that 18–24 months is 'the minimum period of residence required to achieve most of the specific therapeutic goals'.[18] (Long-term and semi-permanent or permanent facilities are discussed later.)

Reality-testing

The wish of the resident to be dependent on someone who is infallible, and can perhaps offer a magic cure, is both corrected and frustrated by the capacity of the community to provide reality-testing situations. Distortion of perceptions about oneself and others are characteristic of all forms of disturbance (more so than of *la condition humaine*!). The distortion is reinforced because people lack the confidence or opportunity to test their perceptions, or because they unwittingly invite the response which they fear. The small size of the therapeutic community, its programme of common activities and shared decision-making, and the close proximity of its members, are crucial to establishing the validity, or otherwise, of the individual's viewpoint and hence to making relationships. A man who lived for a year in one of the Richmond Fellowship's houses wrote afterwards: 'It was the first time I had lived in a mixed group. I was certainly disabused of a myriad phantasies during my year . . . I made valuable friends in the community, including my first real attempt at a relationship with a woman.'

On a less personal level, alienation from society can be alleviated through reaching a clearer understanding of the relationship between leader and group. Tom Main, in Chapter 1, comments that the problems of distance of worker from management, and the governed from government, are not simply a matter for regret: 'Often they lead to regressions . . . The world becomes a place . . . with selfish bastards in the high places if one is low in hierarchy, or greedy idlers in the lower places if one is high in the hierarchy.' Note that the phantasy can be a two-way event, especially in large systems. Through face-to-face encounters in the therapeutic community, staff may learn, along with residents, about the importance of sharing and of valuing each member's contribution.

The Sick Role

The philosophy and programme are designed also to reorientate the resident away from the self-image of 'patient' and towards a realistic assessment of himself as a participating member of society. It is a task which runs counter to the predominant view held by developed Western societies, that it is humane to classify the disturbed person as ill. The issue of 'treatment' for the mentally ill has become implicated in the general mechanistic view of illness in the Western world, and its denial of the patient's responsibility and resources. There are now signs that concepts of disease are gradually undergoing reappraisal and change, not only in the field of mental disturbance (originating with Freud and reinforced recently by R.D. Laing and others), but also in physical medicine, stimulated by radical thinkers such as Ivan Illich. In the present climate of opinion, however, the individual is still buttressed in the sick role by social attitudes to disease. His passivity and inability to fulfil normal social roles are accepted as part of the package.

The individual is further encouraged to retain the sick role by the fact that illness is the only socially sanctioned role in which he can be dependent and vulnerable. A request to have time out for reorientation would hardly be appreciated by the employer and would inconvenience the work group. Joseph Berke in his account of Kingsley Hall (Chapter 5) contrasts the deficiencies of modern Western society, in this respect, with the ancient Greek practice of retiring into a cave to experience a healing dream. Present-day opportunities for retreat are conceded largely to the sick, with the exception of religious retreats; these, however, may not free the individual for self-discovery, since they are liable to reward certain practices and beliefs, and to penalise the unbeliever with a sense of failure and isolation. When normal social networks fail, there is no system, outside the medical or penal system, which can contain the distressed person. For the individual who, for instance, questions the sense of continuing to live in an uncaring society; feels unable to choose the right course in a potentially damaging situation; is experiencing pain through personal relationships, or lack of them; for those encountering ethical and emotional problems of this nature, space and acceptance are needed. In the absence of such an environment, the person may deny his needs and convert them into the acceptable face of illness. Alternatively, he may continue to function, but without coming to terms with himself.

Provision for acknowledging personal needs and partial relief from social pressures, may in themselves enable the individual to resist the sick role; in addition, therapeutic communities actively discourage the sick role by means of various strategies. Both Phoenix and Overing (Chapters 6 and 9) act vigorously in the early stages, so as to annihilate the 'patient' self-image. The newcomer is encouraged to identify strongly with the group culture and the sick role is challenged in both communities by a strict stipulation about attendance at the daily activities; it is felt that the structure is a necessary aid to residents in overcoming their manipulative use of their problems and symptoms.

Spring Lake Ranch and the Richmond Fellowship are less coercive, although staff may make a strong stand against habitual 'truancy', and ultimately sanctions may be used if routines are not adhered to. The absence of stringent rules calls for greater understanding and judgement on the part of individual staff. As a general rule, however, it may be stated that opting out of the work programme is seen as infantile avoidance of the responsibility which people can and should exercise within the community. While regressive desires are acceptable, and may be ventilated, they are not viewed as the sole factors governing behaviour.

Testing-out Behaviour

Testing-out tests two things: the extent to which the caring person actually cares (involving his personal basis for his actions and convictions), and the extent to which he is skilled and consistent (involving his ability to distinguish need from manipulative manoeuvres, and to respond appropriately). Many a newcomer can begin to profit by the community only when he has established trust through a period of testing-out. The testing of limits is of primary concern to Thomas Barton (Chapter 9) who focuses on the needs of volatile, anti-authoritarian young men, but any staff member in a therapeutic community has to learn about the forms which this may take. The context in which staff respond is the community structure, which defines certain limits which are considered necessary for the funtioning of the group. Common limits are: adhere to the programme; pay your rent; refrain from violence. Communities to help alcoholics and drug addicts usually have rules against drinking and drug-taking. All of these limits, besides the purposes for which they were evolved, have the additional value that they give the resident a framework within which to test ideas of his own power, and of the authority and consistency of the staff; they also assume that the resident has control over his own behaviour. Barton, speaking of eviction for non-compliance with rules, says: 'It is sometimes beneficial . . . probably because it is an experience in learning that parenting figures at some time mean what they say, and also because it is a refusal to accept pathological behaviour as inevitable.' However, as residents' problems are real and their options few, the use of sanctions should be a last resort; sanctions are rarely needed when staff can demonstrate in other ways that they mean what they say – and that they care enough neither to evict nor to compromise.

Group Issues

It has already been stated that the individual is inevitably a member, at least potentially, of a social group, and that his thinking and behaviour occurs in the process of interaction within the group. The therapeutic community is designed to produce group cohesion and a high level of interaction, with the aim of constructive behaviour, but in the anticipation of some resistance. The conflicts and obstructions which emerge are then recognisable as defences arising from unmet individual and group needs, often of an infantile nature. The kinds of events which evoke defensive reactions are well known: among them, loss or breakdown of a member resulting in grief, anger and guilt; conflict over rules, activating difficulties in self-assertion or in acceptance of authority or limits; sexual jealousy and rivalry, and other situations of 'unfair advantage' which result in unfavourable comparisons and loss of self-esteem. Skilled staff are able to give leadership in clarifying the feelings underlying group behaviour, and to demonstrate that 'bad' feelings need not be destructive of relationships; clarification is also needed where the community chooses to make certain unpopular communications through a particular member.

Individual actions and reactions always occur in the context of a group, but in the context of one-to-one therapy this fact can sometimes be minimised or overlooked in favour of the more immediate dyadic relationship. Members of the therapeutic community have the interactions of the group constantly before them, and are therefore in the most favourable position to assign them due significance and to perceive the many facets of the individual.

Special Needs

The Group Home

Amongst modified forms of residential provision based on therapeutic community principles, the group home has probably received most interest and support. From its beginnings in the early sixties this model has proved attractive financially, and has offered a compromise between companionship and privacy. The economic and planning features which have enabled this form of community to become widespread are: the small size of the group (normally not more than eight people) which can be accommodated in a family-sized dwelling, possibly rented from the local housing authority; the lack of formalities at the planning stage (no planning permission is needed where the group shares facilities such as a kitchen and bathroom); the payment of a moderate rent which can be met, if necessary, by social security benefits; staff, where employed at all, who are non-residential and work part time.

Group homes vary somewhat in their purpose. A major distinction must be drawn between those which offer a permanent home, and those which offer transitional accommodation. As described in the MIND/NAMH booklet,[19] the concept implies a permanent home, which will normally cater for people of middle-age, who would otherwise be long-stay patients in psychiatric hospitals. Other residents may be those who have largely recovered from an acute breakdown and have no suitable permanent home. A preventive function may be fulfilled in providing for the isolated elderly.[20] Not all homes, however, are permanent; a postal questionnaire sent by the Richmond Fellowship in 1973 to fourteen group homes run by local authorities revealed that five of these were transitional. The five group homes run by the Richmond Fellowship allow for indefinite stay, but encourage a progression to less supportive accommodation; in addition, five community residences provide a substitute family and a greater measure of support for long-stay residents who would otherwise need to remain in hospital, or be liable to relapse.

In general, criteria for admission reflect the lack of staff presence: problems which are unpopular in any community are doubly so in the group home (for example, addiction, tendency to overdose, unsociability) whilst there is considerable emphasis on ability to mix with others, fulfil practical tasks and, in some homes, to hold down employment.

Support to residents varies greatly. In some cases, local authority or independent social workers are allocated to the home. In others, voluntary helpers or domestic staff may keep in contact with residents, be available for advice, mainly on domestic matters, and also liaise if needed with the local psychiatric services. Most homes emphasise the need for group cohesion and co-operation, although the extent and nature of the support provided to further these aims may be very limited. Where social work staff are employed, their task is usually felt to include enhancing group interaction through encouraging open communication and the resolution of conflicts. It is not intended, however, that the level of interaction should be intensive. Even in one atypical group home, in which the age-group was lower and the level of education higher than usual, the house ethos was described by one of the residents as 'not treading on each other's neuroses'. On the other hand, part of the aim of the house was recognised as 'people learning to understand and come to terms with their inner conflicts'. It is perhaps significant that the input of the staff member for this home was almost full-time, and that she was seen as the facilitator of communication, and capable of controlling excesses: 'We're more likely to let go when she's around; she can repair the damage.' It may be conjectured that homes where the staff input is less, either in terms of time or group skills, will be relatively more inhibited about expression of opinion and feelings. It is evident that residents who have a diminished coping ability, and lack confidence, are likely to need assistance in relating as a group – and indeed may need the intervention of staff where it becomes necessary to curb very disruptive behaviour. It is accepted that so-called well people may have a limited tolerance for disturbed behaviour, but all too often it is assumed that socially impaired people will be able to tolerate one another, to whatever extent irritation or provocation may take place. It is essential that group homes should not expose residents to this form of distress, but should provide for residents' emotional as well as physical needs.

Adolescents

Adolescents require certain environmental conditions, which are appropriate to their developmental stage, and it has been found necessary in the Richmond Fellowship to adapt therapeutic community principles accordingly. This formative age imposes intensive pressures on the adolescent in terms of physical, social and emotional development; differentiation and separation from parent-figures is proceeding unevenly, concurrently with the powerful need to seek acceptance in a peer group, and to begin to explore adult relationships and roles. A fund of energy and motivation is available, which needs to find expression in appropriate activities.

The developments, feelings and problems which exist even in a 'normal' adolescence are powerfully described by Simone de Beauvoir in her autobiography, *Memoirs of a Dutiful Daughter*. Of the physical changes of puberty, with their accompanying emotions, she writes: 'I looked awful; my nose was turning red; on my face and the back of my neck there were pimples . . . embarrassed by my body, I developed phobias: for example, I couldn't bear to drink from a glass I had already drunk from.' Puberty brought not only anxieties but also *sexual desire*: 'I would often let my gaze wander idly over the bits of old newspaper hanging up in the lavatory. In this way I read a fragment of a novelette in which the hero applied his burning lips to the heroine's white breasts. This kiss burned right through me . . . my daydreams were crystallized around that image.' The young Simone rebelled against parental authority and norms, yet with accompanying insecurity: 'I had lost the sense of security childhood gives, and nothing had come to take its place. My parents' authority remained inflexible, but as my critical sense developed I began to rebel against it more and more.' Yet growing independence was accompanied by a need for confirmation by her father of her new sexual identity: 'As long as he had approved of me, I could be sure of myself. For years he had done nothing but heap praises on my head. But when I entered the "difficult" age, he was disappointed in me . . . Not only did he fail to conceal his disillusionment from me, but he began showing more interest than before in my sister, who was still a pretty child.' Longing for her father's approval was accompanied by rivalry with her mother: 'But my real rival was my mother. I dreamed of having a more intimate relationship with my father.' And with the realisation of growing up came phantasies about adult life: 'One afternoon I was helping Mama to wash up; she was washing the plates, and I was drying; through the window I could see the wall of the barracks, and other kitchens in which women were scrubbing out saucepans or peeling vegetables. Every day lunch and dinner; every day washing-up; all those hours, those endlessly recurring hours, all leading nowhere: could I live like that? An image was formed in my mind, an image of such desolate clarity that I can still remember it today: a row of grey squares, diminishing according to the laws of perspective, but all flat, all identical, extending away to the horizon; they were the days and weeks and years. Since the day I was born I had gone to bed richer in the evening than I had been the day before; I was steadily improving myself, step by step; but if, when I got up there, I found only a barren plateau, with no landmark to make for, what was the point in it all?'[21]

Adolescent turmoil, here so vividly conveyed, clearly requires in the adult great sensitivity, together with recognition of the need for boundaries, and for opportunities for self-expression, and the development of confidence and skills.

The Richmond Fellowship Staff Manual chapter on adolescent houses states: 'In general terms, adolescents are people in formation and are consequently in a phase of development in which activity and exploration of new and alternative roles are important. It is vitally important, therefore, that the house should provide a higher degree of structure than that normally required by adults, so that this exploration can take place in a secure situation.' It is not, however, intended that the resident's time is monopolised by organised events; time to reflect and assimilate new experiences is equally important, as is stated by Diane in Chapter 12.

Special considerations which may not be prominent in adult communities include: the need for staff to model *socialisation*, since the peer group cannot adequately do so; a higher degree of organised activity; a higher staffing ratio in order to respond adequately to individual needs and to testing-out behaviour; planned involvement of parents or other parent-figures with whom the adolescent is still actively engaged over issues such as dependence; close links with local educational and employment resources; and awareness of legal considerations and obligations.

Issues of identity and authority, which are evident in de Beauvoir's reminiscences, form a large part, albeit unconscious, of the adolescent's preoccupations. The desire for autonomy and the capacity to exercise it, which are sometimes out of phase, need to be explored in a relatively secure setting. Recognition of these issues is encouraged in the Fellowship's adolescent units and discussed in the 'Welcome

Document' which is presented on arrival:

> For a lot of new people, this is the first time you have lived somewhere where you carry responsibilities for yourself, have to make more decisions and have the chance to show concern for the others living with you. To help the community learn from experience and through this grow and mature, all residents and staff come together for group meetings . . . Groups give you a chance to talk about things that matter to you, your expectations of yourself and your future, your problems, and to help you get on with others more easily. Sometimes it's difficult to be honest and tell other people what you think of them or of yourself, what you like and dislike. Sometimes it hurts a bit to hear how others see you, but most people in the long run find it makes them happier and more confident. It is helpful, when things feel difficult, to remember that some of the others have similar problems.
>
> When you come up against requirements, you may think the staff are like your parents, your teachers, or probation officer – 'authority figures' – with whom you may have clashed in the past. In this House we believe, in time, you can find authority *within yourself* and recognise and sort out problems that have made things difficult in the past, so that the authority of others can be respected also. Staff carry authority but their main job is not to tell you what you should do, but help you find out from experiences from the past, both bad and good, what you want in life, whether it is worth having and how best to go about achieving it.

The Family Unit

Residential care for families in trouble has been designed on various models, ranging from relatively self-contained units within the residential setting to the therapeutic community which by design is minimally adapted to the nuclear family. The latter is the model described by Kelly (see Chapter 11). Families have their own accommodation, mainly for sleeping, but kitchen, dining-room, sitting-room and playroom are communal, and there is maximum interaction with the other families, as well as with unit staff. The therapeutic programme ensures that in many ways the community functions as one large family network, rather than as several nuclear families; the resultant cross-family interactions are a powerful source of both stimulus and learning.

Admission of a family to residential care would seem indicative of problems which are both severe and intractable, i.e. they have not responded to other forms of help, and this assumption is borne out by an analysis of referrals to the Richmond Fellowship Family Unit during the year 1977. Of the 42 referrals made, 50 per cent showed a psychiatric history in one or both parents. Other frequently occurring circumstances included crime, violence inflicted on the children, alcoholism, prostitution, subnormality in the parents, children born of incestuous relationships and deprivation or abuse in the parents' own childhood. Six-sevenths of the families referred included children who were either on an 'at risk' register or under a care order. In general, presenting problems at the time of referral include such factors as: psychiatric disorder in the parent(s); neglect or abuse of the child(ren); marital disharmony; lack of basic parenting skills, notably amongst one-parent families; serious management problems; and family crises. Not surprisingly, in view of the burden of misfortune, disadvantage and incompetence borne by these families, a major problem common to all families admitted to the unit is perceived by the staff as being *lack of self esteem.*

As noted by Kelly, it is common to find that parents and children may have been separated for up to one year before referral, through removal of either parent(s) or child from the home, and this is perhaps a major indication for the use of the residential setting. These families are not required to uproot themselves from a familiar base and established mode of functioning as a unit; on the contrary, they may be in need of the opportunity to re-establish bonds on a more stable basis.

Methods of effecting change in families which have experienced severe problems, poor quality of family life and long-standing lack of self-esteem, would seem to present a particular challenge. Interpretative methods of family therapy are employed in the unit programme; however, additional or alternative methods of therapeutic intervention, such as reassurance and advice, are also indicated, and some of these are described by Kelly in Chapter 11. In addition to the concept of the family as a system, it is interesting to note the use of the multi-family environment as a larger, less emotionally 'loaded' system, in which opportunities to observe and learn can be more fully used. It is noteworthy also that, as pointed out by Kelly, staff often appear to be at their most effective when acting indirectly rather than directly on the family system: that is, when maintaining the structure of the community which thus serves as a model of a 'family' which is flexible and compassionate but nevertheless able to set boundaries, and maintain a balance between the needs of its different members. It would seem that many of the families need this opportunity to internalise such ways of functioning, which may be totally novel to them.

Leaving and Reintegration with Society

The goal of leaving presents one more paradox in the therapeutic community process: the paradox of finding a home in order to leave it. However one may rationalise it, this remains a difficult and often painful issue. It is true, of course, that a biological family raises children in order that they may leave and set up their own homes; however, people who have suffered deprivation and damage in their lives will have much greater difficulty in dealing, first with their dependence, and then with separation.

There are similarities for the resident leaving the therapeutic community with the situation of the adolescent who is preparing to leave home. The degree of awareness of conditions in the 'outside world' will vary, as will the resident's precarious sense of identity and his sensitivity to his own role in social situations. Appropriate self-awareness is necessary in order to adjust to and engage with society. Either overconfidence or lack of confidence may be a hazard, and any pre-existing lack of confidence may be exacerbated by the fact or fear of stigma.

The ways in which various communities prepare their residents for leaving will be looked at later. A first step, however, and one which is emphasised in the theoretical papers, is for the community to structure itself so that there are channels of communication with the neighbourhood and with society generally. Dr Main points out that his experiment at Northfield Mental Hospital during the war was concerned to be socially syntonic: 'It was believed that part of this community's task was to enlist the sanction of relevant authorities for our activities – trades unions, local townspeople and army authorities. We were determined to survive, not to die a heroic death.' Perhaps the presence of the Nazi threat was a help; nothing concentrates the mind so wonderfully as an external enemy! But most theorists make the same point: the community must be in touch with society, and furthermore, although its internal values may differ, in the end it must be able to live within society's values. This is not to say, however, that the influence is only in one direction; if community and neighbourhood are in touch, then the community has an opportunity to influence others. Elly Jansen states: 'The Fellowship was started particularly to try and provide a forum for the community and the mentally ill to meet . . . It was started as a kind of educational programme for the so-called well to accept a bit more of their own madness, in order to be able to relieve the mad from the excess that had been pushed on them.'[22] The process is slow because the permeation of insight meets with resistance among the 'well' as it does among the 'sick'; yet it is only when the community takes this direction that it can undertake community care.

Different communities vary in the extent to which they set out to re-educate society. As stated, the Fellowship has this as an explicit aim, and its policy is to advertise its entry into a neighbourhood and to canvass support by individual visiting. It then establishes bonds by means of a structure of house committees and groups of friends who are the keys to further neighbourhood involvement. Neighbours who involve themselves personally and appropriately in the community are warmly appreciated, partly because they are a bridge to ordinary life. An ex-resident from a Fellowship house wrote of 'Joan': 'She appears unfailingly each week to "do typing", but her activities are soon recognised to be much more than this. Living around the corner from Croft House, she invites people to her flat for music and a cup of tea or glass of sherry. There is something very helpful in this experience, taking one from the community into an ordinary living situation.'[23] For some organisations, however, this is not an important part of their programme. The Arbours Association adopts the strategy of arriving in a neighbourhood as unobtrusively as possible, on the grounds that the house should not be singled out for special attention or placed in a special role. Any disturbances which may arise are dealt with according to the circumstances, and may sometimes involve a staff member in interpreting someone's behaviour to a neighbour.[24] Communities which site themselves in isolated areas, such as Spring Lake Ranch, do not have a similarly pressing motivation to form connections with the locality.

However, as has been stated, the concept of community care, and particularly of preventive care, depends eventually on public awareness of the nature of disturbance and of society's contribution to it. When the level of awareness becomes sufficiently raised, it may be possible for people to request help for themselves before reaching a crisis. In a different terminology, Harry S. Brickman writes: 'The prevention of mental illness, a phenomenon so thoroughly contingent upon social events, must reflect the most sophisticated ecological awareness of the social structure in which the deviant exists, as well as an awareness of how that social structure can accept his deviation while assisting him to overcome whatever personal or interpersonal disorganization he may be experiencing.'[25]

Meanwhile, we remain at the stage of seeking ways of reintegration, and communities deal with this problem mainly by working with the residents. The Richmond Fellowship places emphasis on each resident attending one-to-one counselling sessions, in which problems are identified and goals, albeit flexible, are set. The process of working towards leaving is therefore built in from the beginning. Phoenix House, after an intensive induction period which removes the person almost totally from the outside world, allows a gradual re-entry into society and encourages members in the later stages of their residence to spend periods away from the house, and to seek employment. Spring Lake Ranch helps individual members to make the arrangement most suitable for them, perhaps first working away, or living away but working in the community, before the final departure. All three organisations devote much effort to support after leaving and encourage ex-members to keep in touch, not only with the community but with a network of other ex-members, staff and friends.

Problems of leaving, and the application of learning in a therapeutic communities to 'ordinary life', have been studied particularly in relation to clinical settings.

Robert N. Rapoport in *Community as Doctor* states:

> The Unit staff [of the Henderson Hospital], while overtly stressing their subscription to rehabilitation goals and the attempt to make the hospital more like an ordinary community outside, have in fact developed a specialised therapeutic programme geared to their ideas of the treatment requirements of patients with disruptive personality disorders. Their notion that treatment and rehabilitation are being simultaneously and conjointly pursued blurs the actual continuities and discontinuities between treatment programme and compelling rehabilitative needs. *They are sensitively aware of the treatment world in which they are immersed, but take less account of the outside world. These worlds are willy-nilly different and function according to drastically different norms* [our italics]. The failure to distinguish between these conceptually different sets of goals leads to an insufficient attention to the problems of differentiating treatment stages, grading experiences, and providing

for adequate transitions between one stage and the next.[26]

On comparing 'outcome' of treatment with a control group it was found that no significant difference from the control group existed for those who had been in the unit for two weeks to six months (one-third of both groups improved). There was, however, a significant difference regarding outcome for those who had stayed in the unit for over six months: 50 per cent showed significant improvement; this is a difference of over 16 per cent. However, those who did best in terms of treatment norms (the aggressive) had a poorer rehabilitative record than the more docile patient. The follow-up evidence shows that those who were most disruptive in the unit are not sufficiently weaned from acting out before their discharge. 'Therefore, for the aggressives, there is a severe discontinuity between the Unit and the outside, between the behavioural adjustment in treatment and in rehabilitation.'

In the Richmond Fellowship it has been found that generally at least a half-year commitment is needed to bring about any stable change. The ethos in the Fellowship is in any case profoundly different from the setting studied by Rapoport. During the experimental period in 1959, some clear principles were evolved. First, whatever time and thought might be given to discussion of new proposals, the final responsibility of setting the boundaries lay with staff. Whilst the Fellowship was considered daringly democratic by other agencies in the field of residential care, its own view was that it had to maintain clearly defined limits to the democratic decision-making process. It was felt that the residents would have to cope with the right of others to make decisions and could not expect much democracy in their lodgings or at work. Some 'reality demands' are therefore appropriate, although artificial and petty restrictions should be avoided. Whilst ample time is given to the exploration of obstacles to coping with life in society (including early and contemporary ways of expressing conflict), from the start, the stress is laid on the question: 'What do you want to achieve whilst you are here? – What are the problems that make it impossible to cope and what therefore should be the ultimate and intermediate goals?' The return to society at large, and what is needed to achieve this, is part of each individual review.

In a community-based therapeutic community there is in addition the advantage that links with neighbours are operational. The fact that most people have a part-time or full-time job at least for periods during their stay reminds everyone of what society requires. In addition very specific survival skills are taught. The work groups inside the house, apart from imparting domestic skills, look carefully at the ability of each individual to do a task well, to observe time limits, to work with peers and to exercise leadership or accept it from others. Role play is practised to help residents explore how they may be successful in finding a job or lodgings; it also helps them to identify with the critical employer and with the landlady. Leavers' groups, finally, meet to discuss the problems they will have to contend with, and they explore these and their solutions in anticipation. In addition there is a well-established tradition of aftercare, which includes counselling where necessary. It is considered important that residents should be able to return for an evening, a meal or a few weekends, to the house where they stayed, and this informal contact may continue for years; after all, the relationships made were significant.

For those who do not seek to stay in touch, staff have a responsibility to make contact by correspondence after half a year and one year, to establish how ex-residents are managing, as well as to demonstrate concern for the ongoing welfare of the residents concerned. In addition, one senior staff member devotes the greater part of her time to ex-residents who want to talk, or may be in need of regular counselling sessions. These measures and operational conditions help to alleviate or avert the problems revealed by Rapoport and perhaps point to the community-based therapeutic community as the preferable situation for orientating the resident towards re-entry into society.

The Next Step

The question of leaving – to what? – is being given much thought. The isolated conditions in which many people live are stressful at the best of times. Ideas are therefore materialising whereby a number of ex-members of the community may share facilities, and derive support from one another.

There are as many forms of this next stage of provision or lifestyle as there are of the therapeutic community. The point in common between them, however, is probably that they tend to focus more on interdependency than on dependency on professionals. Therapeutic communities aim at training people in self-awareness and awareness of others, but all too often assume that once they seem ready to leave, they are fully equipped to deal with any problems that may face them in life. One of these problems is obviously that of loneliness; and the fact that much of the input of the therapeutic community is based on its existence as a group, means that many departing residents will feel lost in any setting that does not provide this support and interchange.

This is not to suggest that residents have been incapacitated in terms of leading 'an ordinary life' (of which definitions are problematic). Much of what has been written above underlines the increasing tendency nowadays to live in groups, as a chosen way of life rather than a proof of personal inadequacy. It is difficult to convince many authorities of this, given that most still think in terms either of the nuclear family or of solitary living, but it is the experience of the Fellowship, and other organisations such as MIND, that social isolation often precedes, if it does not precipitate, mental breakdown. It is therefore in many cases counterproductive to return residents to such a situation, however much confidence they may have gained. This is not to say that all those who have passed through a therapeutic community, for whatever reason, should choose to espouse group living: many will be able to cope with returning to their families, others will have developed sufficient confidence and social competence to live alone. But there remains a substantial proportion of residents whose anxieties at leaving the therapeutic community are very realistically decreased by the prospect of being able to share accommodation.

Such provision covers a spectrum ranging from supervised 'three-quarter-way houses', which by their very definition suggest a transitional facility, a next stage in the process of rehabilitation; to a house rented from the council or a housing association by a group of ex-residents, who are the direct tenants of these landlords. They benefit from no social work supervision other than would be accorded to an ordinary citizen. In between there are many degrees of autonomy. Group homes, whether run by MIND or local authorities, tend to supply a certain amount of support, whether from social workers or volunteers, but this would generally be non-resident, and based on a concept of befriending and crisis intervention. The Fellowship is experimenting with various degrees of support, from a staffed house divided into self-contained flats, running a weekly communal meeting and offering individual counselling if required, to projects manned by volunteers or a group of better-adjusted young people sharing a house with ex-residents, rather on the Patchwork Community model; the latter models have the advantage of not needing local authority support, as the projects are self-financing, thus adding to the community's sense of independence.

Every departing resident will obviously have different needs: it is up to the various organisations, and workers in the field, to seek out and provide a range of options that will meet the needs of different individuals at different times, and enable them to use the awareness and the strengths they have gained from the therapeutic community in a more open and independent setting.

The commentary on the chapters in this section has discussed issues of aim and structure. Much of what has been said refers indirectly to the role of staff, which is more fully explored in the section on staffing.

Notes

1. K. Jones, *A History of the Mental Health Services* (Routledge and Kegan Paul, London, 1972).
2. Ibid.
3. A. Julia, 'A Hostel for the Mentally Ill as a Stepping Stone in the Community', *New Thinking About Institutional Care* (Association of Social Workers, London, 1967). See also Chapter 25 below.
4. R.N. Rapoport, *Community as Doctor* (Tavistock Publications, London, 1960).
5. M.S. Schwartz, 'What is a Therapeutic Milieu?' in M. Greenblatt *et al.*, *The Patient and the Mental Hospital.*
6. J. Guindon, unpublished paper presented under the auspices of the CEC at its 47th Annual International Convention, Denver, Colorado, April 1969.
7. Ibid.
8. See A. Foster in R.D. Hinshelwood and N. Manning (eds.), *Therapeutic Communities: Reflections and Progress* (Routledge and Kegan Paul, London, 1979), Chapter 26.
9. M. Klein, *Contributions to Psychoanalysis 1921–45* (Hogarth Press, London, 1949).
10. A. Clare, *Psychiatry in Dissent* (Tavistock Publications, London, 1976), p. 186.
11. Ibid.
12. R.D. Laing, *The Politics of Experience* (Penguin, Harmondsworth, 1967).
13. Clare, *Psychiatry in Dissent.*
14. J. Henry, *Pathways to Madness* (Vintage Books, New York, 1973).
15. Clare, *Psychiatry in Dissent.*
16. *National Schizophrenic Fellowship News* (December 1978).
17. G. Nash *et al.*, 'The Phoenix House Program – The Results of a Two Year Follow Up' in G. De Leon (ed.), *Phoenix House: Studies in a Therapeutic Community 1968–73* (MSS Information Corporation, New York, 1974). However, the authors point out that variables between voluntary and compulsory groups were not studied.
18. G. De Leon, 'The Influence of Time-in-Program on Change in Resident Drug Addicts' in *Phoenix House.*
19. MIND/NAMH, *Group Homes* (MIND/NAMH, Leeds, 1972).
20. L. Christakis, 'Creative Housing for Older Persons', unpublished paper,

Washington, DC, 1975.

21. Simone de Beauvoir, *Memoirs of a Dutiful Daughter* (Penguin, Harmondsworth, 1963), vol. 1, pp. 101–7.

22. E. Jansen, unpublished transcript of a Richmond Fellowship staff workshop.

23. N. Jones in *Keep in Touch Newsletter*, no. 3 (October 1974).

24. See J. Berke, *The Butterfly Man* (Hutchinson & Co., London, 1977).

25. H.S. Brickman, 'Mental Health and Social Change: An Ecological Perspective' in H.P. Dreitzel (ed.), *The Social Organization of Health* (Macmillan, New York, and Collier-Macmillan, London, 1971).

26. Rapoport, *Community as Doctor*, pp. 212, 222–3.

1 SOME BASIC CONCEPTS IN THERAPEUTIC COMMUNITY WORK (UK)

Tom Main

By the end of the Second World War, several psychiatrists in the British army were aware of a sort of truth in General Montgomery's one-eyed monolithic edict that there were no bad soldiers, only bad officers. These psychiatrists, efficiently trained in the medical model of disease, had manfully diagnosed various kinds of personal breakdown in the soldiers sent to them, and had fought for humane recognition of each patient's plight. But they then ran into a fact that was awkward for their medical model of personal illness. This fact was that some army units persistently had a higher incidence of breakdown than others, and the breakdowns seemed to be characteristic, both in and out of battle, not so much of the individual as of the ways certain units treated their soldiers. Further investigation showed that a high incidence of psychiatric disturbance in a unit was also accompanied by other signs of trouble: high VD rates, crime rates, absence without leave and high sickness rates. Conversely the collected figures allowed the recognition of other units in which the incidence of these disturbances was low. Faced with these facts, the psychiatrists now began to speak less about the interesting personal pathology of their patients and more about the nature of the units which referred them. Without abandoning the medical model, they no longer relied solely on it for total diagnosis or treatment, but began to think in terms of the social pathology of whole units, about unit cultures and mores, social systems, types of leadership, unit social values, a unit's stratification of power and of responsibility; formal and informal communications systems; different kinds of officer-man relations; interpersonal relations optimal for stability and effective soldiery.

For medical men reared in the study of individual pathology, this was a new world. A distinct relation between individual health or breakdown and social health or social pathology of the various units was easy to observe, but far from easy to encompass in one embracing theory. Indeed, it is still true that we have no adequate general theory of psycho-social pathology or treatment. We were humbly aware that, for decades, professional soldiers had been sure about these empiric facts even though their concepts of *esprit de corps* and morale were at once vague and idealistic, and their methods of promotion were variously inspirational, moralistic, homespun, pragmatic, intuitive and sometimes unsure. With that fact to guard us against hubris in our new vision we were also lucky to be guarded against amateurism by our encounter with fellow workers in the army who were variously social anthropologists, sociologists, social psychologists and psychoanalysts. A new kind of psychiatry, social psychiatry, became a possibility, and the study of the working of whole social units and their effect on individuals became a legitimate activity for psychiatrists and other applied social scientists. (It was this group of colleagues who founded the Tavistock Institute of Human Relations after the war.)

A second matter is relevant to my subject. Coincidental with the above, group therapy, hardly known before the war, grew steadily in the army, led by Foulkes and extended to the treatment of a whole ward by Bion, while Maxwell Jones in the emergency medical services had begun his first experiments with discussions and psychodrama with large groups of patients. The methods of these workers varied, but they had in common a recognition that patients' living relations with each other and with their doctor was a field of powerful study for insight and change. Such group studies were not, you will notice, about the illness on the medical model, but about the disorders of their living relations uncovered in discussion with each other and the forms and effects of these.

At Northfield Mental Hospital, I had the opportunity to put together these two insights – the significance of a social system for deciding the health or illness of an individual and the fruitfulness for personal change of group analysis – to create this third idea: the possibility that a hospital might become therapeutic as a social organisation, no matter what individual treatments were or were not offered. Not only patients' behaviour and relations but staff behaviour and relations were, therefore, areas relevant for study by all. The experiment was aimed at creating together a social system based not on the medical model of a healthy knowledgeable staff and sick obedient patients, but upon the joint recognition of each individual's capacity and limitations for performing essential tasks, and with participation by all in arranging that these be carried out. Where problems arose and failures occurred these would be subjects not for discipline but for investigation as failures of interpersonal art. The experiment at Northfield led to a high degree of collaboration between patients and staff as joint community members. The major outlines of the social structure and the roles it enmeshed were clear; the army system had seen to that, but the way this structure and the way these roles were sustained became more thoughtful and sincere. The study by all of each other's needs, assets and liabilities led to dramatic changes in the relations within the community. Not only patients' needs and problems but staff's needs and problems were shared openly. There was soon less frustration for all in the community, and more recognition and use of diverse human ability. There was much spontaneous activity for the patients and staff in purposeful and responsible work, not only inside the hospital but outside as well. I think it also developed the first industrial therapy unit; many of the patients used also to work in what is now the BMC factory at Northfield.

In all this, and perhaps this should be stressed, *all*, both patients and staff, were concerned that our activities should be socially syntonic in the widest sense possible, acceptable both to the army system in which we worked, and to the civilian world in which the hospital was located. It was believed that part of this community's task was to enlist the sanction of relevant authorities for our activities – trades unions, local townspeople and army authorities. We were determined to survive, not to die a heroic death.

As the first therapeutic community, Northfield has its own historical importance. It demonstrated that a hospital need no longer be conceived and administered as a place where the treatment of illness comes first, with relative disregard for the wishes of the owner of the illness, but could become one where the owner of the illness can be recognised as a singular being, singular in need and ability, could be respected and perhaps helped to grow, even though in hospital. It also demonstrated that treatment and administration can be thought of as one total clinical activity which needs the active participation of patients, if staff are not to be pushed into carrying massive and inhuman burdens of responsibility for everything, good or bad, and for events the creation or solution of which lies in others' hands.

This experiment, the first 'therapeutic community', ended shortly after the war, too quickly perhaps for its pioneer enthusiasms to be tested in a less excited reality, but late enough for the concept to have taken root in many places all over the world. The term 'therapeutic community', however, is often misunderstood and in some cases misapplied. Sometimes it is used to dignify merely one specific procedure, such as a weekly ward meeting, sometimes to describe any place in which medical treatment is offered. In my view, if the term is to retain any distinct meaning, it should define not techniques or procedure but a particular type of social organisation. It involves the total community in a culture of enquiry into the nature of the social processes within, and how far these truly succeed or fail in caring for the specific individuals in it, both patients and staff. I mention staff, not only because they too are human beings, but because culture spreads from the top in any hierarchy, and as staff are or are not cared for, so they will care or not care for their charges.

The concept allows a particular way of evaluating all social organisation. Every human organisation is a social and interpersonal setting which either extends or cramps the personality of the individuals within it, and is variously therapeutic or anti-therapeutic, creating increased or decreased health. The concept offers a framework by which to view hospitals, halfway houses, work places, factories, townships and, yes, military units. The incidence of disturbed individuals in an organisation will perhaps in the future be taken to measure what the organisation does in the way of anti-therapy. Sickness rates, absence rates, staff turnover rates, alcoholism, mutinies, strikes, suicide rates, psychiatric breakdowns, delinquencies, are some of the things that we can be fairly sure about as being yardsticks of the society in which they are found.

But it is early days. The practical problems of identifying the effect on the individual of different social organisations are immense, and although politicians and industrial managers sometimes seem sure about causes and effects, their methods of treatment are often as merely inspirational, moralistic, homespun, pragmatic, intuitive and unsure as any professional soldier's. The search for knowledge by investigation and experiment is all too rare, and we do not even have an adequate general theory of psycho-social development upon which to found either investigations or treatment. Like professional soldiers, politicians and managers, much psychiatric work is still at a level of pragmatism and intuition, sometimes little more than an act of faith. Alfred Stanton reminds us that in some not very precise way, it has been known and well known that respectful treatment of patients with psychosis favours recovery, but he too asks for research directed towards accurate and specific identification of those patterns of interaction or transaction with other people, which characterise different types of disorder. Only thus will milieu therapy be differentiated sharply from good custody, and therapy from uninstructed humanitarian help.

I believe that it is because we have not yet succeeded in identifying clearly enough the specific transaction patterns and needs of the various types of disorder that we who are concerned with therapeutic organisations find ourselves in disagreements over how such therapeutic communities should be run. It is by no means true that schizophrenic patients, who are well known to deteriorate in situations of high emotional pressure and demand, will benefit from the kind of community which Maxwell Jones designed for psychopaths, wherein they became accountable to large meetings for deviant behaviour. It seems to me that we make a mistake if we judge each therapeutic community in terms of the others. Rather we should judge each in terms of its capacity to understand the particular kinds of people in it, and to devise particular psycho-social processes to meet their particular needs.

Stanley Eldred, in a recent masterly review entitled 'Research and Therapeutic Milieu', points out many problems. 'We are beset in our research methodology by one abiding fact which makes exactitude and control of research design far from ideal.' This is as David Ruhr remarked, 'Patients don't hold still like they should.' A simple example of this difficulty is seen in the problem of follow-up. If it is to be concerned with more than trivia, it is discouragingly effortful and expensive, and yet may still be unsure. The location of the ex-patient, his relatives, his doctor, his employer and his social associates, the obtaining of their collaboration and the design of scales to measure their communication is a daunting task. Insofar as statistical problems arise over psycho-social matters, it is Helen Sargant who observed, 'Soon we run into such apparently insurmountable obstacles that it may seem better to switch our interests.' Phillip May points out the difficulty of contamination in follow-up. The ex-patient is now older, subject to changes in his environment, accidents of fate, and the effect of intervening treatment by others. He attacks convincingly the holy cow of long-term follow-up studies, and makes clear that we must be content with follow-up of reasonably short duration.

But given the need for scientific humility about our theories and research problems and results on the one hand, we are not helpless on the other. We can have some certainty about careful observations, and can essay general statements about them which can be generally tested. We can borrow and use established insights from the social and medical sciences to extend our powers of analysis and we can fall back on much established knowledge. And now for a few landmarks, a few among many. Goffmann, in his book *Asylums*,[1] confirmed and showed in detail the usefulness of viewing the medical organisation not in terms of a medical model concerned with diseases and treatment but in sociological terms concerned with the interpersonal and social processes it contained and the effects of these on the people in it. Scathing about the dehumanising procedures he found and the hidden severe disciplines of deviance, he none the less showed the compelling authority of the sociological viewpoint for reviewing what organisations do to the people in them. In 1959 Russell Barton, in his book on institutional neurosis,[2] had shown that this syndrome, although widespread, was under our noses but unobserved in mental hospitals. This severe, crippling, tragic upset of mental life, was not the result of mental illness; he showed it was simply a long-term reaction to the dehumanising social organisation of the hospital itself. Its features of blanket apathy about work, personal relations, dress, speech, and body cleanliness had been previously interpreted as the result of irreversible brain pathology on the medical model. Russell Barton showed this was false, that the syndrome was reversible, and that it could be prevented if the social structures, the roles, the relations and the culture of the hospital were altered. Our views about the very nature of chronic psychosis had to be reviewed because of his work. Stanton and Schwartz in their studies of individual patients at about the same time showed that particular symptoms such as incontinence and catatonic excitement, hitherto regarded as intrinsic to an illness of the patient, were in fact reactive to crises in the social environment, the patient's ways of participating in confusing, hidden tensions between the staff. They showed that resolution of staff tensions by open but usually painful staff discussion led to disappearance of the symptoms, even though the patient knew nothing of such discussion

Findings of this order led immediately to alterations in hospital organisations and practices throughout the world and have been one of the elements in the reduction of occupied mental hospital beds in Western countries, but they also raised some important questions. Certain controversial workers, and prominently R.D. Laing, have come to regard their patients as never having had any personal illness at all, but simply as sensible people reacting to adverse circumstances, both now and in the past. Others have designed institutional changes which correct or avoid iatrogenic illness, and have been so impressed by the changes in their patients that they have been content with these and have failed to study the patients' essential illness.

It is certainly a major advance that some hospitals are much less anti-therapeutic as social organisations than they were, and there is no doubt that their patients are much the better for this. The avoidance of iatrogenic illness is a major historical advance and where this has been achieved it has been the result of careful, sociologically skilled, persistent effort. It alone has required the detailed consideration of total communities, staff as well as patients, the patient recognition and resolution of resistances to change, and new staff training systems, as well as the obtaining of social sanctions for many difficult procedural changes. The insights gained by our recognition of anti-therapeutic effects in psychiatric institutions and how to avoid them may have major applications in all organisations: general hospitals, factories, offices, prisons, geriatric homes, maternity hospitals, schools, indeed wherever people are in danger of being administered as standard dehumanised units by others who have been put in the equally inhuman position of having to know best. It is now possible and easy to recognise crude and dramatic syndromes reactive to our social organisations and to take steps to avoid them, but vigilance must be eternal. We may in our changed methods of social organisation create quieter and more subtle changes. Perhaps that is what we are in the process of doing today; for the avoidance of anti-therapy is by no means easy.

The need for humility and work remains. And the question arises, 'Is the avoidance of anti-therapy enough for a therapeutic community?' What about patients, ill in their own right and relatively free from reactions to adverse circumstances? For communities which aim to be positively therapeutic it is necessary to relate the social process to the psychopathology it treats. It follows that because of the various psychopathological states, one kind of therapeutic community will not do for all. Even although it is impossible for one worker from one field, such as myself, to indicate without pretentiousness the different kinds of social processes needed for the different fields of pathology, it is possible to attempt some general statements about general psychopathology, and general social process. It may be safe to begin with some of the basic requirements that ordinary people need from their social environment.

Experiments in sensory deprivation have shown unequivocally that bereft of information from the world around him and thrown back only on his internal resources, an individual is liable to become hallucinated, deluded and psychotic. To put this in another way, relations with the environment are essential to mental health. One identifies oneself, and experiences one's resources and minimises distortion of reality, through relations with others. This is not an all or none matter, merely one of degree, because all environments deprive one more or less. Allow me a caricature of organisation man. The independent craftsman or trader becomes increasingly rare, so that today most of us are employed by large corporations. The average man's daily schedule is not under his own control. It is decided by others, together with whom and when he will work, and for how long each day, and when he will have holidays and for how long. But he rarely knows who these others are; all he knows is that his own wishes do not matter much to them. His promotion will not depend on his own wishes or efforts, but will be decided by rules made by unknown others, often by an anonymous higher body. So with his money rewards. In the fashioning of the daily routines and work rules and regulations around him he will have little or no personal choice. These too will be decided by some higher individual or committee he has never met, never sees, with whom he has no relations, and with whom he cannot talk. His ideas about how to make his own work easier or more efficient, more interesting or more rewarding, he will usually have to keep to himself, or his peers. He usually has no personal relations with the very people who indeed fashion the main outlines of his working life, only with his immediate fellows and his immediate superiors, who in any event may be as gripped by the system as he is. No allowance is possible for the way his talents and tastes may differ from those who work alongside him. He can rarely appeal against his fate in a significant way to higher authorities, who make these higher decisions. My caricature concerns the underemployment of personality assets and the degree of anomie in which many an individual works, largely unrecognised as a person, largely unrelated to the purpose of the corporation or the people in it who employ him.

Under such circumstances changes in mental health may arise. The poverty of working relations, the lack of sense to the worker about decisions he must fall in with, the fact of being unimportant, and many other minor, general frustrations lead notoriously not merely to failure of enthusiasm, not only to relative apathy; thin collaboration over policy leads not merely to loss of enthusiasm and limited experience of oneself and one's assets; often they lead to regressions, with the reactivation of primitive infantile ways of feeling and thinking, and the need to dispose of aggression in other ways than in adventure in living and working. Mature relations with the world being unrewarding, mature recognition of others tends to be slowly replaced by a certain narcissistic withdrawal and preoccupation with the self, and so to mental splitting and primitive projection mechanisms with the world now seen as containing inhumanly good and inhumanly bad figures. Relations assume distorted and infantile psychotic forms. The projection of aggression and malice arising from frustration means that the world becomes not a place for rich interest and collaborative satisfaction but for suspicion and wariness about ill-will and possible exploitation, with selfish bastards in the high places if one is low in hierarchy, or greedy idlers in the lower places if one is high in the hierarchy. Although still within the limits of normality such a person is no longer in full mental health. I hope this condensed and caricatured statement will suffice for its corollary that for mental health the personalised individual needs active collaborative relations with personalised others. It seems that he, with his assets and liabilities, tastes, foibles and idiosyncrasies, needs to be reliably recognised, known and accepted, and respected in agreed reciprocal endeavours with others whom he knows in like depth. These relations should probably be of a kind which fully employs the resources and neither under-employs nor overemploys them.

This viewpoint which concerns both the internal life of the individual and his external relations with others allows us the hope of developing a theory of psycho-social development and points to some general considerations about social environments which do seem actively to promote mental health. In these the individual is steadily recognised as singular, and his efforts to maintain his personal identity are welcomed. This means a minimum of staff-decided routines and behaviour and standard practices which he must fit, but means his participation with others in the community in the fashioning of techniques and practices that will seek out and solve the ordinary problems of work and play that face him and everybody else. It also means a certain stability of post in the staff personnel, so that he can relate reliably and in depth to somebody he can count on. Conversely it means that the personnel who are involved with him must have time and share opportunities to get to know him well as a person, with assets and tastes, and not merely occasionally because of troublesome behaviour. His ambitions and tastes are not thought of as time-consuming nuisances which need discipline but rather as community assets, and their employment is encouraged and facilitated. Where crises of the community arise, practical or emotional, his help and and his ideas in solving these are sought, even demanded, up to the limit of his capacity, whether these be problems about staff or fellow patients. His capacity to interact with others is given major freedom. The sick person's liability to distort reality does not in these organisations serve the staff as an excuse, by categorising this as a symptom of sickness, to keep distance from him. When he misunderstands people or events his distortions are seen as an opportunity for critical enquiry into blocked communication for clarifying reality to him and for identifying the particular anxieties which beset him. Such communities recognise that annoying inefficiencies and mistakes are usually the result of interpersonal problems of failure to understand (and I do not mean agree with) others. Such failures are as common among staff as among patients. There is therefore much provision also for staff discussion to seek common understanding and agreement about difficult problems, administrative, clinical or interpersonal, and to fashion mutually informed understanding about particular patients or events.

Because the culture aims at freeing the initiative of patients so that they may undertake responsibilities, it has the same aims for staff. It is careful that junior staff who particularly work at the patient/staff interface are empowered and supported in their initiatives in discharge of their professional roles. The way the staff members are cared for and taught, related to and recognised as singular people, is their model for how they will treat their patients. To avoid confusion among the patients and staff, clarity about the social structure, the roles and their attached tasks and responsibilities and the relations between these roles, both up and down the hierarchy, is essential. Responsibility for what and to whom defines each staff role. Nursing is less about performing functions and tasks, which help distancing from people, than about the needs of whole people. For example it is desirable that each patient knows and can relate to his personal nurse on duty for all of his needs rather than have to go to several different nurses and several different staff for his different needs and functions. The nurses or their counterparts seek not to do things to patients or for patients, but with patients. Their patients are theirs and they are their patients'. Just as the patients will meet in small groups for work-planning, work tasks, or for therapy, so there will be staff groups for sharing of day-to-day information or for professional seminars. The culture is one entity, a patient/staff culture, not one for staff and another for patients. So, the therapeutic community has crystal-clear staff roles, surely and reliably, but the patient role is fashioned by what he can do in the assumption of power and responsibility to produce what one might call a joint investment corporation, in which the views and assets of all are known and respected. Insofar as permissiveness goes, the community will be alert to the abnegation of responsibility by staff when the going is hard, and will examine the hard-going, and will be equally alert to the abnegation of responsibility for oneself and for others that is common in mental illness. There is clarity about the difference between freedom of contributions and social irresponsibility. (Social sanctioning springs from care and interest whereas permissiveness can be a Pontius Pilate act of exasperated refusal to care.) A therapeutic community, if it is to be a useful model, requires of its members a sober hardheaded awareness that no one community setting can be effective with all types of patients. It is fashioned by and for a particular population. Its members also require of each other an interest in what the society around it can and cannot sanction.

These then are some general features about social environments which may have some universal applicability. They revolve around the recognition of assets of the members, the examination of the distortions of human relations, with endeavours to repair, support and nourish the growth of personal identity. Again it may need emphasis that pure models are not for worship, but are mere guidelines for development in different circumstances, and that different psychopathologies need different social processes, especially designed for the special nature of the people they treat. Similarly with any therapeutic community there will be staff with special skills, and the clear differentiation of these skills may have to be refreshed regularly in discussion to avoid amateurism when professionalism is needed. That is to say, the staff members themselves may need help to maintain recognition by all of the singular professional competences of special staff for special tasks and of the different personalities of staff.

Staff rivalries and envies are inevitable in all communities, therapeutic or not, and need not only tolerance but recognition, open discussion and understanding by all, rather than appeasement by role-blurring. Only by truly respecting the different professional roles and skills can real teamwork come about. Certain staff, usually medical or psychotherapeutic, may be required to investigate especially the illnessses and incapacities of patients and to prescribe and monitor drugs; for the concept of a therapeutic community does not exclude these. Indeed, they operate best in a society which is concerned with whole people. Other staff will be particularly concerned with working relations, with social assets, potential and talent, and the facilitation of their use, with joint enjoyment of problem-solving – in a word, with social relations. The sharing of a joint policy thus does not mean that every staff member attempts everything, rather that he or she accepts distinct responsibilities for contributing towards the whole with the differentiated team members relying on each other.

You will note I have not much discussed group meetings or procedures, for while they are essential details within a total design they do not by themselves define social process. The therapeutic purposes of facilitating interaction and understanding, of joint law-making rather than staff law-giving, of solving problems not by fear but by enquiry, of recognising and respecting personal identity and assets and of maintaining a culture of enquiry into problems, seems to be the essence of a therapeutic social approach. The procedures springing from this approach will be fashioned and refreshed and refashioned according to the changing needs of a slowly changing patient population – otherwise they may in time become mere hallowed but lifeless routines instead of techniques to pursue agreed purposes. Above all a therapeutic community can not be other than responsive to changing populations.

Notes

1. E. Goffmann, *Asylums* (Penguin, Harmondsworth, 1968).
2. R. Barton, *Institutional Neurosis* (Wright, Bristol, 1959).

2 THERAPEUTIC COMMUNITIES: THE IDEAL, THE REAL AND THE POSSIBLE (UK)

Elisabeth Shoenberg

I once knew a man who was always looking for the ideal girl. He classified girls as 1st class, 2nd class, 3rd class, pass and unclassed. Search as he might, he never actually met a 1st class girl, and eventually considered himself lucky to marry a 2nd class one. I feel that those of us who work in social psychiatry are in a very similar position. Few of us are lucky enough to be involved in anything as good as a 2nd class community. We keep before us the platonic ideal of what a 1st class therapeutic community should be, and use this concept of the ideal both for hope and despair. Lately there seems to be more despair than hope. What is this ideal?

The concept of the therapeutic community was originally a revolutionary one. At a time when psychiatric hospitals were essentially custodial and repressive, it reintroduced the ideal of mutual care and the opening up of communication between otherwise isolated individuals through the sharing of suffering, of healing, and of responsibility for each other. I say the reintroduction because it was of course a very old ideal, and a very durable one, which has kept reappearing in various guises throughout human history. It is known basically as brotherly love.

Sometimes it has appeared as a religious ideal. All the best-known religions have produced organisations for community living and mutual care – monasteries, convents, lamasaries, ashrams. Other communities have been inspired by social and political philosophies: the phalansteries, the kibbutz and the commune are all examples of these.

Mental health now follows God and social justice as a cause for seeking brotherly love. Each generation has re-expressed the ideal that was there before, and whether it is attributed to God, social justice or merely efficiency, the ideal of brotherly love seems indestructible. Unfortunately, the hidden ideals of greed, hatred, murder, war and pollution seem equally indestructable, so that each new generation rediscovers the ideal of brotherly love as a new necessity for the new men, but has to fight the same old enemies of indifference and selfish isolation.

How do we discover it afresh now, in our time? Today one scarcely dares to mention brotherly love. It seems a phrase too stale, too banal, too worn out by pious hypocrisy. Indeed, if one does say it, the brothers who spring to mind are Cain and Abel. Yet, though we are surrounded by the most appalling and cynical acts of genocide, thuggery and rapacity, that indestructible spirit of caring is asserting itself once again very strongly.

The religious formulation still persists, despite all the acts of bloodshed, persecution and torture done throughout history and today by those who proclaim the doctrine of divine love. Man is crucified afresh each day. The Inquisition tortured and destroyed in the name of Gentle Jesus; Protestants and Catholics still kill each other; Muslims and Hindus have communal strife.

The political formulation persists too: fraternity, equality, freedom. These great and genuine ideals still move us despite the crimes that are committed in the name of liberty; despite the revolutions that have repeatedly devoured their own by guillotine, concentration camp or merely politics.

Now, we have a psychiatric restatement of the religious, political and sociological formulations of this old ideal. I find this very hopeful because it suggests a real attempt to discover something of the true nature of man's isolation and his strange, sad position as a sort of vulnerable predator. In the past and the present, religious, political and sociological action in support of man's love and care for his neighbour have each led to intolerance, persecution, cruelty and massacre. Will psychiatry do the same?

In this latest approach to an old and tragic problem, those concerned with psychiatry are dealing with people who are labelled ill. This concept of mental illness is a very hot potato and I don't propose to burn my fingers on it. Is there such a thing as mental illness, or is it merely an artefact caused by the deforming pressures of our society? I fancy it's sometimes mostly one, sometimes mostly the other, and usually a bit of each. But whatever the various and complex truths, half truths, nonsenses, speculations and dark suspicions with which we try to answer this question, we do know that people who get labelled 'psychiatric patient' have one thing in common. This is, in greater or lesser degree, an awareness of difficulty in coping with interpersonal relationships. This often disabling difficulty, this inability to communicate and accept communications, can be dealt with in a number of ways.

In its most extreme form, one traditional method of treating this problem of interpersonal relationships is to label the incomprehensible communication 'madness', and to push out of society the person who can't find his role in it. This was the old approach of putting lunatics away, locking them up with their alarming and incomprehensible feelings, and refusing to try and understand them. In the words of Tom Lehrer, 'If you can't communicate, the least you can do is shut up!' This is what mental hospitals used to be for, and still often are, despite lip service to the therapeutic community. Just crowding a lot of sad and lonely, self-isolated people together into a hospital ward, or a hostel, or a home, does not automatically make them into members of a community. Indeed, it may increase their isolation, institutionalise their aloneness, and merely create a very damaging lonely crowd. If we are to create a therapeutic community out of their separate lonelinesses, there must be a conscious and sincere attempt to use the therapeutic potential of all the patients and all the staff, and to open up communication not only between the patient and himself, but between patients; between patients and staff, and staff and staff. I think the last of these is the hardest. This inevitably demands a breaking down of hierarchical barriers in communication. When this is done, each member of the community – staff or patient – develops his full value as one who not only receives help but gives it.

But can we come together with strangers as brothers? Can we care about their feelings, anxieties and joys and share ours with them? Succeeding or failing in doing this is basic to the whole idea of the therapeutic community. It is equally basic to our being able to tolerate starvation, bombing, defoliation – the destruction of whole peoples, as long as they are far away, somewhere out there in the dark. Actually, when we do tolerate all that, it's really we who are in the dark. If I may quote Tom Lehrer again, he tells a story which I thought very funny at first, but later came to realise sums up the problem of loving your neighbour very neatly and very cynically. He tells of getting a letter which said, 'Darling, I love you and cannot live without you. Marry me or I will kill myself.' He was most disturbed and worried when he read this letter, until he took a look at the envelope, and found it was addressed to 'Occupant'! It really is quite difficult to love one's neighbour. To do so one needs to know him. He must be known as a real person – not just the 'Occupant'. That real person may be quite hard to accept and interact with, and this is where a purpose-built therapeutic community can be a great help, as a workshop of human relationships.

The ideal therapeutic community has staff and patients encountering each other as real, often fallible, people trying to fight their way together through obstacles of fear, phantasy and sorrow. By interaction with others they develop a capacity for self-acceptance and internal communication as part of self-realisation. The usual way of facilitating this is by regular group and community meetings which all participate in as part of the total community experience.

The form and content of this community experience are not static, unless the community is dead or dying. It started as a revolution in communication and relationships, and is now undergoing a radical change. People who helped to make this revolution, and were enthusiastic in developing new forms of dynamic organisation, get very worried when newcomers want to change these settled forms of organisation, because what's happened is that this revolution has in itself become institutionalised.

The death of Denis Martin was a great sorrow for those of us who knew him and knew his work. But one of the many things that will live on in his work at Claybury is that – unlike the original pioneers of the therapeutic community who worked in small, select units with patients who were homogeneous and rarely psychotic – he was a pioneer in introducing the therapeutic community approach to a very big mental hospital, to treat every kind of patient in every kind of ward. This meant that the conventional ways of working with carefully chosen patients, and often equally carefully selected staff, had to be adapted freely. Techniques grew, changed, modified, took on a life of their own. We argued, experimented, constantly changed. What had worked well with one group was inappropriate for another. Staff needs and problems changed enormously too, in step with the vast social changes that we have all been living through.

To my mind there is only one thing that does not need to keep changing in the successful therapeutic community, and that is the importance of opening up communication and keeping it open. Everything else can and should constantly change, evolve, and respond sensitively to changing needs so that it can let the members find tomorrow's answers for tomorrow's problems.

I have been discussing patients and therapists, but the idea of a therapeutic community is not limited to the psychiatric hospital, hostel or home. The difficulties that people have in breaking out of their isolation are not limited to those labelled psychiatrically ill. They are part of human experience, and particularly so for people who live in our fragmented sort of society, where the need to belong to a community, a recognisable group, is great. The more our society breaks down traditional naturally occurring bonds, the more people try to recreate them in different forms. Many try to escape from their isolation by setting up groups and organisations in which the cultivation of interpersonal relationships is the sole object instead of the by-product. When they do this, the word 'therapy' seems to creep in. I wonder why!

Some of these new, purposeful organisations are at a seemingly superficial level. Others, such as the encounter groups, seem to consider some sort of therapy as one of their aims, and this really worries me. Do we have to be sick to encounter each other and ourselves? Must our community be therapeutic? People use this term 'therapeutic community' so loosely as to make it quite meaningless. For instance, a parson once said to me very proudly, 'My whole parish is a therapeutic community', and he seemed affronted when I asked: 'Why? Are all your parishioners ill then?' He really only meant that it was a closely knit community of people who knew each other well, who helped each other, and were able to talk to each other frankly in a caring sort of way. That's admirable, and it's not as common as it should be, but you don't have to be in need of therapy to aim at and achieve a well functioning community.

The need for a therapeutic community is intimately related to the isolation that so many people experience within our society. The success of a therapeutic community is equally intimately related to the support that it gets from society. Ideally, the person who cannot cope with the tasks of living, and requires in-patient treatment, needs to relate his membership of the therapeutic community within, to the society without that he came from and will return to. Within the hospital, or other therapeutic organisation, a network of relationships is set up. Each new member is absorbed into it, so that he gradually learns new ways of examining and communicating his own feelings as well as responding to those of others. He is stretched in his emotional understanding and sincerity, learns new ways of using his potential, and develops new social skills. The staff, composed of people trained in different disciplines are developing and learning and being stretched too.

There are many ways of organising such a community, but most agree that the quality and depth of the experience – and therefore of what can be achieved – appears to bear some relation to the number of meetings. If there are too few, communication tends to congeal. If too many, it is just possible that communication may undergo a sort of paradoxical inhibition. Most of us feel that a daily community meeting, with a variety of small groups as well, is desirable.

This intensive communication, within the protected treatment situation of social intimacy, warmth and openness may be something very different from life at home. It is therefore very important to involve relatives in the treatment situation wherever feasible, so that they can share in changing and developing.

Being in hospital is only an incident in a patient's life, but it is an incident which can crucially affect how his life is lived subsequently. We talk of halfway houses as part of rehabilitation after hospital, but we must also consider the hospital itself as a halfway house. Halfway to what? All too often even a good therapeutic community in a hospital can be halfway to losing one's footing in society. Even the shortest stay in hospital may foster traits of dependence which can be utterly ruinous. People may indeed recollect the warm friendliness when they are alone in a bedsitter, or lonely housewives at home, or without friends, or unemployed. They may seek outside the companionship and understanding that they found in hospital, but it is not forthcoming.

As members of the hospital therapeutic community, the hospital took them halfway towards being members of the ordinary outside community, but it is not far enough for many: halfway to living and communicating with others; halfway to social and personal responsibility; halfway to rehabilitation. But where is the other half?

There is a handful of group homes, a tiny number of hostels and sheltered workshops, a few clubs, a grossly undermanned and over-burdened social service. So people stay on in hospital when they could be discharged if they were able to get support outside the hospital. They linger on in hospital waiting for a place in a halfway home, waiting for a room, waiting for a workshop, or because their homes have closed up behind them. If the psychological moment for discharge is passed, the impulse to attempt independence may pass too. Their capacity for independence is threatened by institutionalisation, and they may end as chronic patients preferring a caring, but crushing, institution to the bleak, rejecting outside world.

We are supposed to have put an end to all that by substituting a dynamic therapeutic community for custodial care. But the problem of institutionalisation within our communities may arise not only from the difficulties of re-establishment in the outside world, but also from our misplaced enthusiasm. Sometimes, for instance, a patient may improve a great deal. Though he still has many problems he's now superficially well. He's doing well in group therapy, works through a lot of material and is really a great help to the group. At our staff meeting (we meet once or twice a day) somebody says 'What about discharging him?' 'Oh no, that would be a terrible pity . . . he's just getting somewhere, we must go on . . . ' And so we might go on until that happy impetus to go out and get a job and get on with ordinary life has passed. It's rather like the advice to deal with the impulse to take exercise by lying down until it goes away. There is a real danger in doing this. We can keep people working away at their problems until psychotherapy becomes their established way of living, instead of their way into life. The seductive form of the warm, helpful, therapeutic community must not blind us to the danger that it may cause just as destructive institutionalisation as the bleak, custodial, closed hospital.

This is surely the time when we need to take our staff and our skills into the outside community. I mentioned that hospital admission should be only an incident in the total treatment of a patient and his illness. Many of us are trying to avoid that admission altogether, or make it very brief, by seeing the patient in his home setting against the background of his own community, and treating him there. But how can we do this without solving some of our staff problems? Not only are many hospitals grotesquely understaffed, but the best use of the existing staff is not made. When we talk of therapeutic communities we always think of the patients, but the staff are members of it too, and when their problems become overpowering, what is the effect on their contribution to the community? In some hospitals, the majority of students and junior nurses now come from abroad, as do quite a few of the doctors. Young, far from home, perhaps in very alien surroundings, dealing with very alarming people from a foreign culture, they struggle with problems of homesickness, loneliness and adaptation to a new way of life. How much help *do* we give them, how much carefully planned help *should* we be giving them with language and local ways, as well as friendship and gratitude for what they bring to our hospitals? It may well be that, just as a therapeutic community for the sick offers much that can be carried over into society at large, so the informal league of nations within our hospital community may help to show the way to an international and peaceful culture.

But this seems a long way off. In the meantime, we haven't enough staff to cope adequately. The stress on the overworked staff has immediate repercussions on the quality of the community and what can be achieved within it. It is bad economic thinking too. *Economy on staffing is extravagant, for it leads to increased expense on keeping some patients who would be able to leave, if we had enough staff to allow for more intensive work, and if the resources within the outside community were adequate.*

So, whether we think of the therapeutic community in its ideal form or as it actually is, we cannot pursue it in isolation from our whole society, any more than we can conceive of our patients without thinking of them in their social and family settings.

Let us consider what we are asking for in terms of the possible as well as the ideal: the practical possibilities within the real situation. What is happening now? The revolutionary communities which were set up in the 50s and 60s have now become the establishment, and the dynamics of today are producing fresh forms and revolting against the classical modes of therapeutic communities. Do we need the sort of staff we are accustomed to demanding? Does the future of the therapeutic community rest with the professionals? Do we need more and more of them, or are we perhaps moving towards some quite new phase?

When we consider these questions we are as likely to find the answers in sociology and anthropology as in medicine. Psychiatry involves a partnership with these sciences (or pre-sciences). Vast social solutions, using the vast social and therapeutic potential of the patients as part of society instead of being alienated from it, may well lead us to working outside the institutions in a new type of therapeutic organisation. I think it's likely to be an organisation in which the professionals will do less dictating and act more as resource people. We are clearly moving out from the classical intra-mural, closed therapeutic community into working within the open community of people at home. Not only are our staff working through crises with families in the community, but non-professional community members are increasingly being involved in primary mental health care. This way of working with the actual resource people of the local community itself is a very promising development which is already being worked out with considerable success in some developing countries, for example, southern India. Conversely, the members of therapeutic communities may have an important role in helping us to deal with our problems as citizens of a very sick world. It may well be that the lessons that our patients teach us and themselves will have to be learnt by the 'sane' organisations of the world: these are the communication skills they have learnt as sick people, which are so lacking in the 'sane' world.

Let the shape of therapeutic communities to come arise from feeling, listening, sharing and caring, as a sensitive response to each other's changing needs in a changing society.

3 THE HALFWAY HOUSE AS A THERAPEUTIC COMMUNITY: A USEFUL MODEL OR A BURDENSOME MYTH? (USA)

Howard A. Hoffman

Our effort to define, describe and measure what therapeutic communities are, is a timely and important endeavour. In the United States, we are at a time when fiscal intermediaries, the government and private insurance companies, as well as the consumers, our patients, are raising questions about what we are doing, why we are doing it and whether it works. They are also saying, 'whatever you're doing, it costs too much'.

I recently attended a meeting where medical directors from many of the leading private psychiatric hospitals in the United States attempted to define milieu therapy. Significant in our motivation to do so, was the fact that private insurance companies have refused to pay for treatment in psychiatric hospitals, as soon as they find out that the patient is receiving milieu therapy. At the end of the meeting the group was split between those people who felt that using the term should be abandoned because it was a cop-out, an excuse for muddled thinking and poorly defined treatment objectives; the other half of the group felt that it was a cop-out to abandon the term, that indeed, we had to devote ourselves to continued work at definition. Those of us who work with therapeutic communities are *convinced* it is the right approach. When asked to substantiate our 'feelings' with facts and follow-up studies, we lamely retreat to discussions of the methodologic nightmares involved in doing controlled research in the field.

Since the early days of the Belgian colony Gheel, eight centuries ago, there have been people dedicating themselves to helping the emotionally disturbed, by harnessing the therapeutic potential that can be found in organised social systems. As Bochoven in his scholarly article on the history of moral treatment in American psychiatry[1] points out, 'Plato laid the basis for human understanding when he wrote, "it may almost be asserted that all intemperance in any kind of pleasure and all disgraceful conduct is not properly blamed as the consequence of voluntary guilt. For no one is voluntarily bad. But he who is depraved becomes so through a certain habit of body and an ill-governed education. All the vicious are vicious through two most involuntary causes, which we shall always ascribe to the planters rather than to the things planted, and to the trainers rather than to those trained." Hippocrates declared that behaviour in psychosis was due to brain diseases, and decried the belief in demon possession.' These elements of understanding were lost to mankind through the Dark Ages.

In the eighteenth century, as humanitarian care replaced the abuses derived from superstition and misplaced religious interpretation of symptoms, we entered into what has been called the Golden Age of psychiatry, the moral era. Medical historians have referred to this as the first of the three major revolutions of psychiatric thought. Stresses of a psychological nature were referred to as moral causes, and moral treatment meant that the patient was made comfortable, his interest aroused, friendship invited and discussion of troubles encouraged. (The insane came to be regarded as normal people who had lost their reason due to psychological and social stresses.) This treatment reached its peak between 1820 and 1860, and was led by such people as Pinel, Tuke and Rush. In 1887, John Butler of the Hartford Retreat in his book, *The Curability of Insanity and the Individualized Treatment of the Insane*,[2] pointed out the importance of scrutinising the hospital environment to define and remove whatever is distressing or disturbing. He insisted that a cheerful, sympathetic atmosphere and aesthetic appeal were essential for the care of many patients; his goal was to make hospital wards as homelike as possible. He believed that confidential interviews with patients were essential, but he was convinced that the turning point in many a patient's illness took place in group discussions. He also insisted that appropriate social influences could not be maintained if hospitals were allowed to care for more than 200 patients at one time, and he considered monotony to be the greatest obstacle to be overcome in mental hospitals. Moral therapy, however, was quietly abandoned in American and British mental institutions after 1860, and was later almost completely forgotten until the 1950s. But in 1953 the Third Report of the World Health Organization Expert Committee on Mental Health concluded, 'The most important single factor in the efficacy of the treatment given in a mental hospital to be an intangible element that can only be described as atmosphere.'[3]

The second major revolution in psychiatric thinking has been described as the Freudian or analytic era. Extensions of the analytic model focused treatment on the diadic relationship. There grew up the polarising positions that implied that treatment was involved with personality change, whereas social adaptation was considered to be rehabilitation. We are currently in the third revolutionary period; that is, the era of community psychiatry or its basic science, social psychiatry.

In the era of social psychiatry, the exclusiveness of the diadic relationship and the implication that this was the *sine qua non* of treatment, began to be questioned. The overly polarised relationship between treatment and rehabilitation was also questioned. Social psychiatry extended into family relationships, societal, cultural, economic and legal areas, all of which were felt to affect behaviour. It is in this context that therapeutic community concepts flourished. Non-hospital-based treatment settings also began to be established, and predominant amongst these, the halfway house.

Any discussion of therapeutic communities must include such names as Maxwell Jones, Thomas Main, Allen Kraft, Thomas Detre, and Ken Artis as some of the important innovators and implementers.[4] In addition, brilliant theoretical and descriptive work has been done by Rapoport, Stanton and Schwartz, Caudill, and Almond.[5] I would like to add to our information a description of some of the essential elements to be found in any therapeutic community. I will then discuss the concepts in the context of halfway houses, pointing out where these ideas are well applied, and where they become burdensome.

My experience with therapeutic communities has been primarily with in-patient units in psychiatric hospitals. These have included a therapeutic community in a university setting at Yale University, in a research setting at the National Institute of Mental Health, and now, a private mental health centre, The Psychiatric Institute of Washington. I was also consultant, for five years, to the first Richmond Fellowship Halfway House in the United States, Kalorama House in Washington, DC.

Much of distressed human behaviour may be seen as faulty social learning, which has interfered with an individual's capacity to cope. Role theorist Sarbin[6] has pointed out the simple formula that behaviour equals the characteristic self, plus the social role one is enacting at any time. Thus, in looking at the interaction between patients and staff, one assumes that every behavioural event is governed, in part, by the expectations, values, rewards and identifications which characterise the particular social role being enacted. To understand total behaviour, therefore, it is important to examine what part of behaviour is related to the patient's self, and what part is role-determined action. Accordingly, to understand patient behaviour in a psychiatric setting, an awareness of the environment and its social system is important.

In most traditional psychiatric settings, patient experiences are rated and placed in a very distinct hierarchy according to their value. The hierarchy is communicated in both overt and covert ways, and is implicitly accepted by the staff. When the staff accepts a hierarchy of values, they easily communicate this to the patients. At the top of the hierarchy, in these traditional settings are transactions with the doctor. These are usually the most brief of the experiences the patient has. At the bottom of the list are those experiences the patient has with the nursing staff, generally the lowest-ranking member of the nursing staff, the aide or orderly. These are frequently the longest transactions. The staff members at the bottom of the hierarchical list conclude that their experience with the patient is of relatively insignificant value and that they are present to keep the patient comfortable until the important event occurs.

In a traditional medically oriented facility, then, there is almost an inverse relationship between the amount of time spent with the patient and the importance accorded to that contribution. This clearly is an inefficient educational model. The more time spent with a person, the more it is likely that effective influence will occur, provided that the social system is a reinforcer. Much that we do in treatment is educational. We teach our patients to recognise their feelings, we teach them about family dynamics and relationships, we teach them effective communication, we teach them about insight and we may even teach them certain tangible interpersonal social skills.

Therapeutic community advocates say that this traditional environment is not only inefficient in its utilisation of personnel, but that it also robs the organisation of creative input from all members. The therapeutic community does not assume an *a priori* position about the origin and value of therapeutic experiences. In fact, each member of the community has an important contribution to make. The therapeutic community is, therefore, a specific treatment method, as specific as psychoanalysis or somatic therapy. When it is working at its best, it is comprised of many different therapeutic inputs. It is a social structure which is designed to be the primary instrument in the helping process, where all interactions and relationships are relevant and potentially therapeutic. The staff members must strive for the condition where they are able to prize the importance of their own contribution, and respect and value the contribution of their colleagues, regardless of their hierarchical position.

I would now like to discuss some of the elements that I think are important and common to all therapeutic communities. The first of these is awareness and sensitivity of the community to its own 'value system'. What does the community believe in, what does it expect from patients and what are its goals? Because of the powerful psychological impact this organised social system can make on the patient, it is essential that values, the cultural attitudes of the community, be continually identified, examined and modified. The leader of the community must decide how self-contained the community will be. To put it another way, how porous will the boundaries of the community be? What influences beyond the control of the community itself will be encouraged, tolerated or excluded? The more closed the system is, the more powerful influencer of behaviour it can become. It has been suggested that therapeutic communities can be seen as a form of brainwashing. Robert Lifton, in his book, *Thought and Form and the Psychology of Totalism, A Study of Brainwashing in China*, said, 'The penetration by the psychological forces of the environment into the inner emotions of the individual person is perhaps the outstanding psychiatric fact of thought reform. The milieu brings to bear upon the prisoner a series of overwhelming pressures at the same time allowing only a very limited set of alternatives for adapting to them. In the interplay between person and environment, a sequence of steps, combinations of manipulation and response, take place. All of these steps revolve around two policies and two demands; the fluctuation between assault and leniency and the requirements of confession and re-education.' In fact, there are many similarities between a therapeutic community experience and what Lifton has described. However, rather than enslaving, the treatment experience can be a liberating one for the patient, freeing him from psychological constraints.

Most patients are interested in knowing what the staff expects of them; therefore, staff members need to be clear and consistent about behaviour they want to positively reinforce. Since most therapeutic communities emphasise the healthy integrative aspects of the patient's personality, it is important to examine the consistency with which this cultural value is communicated. Significant therapeutic experiences occur when the patient, with his own attitudes, ego ideals and family values, abuts against the cultural value system of the therapeutic community. This cultural interface is the locus for much work. Empirical observations have shown that patients who can allow themselves to become identified with the ward values have a better hospital experience and have satisfactory discharges.

It may be difficult, however, to transmit and translate the experiences in the therapeutic community to life outside. Recognising this factor, some hospital therapeutic communities bring the family in. As a result, the family is forced to look at, define and relate its value system to that of the community. Halfway houses need to scrutinise carefully the issue of applying the community's values to life outside. Since many patients will use the halfway house as a transitional object in order to separate from their families, the family may not be the appropriate aspect of the outside world to integrate into the treatment.

The second element in therapeutic communities I want to mention is that of 'open communication'. This is a simple concept but is difficult to implement. In the therapeutic community, all transactions have therapeutic potential; that is, patient/staff, patient/patient and staff/staff. This last, staff/staff, takes special work. In the book, *The Mental Hospital*, Stanton and Schwartz hypothesised that covert staff hostility yielded overt patient acting-out. When a staff is in conflict the patients will sense it and act out in an attempt to get the staff to stop fighting among themselves and resume a more staff-like position. In the therapeutic community it is essential to open up this type of communication. There must be a willingness on the part of all community members to be candid about their feelings, perceptions and needs. The staff must be willing to share, but not burden, patients with staff difficulties for example when those difficulties affect staff availability. The acknowledgement that the staff has problems and is trying to solve them is far preferable to the staff pretending to be maximally functioning.

Many therapeutic communities allow most of their meetings to be attended by patients. Case discussions, planning sessions and staff meetings all may be held in the presence of patients who are interested. This can allow the patient to interact with the staff around the staff's perception of his behaviour, while also helping unmask some of the mystique that accompanies psychiatric treatment. Too often families and patients seek psychiatric treatment for what I call the 'car wash' concept of psychotherapy; namely, one deposits a patient at one end, something mysterious happens in the middle, and he is picked up at the other end with everything different. Patients, as well as families, often feel that they cannot be part of the decision-making about their own lives because they do not have the required expertise. This dependency on 'staff omnipotence' enhances the inherent distance between patient and staff and should be discouraged. By observing staff members in their struggle to make decisions and contend with their own problems, inadequacies and frustrations, the patient may develop a model for problem-solving – that is, if the staff *is* solving problems. As one patient put it when sitting in one of our more deadly staff sessions, 'My God, if I had to sit in many of these meetings, I'd *really* be crazy.'

To achieve open communication, the bureaucratic model of communication must be overcome. This is where positions talk to positions, rather than people talking to people. In the therapeutic community we attempt to flatten the vertical administrative hierarchy for communication purposes. It is important, of course, that the administrative structure remain vertical in order for staff members to know their responsibilities, but for the purposes of communications it must be made horizontal. Therefore, staff at all levels are not only encouraged, but are expected, to give adequate, honest feedback to the leadership. When staff at all levels feel responsible for sharing their observations and suggestions, there can truly be an opportunity for creative innovation. The staff in therapeutic communities are encouraged to be 'real people' utilising, rather than hiding, their own personalities. Staff are encouraged to recognise and express their own feelings and to give feedback. The patient then has a chance to learn about the impact he is having on others.

The third element is the need for patients and staff to participate in the decision-making process. There is no better way to communicate the expectation of healthy behaviour on the part of patients than by having them take part in decisions. As many areas of responsibility as possible should be delegated to patients. The staff, of course, must remember that delegation of authority is not abdication of responsibility. It is in the fulfilment of this element of therapeutic communities that patient government activities flourish. For patient government to work, it must be real; not that the patients can decide things, as long as they decide them the way staff would have anyway. Therefore, if the staff cannot live with certain decisions, then that area should not be delegated. Confusion may arise around the notion that the therapeutic community is a democracy based on the principle of one man, one vote. It is not true that all members are equal; a clear sense of who the leader is and what his prerogatives are must be firmly established.

Fourth of the essential elements is that of 'overlapping of staff roles'. This is sometimes known as role-boundary diffusion, and at times, role-boundary confusion. This can allow staff members to interact with patients and each other without being limited by their assigned community role. As a consequence, certain decision-making as well as leadership responsibilities are assigned not merely on the basis of one's staff position. Specific tasks need to be accomplished, but there can be overlap in assigning them. Some hospital-based therapeutic communities have gone so far as to choose leaders based on leadership ability, rather than merely assuming that all leadership should be invested in those with medical degrees. This, of course, is an area of considerable stress for traditionally trained staff who in many cases have never been questioned about their decisions and observations. Nursing staff from traditional settings, who are frequently silent handmaidens, are encouraged to present their points of view and allow themselves to be recognised as individuals. Each staff member is encouraged to maximise those inherent human qualities which are brought to the job.

The next element is the 'integration of treatment and rehabilitation'. Most therapeutic communities, being reality oriented, see work and play as important facets of life; therefore, social and vocational rehabilitation activities are seen as integral parts of the total treatment plan. Rather than utilising just occupational therapy and diversional activities, therapeutic community programmes may add activities related to here-and-now issues, stressing the skills needed in coping with the activities of daily living, including work and play.

The last of the elements essential in the development of a therapeutic community is the need for administrative support. There is much about the system I have just described which is clearly anti-organisational; therefore, one must have a clear mandate and the active support necessary to develop such a programme. This is particularly so if one wants to develop it as part of a more traditional organisation. Well-established roles and prerogatives are threatened by therapeutic communities, and therefore mere lip service of support will not be enough when the challenges come.

I would now like to apply these concepts to halfway houses. The first of the elements I discussed was a clear definition of the community's value system. This is a vital issue and strikes at a core problem for many halfway houses. It touches on the crucial definition of leadership, decision-making and boundaries of the community. The very first question a house has to decide is, what is its treatment mandate? How much responsibility for treatment can it take, ethically and legally? Where will it be along the responsibility continuum, with at one end a Synanon type of house, assuming total responsibility for all aspects of its member's life, and at the other end the friendly rooming house? The house has to decide about its philosophy of treatment and goals. 'Is it better to be in or out of the house during the day?' is a question that must be answered before a coherent treatment philosophy can be developed. Some halfway house therapeutic communities feel that spending the day with the programme in the house is necessary before a successful adjustment to the outside can be made. Others feel just the opposite. The halfway house therapeutic community, because of its small number of staff, can more readily assume programme consistency; that is, if its leadership and communication amongst staff are effective.

The role of the doctor in the programme needs to be clarified. Some houses want no part of any physician; others use only his MD as a necessary, legitimising evil. Others value him as a consultant, and still others are dependent on him for leadership. A perplexing situation exists in the United States in this regard. Because of current health insurance guidelines, no insurance coverage exists for programmes unless they are clearly under medical supervision. Since most halfway houses do not have full-time physicians, the patients are therefore not covered. It may therefore cost the patient less money to remain in the hospital, although it is no longer the appropriate setting and the actual costs are much higher.

An important part of any therapeutic community value system is a definition of the limitations of behaviour. How much social or group pressure will be brought to bear? How much regression and aggression will be allowed? The style and extent of limit-setting often becomes a charged issue for the halfway house staff. Private hospitals can use the lever of transfer to another facility as the basis for limit-setting. This is not as easily used by halfway houses, since the alternative is rarely another halfway house, but usually back to the hospital or jail.

All therapeutic communities share the problem of cultural drift, i.e. staff saying and believing that its behaviour is consistent with its value system, whilst in reality the patients of the community perceive a different situation. The community also may develop an unwillingness to look at itself and assess its effectiveness. These two situations, difficult in all therapeutic communities, may even be more insulated from scrutiny in halfway houses because they often are independent organisations unrelated to outside restraining and corrective influences.

The second and third essential elements I described were open communication systems and participatory decision-making. Halfway house therapeutic communities are well suited to accomplish these ends. The small size of staff, the intimacy and support available, as well as staff exposure and willingness to be seen as role models, can all contribute to a sense of openness.

Since most halfway houses pride themselves as being human, non-bureaucratic organisations, the communications network may be exceedingly informal. This approach may be all that is needed in a setting with simple and minimal treatment and administrative responsibility. Most halfway houses, however, do not fit that description and therefore must work to overcome the wish not to formalise communications. It is important for staff and residents to understand basic tenets of group life, tasks of group leadership and group boundary issues. In therapeutic communities, we learn very rapidly that groups can be inefficient and can tend to rehash issues. We must continually emphasise for staff and residents, where decisions are made, who makes which decisions, which are delegated to staff, which to patients and which remain only for the leader. Participatory decision-making may be misunderstood by residents and staff to mean that everyone will have a vote on all decisions. The leader must be firm and clear in letting the community know what areas are his alone. He must help people see the value and place of formal communications. He must retain his prerogative for privacy and delay in responding to staff pressures. This is difficult in informal systems where people come to expect immediate response. Structured meetings in some halfway houses are resisted. In my view, they are necessary to help reinforce group boundaries and differences. Regular meetings with defined tasks are very useful and indeed essential tools.

In our hospital therapeutic community, our formalised meeting system involves the following practices. The leader of the community has to set up regular communication meetings with the outside world: this means the rest of the hospital. He must also have a regular meeting with his head nurse. The head nurse must have regular meetings with the nursing staff. These have to deal with administrative tasks, clinical observations, as well as ventilation of feelings. Then there is a total staff meeting where the various disciplines all meet to examine the clinical work and delineate interface issues.

There is a community meeting, a most important meeting, which is the place to reinforce community values and deal with decisions and feelings within the entire community. There are patient decision-making meetings – these vary depending on the complexity of the patient government system. In addition, there are community orientation meetings for new patients. Family meetings become important to maintain the family's contact with the patient and with the community. There are also meetings set up to communicate with the various therapies that are not on the unit every day. All of these are regular meetings and do not include those emergency meetings that are set up to define and resolve crises. In addition to all of these, there are various meetings that deal with a given patient's individual issues. In reviewing this, it becomes clear why therapeutic communities have been defined as organisations where the staff spend 90 per cent of their time meeting together, and somehow patients get better. Halfway house therapeutic communities do not need to have nearly as formalised a communication system; however, they must recognise the need for a system.

The fourth of the essential elements I noted earlier is overlapping of staff roles. Halfway house staffs are, in my experience, unlike most other mental health professionals. They are highly motivated and frequently missionary in their zeal. They appreciate the effectiveness of organised treatment programmes, yet are often repelled by the forbidding formality of institutions. They are more accepting of human values and life-experiences in prospective staff members than in specific credentials. They are frequently called upon to be generalists – from counsellor to cook, planner to plumber. Those staff who are most effective are able to tolerate the overlapping of staff roles and are able to use themselves as role models.

Most of us psychiatrists working in institutions or private practice have become accustomed to being able to hide from our patients regularly. Phrases like 'let's stop the hour now – our time is up – I have another patient' serve us well. Our patients dutifully leave the office hoping they haven't taken any undeserved time or liberties. We have trained them well. The halfway house staff cannot hide. There is no easy way out to avoid the demanding resident. Besides time, the demands are often for information about the personal life of the staff member. The office therapist may believe that such data are not useful to the therapy, but can the halfway house staff member hold this view? Is it irrelevant for the patient to know how a staff member solved a major life-problem? Is the resident's behaviour inappropriate in asking this of someone with whom he virtually lives? Clarifying the boundary between what is a professional relationship and what is a friendship is a significant burden for many halfway house staff members, particularly new ones. These issues must be continually worked on and must be kept available for scrutiny. This is a responsibility of the leadership.

This leads to another burden for therapeutic community halfway houses; namely the training of staff. There is almost nothing that one can read to prepare adequately for the experience of being a new staff member. The only model that may approximate the concept of the therapeutic community is that of a family, and we certainly don't want to tell new staff that 'working here is just the way your own family works'. They might run screaming for the door. Therefore on-the-job training is required, but organisations that depend solely on on-the-job training are vulnerable to much staff inefficiency.

As mentioned above, the willingness for halfway house staff to be generalists in the true sense of overlapping of roles is necessary. However, although the experience may be meaningful for the staff member while doing it, he may find that the training and experience is not readily transferable to other mental health settings. Although he may be highly valued in the halfway house, he may not be able to move, and thus narrow his career ladder with all the inherent morale problems. (I must say that this has not seemed to bother the halfway house staffs that I have known nearly as much as staffs in larger institutions.)

The halfway house seems particularly well suited to integrating rehabilitation into the treatment programme. There are unique opportunities for real tasks of living to be performed by residents. Some treatment approaches see their task as limited to psychological and symbolic issues, and assume that the patient will learn somewhere else to cook a meal, handle a budget and find social activities. For many of our patients, their parents did not serve as positive role models; rather, they were people to be unlike. It is much harder, of course, to pattern behaviour when it's in the interest of moving away from something, rather than towards. In the halfway house therapeutic community the residents can explore new skills and behaviours modelled by the staff within a supportive environment.

I mentioned earlier the importance of administrative support in establishing therapeutic communities. The administrative aspects of establishing halfway house therapeutic communities have very distinct positive and negative aspects to them. First, it is easier to start a halfway house because compared to hospital organisations, it is a relatively simple one without equally cumbersome bureaucracies and traditions. Complicated licensures and procedures as required by hospitals are generally not needed because of the type of staff attracted, as well as the work contributed by residents.

Although the small size of the staff and its organisational independence has many advantages, it also leaves the halfway house particularly vulnerable, for example, to financial exigencies and pressures which, when subtle, may affect the kind of patient the house will accept and, when blatant, can threaten the very existence of the organisation. In addition, halfway house therapeutic communities are particularly vulnerable to staff instability. Many houses have been started by charismatic, idealistic, zealous people. Unless these leaders train people to take over for them, when the leader leaves, the house may lose its sense of mission and fail. The personality of a house may turn over if two or three key staff members leave in quick succession.

Besides some of the burdens or problems of therapeutic communities mentioned above, there are a few others to mention. The fact that community-based therapeutic communities are still relatively unformulated means that it may take a new staff member three months before he learns enough of the community's language to ask the right questions and another three months before he can make a real creative contribution. Unfortunately this process may lead to a sense of frustration and demoralisation for the eager new staff. Although most staff members acknowledge much personal and professional satisfaction in working in the therapeutic community, the lack of clear role boundaries and the threat of loss of professional identity may produce considerable anxiety. Working in an emotional fishbowl where one's personality is subject to scrutiny adds to this difficulty. It has been said that working in the therapeutic community for six months is equivalent to two years of personal therapy. Because of the introspective nature of the community and the meaningful experiences shared, the staff may become extremely tight-knit and exclude newcomers. It is perhaps less of a conscious exclusion than it is a lack of awareness or recollection of what the integration experience is like for the newest member.

In any treatment programme, the rate of patient improvement will fluctuate and eventually level off. When the patient is not improving fast enough to satisfy the staff, he may feel that he is not tolerated the way he is. This situation can lead to extrusion from the group. A problem of all group-oriented treatment is that the patient's individuality may become lost in the concern for the group. With powerful group processes at work, it may become easy to lose appreciation for a patient's unique individuality, particularly when its manifestations challenge some of the group's beliefs. It must be remembered that individualising a treatment approach is not contrary to therapeutic community philosophy. The community must always be aware also of how residents are going to integrate their experiences to their life outside. This can be particularly difficult for schizophrenic patients who often experience boundary problems within themselves, let alone between themselves and the outside world.

I have mentioned some of the difficulties found in therapeutic communities. However, as hospital-based treatment has its limitations and as hospital costs are soaring, alternative models of treatment must be supported, expanded and researched, and the therapeutic community halfway house is one such alternative. It has been suggested that a major responsibility for those of us involved in psychiatric care is to offer an experience that communicates hope for the future, instead of the sense of chronicity, fate and boredom. The staff of therapeutic communities may at times be harassed, overworked, overwhelmed and anxious – but never bored. Halfway houses are organisations which can at one and the same time be stabilising and normalising but continually problem-solving and evolving. Patients can then find themselves in a milieu of openness to change, which helps them gain the courage to face change in themselves.

Notes

1. J.S. Bochoven, 'The History of Moral Treatment in American Psychiatry', *Journal of Nervous and Mental Diseases*, vol. 124 (1956).
2. J. Butler, *The Curability of Insanity and the Individualized Treatment of the Insane* (Putnam, New York, 1887).
3. World Health Organization, Expert Committee on Mental Health, Third Report, Geneva World Health Organization, Technical Report Series 73, 1953.
4. M. Jones, *The Therapeutic Community* (Basic Books, New York, 1953); T. Main, 'The Hospital as a Therapeutic Institution', *Bulletin of the Menninger Clinic*, vol. 10 (1946); A. Kraft, 'Community Mental Health Center', *Pennsylvania Medical Journal*, vol. 67 (1964); T. Detre *et al.*, 'An Experimental Approach to the Treatment of the Acutely Ill Psychiatric Patient in the General Hospital', *Connecticut Medicine*, vol. 25 (1961); K. Artis, *Milieu Therapy in Schizophrenia* (Grune and Stratton, New York, 1962).
5. R. N. Rapoport, *Community as Doctor* (Tavistock Publications, London, 1960); A.H. Stanton and M.S. Schwartz, *The Mental Hospital* (Basic Books, New York, 1954); W. Caudill, *The Psychiatric Hospital as a Small Society* (Harvard University Press, Cambridge, Mass., 1958); R. Almond, *The Healing Community: Dynamics of a Therapeutic Milieu* (J. Aronson, New York, 1978).
6. T.R. Sarbin *et al.*, *Clinical Inference and Cognitive Theory* (Holt, Rinehart and Winston, New York, 1960).

4 THERAPEUTIC COMMUNITY MODELS: I SPRING LAKE RANCH (USA)

Michael Wells

For more than forty years Spring Lake Ranch has been a living example of an alternative to the mental hospital. It is variously described as a therapeutic work community, a halfway house, a transitional residence and intentional community, and it is in fact all of these. However, it also differs in significant respects from what most people associate with these terms, so I shall try to paint a picture of the people, the place and the life that is lived there.

The two people who began Spring Lake Ranch, Wayne and Elizabeth Sarcka, were in the true tradition of pioneers. They had an idea and an ideal that they turned into their lives. In many respects it was no different from the ideal that has prompted most of the more humane approaches to the problems of the mentally ill within our midst. The Sarckas took into their home men and women who were mentally ill. They believed that if they shared their lives, accepted each person for what they were and joined with them in common work, the people they took in would get better. There is nothing very original in that, except that at the time, in 1932, most mentally ill people who could not live at home were in institutions, separated from society in the dependent subculture of the institutionalised patient. The Sarckas chose to live on a beautiful, abandoned,Vermont hillside farm connected to the highway by a mile-long, narrow dirt road rising steeply from a valley and ending beyond their farm at a magnificent eight-acre lake called Spring Lake. Wayne Sarcka, who always saw everything larger than life, saw not a farm where they settled but a ranch, and so it became Spring Lake Ranch. They set up house with their two-year-old daughter and two young men referred to them by their one psychiatrist friend in faraway New York. This was at the time of the great depression and the Sarckas had no financial backing to supplement their own limited resources, so no one had to ask what to do. It was obvious: survive. They had to patch the house, fix the road, plant crops, tend animals, clear land, eat, sleep and, when there was time, relax and play. Such an undertaking would have been out of the ordinary for most healthy people, but to do it with two disturbed young men from the city, defying the common practice of the time, was thought by many, including their friends, to be foolhardy.

It worked, however, and they survived that first Vermont winter and those first two residents improved remarkably. Their medicine was faith, acceptance, expectation and a lot of shared hard work. By implication the Sarckas must have had conviction, commitment, tenacity and were either foolhardy or had a vision. Wayne's extraordinary energy and inspirational enthusiasm and Elizabeth's loyalty and dogged determination to turn their dream into a practical reality were the building blocks of their ranch. For years they struggled against the climate, which can be extremely severe in Vermont, shortage of money, not enough residents, a lack of acceptance and, I'm sure, at times against each other. But slowly and painfully their idea took hold and grew. Twenty-eight years later the culmination of their work was to incorporate as a private, tax-exempt and charitable foundation, so as to ensure that others could take what they had created into its second generation. That was fifteen years ago and now more than ever we who have followed see the uniqueness of their legacy. Theirs was not a preconceived philosophy expressed through an institution set in place; it was the natural expression of two hard-fought lives growing through time.

Today there are close to fifty people living there, of whom thirty are residents and the rest staff and their families. We live in eleven homes or cottages with all manner of farm and work buildings surrounding us. The latest addition is a half-sized dirt-floored gymnasium. We built most of the buildings, and none are elaborate, just simple framed structures sometimes built to meet an urgent need, often with material salvaged from a house or barn we took down for someone in the nearby towns.

Who comes to Spring Lake Ranch? They are young men and women usually between 17 and 30 years of age. Most come from the metropolitan centres in the East to Mid-West and are referred from private and state hospitals, mental health clinics, psychiatrists in private practice, the courts and friends who know them and us. Most of those who are referred have been treated, often extensively, in more orthodox treatment centres but have not reached the point of being able to take over their lives. Whilst some come here for primary help, more often it is the second or third or even tenth or eleventh try. A scholarship fund supported by alumni and a rate in excess of cost, enables some less well-off people to come, but the majority are from middle and upper-middle-class families. Diagnoses change with the times, but people referred here are afflicted with almost any kind of major mental illness, perhaps the most common being schizophrenia, depression and manic depressive illness. There are also those who may be grown-up hyperkinetic children, those suffering from what is now being called minimal brain dysfunction, adult childhood schizophrenics and so on. Often problems are complicated by the abuse of drugs and alcohol or by encephalitis, epilepsy, anorexia or the effects of serious head injuries.

As significant as what went wrong with the applicant is what went right. We need to know about their assets. Are they likeable? Do they have a sense of humour, sensitivity to others, work or leadership ability, specific skills? How much education do they have, and just how well have they managed in life so far? Therefore, when people apply we ask their physician for records describing previous illness and treatment, and the applicant and parents for background information on early development and a description of their best level of functioning. It is always best for applicants to spend a day or two with us to see for themselves what they will be getting into. Then we can try and decide whether we feel time here might be beneficial. We have to consider the balance of the community, our own limitations, the willingness of the person to give it a try and our own and the applicant's financial situation. Once everyone says yes, there may be a wait of a few weeks until we have a room.

Who will a new resident find working there when he arrives? The staff are almost all lay people with a variety of skills, interests and reasons for being there. In fact, we prefer people of different life-experiences and backgrounds. We want old and young people, rural and urban, a lot of education and a little, conservative and liberal, long and short hair, religious and not so religious, authoritarian and easy-going. That, after all, is what we all have to contend with in life and it is from such diversity that most of us find people with whom we can share common interests and perhaps friendship. The staff seem to fall into three broad groups. Students from Antioch and other work-term colleges come for specific time periods and a peace corps or service type of experience. They bring energy and enthusiasm, high expectations, change, questions, and a refreshing ignorance of our limitations. Then there are married couples with and without children. Sometimes both husband and wife work, sometimes just one. They are apt to stay at least a year and often much longer. Because of family needs, their commitment is split and their less than total commitment often enables married staff to withstand the intense emotional demands inherent in so circumscribed a community and stay involved for longer periods of time. They are, if you like, the glue that holds the staff together. The core of the staff are the single, sometimes older, people who bring their life-experience here and share it on a most intimate level with people whom most would simply rather avoid or wish to avoid. This is an emotionally exhausting life and each person continually struggles to maintain balance and find renewal.

For any of us who work at Spring Lake Ranch the quality of the life we live is what makes it worthwhile. Neither pay nor status provide the motivation to stay on. All of us have to wear several hats: house parent, business manager, work leader, interviewer, cook, driver, recreation leader, maintenance man, farmer. Our specific job becomes the vehicle within which we relate to each other and to the community. We strive to have each person develop his own personality within the needs of the community, and that personal expression becomes our job, our work and sometimes our life. Often there are one or two residents who by their contribution move from resident to staff and sometimes there are staff who move the other way for periods of time. That there is a bridge with traffic either way is important to us. Much is made of the fact that in therapeutic communities you cannot tell the staff from the residents. There are of course differences, most obviously in terms of functioning. Nevertheless, because of the absence of any professional/patient separation, a great variety of degrees of health and illness, and an inherent vulnerability of everyone to each other, the line between staff and residents becomes blurred. It is not always an advantage for very ill patients, but it is essential in any therapeutic community.

What do we do? Life is simple, stripped of much of its sophistication, reduced to working, playing, sleeping and eating. You cannot feel you belong if you do not contribute, and because we have various skills and often almost no skills, work is basic and simple. All of us can load wood into a truck and dig a ditch for a foundation for a house, peel potatoes and hang laundry. And most of us can learn to stack hay bales, feed chickens, bake cakes, wash dishes, perhaps even nail studs into the walls of a new house, gas up a truck, sew curtains or cook breakfast. Most of the work has to be done; some is interesting and challenging, some boring and repetitive. Not only is there variety in the kind of work, but also in the leadership and composition of the crew. One may be assigned a simple task and an easy crew leader, or an exacting and difficult job and an honorary and demanding boss. Sometimes getting the job done takes precedence over people's individual needs, sometimes the work is structured to meet the needs of the person doing it. Staff and residents lead work crews and for everyone involved in the project the predictability of achievement can be a refreshing change from the slow and painful process derived from working at one's problems.

Of course it helps to develop good work habits, skills and work tolerance. More important though is the feeling of belonging and the satisfaction of accomplishment that it can engender. Shared work is perhaps the best vehicle for learning how to enjoy the friendship of others and feel comfortable with authority. While work is expected of everyone, on a basis resembling normal employment, and is assigned and structured, leisure time is simply there, and what to do with it depends on the leadership within the community, the morale and each individual's participation. We can do just about anything: cross-country skiing, fishing, sailing, hiking, riding, playing volleyball, tennis, play-reading, dances and so forth. The choice is endless. Since it is not mandatory, what counts is whether people participate in recreation. For this reason the variety of recreational activities taking place and the degree of participation is often a barometer of the health of the community.

What kind of structure is there? It may be best described as fluid and constantly evolving according to the needs of whatever group is there at the time. There are times when the chain of command needs to be clearly identified and other times, usually when the community has been stable for a long period, that a much more broadly based democratic system is appropriate. Some decisions are made on the basis of a hierarchical structure with the director at the top. Most decisions, particularly those concerning how we live day to day, are more apt to be decided at various community meetings where one man, no matter what his standing, has one vote. All decisions by both chains of command can be influenced by the other. There is a continuous attempt to disperse reponsibility for everything as widely as possible, but at any time the extent to which this can be accomplished varies with the sense of cohesiveness of the group. Rules, policies and procedures are implemented, challenged, rescinded and re-established as the face of the community changes. For example, at the instigation of one resident and after numerous community meetings, we recently changed our entire record-keeping system and the way we use our consultant psychiatrist. A patient's prior records are accessible to him and may be seen at any time. Meetings concerning a resident's progress may be attended by anyone in the community who is concerned, and our consultant can only meet with residents in the presence of another member of the community. This increases the possibility of people helping each other, regardless of their status as psychiatrist, resident or staff member. It also lessens the frightening mysteriousness of illness and the magical expectations that many invest in psychiatry. We try to be a mirror of the people comprising the community, vulnerable at all times to change and modification, building and tearing down traditions, listening to each person and all the people. It is so often within this never-resolved and continuous tension and dialogue that the community comes together and falls apart and the individual grows.

Where and what is the therapy? Ultimately all of us must hope that therapy dissolves into a life that gives meaning, purpose, growth and fulfilment. Therapy is a specific tool to repair or discover what is broken or undeveloped in our life, that prevents us from achieving our goals. For many who come to us, and for their families, therapy has become their lives and everything awaits its result. When we have tried a specific therapy (and we have tried many and still do), those people participating in it are apt to save up problems and crises for the therapeutic session or wait for the miracle-worker or pill to make them better. Since our primary concern is focusing on health and developing assets, we run into trouble with specific therapies. Of necessity therapy focuses on pathology and too many of our residents are already well on the way to becoming professional patients, perhaps the most boring profession in the world. To isolate one function or time and label it therapy tends to leave many feeling that every other time is not therapy and therefore unimportant. Rather than encourage people to save up their problems for the therapeutic session, we try to deal with them as they happen. So we attempt to remain vulnerable to crises as they occur and strive to make the way of life at the ranch a vehicle for growth. We explore the relationship between individual and group needs within the framework of work and play where the demands of each are in continual conflict. Dialogue is continuous and often non-verbal, such as two people at either end of a cross-cut saw felling a tree or helping each other pull a block of ice from the lake, where speech is more physical than verbal. This is not to preclude the very important part that specific therapy plays. Our consulting psychiatrist visits once a week, and brings his professional expertise to bear on those aspects of illness which respond to specific therapy. Medication is clearly of crucial importance and often essential to people suffering from psychoses, mania, depression and so on. For some a specific therapy in hospital, such as behaviour modification, may be called for;

for others a much more structured and controlled environment. Our consultant is truly a physician and works to treat the symptoms of illness which so often prevent his patients from participating in the life around them. He does not do individual therapy nor make major decisions affecting residents. He does, however, work as a consultant on any matters concerning not only residents, but the ranch community as a whole. By contrast we have a mother, father, brother, neighbours, employees and girlfriends in the community where life goes on.

Throughout the year there is a turnover of both staff and residents. Those who leave are usually the students and much healthier residents, at this point often indistinguishable, who have grown into a nucleus of health that carries the morale of the community. We who are left are older, long-term staff in whom tradition is vested. We are to some extent separated from the residents by our age, and experience and growing professionalism. The residents who remain are still cocooned by their illness and unable to shed its mantle or risk relating to more than their problems. Even the new young student staff may be bewildered and uncertain because illness is often masked by the security offered by the ranch community. However, time passes, and as the sense of security that stems from participation develops, friendships are risked and emotional involvements develop, until once more there are young people who begin assuming more and more responsibility for running the community and often changing it. This is the role of son and daughter played out over and over again in all our families to the point where the family is simply not big enough to contain the energy present, so the children, like our residents, leave home, buoyed with the knowledge that they can at least in this setting, structure and discipline their own lives, make decisions and act on them and succeed and fail without the devastating consequences of collapse. Of course, many only travel short distances on this road and some jump right off at the beginning, terrified and unable to leave the protection of a structured institution or home. What makes this whole ebb and flow of life so exciting and renewing is that no two groups of people growing through the ranch are the same. Each leaves his own indelible imprint, not only in a barn built, a new dock at the lake, or a stand of maple syrup, but also in the faces of people who have become friends and not residents.

Leaving is not easy for anyone and must be individually worked out. Some are strong enough to leave us and their families and return to college or take a job wherever they choose, being almost free of the fear of another breakdown. Many cannot go that easily or completely, but then working here as staff may be a useful step or living here and commuting to a job or school each day or undertaking part-time volunteer work in the community. Perhaps work is no problem, so living away and working with us makes more sense. Others leave in a great flurry but collapse within a short time, return and try again, and perhaps even again. Still others with lifelong illness and institutionalism move so slowly and painfully that a foster family or long-term halfway house in the area is indicated. For them the emotional and social stimulus of the ranch coupled with the inherent expectation is too much and a smaller more stable setting is necessary if any growth is to occur. Then there are always those who collapse or simply don't fit or who by their behaviour exhaust our tolerance and patience and leave usually to other more structured institutions. Interestingly, when the next step is state hospital, it is often only for a brief time during which the contrast of what it really means to be a mental patient and what was experienced here as the possibility of independent life becomes clearly focused. The patient works as he never has done before to find the person he is. After people leave, our follow-up work can be extensive in terms of social support, helping people find jobs and providing help during acute episodes that may occur during times of increased stress. At any time we may support as many as thirty-four ranchers who have settled in the neighbouring community.

Whose needs are we best able to meet? That is a difficult question to answer because our many different referral sources see us so differently. Broadly speaking we meet the need of those whose acute symptoms have subsided, but who are still unable to go home or even sometimes unable to benefit from an urban or suburban halfway house, because they are not well enough, nor sufficiently motivated to become involved in day-care programmes, work or schooling. Increasingly over the last few years there are doctors who see the ranch as a primary treatment resource, a place to which to refer patients instead of a hospital. More commonly, agencies refer patients who have not responded sufficiently to more orthodox treatments and who are still unable to move back into the community. As people stay and improve, we do in many instances fulfil the role of a more conventional halfway house with people leaving each day to work in the community, returning in the evening. There is a very real expectation of growth and change for all who come, no matter how chronic their illness, and few residents stay more than one year who do not make some progress. We are then constantly striving to recreate an enabling environment that allows all of us, not just the residents, to be free to risk change and growth. We are learning all the time the basic ground rules of how to live, becoming familiar with and developing our assets, recognising and accepting our limitations; all within the context of simple daily life.

5 THERAPEUTIC COMMUNITY MODELS: II KINGSLEY HALL (UK)

Joseph H. Berke

Kingsley Hall is a former settlement house in the East End of London that was built around the turn of the century. In 1965 Dr R.D. Laing and his colleagues obtained the use of it in order to create a unique community where people who had entered a state of psychosis would be allowed to pass through this experience. The view was that a psychosis is potentially growth-promoting and ego integrative. It is not an illness. Therefore, by not treating it as an illness, people who were psychotic would not be enjoined by their social circumstances to behave as if they were ill.

The building, a rather large red-brick building, is in Bow, deep in the heart of the East End working-class district. It was built by Muriel and Doris Lester in order to help the poor people in the area. From this building many of the pioneering social services, that were eventually incorporated into the National Health Service, began – simple things like nurseries for children, soup kitchens, discussion centres and adult education. After the war the building was used as a student hostel, but the Lesters were upset that many of the pioneering uses to which it had been put seemed to be fading into the background, into newsreels and memories. I think this was one of their reasons for deciding to lease the hall to Dr Laing and the group known as the Philadelphia Association, who had been looking for some time for a place in which they could put their ideas about psychosis and schizophrenia into practice. Their view, and a view which I share, was that what is commonly known as schizophrenia or psychosis, is not an illness. We completely reject the medical model, as we feel that it is a theoretical construct, imposed upon most emotional sufferers, who for historical reasons suffer an injustice, in both the experience itself and the social environment – other people, who give the label of 'mental illness'.

Psychosis is a waking dream. It is an alternative state of reality from which it is difficult to exit. Some people are completely immersed in the dream, other people are immersed in the dream but also have a certain awareness that they are not in the dream. This experience is akin to some extent to an LSD experience. During the first parts of the drug experience one is completely in the experience and often unaware of usual social reality. Later one can be aware of both everyday reality and the drug state. Schizophrenia, in contrast, is a diagnostic label, applied to people because they are socially bothersome. It was once estimated that a person has to bother over a hundred other people in order to be diagnosed schizophrenic. The bother consists of doing things, thinking things or experiencing things which cause distress to other people.

The idea that regression, the flight from adulthood into infancy, or psychosis, the flight from accepted reality to an altered state of consciousness, may be a creative experience has been expressed by numerous writers. The distinguished British psychoanalyst, D.W. Winnicott, saw both regression and psychosis (they may occur separately or simultaneously) as the means by which many individuals seem to shed their false fronts in order to reach a new and vital relationship with themselves and the world. Dr Winnicott advocated a greater tolerance of these phenomena which he termed mechanisms of healing and readaptation. Moreover, he suggested that special provisions should be made so that people would be able to complete the breakdown of the old self once it had started.[1]

The essential observation is that the breakdown is a cyclic event which includes a period of psychic fragmentation leading to a period of emotional reconstruction. The Polish psychiatrist, Kazimiera Dabrowski, has called this first phase 'positive disintegration'.[2] In many situations, he sees it as the necessary first step for the birth, development and integration of the personality. Similarly, the American psychiatrists, Don Jackson and Paul Watzlawick, regard the acute psychosis as 'a manifestation of growth experience' which may lead to a rapid, long-lasting and successful therapeutic change.[3]

These conclusions are supported by the published accounts of several people who have gone through both phases of fragmentation and recovery. John Thomas Perceval provided one of the first and certainly one of the most illuminating of such narratives.[4] Born in 1803, he was the fifth son among the twelve children of Spencer Perceval, the Prime Minister of England who was assassinated in the House of Commons in 1812. He had a conventional childhood for a young man of his class and in his teens he was commissioned as an officer with a cavalry regiment, the 1st Foot Guards. Early in 1830 he relinquished his commission and became closely involved with an extreme evangelical cult in Scotland. The members of this cult were called Irvinites. They spoke in an unintelligible gibberish which they believed to be the language of a foreign people. But these people found it hard to put up with the increasingly erratic behaviour of Perceval. As a result he left them and went to Dublin. There he contracted syphilis. Although he made a rapid recovery, he began to be increasingly bothered by voices. Eventually his brother came and committed him to a mental hospital near Bristol. He remained there for over three years, possibly because he came from a socially prominent family who did not want to be embarrassed by him at home. Then in 1834 he left hospital and took a wife. In subsequent years he wrote his books, had four daughters and lived to a ripe old age.

He describes the onset of his psychosis: 'I was tormented by what I imagined was the Holy Spirit to say other things, which as often as I attempted, I was fearfully rebuked for beginning in my own voice, and not in a voice given to me. These contradictory commands were the cause, now, as before, of the incoherency of my behaviour, and these imaginations formed the chief causes of my ultimate total derangement.'[5] The voices continued to torment Perceval throughout most of his stay in hospital. But the pain diminished when he began to realise that the voices did not come from outside himself, rather from inside himself. Moreover, they were not meant to be obeyed literally, rather to be understood metaphorically.

A vision marked the turning point in his struggles. He recalled that he was often tempted by the sight of naked women. One day he saw the image of a 'female of great beauty', 'a creature of flames', someone who was married to one of his friends. 'She appeared to descend from heaven unto me, when I was lying on the grassy bank in my wretched prison-yard, and uniting her spirit with my person, filled me up with comfort. "Surely," I thought, "she is praying for me, and her prayers are heard and her Spirit is living in me." I was then, perhaps, bordering upon frenzy or upon melancholic madness, and *thus the Almighty condescended to heal by the imagination that which, by tricks on the imagination, he had wounded, broken and destroyed*' (my italics).[6]

Because psychosis is cyclic it has often been described as a 'journey' or 'trip'. Gregory Bateson, the anthropologist who edited Perceval's *Narrative* remarks: 'It would appear that once precipitated into psychosis, the patient has a course to run. He is, as it were, embarked upon a voyage of discovery which is only completed by his return to the normal world, to which he comes back with insights different from those of the inhabitants who never embarked on such a voyage.'[7] For Bateson the acute psychosis is a vast and painful initiation rite conducted by the self into the self. It is the definite means by which the ego sheds its skin and is renewed.

Dr R.D. Laing has commented on the mythical or archetypal politics of this voyage. He sees it as a retreat from all outer concerns into an inner world of space and time completely removed from all usual constraints and prohibitions. The initial phase is a going backwards into the 'self', into the 'womb of all things' (pre-birth). The return is a passage from inner to outer, from regressions to progression, eonic time to mundane time, from 'cosmic fertilization to an existential rebirth'.[8] This 'going into the self' is not a universally accepted expression of madness. On the contrary, there are cultures where the death of the ego and the reintegration of the spirit are an integral part of the ceremonial movement from child to adult or from adult to man of knowledge.

In many other places, both past and present, this experience has been deliberately invoked as a means of healing. It was a common practice, for example, in Ancient Greece. The sick came from all over the ancient world to seek cures at the temples of Asklepios, Demeter and Trophonius (Zeus), by means of 'incubation'. Literally, incubation means 'lying on the ground'. The initiate was expected to spend a night in a cave, alone, lying on the ground in preparation for a dream or vision that would, in itself, cure him. Although incubation had many variations according to each particular temple, the incubant was invariably accorded respect by the priests and held in esteem by his friends and relatives. Perhaps this is because the procedure was occasionally physically dangerous and often frightening. Once at a sanctuary, he would bathe in sacred waters or drink from a sacred fountain. Then, as part of the rite of purification, he may have been asked to fast or eat special foods. Honey cakes were common because there was considered to be a link between honey and prophecy. Finally, the incubant would be dressed in swaddling clothes made from very fine fabrics. The Jungian analyst, C.A. Meier, points out that, once the sacred rite had begun, the incubant was for all apparent purposes a prisoner of the gods. They determined how long he could stay, what food or drink he could consume and when he could leave the cave.[9] This is a way of concretising the situation whereby, in undergoing the incubation, the incubant is putting himself in the hands of his unconscious. He then waits for the appropriate message from the unconscious in the form of a 'right' dream or vision. When it comes, it needs no interpretation and the disturbing symptoms which brought the person to the sanctuary simply disappear.

These situations, these examples, have to do with the background to the whole Kingsley Hall experience. Kingsley Hall itself, as a community, had no formal structure. There were a number of people living there together, some who were psychiatrists and some who had been patients in mental hospital. Sometimes they had their wives with them or their girlfriends, sometimes not. There were about twenty-five people altogether. At any one time there might be three or four people who were actually psychotic. People who were psychotic were given space, they were given company if they wished, or not, and they were given a great deal of physical support if necessary. It was a feature about life at Kingsley Hall that as people were not considered ill, they did not have to be treated. No drugs were given to anybody. There were no staff and no patients, and there was no formal structure of doing things around the Hall, yet things got done. There were people who were 'up' and people who were 'down'. The people who were 'up' or capable of functioning in a more usual social sense looked after the Hall.

Amongst the people who were at Kingsley Hall was one very remarkable woman whose name is Mary Barnes. She had spent several years in mental hospitals as a catatonic schizophrenic and she was for a period in the Richmond Fellowship. Before that she had been a Sister Tutor, and had also served as an officer in the British army as a nurse. She had many similar ideas about regression as a form of going back into the self, an opportunity for renewal. Mary was essentially looking for a place where she could go through such an experience. I would like to read from one of her accounts, because it describes a lot of the ideas and feelings involved in Kingsley Hall, not only for her but for other people as well. She writes, 'Flection: the art of bending or the state of being bent. That's how I was at Kingsley Hall, bent back into a womb of rebirth. From this cocoon I emerged, changed to the self I had almost lost. The buried me, entangled with guilt and choked with anger, as a plant matted in weed, grew anew, freed from the knots of my past. That was Kingsley Hall to me, a backward somersault, a breakdown, a purification, a renewal. It was a place of rest, of utter stillness, of terrible turmoil, of the most shattering violence, of panic and of peace, of safety and security and of risk and reckless joy. It was the essence of life. The world, caught, held, contained, in space and time. Five years as five seconds, five seconds in five hundred years.'

I first met Mary two years before in Dr Laing's office just as I was about to return to the States to complete my training: she was a small, broken woman, crying and weeping. Then I met her again at Kingsley Hall and I was horrified to discover that she was living in a bed of shit, was thin and emaciated, so thin that it was felt that she couldn't even be sent to hospital, as we might be prosecuted by the medical authorities for keeping a person like that. The question was what to do with her. It was not just a psychological problem, but a medical emergency. At the community discussion, I said, 'Well, I'll have a go at forming a relationship with her and trying to help her.' We agreed we would give it a few days and if it didn't work we would just have to send her to hospital.

I don't know why, but she seemed to remember me from two years previously. She didn't say anything when I told her she'd have to go to hospital or allow me to feed her, but responded when I fed her with the baby bottle Soon after, she began to get together and work through this experience with me. One interesting facet of this had to do with her very socially unacceptable habit of smearing shit. She liked to play with the shit, it was her way of making babies, with her faeces; as Sister Tutor she used to go to work at the hospital, and in between taking care of patients she used to go to the loo, take out her faeces, play with them for five minutes, clean up, and go back to take care of patients. For obvious reasons, both the smell and the mess, we told her she could do this in her room but not other parts of the Hall. She did not take any notice and she used to go around and make large faecal paintings which were caked on the walls of the dining-room and elsewhere. It struck me that there was energy in those paintings and much later I suggested to her that she should paint instead of smearing and gave her paints. She then initiated a torrent of painting, and there wasn't enough room in the Hall; there were not enough colours for her; there wasn't enough paper and not enough paint for her. Paintings were from her inner world, which is really a similar means of helping her – a means by which she met her unconscious. I won't go into it in great detail because it's all written down in a book we wrote together called *Mary Barnes: Two Accounts of a Journey Through Madness* in which she gives her account of what happened and I give mine.[10]

It is often asked, 'What happened to Kingsley Hall and Mary Barnes?' Kingsley Hall continued until 1970 when the lease on the building ran out and the community had to disperse. Thereafter, two new groups concerned with carrying on and developing the work of Kingsley Hall came into being. One was initiated by Dr Leon Redler. He rented some short-lease houses in poor repair from a North London council and started the 'Archway' communities. They have been portrayed in the film *Asylums*, and have eventually become part of the Philadelphia Association.

Dr Morton Schatzman, Vivien Millett, my wife Roberta, myself and others formed the Arbours Association. The temporary dwelling places where the Israelites lived in the wilderness after their exodus from Egypt are called 'arbours' in the New English Bible. We wished to provide comparable support and shelter for people in emotional distress and crisis. Dr Schatzman and Ms Millett created the first Arbours household in their home. Subsequently we sponsored two other long-stay communities in South and West London and a short-stay crisis centre in North London where people can have intensive interpersonal help, whether individuals, or couples, or entire families.

Mary Barnes went to stay in a self-contained flat in Hampstead after leaving Kingsley Hall. Two years later she moved into one of the Archway communities as she felt lonely living by herself. In 1975 she moved to her own cottage in Chagford, Devon, where she paints, is writing another book and endeavouring to help others who are beginning the journey which she has passed through.

Did Kingsley Hall succeed? It is an irrelevant question. It did no harm. It did not cure. It was simply a place where some people encountered selves, lost, distorted or forgotten. Given time, given luck, some were able to hear the beating of their hearts and elucidate the rhythm.

Notes

1. D.W. Winnicott, 'Metaphysical and Clinical Aspects of Regression Within the Psycho-Analytical Set-up' in *Collected Papers: Through Pediatrics to Psycho-Analysis* (Tavistock Publications, London, 1958), pp. 278–94.
2. K. Dabrowski, *Positive Disintegration* (Little, Brown, New York, 1964).
3. D. Jackson and P. Watzlawick, 'The Acute Psychosis as a Manifestation of Growth Experience', *Psychiatric Research Reports* (16 May 1963), pp. 83–94.
4. J.T. Perceval, *Perceval's Narrative: A Patient's Account of his Psychosis, 1830–1832*, edited by Gregory Bateson (William Morrow, New York, 1974).
5. Ibid., p. 32.
6. Ibid., p. 308.
7. Ibid., p. xiv.
8. R.D. Laing, *The Politics of Experience* (Penguin, Harmondsworth, 1967).
9. C.A. Meier, 'Incubation at the Oracle of Trophonius', *Ancient Incubation and Modern Psychotherapy* (Northwestern University Press, Evanston, Ill., 1967), p. 109.
10. M. Barnes and J. Berke, *Mary Barnes: Two Accounts of a Journey Through Madness* (Penguin, Harmondsworth, 1973).

6 THERAPEUTIC COMMUNITY MODELS: III PHOENIX HOUSE (USA)

Mitchell Rosenthal

The Phoenix House organisation has eleven houses, through which we are treating about 1,000 people. The population of the houses has an average age of twenty-three years, but ranges from eleven to sixty-seven. We have even had people as old as seventy-five in the community, who have been addicted for over fifty years! The membership is 46 per cent black and 19 per cent Puerto Rican, the rest being mostly white with occasionally an Asian or American Indian.

I think that the therapeutic community offers the single greatest hope, as a new social force, of bringing about positive change for individuals in need of help – individuals whom society defines as disordered, who may now be confined in our jails, mental hospitals or other custodial institutions. Traditional institutions are failing. The family unit, which is still the best mechanism known to man for child-rearing, is falling prey to urban population shifts, ambiguity of parental roles, sexist warfare and rapidly escalating rates of homosexuality. Colleges and universities have failed to grasp the imagination and hearts of our youth, who now cynically use them more and more as technical and vocational career centres. These institutions have failed to fill the humanistic moral vacuum left by diminishing religious institutions and decaying political leadership. Big business has done little more than to compete with civil servants to create a monolith mentality devoted to cradle-to-grave security. It is paradoxical that, although a relatively small movement, therapeutic communities have the potential to revitalise so many institutions. What can they provide? First, they can repair the victims or casualties of our own failing families; sometimes they can restore the vital balance to keep a family intact. Secondly, they can re-enfranchise a vast army of disadvantaged people. Blacks, browns, yellows, whites; men, women, children, rich or poor, young or old; mentally ill, drug addicted, alcoholics and former felons – all stand the greatest chance for a changed life through a therapeutic community. Thirdly, our colleges, universities and even big business can borrow a philosophy and a methodology that allows for human growth through totally open communication.

Several factors however stand in our way. First, society is ambivalent about allowing disenfranchised members any power. In America the hopeful exuberance of the Kennedy sixties has given way to the cynicism and grimness of the post-Watergate recession. There seems to be little current sympathy for any major programmes for human renewal. This is not just the political leadership, but strong grass-roots feelings that the poor, the welfare-takers, have received enough. When money is scarce perhaps this is not unreasonable. The sense of enough is also created by the fact that black Americans seem to have made great strides towards equality. In the early sixties a black taxi-driver in the South could not pick up a white passenger, let alone go to a white university. Today there are many organisations to aid the poor black, and almost none to assist the disadvantaged white. Meanwhile our cities, which are the cauldrons or incubators of so much disorder and of so many socially disordered people, are facing fiscal collapse. The anger and fear produced by this kind of fiscal uncertainty makes a commitment to the needy unlikely. This need not spell doom to therapeutic communities, since it could actually force them to a greater self-reliance and business development.

Secondly, institutions which have been the custodians of the poor, do not want to give up their power. Mental health workers do not want to turn over their keys and their roles to former patients, any more than correction workers want to allow inmates a say in how our jails and their programmes should be run, but the essence of the therapeutic community is sharing of power – the fact that one may enter one hundred per cent patient, but leave one hundred per cent staff. Of course, this is the essence of good organisation, as Sigmund Warburg said – to make oneself dispensable. This all sounds very reasonable. But every time I have begun a therapeutic community, in a prison, a hospital, a military institution, the greatest resistance comes from the existing staff, who are more concerned with their territory and their power than with the long-range well-being of their patients.

Finally, perhaps the greatest weakness of all is the lack of forceful and potent leadership to emerge from the therapeutic communities themselves. True, many charismatic figures have been responsible for developing the new therapeutic communities and staffing the old ones, but they represent only a fraction of those who have potential for this work, that is, those who are intelligent, sensitive and psychologically orientated. Many of these gifted people have been patients and opt to get out of the system. Sadly they no longer wish to stay in touch with the pain of others – that probably comes too close and keeps old wounds open. This is not surprising. Yet without commitment from those who have overcome their own handicap and their own illness through participation in these methods, there may be no therapeutic community movement. Intellectual awareness and ability are not enough; therapists and administrators can only be trained by going through the very process itself. Our hope is truly the people we help.

Treatment efforts are usually based on a model of disorder, its characteristics and its amenability to specific interventions. Contemporary models of drug treatment rest on the logic that the problem of drug abuse, misuse and addiction is a problem of the individual, and of his physiological and psychological characteristics. Drug abusers and addicts are easily described as suffering from metabolic disorders, or as being dependent and inadequate personalities. Based on these models of addiction are treatment regimes focusing on biochemical or intrapsychic processes. The individual is conceived of as the unit of treatment, and efforts are aimed at altering his internal make-up or his metabolic balance. Focusing exclusively on individual psychology or physiology has resulted in every conceivable effort to deal with the drug problem, yet the attempts have yielded a record of success that is very bleak. An alternative conception which I am suggesting is that the problem of drug misuse does not merely reside within individuals; if it is located anywhere, it exists in the complex relationship patterns of persons and their social context. In the past, transpersonal dimensions of the drug problems were passed over as influences which were regarded as important but not central to the question. A major conceptual reversal of the approach to the problem is required.

A conception of treatment must therefore, at the very least, include efforts to change the social context in which the addict is located. A treatment programme should not be based primarily on a medical model, but on a social system model of group maintenance and development. Treatment should be primarily devoted to an attempt to reterritorialise the addict in terms of social location and movement. One can think of the environment of the person before entry into addiction as a drug landscape. The significant locations for social contact in that landscape are designed for the procurement and use of drugs. The routine daily pattern of the drug addict's life is described as an orbit plotted for drug-takers. In a very real sense, the everyday landscape is saturated with opportunities and commands to use drugs and avoid the alternative options. And so long as the addict remains part of that landscape, he cannot be expected not to use drugs. Moreover, what is important about the drug landscape is not so much the availability of drugs and the frequency of opportunity for their consumption, as the exclusiveness of drug-taking activities. In reterritorialising the addict, the effort is directed towards locating him in a more drug-free environment, to be sure, but the primary goal is to place him in a field where the strongest influences are those which tend to involve him in human activities other than drug-taking. Treatment programmes must compete successfully against the addictive social system of which its members were originally a part. This is accomplished through the construction of a new social landscape, and the reconnection of the addict with the community whose values and modes of operation are antithetical to the community within which he originally became addicted.

Congruent with such an alternative model of addiction, the following requirements are on the list for an effective treatment programme. One, the norms governing the behaviour of all members of the treatment organisation, professionals and addicts alike, must serve the purpose of the organisation, that is, to create an alternative social network which can successfully recruit members out of the addictive community. At least some norms of the treatment organisation must be in direct opposition to those held by the addictive social sub-systems. Most members of the Phoenix programme who have participated in it for any length of time are able to describe its operation and purpose with clarity and accuracy. Almost any senior resident can and is called upon to guide visitors and explain the programme. This ability to act as spokesman for the programme can be taken to indicate that the induction into its norms and purposes has been very effective. The ideology of staff and residents alike is strongly anti-drug. Drugs are considered as agents of internal pollution, and a cop-out. Members who manage to gain prescriptions for drugs through physicians are subject to severe criticism.

Two, the formation of sub-groups which are loyal to the norms of addict culture must be prevented. The formation of sub-groups can be discouraged through the replacement of the traditional staff/patient dichotomy with a developmental continuity, so that there is a gradation of levels of authority which includes all members of the organisation. In this way, exclusive interaction between new recruits to the organisation is minimised, and the opportunity for interaction between new recruits and older members is enhanced. The formation of sub-groups at Phoenix House is prevented in various ways.

First, admissions are on an individual basis, so not more than a few addicts enter at any one time. This is of course quite different from the entry patterns of schools and other training organisations, including the military. If a number of new members enter together, it is more likely that they will be able to reinforce values at variance with those of the organisation which they are joining. Furthermore, when a new member enters an institution, he is inducted into a social role by the older members. In traditional treatment programmes, new patients and new staff members go through quite different induction processes. They are inducted into different roles by different groups of preceptors. In contrast, Phoenix House operates to blur such distinction. Patients and staff alike are first and foremost members of Phoenix House. We don't use the term 'patients' but rather 'residents'. Virtually all members have similar social histories. Role position within Phoenix House is not determined by membership in one or two groups, but instead rests on progressive induction into and development of the performance expected by all members. Although there are some distinctions between older and newer members, the distinction is based more upon day-to-day performance than upon externally imposed criteria. New members eventually become older members, and are not confined by pre-selection within a lower-status group.

Three, a high degree of social control needs to be exercised over all members. Positive and negative sanctions must be strong and visible. Among these will be procedures for status changes, rituals of honour and dishonour, and informal yet well-functioning channels for the expression of interpersonal approval and disapproval. Such social control mechanisms maintain the organisation's purpose and strengthen the commitment of individual members to the programme. In Phoenix House a high degree of social control over all members is achieved by several means. The most potent positive sanction for conforming to the normative standards of the community is formal status increase, which involves ceremonially conferred titles and increased authority and privileges. This means of control is facilitated by the organisation of Phoenix House, which is a formal status hierarchy in which every member occupies a specified position. Positive sanctions are continually expressed in the positive regard members of the community show each other. Negative sanctions are imposed upon those who violate the norms of the community. These consist of formal status reductions, again ceremonially marked with loss of titles, authority and privileges, and of dramatic visible stigmata, such as a shaven head and the wearing of a humiliating sign. In the case of more minor and more frequently occurring norm violations, negative sanctions take the form of on-the-spot pull-ups, or verbal admonitions from other members. All members of the organisation must be induced to enact the role of agent of the organisation's normative system, both through conforming to the norms and by issuing sanctions for the non-conformity of others. A strongly enforced norm at Phoenix House is the rule that all members, even the newest, must continually monitor the conduct of all other members with regard to the community's normative standards. Each member is expected to impose informal negative sanctions such as pull-ups when a minor norm violation occurs, and to make major violations known to the community as a whole, so that formal sanctions can be applied. The rule compels each member of Phoenix House to act as an agent of the community's normative system.

The pressures of social controls must in turn be matched by the opportunity for personal gratification for those members of the organisation who abide by its norms. A sense of community and comradeship, pride in collective accomplishments, a range of exciting activities and the option of continued involvement in the organisation, are among these gratifications. Membership of Phoenix House appears to recompense most participants for the sacrifices of freedom which are required. The visitor or observer is impressed by a strong sense of community and a sense of being genuinely cared about by others. Phoenix House members work hard, but each member's work is highly valued and each is able to see the contribution his work makes to the total functioning of the house. For example, a resident might say, 'I can show you around the house. This is my house and I feel good about it. I can show you what I've done to fix it up.'

Finally, there is the gratification of being involved in a dramatic, emotionally charged process, which results in visibly positive changes in oneself and in all those one is associated with – for some, a sense of being saved and saving others. As one member said, 'Even the balance of experience is altered. You learn to see every bad experience, every personal crisis, as an opportunity, and if you get through it without using dope you really feel good.'

Position in the status hierarchy of the organisation should be determined by universalistic criteria. Any member of the organisation can have the opportunity of rising within the status hierarchy as his commitment to the norms and values increases. Movement within a hierarchy should proceed through a sequence of formally defined stages, marked by the community rituals attendant upon the passage from one stage to another. Positions within the status and authority hierarchy at Phoenix House are allocated on the basis of conduct within the community. The absence of traditional staff/patient dichotomy enables any member, regardless of his lack of extrinsic credentials, to rise high within the hierarchy if his performance warrants it. In fact, any member can realistically look forward to becoming a director of this facility. Moreover, the most senior members of the hierarchy may be challenged – perhaps by the newest person in the community – through the encounter groups, which are totally peer-structured and provide a parallel system to the hierarchical one. If abuses of power should occur, therefore – which they well may – you have a very important balancing force which tends to stop the hierarchical power from corrupting.

There must be a high rate of interaction among all members of the organisation. This increases group cohesiveness, permits the development of interpersonal skills, ensures the widest scope for communication and permits a high level of monitoring among members and therefore of social control. Phoenix House ensures a high rate of face-to-face interaction among all its members by several means. First and most important, the organisation is not permitted to grow too large. Houses are kept to a population of seventy to eighty members. The house is then further broken down into clans, of usually no more than fifteen to twenty members responsible to one clan leader. The formal activities of Phoenix House are designed to maximise contact amongst members. The day is highly structured into work activities, group meetings, seminars, intensive encounter groups, recreational activities and so on. Members are systematically rotated about within this complex activity structure so that each member is daily placed in various types of interaction with a large number of other members. There is also the shared norm that one should get to know all the other members of the community and not spend much time by oneself or with the same few friends. The interaction among all members must encompass a wide range of interactional modalities, discussions and co-operative work efforts, and a wide range of emotional expression must be encouraged, so that the interactional potential and skills of the members may be developed to the fullest. The formal activities are designed to bring about not only a high rate of interaction among the members but also to encompass a wide range of modes of interaction. There are a variety of activities in which members are involved, requiring a variety of behaviours, so that interaction is not restricted to a limited, stereotyped set of role relationships, but allows the relationships between members to develop to their fullest richness and complexity.

Phoenix House attempts to strike a balance between isolation from the larger social context and involvement within it. In the early phases of membership, isolation is predominant. At the induction centre where all members spend their first stage of residence, generally for three weeks to a month, even looking out of the window is discouraged. Isolation at this stage of membership acts to intensify commitment to the organisation and to prevent the intrusion of conflicting demands, for example from drug-using buddies or family members. The means for isolating new members of the group involve the establishment of new interactional territories, bounded by physical space which constitutes the drug-free social landscape, peopled by fellow members of the community who are committed to developing new behavioural and interactional patterns. Isolation itself is no novelty for the addict; the drug landscape itself is typically quite limited. One of our people said, 'When I was dealing, the guy I got the stuff from brought it to my room. I stayed in that room with a bed and a TV, a radio and about 2,000 magazines. I never went out of it for three and a half months. If I wanted food, I sent out for it. I didn't want to leave – I had everything I needed.' The difference at Phoenix House is that the isolation serves the function of re-territorialisation, an abrupt move into a social landscape where the strongest forces pull for involvement with other people rather than with dope. In the later stages of membership, when members are firmly committed to the community, emphasis is placed on gradual re-entry into the larger society. At this stage members are encouraged to become engaged with the outside community, spend periods of time away from the house and become employed outside. This amounts to gradual extension of the senior members' territory, with Phoenix House as its centre. Eventually, having gained self-confidence and the trust of fellow members, and being no longer dependent on a source of drugs, the territories of members are enlarged far beyond their previous limits. For example, one of our members said, 'I just went to the West Coast to speak at a National Women's Liberation Conference. It's great to be so free. I never thought I'd go anywhere except maybe the jail.'

The Phoenix House programme provides for membership of sufficient duration to allow deep involvement in the organisation to develop. The average length of residence was formerly eighteen months to two years, and has now fallen to about twelve months. Although we encourage people to stay eighteen months, most people leave against advice. But new members are exposed to many more senior members who have developed a strong commitment to the programme and value system, and who have extensive changes in their capabilities, status and lifestyle. The impact of this exposure was described by one of our residents who said, 'When I first came to Phoenix, I was so impressed with all the people. They seemed so strong and together. And then I'd hear them tell about how messed up they'd been, or how they still got scared of something, and it made me feel like I didn't have to hide anything. And I couldn't hide anyway – these people were hip to my whole game.'

Even after members have moved out and re-entered the larger society, they are still encouraged to maintain some involvement in the organisation. Many of them return to the house regularly for visits and encounter groups. They also see fellow graduates of the programme socially, and in times of crisis, as they tell us, they continue to be guided by the norms of the Phoenix community. For the street addict, the available interaction partners are limited to other addicts and such representatives of the 'straight' society as police, correction officials and help professionals. Individuals belonging to these groups are seen as untrustworthy and are exploited. The experience of such isolation is illustrated in the following quote: 'I had no friends. They were just people I associated with, but it was no more than just a business. I knew they'd knock me over the head and take away my dope if they got a chance, and I would have done the same for them. When you're using drugs there's no such thing as a friend.' Phoenix House members do not have friends who are currently using drugs. However, they interact with a large group of other members who are concerned and helpful, and with members of the Friends of Phoenix organisation, who are in large part persons from all walks of life, people to whom addicts would not normally have access. One of our people said, 'The biggest thing I got out of Phoenix, besides my very life, was friends, people who accept me for who I am, not just to get something from me.' The addict who enters the Phoenix programme finds a ready-made social network to accept him. When he leaves, the network remains available. There are persons to telephone, visitors to live through a crisis with, or to be with when one is tempted to go back to drugs. I might say that most of our people, in seeking employment, end up being employed somewhere where another member is already employed. Their first apartment or home after Phoenix is generally with a room-mate who also went through the programme, so that in effect they leave with a network of five, twelve, perhaps twenty people, whom they remain very close to, and with whom they continue an intense relationship long after they have formally left.

Phoenix House is sensitive to the needs of building its prestige and charisma within the larger community. Through an extensive formal programme of public relations, involving the public and private agencies concerned with addiction problems, through our own Phoenix organisation and the encounter groups run regularly for interested non-addicted people, through sponsorship of drug-free rock concerts and art festivals and through work with the media, Phoenix has attempted to build a strong and positive image. All of this goes to maintain a large sense of family, a sense of a network to which people can continue to relate.

7 THERAPEUTIC COMMUNITY MODELS: IV THE RICHMOND FELLOWSHIP (UK)

Elly Jansen (Transcript)

All workers in therapeutic communities are concerned to extend the provision for people who should not or need not be in psychiatric hospital. We know that hospitalisation is a very expensive and very extreme measure, yet we all, it appears, feel somewhat impotent to provide an alternative solution. How are we going to use the resources that we have between us to achieve something more and something better?

Obviously we need to learn from one another; we have also, I think, become aware of the limits to what we can learn. When I went to America for my first sabbatical, after having worked for seven years with the Richmond Fellowship, I went very much with the notion that I was going to learn short-cuts and miraculous ideas, in order to do the job quicker, better and with less personal suffering and less cost. I did not actually find such ideas, although I learned quite a lot. There were a number of houses that reflected somewhat the approach that is professed by Spring Lake Ranch – one of the communities that I have visited many times, then and since. It is one of the models that most resembles the Fellowship, because of its mixture of 'ordinary people' living together as equals, yet with an ongoing concern to help people to make progress. When I first visited, the community was hardly interested in groups, and I was one of those who recommended that people get together and create a forum for discussion of responsibilities – not only those of a domestic nature, but also those of a personal nature. That was the contribution which I made at the time. Something I learned there, of which I had not been particularly aware before, was how much natural surroundings can do to help people to feel differently about life. It can of course give a misleading view: most people who go to a rural community will sooner or later end up back in the city. At the moment, however, we are making the opposite mistake of saying that everybody who leaves mental hospital must be brought back at all costs right into the heart of society. We must remember that some people may love living in the country, and may acquire the serenity of it.

Rather than just giving an account of the Fellowship model, which is described elsewhere, I would like to put it into a context of other models and views. Kingsley Hall was a very interesting project, in the initial planning of which I was involved. However, the views of Dr Laing and myself diverged, so that I felt eventually that the only thing to do was to part company and observe what would happen to the experiment. I feel now that this was the right decision. It would have been difficult to have an approach which is basically a treatment approach allied to what we see as basically a rehabilitation approach. Of course, you can have quite a debate about what is rehabilitation and what is treatment, because you can say that within the rehabilitation programme you have all the treatment needed – and the other way round. Looking specifically at Kingsley Hall, however, I think that twenty or twenty-five people had their lives put in disarray by one or two people. A very high percentage of people, therefore, needed to have a very costly involvement, and as a model I think that it is not going to work; and it is not going to work for various reasons. First, the number of helping adults who have to be involved is too high. Secondly, the need for structure may be called a defence against anxiety but I think that it is an *appropriate* defence against anxiety. If people are in pieces they may need to regress, yet one thing that you have to give them is some structure, some harmony and some place where they can rely on finding these things. The idea of letting things happen and that if shit hardens on the wall then in two years' time it won't smell, is not an idea that many people can live with for very long. Neither is it likely that it is of any help to the regressed person, who can hardly feel cared for. The debate as to the value or otherwise of a structured or totally unstructured community is linked of course to one's views as to the nature of schizophrenia and as to how far one views this condition as being entirely a response to a schizophrenogenic environment. It has been said that there are no bad soldiers, only bad officers – yet if you have any commonsense, you know that there are both. There may be people who create a response in others that may be given a certain name, schizophrenia or any other; and there may be people who suffer from a particular disorder labelled schizophrenia that has a particular effect on the environment. I think that they both very likely exist, and it is no good to say that all the mad are sane and all the sane are mad, as implied by R.D. Laing. The fact that one person in Kingsley Hall, Mary Barnes, got well has, I think, quite a lot to do with the tremendous amount of attention and hero-worship which she had and still has. Maybe some other people would in fact get better if one could put them in a position where they could play a very major role.

With regard to the Phoenix houses, the ultimate aim of getting to the top savours to me a little of the aims of the public schools in England! You have to forbear with cleaning the lavatories because the day will come when you can order someone else to do it. That is doing Dr Rosenthal something of an injustice, because I feel that his general ideas certainly have improved a great deal upon the original ones of Synanon, which in reality is a totalitarian alternative organisation. The idea is that you give your life to it in the same way as you give your life to a monastery. In the future you don't earn a living, you are owned by the community, and if you leave it you become a traitor. You cannot leave it on the reasonable grounds that you feel the right time has come for you personally to do so. That, I think, is in itself an extremely repressive answer, and I have myself seen the punitive nature of Synanon and could never agree with it. It is claimed that Phoenix House depends on honour and dishonour, reward and punishment. To this day I wonder whether it isn't possible for drug addicts, like the rest of us, to respond simply to being told by a friend, who also happens to be a member of staff, that they're behaving like a bastard, or that they 'make someone sick'. This does not involve the staff member in adopting methods which make him a superior in terms of power – 'I can give you punishment or reward and that is where you stand in relation to me.' This is something that I have never quite been able to accept. Many people in the drug abuse field say that the drug addict is very dependent on punishment and that therefore punishment is necessary for rehabilitation. The addict is punished and then when he has made his atonement he punishes others until they have made their atonement. I would very much like to have the time to go into that argument further. What I found most encouraging was to learn that people leave after one year, and that they are in fact encouraged to go back into society, rather than to form a totally different kind of 'superior', separate society.

In all the halfway houses and therapeutic communities I think we have somewhat the same goals. The structures are obviously different, as they need to be for different groups of residents. They also need to vary for different staff. People have different talents and abilities which need to be used. They also have different convictions, according to what they have been in touch with, how they have grown up, what their areas of difficulty are. Rather than going against these, it is preferable to utilise them provided that one is reasonably aware of where the strengths and weaknesses lie. So it is quite important that, for example, in an organisation like the Richmond Fellowship, there exists a wide variety of houses so that not only residents but also staff can find the house where they fit in best. A valuable attribute in staff is a questioning attitude. Sometimes, it is true, we have the extreme situation of people who assert: 'I want to do my thing and I will continue to do it regardless of the nature of the organisation, the money it provides, the strengths it has, the organisational patterns it has, and the responsibilities that are delegated.' It is terribly important that there is agreement on certain external constraints on boundaries and principles whilst at the same time there must be maximum flexibility for the staff to use their scope and creativity. In each house, as well as in the organisation, a *modus vivendi* has to be worked out and the question is always, how do you do that? You start, it seems to me, with the things that you cannot help possessing: your commonsense, your intention, what you have learned is practicable in life, what you feel is of importance to yourself. What is important for yourself is to be valued as a person, to be listened to when you have something to say, and to be listened to even if at times you feel like saying it nastily; but also to be checked and to be told, 'You don't need to do it that way, I'll listen anyhow.' Then our residents bring a lot of contributions and interest too. This contribution is not always recognised; for instance, when the Fellowship first started, I was much criticised by professional bodies because I lived on an equal footing with the rest of the residents, trying to find a way in which we could learn and live together. We were entirely without a model to start with, but definitely committed to finding one.

As soon as new staff enter both house and organisation, these staff also bring their needs and their ideas, which need to be introduced and to influence the way things are done. Therefore, an organisation must have an identity responsive to change; but in order for it to undergo change, that identity must be there to begin with and it must survive. Thus it is tremendously important that there be an on-going group of people who have thoroughly learned the lessons – often costly ones – of this type of work. In this way the organisation retains a nucleus of people who become the philosophy carriers, and who should have the task of evaluating the new ideas, so that one doesn't blow over with every new wind that blows. Total absence of structure is, I believe, not just asking for the kind of trouble which some people think is therapeutic, but is really creating, for a maximum number of people, a situation that is literally not liveable in (besides being unhelpful to patients). In a situation where staff have the role of mobilising residents to help one another, staff themselves need to be very aware of themselves, and to understand what people can tolerate and can actually accept. At the other extreme, there are communities which are largely custodial, which provide kindly, or not so kindly, shelter, a very clean place often, but with no personality, and allowing no individual expression; a place which does very little to help a person and to make life more welcoming and enriching. There is also the 'parental' organisation, which to some extent is the model, rightly or wrongly, of the drug addiction communities – yet it is my view that 'parenting' can be more satisfactorily achieved than by the totalitarian and punitive model of Synanon. This, however, is a model that is *apparently* successful – although I do not think that the results have ever been fully assessed, in terms of the residents' ability to leave and maintain themselves in society. It is interesting in this context to note that people are always terribly interested in sanctions because the idea is ever present, understandably, 'What am I going to do if I can't cope with this individual, or this individual won't behave?' The whole secret of the functioning of the therapeutic community is on the one hand, not to be repressive – not just to say, 'If you want to stay here you have to fit in with us' – and on the other hand, not to allow people to use the house entirely as they think fit, without bearing in mind what they are there for and how they are going to use the time. Between these two extremes – *laissez-faire* attitude and expelling people for bad behaviour – lies the whole of our work: the motivating of residents in the direction of greater responsibility and autonomy, and greater acceptance and love of themselves and others.

In the Fellowship, we have from time to time gone in opposite directions, and this is to be expected. A new idea comes in and in no time it has become a dominant practice; for example, there was a time when everybody felt that group meetings were extremely punitive. There was therefore a period when the focus was on the individual interview, which fostered great dependency and an insatiable demand for more and more staff, because in a dependency situation it is Parkinson's Law which operates. On the other hand, we reached a point where the group became overvalued and in fact exercised tyranny: the group must know and be told everything. The basic need that every human being has, to have a person in whom he can confide, is a very important one, and one which in this situation was violated. I was concerned to learn recently of a new practice at Spring Lake Ranch, whereby if somebody is talking to a psychiatrist, another person has to sit in. If a third person is the object of a complaint that psychiatrist should be able to say, 'That is something you should bring up in the community group.' But I feel that something is wrong if staff have reached a point where they are no longer willing to allow individual communications. The group, after all, is not everything in the lives of any of us. There has to be a distinction maintained between openness and what I would call indiscretion, and between confrontation and tyranny.

In the therapeutic community, the basis of the approach is that people are equal as human beings, although one hopes the staff will have a particular capacity to mobilise the community. In the Fellowship we feel that there must be a very careful balance maintained between accepting people (and helping them to accept themselves) without imposing a lot of conformity or repression; and on the other hand, providing a challenge for people to behave in as mature a way as possible. We feel that stretching them is not a negative thing; on the contrary that it is useful, provided that people are also given the support to be able to cope with the challenge. If you live in a community you anyway soon reach the realisation that certain things are a basic necessity. For instance, if people don't do their share of the chores the whole household goes to pieces and on the whole people don't like to exist in that way. There is a necessity, not only for the individual to survive somehow amid his possessions, knowing that he can easily clean himself up – but for the household collectively to survive through the co-operation of its members, to have a time to meet at table, a time to meet during the week, and to know that at certain times of the day the place will be clean enough, not just for yourself (although that is important) but for the neighbours down the road. For if we say that we really want to be part of the community again, we cannot ignore the fact that there are standards in the community and that although standards may sometimes be higher than the ones we can or wish to maintain, nevertheless ours must be reasonably close to what the neighbours would feel is acceptable. There is the theory that people must give expression to the way they feel and therefore if they feel depressed, their clothes will be on the floor, their shoes dirty and their bed unmade. This also works the other way, and in that case you have a very depressing effect and a circular one. If people can be helped to adopt reasonable habits and to create some structure, this has a good effect, as I have witnessed. And the structure does not need to be imposed in an autocratic way: it can be created by raising morale, through a process of involving residents in what we are to make of this house, what colour this room shall be, what kind of curtains it shall have, and so on.

There are of course very specific areas in which we feel we need to try to motivate residents to change, and one of those areas is work. It may seem punitive, but I found great comfort in seeing the emphasis placed on work at Spring Lake Ranch where in fact it received greater priority than at the Fellowship. There, everybody starts work at 9.00 a.m. and works until 3.30 p.m. or 4.00 p.m., undertaking a significant task. It is interesting that people are not yet asking for money to do that work, but I believe that a law was pending in 1974 in the United States under which, even if patients do work that does not bring any benefits at all to the community, they will have to be paid for their labour. The question then arises: when do you work to get yourself back into good working patterns and when do you work because you are providing a service to the community, rather than to meet your own need? In the Fellowship, adult residents are normally expected to be up by 9.00 a.m., having breakfasted or not, and to work until 11.00 a.m. on cleaning and tidying the house. Then there are several meetings a week to discuss work attitudes. Leadership of the group can rotate so that a person in turn can not only have the leadership of the work, but also the leadership of a group looking at work, and at how you relate to peers, to seniors and juniors, what you think of authority, whether you can, in fact, when you return to that strange outside world, cope with the problems it poses, and how you can adjust to its requirements, and at the same time make your own needs known in an acceptable way.

The other strong emphasis of the Fellowship is on resocialising people. As you may know, we have a firm philosophy of working in and with the local community, although from time to time we fall down on it. There is always a tendency when things become difficult internally, to close the doors and say, 'No outsiders in; they require extra work, and extra attention which we cannot give.' When that happens we in fact cut ourselves off not only from important resources of people who can help us and help our residents, but also from part of the task which we exist to fulfil. This is to educate the local community to accept people who are in difficulty, and to mend the dreadful split whereby you categorise people as 'sick' and 'well', by enabling people to understand themselves. We have found that the residents, because of their learning experiences in the houses, become excellent people to assist others in understanding relationships, and in a way it is perhaps surprising that we do not have more staff who have themselves participated as residents in the therapeutic process.

There is, as I began by saying, a need to proliferate both halfway houses and a variety of models. We have developed practical ideas of how a house can function, how it can be accepted in its locality, and how it can influence the local community as well as benefiting the residents. The question now is, how can we provide more? The Fellowship has addressed itself particularly to this question by stating that new staff must learn the job, not by being thrown in at the deep end but by joining a house where there is an experienced staff team in order that they may have the benefit of a learning situation as, for example, in a teaching hospital. This type of work cannot be undertaken by taking a social science degree or any other degree, although they have their value; you can actually only learn this job from the inside, from being with people and from becoming reasonably comfortable with being uncomfortable. It is necessary for staff to learn where their own needs lie and how these can be met outside the work situation, so that when they are interacting with residents they are objective enough not to be overwhelmed, yet compassionate and caring enough to identify. It is only when staff have reached that point that they can actually do this work for many years without going under. If they cannot reach that point then staff may, out of their feeling of impotence, frustration and anger, tend to recreate the problems they have with residents in their relationship to management, who then need to be perceptive and skilled in seeing at what level what type of support or intervention is required.

The basic point is that we need people who have the commitment and ability as practitioners to do this work, and who have the commitment and ability to train others. We need new people who have good ideas, and who also have the discipline and perseverance to work collectively, rather than to start projects in isolation from one another. Joining forces is not the answer to every ill; old constraints may be lost, but inevitably there will be some new ones. Yet in the Richmond Fellowship we have found that the constraints of joint work are outweighed by the advantages; especially the support of peers, which is just as important for staff as for residents.

Whatever the model, whatever the system, whatever the concepts, it is ultimately the quality of the staff that makes a project succeed or fail. If there is a need for many houses and many workers, there is a greater need for clarity and commitment, and for each individual worker to see the essentials. And when that is achieved we still need the quality of the various staff teams who will jointly create a human and successful enterprise.

8 A THEORETICAL APPROACH TO THE HALFWAY HOUSE (USA)

Sue Harris

The number of halfway houses has been increasing recently, but has been largely restricted to the field of drugs and delinquency. Federal agencies have so far not concerned themselves with learning how to organise such 'sheltered' situations for the schizophrenic or psychotic as a transition between hospital and community during a period when patients are under emotional stress. The absence of statutory financial provision has kept the halfway house from being among the real and/or theoretical alternatives for care in the United States.

Historically, several models for the practical and ideological organisation of halfway houses have been created in England but have met with little support from the psychiatric community in the United States. Without a theoretical orientation fitting the needs of the psychiatric patient, primarily the schizophrenic, the professional community here does not see the urgency in developing the halfway house concept and pressuring for government support. The Richmond Fellowship, founded in 1959 by Elly Jansen, is the most developed theoretical and practical system of therapeutic community approaches. Numerous halfway houses have been set up by the Fellowship in England, Australia and the United States, providing a network of initial support, pooling of information resources, expertise and training. Kingsley Hall, developed by R.D. Laing and his followers is the other well-known theoretical and practical approach to the therapeutic community concept in England.[1]

Currently in the United States only 'domiciliaries' and institutions have arisen to provide lodging for patients discharged from mental hospitals. These are apparently atheoretical, private financial ventures, having little or no community support and less federal and state interest and supervision. Since these domiciliaries are actually real-estate ventures, much like the private 'old age home', information fed to the medical profession has been incomplete, biased and often cynical.

In the United States a practical orientation to the concept of the halfway house, its organisation, needs and facilities, must be clarified to include the predictable difficulties and problems of schizophrenics in giving an approach to necessary interventions in the halfway house situation. This chapter is an attempt to describe a useful theoretical orientation towards schizophrenia and the schizophrenic experience in the adolescent and young adult.

Until puberty, the process of becoming human is almost totally in the hands of the parent-figures, who remain the central, most powerful influence on a child's life.[2] This influence includes providing the validation for most new experience and functioning, as well as the evolution and maintenance of restrictions on experience and functioning.[3]

With adolescence comes a new state of affairs. Whether or not the adolescent is ready, the responsibility for getting on with the process of growth is his own. The organisation of life to include the relevant experiences needed for further personality development is up to him. By puberty, the parents have already passed on all values, useful and harmful, which they could make available. Thus any capacities the parent has for intimacy or productivity have already been passed on to their offspring. At this point in the life of the adolescent, the function of the parent, despite societal preconceptions, is primarily that of financial support. The adolescent needs to organise his own means for the expansion of caring into the world of his peers.

The particular developmental tasks of adolescence include establishing cherishing of others who are not automatically acceptable to familial ties, acceptance of sexuality, developing competence and the ability to earn a living, developing new kinds of relationships with peers (i.e. the stranger, acquaintance and friend) and leaving home. Ready or not, the adolescent is driven to leave home and establish a new independence. This real and symbolic break with the family as the primary source of values, knowledge and caring is met with great uneasiness, anxiety and resistance. Figures show a continuously high rate of drop-outs in the last year of high school and first year of college, and many of these young adults return home, to wait, and hope, and maybe try to leave again. Culturally, late adolescence is prone to much anxiety over these very real transitional issues. More intense states of anxiety include disruption of consciousness and emotional chaos, commonly called the acute schizophrenic break.

With psychiatric intervention and management, the outcome or resolution of such psychosis can be toward greater independence, a decrease in anxiety and lessened fear. Left alone, these psychotic periods are often resolved by more reliance on the known interpersonal quantities, such as parents and family, less movement towards financial or economic independence and learning, and increased fear of peers including strangers, as well as fear of motion towards intimate relationships of any kind. More rigid personality structure and increased phobias develop with obsessive preoccupations over matters of security, prestige and normality. The bravery necessary for living becomes a dream of the past. In this alienated state, the young adult is treated with short-term hospitalisation, drug maintenance, and a quick return to his immediate family. This situation is culturally acceptable and even conventional; it is seen by our medical professional community as a necessary evil since funding for other alternatives is not available except in wealthy families or from smaller, private agencies, if at all.

However, the sixteen to thirty-year-old returning home must make peace with the process of being a fifth wheel, no longer a child, yet committed to that role in the eyes of the parents who cannot see their child as an adult. This child role can continue even through middle age or old age, in part depending on the ability of the individual to mature and in part depending on the intensity of parental possessiveness.

Having gone 'crazy' a person acquires a new and often self-conscious definition – not surprising, when even professionals see schizophrenia as a disease that is incurable and to be contained via drugs and medication, diet and shock. There is a tendency on the part of the family and hospital to support old parental prohibitions and at this stage to impose even greater restrictions based on the adolescent's new definition as a schizophrenic. To illustrate: a young man, isolated and evidencing difficulty at school, has gone into the army and is suddenly able to study, think and even get through the training programme. He 'hangs out' and dates girls. He suddenly experiences intense anxiety and, in a moment of despair, attempts suicide and is hospitalised. While in the hospital he is incapable of speech, is extremely confused and frightened. Treatment prescribed is somatic with recommendation of discharge from the army home to his parents. The army experience is remembered as a dismal and frightening failure. The young man is returned home to his parents who are willing to accept him and his failure. The resulting interpretation by the patient, the doctors and the community is that the army experience was too much for him and that he would do better in a protected environment. Dulled and stunned by the experience, with periods of amnesia and much residual dread and despair, the young man is certainly incapable of any functioning near the level of his army performance. Clearly he cannot stand too much new experience. The obvious interpretation is that he has transcended his limited capabilities. Thoughts of alternative forms of independence are shelved until he is 'rehabilitated'. The shame of a 'nervous breakdown' puts serious limitations on the expansion of social contact. The young man is pushed towards greater alienation and further into association with family and a new definition in life. Future attempts at leaving home are met with intensely forbidding gestures from the parents, now supported in their lifelong fears by the patient and the hospital staff. Staying home is experienced with increasingly unmanageable rage; but the young man's experience is dulled. Life is flattened, and passive acceptance becomes the norm. The increasing rage is volcanic and periodically unmanageable without hospitalisation. The future of this young man and many others like him has been decided. He has embarked on a new career, that of a professional schizophrenic.

Problems of the Adolescent and Young Adult Schizophrenic

The issues around which the adolescent most usually has a schizophrenic episode are those which centre on the developmental task of leaving home. This issue, as it symbolises individuation, involves making the transition from orientation towards one's parents as audience and validators to an orientation towards one's peers as validators. Validation is the process of friendly recognition of another person's experience, including needs and functioning. Leaving home also involves learning and putting to use some very concrete skills such as earning a living, maintaining one's person and apartment, and negotiating social relationships with strangers and acquaintances in the work situation, the living situation and, generally, the world. You can't support yourself if you can't hold a job. You can't hold a job if you can't take public transportation or drive a car or get through a job interview. Even the most isolated jobs require initial contact with a boss. Most jobs require getting along with a boss and fellow workers.

In addition to the issue of work, there is also the problem of managing money. In order to maintain independent living arrangements it is necessary to organise a means of paying one's bills, living in an household of some kind, having presentable clothes to wear, organising meals and sleeping arrangements. Adolescents who cannot manage these apparently simple aspects of living are often among the schizophrenic casualties of this transition period.

A hospitalised patient once told his therapist that, after a hospitalisation, he had been supported in an apartment by his parents. He was pleased with his new living arrangements. Since he was considered too disturbed he was relieved of the necessity of having to look for a job or manage money. His parents could afford to support him in a separate apartment. Nevertheless, he still had to figure out how to organise his apartment and take care of food and clothing. His pitfall was the laundry. Every day he would take his dirty clothing and deposit it in a chute in the hallway that he imagined to be the laundry chute. He could not understand why he never had his laundry returned to him by the management. It was only later that he learned he was using the incinerator for a laundry. Such extreme incompetence was actually contrived by the patient, who must have known better. Nevertheless, his story has as its purpose the dramatisation of his profoundly held conviction that he was totally incapable of caring for his needs on even the simplest level.

An even more tragic situation is that of the financially supported young adult schizophrenic whose parents use the withholding or manipulation of funding to deter further moves towards independence. If the young person has no concept of financial management or holding a job, he can for reasons which are not easily contested be quickly brought to his knees.

The capacity for basic competences, such as organising a household, managing money and holding a job is usually not so much the issue as acceptance of peer validation. The more serious defect is the inability to maintain relationships which validate such competence. In the case of the professional schizophrenic who has been through the shuttle between home and hospital numerous times, the primary validators remain the parents who are totally convinced that their offspring is incapable of managing even the simplest task. Since the parents remain the primary validators, the schizophrenic must be as they see him. The incompetence increases and is farced, as in the case of the young man and the incinerator, and it is maintained as part of the new way of life.

The young schizophrenic maintains a focus on the parents as audience and a childlike status. The central issue for the adolescent in establishing an adult role in society is the source of validation. If validation continues to come from primary relationships within the family and these primary relationships cannot validate new needs for independence and competence, the adolescent is destined to live out the limited parental expectations of childishness, incompetence and stupidity most commonly associated with schizophrenia.

The focus of the young schizophrenic is primarily on the mothering figure. If the mother enjoys alternative sources of validation for her child with peers outside the family, there would be the possibility of later validation for more adult functioning, and the prognosis of any period of severe disorganisation would be improved. The reality for most of those who have been through severe schizophrenic episodes is that they can accept no validation outside the family which might give credence to their capacity for adult competence and relatedness.

The Halfway House

The halfway house, by creating and containing the central interpersonal experience, is a means for transition from the period of severe emotional disorganisation to the ongoing period of reliable adult functioning. The halfway house relates primarily to the needs of the adolescent or young adult schizophrenic coping with the issues described above. After the hospital, the halfway house provides the next experience of living with peers and organising a large household. As such, it includes the expectations that the particular patient will contribute work and involvement in the organisation of such a household. The expectation of the house is that the resident will function in goal-directed activity with others, hopefully with some enthusiasm.

The resident of the halfway house is encouraged to use the group for support and progress towards eventual self-support and autonomy. Use of the resident group and group leaders for help with the goals of establishing interdependence and self-support constitutes the significant step of making use of peer instead of parental validation. The validation is for the appropriate goals of adolescence.

A halfway house should include groups organised to maintain the household, that is, the cooking, cleaning, shopping, finance and maintenance. There also need to be groups organised to discuss the core issues for halfway house residents' groups on how to get and keep a job, how to find an apartment and deal with landlords, how to get back to college and organise a meaningful education, how to take care of one's health and get adequate medical care, groups that share common experiences with family, sex, social relationships and give mutual support around these issues. These groups need to be programmed into daily routine of the halfway house as is the case, for instance, in the Richmond Fellowship. Leadership for such groups will probably come initially from staff members with more experience and comfort, but should be extended to residents as they develop a sense of membership and autonomy. Administrative decisions and policy should remain clearly in the hands of the staff of the halfway house, but participation and contribution of skills impart leadership that is essential for the resident to learn. In addition, needed skills can be shared among residents and taught by residents. The goal should always be to increase group participation, self-respect and competence.

In addition to participation in groups organised around specific goals, the experience of living with continuity in a group among peers is essential for the halfway house resident. The continuity of daily living in a group provides an alternative to the chronic mood of isolation and despair usually felt by the adolescent or young adult relegated to the role of the schizophrenic in the context of the family. Contained in the experience of group living is the opportunity to make choices of acquaintance and friend, to organise one's own activities, to extend one's interests in directions beyond the scope of one's family and to notice the possibility for considerable variation in the ways in which people live their lives.

An adequate halfway house arrangement should be able to recognise that the process of learning new functions may involve periods of regression, disorganisation and inability to function and therefore facilities for such periods should be provided.[4] These facilities might include readily available means of rehospitalisation should a resident require some period of reorganisation, although it is envisaged that usually the necessary support could be given within the framework of the halfway house.

The purpose of the halfway house should be transition to, or progression towards, living in the wider community. Therefore, it is essential to maintain contact with the outside world and its requirements with a view to helping the resident prepare to cope comfortably with that world. There is no requirement that either the staff or the resident see the larger world as particularly ideal or rational. However, it is important to see the ability to get along in the world as an indispensable prerequisite to adult status.

The period of preparation should be finite but non-rigid and consist of specific steps towards eventual functioning in the outside world. Such preparation involves role-playing with staff and residents, sharing of information and advice, practical assumption of responsibility in the house, and eventual involvement with real experience outside. Preparation should also include expectation of a number of mistakes as the novice adult attempts to learn how to function in the world.

Sometimes the best way to learn how to work is to get fired from a number of jobs. After a series of experiences at different jobs with different bosses and finding out what not to do, the resident can settle down, do what's acceptable and competently hold a job.

The most pressing problems in the establishment of a halfway house are finding the means for financial support, and finding perceptive friendly staff.

The residents' problems are precisely around the issues of self-support and competence. Rarely do they have access to funds to pay their way. If the family has money, support can be accepted from them as long as the halfway house is not dependent on its maintenance from this source. Control over the halfway house and, incidentally, over the residents, must not be the price of such financial support.

Money to establish and run a halfway house is not readily available through federal and private grants. In addition, the requirements for grants are very stringent, with many restrictions and regulations for construction to meet government requirements.

One method often used to pay the rent is the collection of SSI (Social Security and Invalidity benefits) from the residents. Such payment is totally inadequate to meet running expenses, and removal of the resident's whole SSI cheque leaves him totally penniless, without the autonomy involved in having spending-money.

In addition to monies required for rent and maintenance, sufficient funds need to be available to pay salaries high enough to attract suitable staff. Training and supervision for staff must be part of the programme in order to support and develop staff members and to provide sufficient motivation to stay with the project.

Education and preparation of the surrounding community is another major issue. The staff of a halfway house need to establish early relationships with key people in the wider community, in order to orient them to the nature of mental illness and the real problems of the residents. The wooing of skilled and retired members of the community as contributors and participants in the halfway house programme is needed to help in building constructive interactions. Such orientation might take place through conversations, parties and get togethers of various kinds, like neighbourhood and tenants' association meetings. An example of structured contact with the neighbourhood is provided by the Richmond Fellowship which establishes local committees to provide a link between house and neighbourhood, and to facilitate social integration and provide work opportunities and practical assistance.

For most communities, the prospect of having a house full of 'loonies' right next door is extremely unwelcome. Fears and phantasies surround the spectre of mental illness: bizarre behaviour, aggression, possible vandalism. Forcing a halfway house on the surrounding community without preparation or communication can establish a barrier of hostility which is hard to break down, and is detrimental to the halfway house resident who wishes to establish a viable foothold within the community. Instead, what is needed is good public relations, re-education and much interaction. The establishment of ongoing communication and co-operation with people in the area enables the resident to use the community as a source of validation.

The task of establishing relationships with the neighbourhood also involves orienting the residents to the need for relating to the community. Instead of establishing an elitist group that looks down on the 'straight' outsider, an atmosphere of curiosity and friendliness needs to be established and the staff need to encourage participation in neighbourhood activities. Part of the importance of peer validation is the concept that it can expand indefinitely and that choice is possible and change is acceptable. Validation can and must come from an increasing number of people. Part of the job, therefore, of the staff of the halfway house is to introduce the possibility of new validation from peers outside the halfway house, to insist on establishing connections with the outside world, and to see the members' interaction as valuable, even if it is temporary or culturally seen as problematic.

Relationships with those outside and inside the halfway house community should be egalitarian and conducive to increased expansion of functioning and relatedness. Staff need to be ready to relinquish strong ties with residents when it is appropriate. The relationship between the parents and the resident tends usually to be hierarchical or authoritarian rather than egalitarian. The young schizophrenic's problem is the inability to leave home and the exclusive focus on the mothering figure, with inability to form viable alternative validation. There has to be an understanding that a minimum of a certain number of nights must be spent at the house for a resident to be considered a resident and that daytime hours should be spent on the projects of developing learning skills, competence and self-support.

The problem with schizophrenic family relationships is not just the family's tendency to hold onto their offspring and to infantilise; there is also the strong pull on the part of the offspring to go home, to repudiate the experience of independence and to return to mother. Many halfway house residents have been extremely dependent on the mothering figure. The staff of the halfway house need to be aware of the central problem of most of its residents, that of the over-importance of the mother and finding new sources of validation beyond the parents. No matter how angry, morose, psychotic, frightened or despairing the resident becomes, his need is not for his parents. Understanding and protection at these times should be made available in the halfway house. Any child may become homesick at camp or boarding school for his or her parents. That is not the signal to send the child home but rather to provide alternative comfort and to involve the child in more absorbing activities.

It is desirable for each resident to have an individual therapist to meet at least once weekly. In addition to a solid relationship with one of the staff members at the halfway house with whom employment, management and household issues and emotional problems relating to the community are discussed, an analytic relationship with a therapist can provide an important nurturing situation for residents – in which deep-seated problems may be resolved. At the Richmond Fellowship there is an understanding between the resident and the staff that communication will be maintained between therapist and staff regarding the resident. In this way, there is the clear recognition that both the life in the therapeutic community and the therapy sessions are a part of the therapeutic process.

The daily routine described by Elly Jansen and the staff of the Richmond Fellowship[5] is a good model of the type of halfway house needed for the transition from hospitalisation to productive life. There are, first of all, 'high expectations' for the resident within his individual limits. The resident is expected to learn to live with other people, carry a share of household chores, become competent, caring, self-supporting and to establish a viable way of life in the world at large. High expectations are intrinsic to validation. The group is a powerful source of validation for practical and interpersonal competence. There is an active and positive relationship maintained with the outside world that is seen as the eventual goal of the resident. In a number of cases the relationship with the family of the resident is seen as a significant cause of exacerbation of the problem, and in any case residents need to seek independence from their families.

Summary

This theoretical orientation to the schizophrenic experience in adolescence and young adulthood is consistent with the concept of schizophrenia as a phenomenon resulting from inadequate and insufficient interpersonal relationships and the ensuing inadequate competence in the adult world. The halfway house has been described as ideally providing a real interpersonal emotional base and training ground for competence during the transition period between an acute psychotic episode and return to the outside community as a functioning member of society. An attempt has also been made to outline problems likely to be encountered in the process of organising and maintaining a halfway house and to indicate already successful models of halfway house organisation.

Notes

1. See M. Barnes and J. Berke, *Mary Barnes: Two Accounts of a Journey Through Madness* (Penguin, Harmondsworth, 1973).
2. J. Pearce and S. Newton, *The Condition of Human Growth* (Citadel, New Jersey, 1963).
3. H.S. Sullivan, *The Interpersonal Theory of Psychiatry* (Norton, New York, 1953).
4. See Pearce and Newton, *Human Growth*; K. Andrews, 'A Study of Parallel Play and its Effects on Preadolescent Art Work in a Museum Setting', unpublished dissertation, Union Graduate School, Yellow Springs, Ohio, 1977; E. Jansen, 'The Role of the Halfway House in Community Mental Health Programmes in the United Kingdom and America', a lecture given to the 125th Anniversary Meeting of the American Psychiatric Association, Miami, Florida, 5–9 May 1969.
5. The Richmond Fellowship of America, 'House Principles and Program', 1977.

9 LIMIT-SETTING FOR LATE ADOLESCENTS IN AN ADULT PSYCHIATRIC HALFWAY HOUSE (USA)

Thomas F. Barton

> The testing phase . . . extends from the beginning of treatment to the control of acting out and the establishing of a therapeutic alliance. It is obviously crucial. If its ingredients are not recognized and properly handled, the remaining hours or even years of therapy may be rendered ineffective.[1]

> Another dynamic motivating the test is to determine if the therapist 'cares'. The parents have usually felt too guilty to set limits, which the patient has interpreted as further evidence of their lack of caring.[2]

What this chapter will try to do is organise impressions gathered during two years' work as a resident counsellor in a well-functioning, high-expectation halfway house, with particular emphasis on experience with men between 18 and 24 years of age.

Although they come from a variety of ethnic and experiential backgrounds, these men have more in common with each other than with patients in the over 24 age-group. The difference is visible and striking. The older patients move with more hesitancy, tend to be sedentary, much more masked, less energetic, and tend to act-out verbally. The younger group give a physical appearance of strength and vitality, restlessness, wider ranges of expressed feelings, and tend to act-out through their behaviour, by cutting rehabilitation classes, for example, drinking, playing radios at volumes unacceptable to the neighbourhood, and so forth. Another crucial difference is that many of the older residents see themselves as 'mental patients', while the younger group often reject that label, seeing themselves as people who are 'fucked up' in one or more ways, sometimes dramatically and irreversibly so.

During my period at this facility, eight men in this age-group have been accepted as patients/residents. Most were considered by their families, the mental hospitals referring them, and occasionally by themselves, as insane. The most common hospital diagnosis was one or another form of schizophrenia, usually chronic. What they did have in common with the older group was the experience of being treated as mental patients by family and friends. All had experienced the infantilising process of hospitalisation, and the associated infantilising attitudes of some hospital personnel.

They also had in common their interaction with the halfway house staff, which was the same for older and younger residents: refusal to treat them as fragile, helpless, sick children, and refusal to deviate for any or all of them from the basic rules of the house.

Specific examples may be helpful in understanding what that means.

Bob M., age 22, appeared for his intake interview in August. He was required to come from Jacobi Hospital for the interview unescorted, despite the efforts of his social worker to 'come along and help out'. We refuse to see applicants on any other terms for several reasons. First, there have been too many instances of hospital personnel trying to force someone into our facility against their will, a situation that emerges quickly during unescorted intake interviews. Second, every man and woman in the house is given to understand from the first that they will be treated as responsible adults, with their own keys to the front and apartment doors; freedom to come and go as they wish as long as they are involved in school, work, or vocational and social rehabilitation programmes every day. They do their own shopping and cooking, and manage their own money. They are told the few basic rules of the house; immediate eviction for any physical attack on another, themselves, or the house; for drunkenness at meetings of the house; for non-attendance at programme or house meetings; for use of illegal drugs in the house; for non-payment of rent.

During the intake interview we learned that Bob had gone into the navy at 18, and been discharged six months later for 'being a manic-depressive'. He took obvious pride in the fact that 'no doctor on earth can help me'. His general attitude during the interview was arrogant, hostile and contemptuous of these idiots asking him such stupid questions. He described how sometimes he would collapse completely, and sometimes his brain would 'speed' and he would talk for hours or days. This led to questions about drug use, i.e. methadrine, and he confirmed he began using it when 16, but quit on going in the navy. He said he was no longer on any drugs except lithium. He obviously derived satisfaction from describing how 'off the wall' he was during these mood swings. ('An admixture of satisfaction with this state of turmoil is never absent.'[3]) He said he wished to live at the halfway house because of 'trouble' with his family, but refused to discuss that further.

We ran through a description of the house and the rules, and he said that on the days he was 'mental' he probably could not get out of bed to go to his rehabilitation programme. We said that if he cut programmes he would first be warned, if he continued cutting he would be suspended from the house for 24 to 72 hours, and if he cut after that he would be evicted. We said that the only acceptable reason for not attending programmes, which he, like everyone else in the house, would have from 9.00 a.m. to 3.00 p.m. five days a week, would be physical illness, in which case he would be expected to be at Jacobi Hospital Emergency Room waiting for treatment. He then asked if he could have help getting up, i.e. whether the staff would get him up. We said no. He asked whether the other men could help get him up, and we said if he became a resident one thing he would have to learn was to ask people other than the staff questions like that since we didn't answer them.

He became angry and said, 'The social worker said you people were here to help me and take care of me.' We said we weren't there to take care of anybody. Our job was to do what we could to help him learn to take care of himself, as everybody else in the world has to do, and we were starting right now. He then said we probably didn't want him to move in because he had been angry with us just now. The reply to this was that his being angry or not angry had nothing to do with it. If he wanted to move in, and understood what the contract was, that was fine, because we thought the house could be helpful. If he didn't want to move in, that was up to him too. We added that there would probably be times we would be as angry with him as he had been with us, and that being angry and expressing it was not only acceptable in the house, but something people who lived in the house were expected to learn how to do.

He decided to move in, and spent the first week leaving the house early in the morning and cutting his programmes in the rehabilitation centre the rest of the day. At the end of the first week, he was warned that if he cut any programmes the following week, he would be suspended for 24 hours. He promptly cut more programmes and was suspended. After the suspension, towards the end of the second week, he began cutting again.

Finally he was called into the staff apartment and told that if he cut his programme one more time during the next six weeks, he would be evicted on the spot. His first remark was, 'But where will I go?' We said that was his problem; if he cut programmes knowing he would be evicted it was his responsibility to find out where to go. Our responsibility would end with putting him and his possessions on the pavement in front of the house with his rent refunded, but that one way or another this 'bullshit' had gone on long enough. This last message was delivered by the house director, a woman, which shocked him as much by the language used as its contents. He became more genuinely engaged than we had ever seen him previously, left the staff apartment, and for the next six weeks attended every meeting in his programme, on time.

Along with this perfect attendance, for the first three weeks, went silence in the house. He would speak to no staff member, and only grudgingly to other residents. He attended the weekly house meeting (for all residents) and the weekly apartment meeting (for the six men in the men's apartment and myself) but would say not one word during the meetings. During the men's apartment meeting several of the other men tried to speak to Bob and got no response. They then asked me, as the staff member responsible for the apartment, to make Bob talk during the meetings, and to them. My reply was that I knew of no house rule requiring anybody to talk as long as they met the rules that applied to everybody in the house in terms of behaviour. I also thought their request that I make Bob talk reminded me of children asking daddy to punish another child. I said my opinion was that by doing this silent number Bob was cutting himself off from other residents, and the staff; isolating himself probably didn't get him much relief for his obviously angry feelings, but that was his problem to sort out, and whatever my opinion was about the childishness of his behaviour, he could stay his whole year without talking if he wanted to.

When I hit the part about Bob's behaviour being 'childish' and 'angry' he looked ready to explode and when I'd finished he yelled loud enough to be heard on the first floor, 'I'm not angry, I'm just bored.' During the rest of the meeting he talked about how much he hated the boring six weeks' evaluation at the rehabilitation centre and the boring groups he had to go to, but what was also being communicated was pride in himself for being able to 'stick it out' at something for the first time since he got sick. At the men's apartment meeting in the sixth week of his programme, he said that he was getting a favourable evaluation for his attendance and work performance, and wanted the men's group to tell him what kind of vocational training he should ask for, or tell him whether he should go on to college. Again he became enraged when I and the other men refused to go beyond asking what he wanted to do.

This pattern has continued: demands for exceptional treatment and/or infantilisation, and anger when it is not forthcoming more and more coherently and insightfully expressed.

Bob's experiences in the house show how staff applied in practice with him the theoretical assumptions that were developed to deal with older, more chronic patients:

1. Patients are neither fragile nor made out of glass.
2. Infantilisation is the worst possible form of interaction.
3. Unless limits are set, and meant, the patient is quite correct in perceiving the staff as uncaring.
4. High expectations tend to encourage maximum performance and change.
5. There is no contradiction between anger and real caring, which means caring enough to let go, and sometimes push.
6. A halfway house is by definition a situation of dependency for the residents, and the staff must make every effort to counteract that by fostering independence.
7. Defeat, retreat into hopelessness, and failure are unacceptable. The worst disservice a staff member can do a resident is accept a self-definition of being a hopeless case, unable to change, even if the alternative is eviction from the house.

This last point requires some development. Masterson quotes one patient as saying:

> They would say I couldn't. I did it anyway and then they would say you will stay in next week. I would go out and there was absolutely no way they could have handled me. I could wear down anyone. No one could have controlled me. They tried everything. They even tossed me out four times. I packed my bags. After a day or so my father would come and apologize to me. He was a pussy. He let me get away with everything. He was playing my game and I always won like with those curfews. I never kept them.[4]

How to reconcile eviction, the ultimate sanction, and its transferential meaning of total rejection by the family, with Erikson's comments on negative identity?

> The patient insists that the therapist accept his negative identity as real and necessary – which it is, or rather was – without concluding that his negative identity is 'all there is to him.' If the therapist is

> able to fulfil both these demands, he must prove patiently through many severe crises that he can maintain understanding and affection for the patient without either devouring him or offering himself for a totem meal. Only then can better-known forms of transference, if ever so reluctantly, emerge.[5]

First, there has to be a clear-cut recognition of the difference between limits and the full range of negative self-identifications. The rules of the halfway house which are grounds for eviction are carefully chosen, and kept as few as possible: the bare minimum necessary to avoid chaos. It was absolutely unacceptable for Bob to cut programmes, and he knew that at the intake interview and he also knew that it was no less unacceptable for any other resident. This was a limit which was set and meant. Before this rule was made, withdrawal into rooms, drug abuse, suicidal gestures, violence and general confusion were frequent events at the house. Mental illness was highly beneficial, since if you felt crazy, you didn't have to get out of bed in the morning and go to that 'dumb typing class' or whatever.

His most overt negative identity, however, was unacceptable, i.e. the mental patient who couldn't go to programmes. He retreated to a second position: the man who never spoke. The clear message he received about that was:

1. It's childish and self-defeating.
2. It's also your right to be childish and self-defeating in this way, not because it's good for you, but because to try to force you to be otherwise would be treating you like a child, and also an inexcusable invasion of your ego boundaries, specifically your right to think, feel and speak for yourself. We don't pretend for one minute we think it's appropriate, or going to get you anything. But for now, we accept it, in that we do not try to force you to change it against your will.

As Meeks put it:

> In short, the adolescent is told that his behavior is none of the therapist's business except that some actions interfere with the therapeutic process and these must be controlled or therapy will not proceed properly. Often, it is also possible to demonstrate that acting out disrupts the youngster's psychological harmony or threatens to harm him. The therapist tries to convey his wish that the adolescent win the developmental war while keeping it clear

that it is the youngster's battle and that the therapist cannot fight it for him.[6]

The sanction of eviction has been applied to four of the eight late-adolescent men mentioned at the start of this chapter, once for using marijuana in the house, once for continued drunkenness, and twice for threats of violence with weapons. Two of the men have shown no improvement since eviction, and two made major positive alterations in their lives immediately following the event.

In summary, of the eight late-adolescent men, the following results have been obtained:

1. Finishing the year of residence:
   - David: In fourth year of undergraduate school, engaged.
   - Mike: Construction work, recently married.
   - Bob: Entering Office of Vocational Rehabilitation-supported school full time.
   - Sy: Has returned to live with father and not working; this is considered an unsuccessful outcome.

2. Evicted for cause:
   - Max: Threat of violence with weapon, in first month. Now drug-free, attending college part time.
   - James: Threat of violence, in third month. Living with mother, not working. Considered unsuccessful outcome.
   - Saul: Evicted for drunkenness at house meetings, in second month. Working, attending college part time.
   - Larry: Evicted for dope-smoking first day of residence. Returned to live with relatives. Considered unsuccessful outcome.

Of the five outcomes considered successful, each man is either working or going to school at a higher level than ever previously attained. Although most have records of multiple hospitalisations prior to admission, none of the five have been hospitalised since leaving. Sy, while not meeting house standards for a successful outcome, has completed a stenotyping school. Mike and David, functioning at the most age-appropriate levels now, were both sent to the house diagnosed 'paranoid schizophrenic'.

Summary

The younger group of men have, as a group, had a somewhat less successful rate of outcome than the rate for the house as a whole, success being defined as no rehospitalisation, own apartment and employment and/or higher education.[7] Their style of limit-testing tends to be different from residents over 25, but the same methods of staff-functioning appear to be as appropriate and useful for this group as for the more practised patients. The younger group of men tend to test limits more directly and overtly, in an active way, and also have a higher rate of eviction for going beyond acceptable limits.

Eviction, however, is sometimes beneficial, and has been explicitly identified by at least two men subjected to it as helpful to them, probably because it is an experience in learning that parenting figures at some time mean what they say, and also because it is a refusal to accept pathological behaviour as inevitable and outside the responsibility of the individual engaging in it – a new experience for most residents used to pathogenic families and infantilising hospitals.

For both the older and younger patients, the initial testing is around limits, usually within the third to ninth weeks, after an initial period of 'good behaviour'. Although the style of the two groups differs, successful negotiation of this testing usually leads to a positive transference to the house and staff, and increasing willingness and ability to acknowledge and work through intrapsychic conflicts. If this increased openness is met by unwavering refusal to infantilise and foster dependency, and with respect for ego boundaries, the outcome tends to be favourable, even for patients with repeated hospitalisations and pessimistic hospital diagnoses.[8]

Notes

1. J.F. Masterson, *Treatment of the Borderline Adolescent* (Wiley-Interscience, New York, 1972), p. 113.
2. Ibid., p. 114.
3. P. Blos, *On Adolescence* (Free Press Paperback, New York, 1962), p. 220.
4. Masterson, *Borderline Adolescent*, p. 114.
5. E.H. Erikson, *Identity: Youth and Crisis* (Norton, New York, 1968), p. 215.
6. J.E. Meeks, *The Fragile Alliance* (Williams and Wilkins, Baltimore, 1971), p. 92.
7. This rate of success would be impossible if the halfway house were not associated with the social and vocational day programmes of the Sound View-

Throgs Neck Community Mental Health Center, located directly across the street, which provides a well-functioning, structured programme of activities for house residents, and counselling on jobs and continuing education.

8. For a detailed description of house organisation, functioning and outcomes, including a cost analysis showing the advantage of halfway houses when compared to the hospital costs, see B. Feitel, 'Residential Rehabilitation for Psychiatric Patients', paper presented at the Annual Meeting of the National Council of Community Mental Health Centers, Washington, DC, 25 February 1975.

10 PSYCHO-EDUCATION AS A RE-EDUCATION MODEL: THEORETICAL FOUNDATIONS AND PRACTICAL IMPLICATIONS (CANADA)

Pierre Gauthier

Psycho-education as a re-education model has been developed for the last 25 years in Quebec, Canada. The purpose of this chapter is to answer, at least in part, the following questions which have often been asked by United Kingdom colleagues:

What are the basic components of the psycho-educational model? What have been, so far, its achievements and its limitations? Are there in it elements which can be used within the United Kingdom context despite language and other cultural differences; if so, what are the prerequisites?

The Epigenetic Principle

As one of its postulates psycho-education adopts the epigenetic principle first inferred by biologists who, having observed embryonic life, proposed that all living organisms develop through a sequence of stages, each one tributary to its predecessor, each one influencing its successor. In other words, life unfolds in a patterned continuous fashion through a series of phases in each of which relatively discrete growth processes occur, followed by a movement of integration. On that basis new growth takes place, to be followed by new integration and so on until maturity and the reverse process of gradual disintegration. Thus each stage of development contains in potential subsequent diversified development, and its determining, although not exclusive, influence on the patterned subsequent phases will follow.

As a corollary to that principle, any impairment, deficiency, distortion or trauma experienced by a living organism at one stage of development will have lasting effects on following evolution. One illustrative example of the application of that principle is the highly publicised case of the thalidomide babies.

The epigenetic principle has been used as a cornerstone of two theories which in turn contribute conceptual foundations to the psycho-educational model, namely Erik Erikson's theory of personality growth and Jean Piaget's theory of cognitive development. Expanding on the Freudian theory of the personality, Erikson proposes that personal development occurs from internalisation by an individual of repeated patterns of interaction with other human beings who are in relatively prolonged contact with him. In that manner certain basic traits are acquired that either favour or disfavour ulterior acquisitions. For example an infant, through constant experiences of being fed when hungry, cleaned when wet or soiled, reassured and comforted when anxious, stimulated in a manner proportionate to his neuro-muscular capacity, will evolve a sense of basic trust *vis-à-vis* the social environment, while the opposite pattern of mistrust will tend to become a permanent feature of his personality if he is continuously exposed to hunger, thirst, physical or emotional discomfort or sheer brutality. Once established, patterns of trust or mistrust will favour or impair his capacity to evolve the subsequent pattern of autonomy, leading him to feel quite capable of mastering his own neuromuscular system or, at the other end of the scale, to become doubtful of his ability to use his body in a directed co-ordinated fashion. From here Erikson goes on to elaborate his propositions of the 'eight stages of man'.[1]

From another point of view Jean Piaget, a biologist turned psychologist, suggests that intelligence develops from the level of the newborn infant's sucking reflex through sensory motor activities, mental representations of relationships between concrete objects, to the level of abstract thinking where one mentally constructs relationships between concepts and systems of concepts.

Another Application of the Epigenetic Principle: Re-education as a Process Unfolding in Stages

Jeannine Guindon, who was the first to provide conceptual backing for and cogently define the psycho-educational model of intervention in a book entitled *Le processus de rééducation du jeune délinquant par l'actualisation des forces du moi*,[2] offers a synthesis of Erikson and Piaget, as well as a number of other theoreticians of personality development or re-education approaches where she also follows the epigenetic principle. In her book and in a more recent publication by my colleague Gilles Gendreau under the title *L'intervention psycho-éducative, solution ou défi?*[3] one finds the following major elements, each one a prerequisite for its successor.

Acclimatisation

The youngster is offered a milieu where his total life is organised around activities which meet his level of interest and are programmed in such a way that

– success is practically guaranteed; the youngster is put in a situation where he has the least chances of being tripped by his own tendencies to failure which usually 'confirm' self-devaluation. He is enticed to produce objectively functional simple physical objects through specified procedures, and to perform mostly in activities where sensory motor skills prevail

– interaction with peers is maintained as far as possible at a low level of intensity

– educators, through their overt and covert behaviour, express an attitude of acceptance without emotional overstimulation. They are also forever present in all daily life situations as well as very explicit as to tolerated and non-tolerated forms of behaviour

– time and space limits are clearly defined.

Control

At the self-control phase of re-education the boy or girl is expected gradually to take charge of his or her own behaviour. They are given more possibilities of choice of means to attain objectives which are established, with their participation, by the team of educators This team is in charge of the group where they will remain until completion of re-education. The establishment of personalised links with at least one educator is favoured, mostly through weekly one-to-one encounters revolving by and large on the experiences he or she is having in the centre, with gradual forays into the past and future. In that manner each individual may construct a clearer picture of his or her own life, with an adequate grasp of cause and effect relationships in interaction with peers, educators and parental or other authority figures.

Finally, the child or adolescent is encouraged to take on, within the group, responsibilities of a concrete nature: care of equipment, cleaning, setting up of materials for activities, care of plants etc.

Productivity

Once a youngster has become able to behave in a coherent self-directed way and has developed sufficient competence in a carefully selected spectrum of activities he is offered the opportunity to plan his own tasks, estimating time schedules and evaluating his own results. He is encouraged to take on social responsibilities in the re-education group he belongs to: to act as representative, team leader in sports, co-programmer of certain group events with educators and the like.

In weekly encounters with his educator (as much as possible the same person throughout the re-education process), some emphasis is put on exploring unconscious motivations and past experiences, and on building realistic expectations for the future. If the family situation offers possibilities of collaboration, much effort is invested in re-establishing or reinforcing links with parental figures.

In general, at the productivity phase, the accent is on quality work and study, responsibility *vis-à-vis* others, and consciousness of self.

Personality

This is the phase where integration of the whole re-education experience is emphasised, culminating in the identification by the youngster of the values he wishes to use as life-guiding principles. His programme in the re-education milieu is largely left to his own decision. The major goal here is preparation for and sampling of work or study in the wider society. In his life at the re-education centre the youngster at times becomes a quasi-colleague of educators, playing a supportive role for his less experienced peers.

In the area of interpersonal links educators favour the establishment of more personal links with same-sex friends as well as responsible heterosexual involvement. In sum, at the personality phase, the youngster is led to construct a synthesis of his whole life-experience, with accent on the evolution accomplished during re-education.

Actualisation of Ego Strengths

Presentation of the psycho-educational re-education process strictly from the point of view of stages or phases would be very static indeed. Let us now try to explore its dynamics.

The basic resource the educator tries to develop is what Jeannine Guindon calls 'ego strengths', meaning those capacities of the personality that are operational here and now in allowing an individual to, in Freudian parlance, accomplish one or more of the following tasks:

– maintain equilibrium between impulses and super ego
– correctly perceive messages from the external world
– engage in culturally approved forms of behaviour.

In more simple terms they are those elements of personality that 'work', while such elements as antisocial, neurotic or psychotic traits can be considered as 'ego weaknesses'.

The psycho-educator, in order to intervene appropriately, has to know about the personality defects of the individual he is in charge of, but it is crucial for him to identify ego strengths because these are the elements he will appeal to by two principal means:

– a tailor-made life-organisation programme made up of a spectrum of activities, a significant part of which are individualised
– the gradual building up of an emotional bond between youngster and educator.

The Role of the Psycho-educator

The role of the psycho-educator consists in two major functions:

– to plan and programme life-experiences, usually in a controlled social environment, for a group of individuals with behaviour or personality disorders
– to share with them these life-experiences on a continuous basis, several hours a day, several days a week.

So he must develop a bi-polar expertise: the capacity to organise and activate a social environment rich in learning experience, and the capacity to use clinically the numerous events cropping up through shared daily life.

Let us now try to expand somewhat on the organisation and sharing of life-experience aspects of the psycho-educator's role. The structuring of a carefully designed spectrum of learning situations, with the development of appropriate space design, teaching equipment and materials is probably a major contribution psycho-educators have made to the re-education field over the last 25 years. By this I mean the design of a whole milieu where Eriksonian and Piagetian theories, as well as much of applicable research by students of group dynamics, have been used to identify components that would create a highly active and motivated life for both staff and youngsters.

To be more specific, each centre articulates the whole yearly calendar around four or five major projects that mobilise the energies of staff and residents: for example Olympic games, a drama festival, a pottery exhibition. These events are planned and programmed in such a way that all or most of the re-education community members, staff or boys and girls, have roles commensurate to their capabilities during several weeks of preparation which usually climax in a major accomplishment involving the local community members or prestigious figures of the wider society. In that manner each category of activity contributing to the re-education process is the focus of collective inputs during a portion of the year.

Utmost care is given in providing a spectrum of activities which covers the major aspects of personality development: scholastic, socio-cultural, which includes introduction to the workings of social institutions normally dealt with by the average citizen (banking, income tax, social security, voting and the like), expressive arts, physical education, sports, nature exploration, crafts and techniques, social reinsertion with focus on contacts with the work place.

The underlying hypothesis here is that personal evolution occurs through doing, accomplishing rather than verbal self-examination, plus analysis of what and how one has accomplished something.

Such activity becomes the object of minute programming so that within each area of competence development the youngsters learn to accomplish individualised and group tasks. Specific objectives of competence acquisition are thus analysed in terms of learning challenges, each challenge being operationalised into a series of tasks that are micro-graduated in order to match closely the actual level of accomplishment and interest of the youngsters.

The other dimension of the psycho-educator's role is to share the life of those he is in charge of and intervene clinically within this situation. To perform this role he must become a group activator (in French, *animateur* which literally means giving soul to, injecting spirit into) with clinical expertise, which requires sound training in group dynamics, minimum mastery of participant observation techniques and good knowledge of personality theory. With these three elements he can then

– gather theoretically significant, valid, reliable samples of individual or group behaviour
– analyse these samples to participate, with other human sciences practitioners, in the establishment of a diagnosis and intervention programme
– review its effectiveness, which leads back to modification of both diagnosis and programme.

One can probably see by now that the professional role here defined borrows from the various disciplines of psychology, pedagogy, psychiatry and other social sciences but tends to define a new way of applying them. By that very process it is hoped that some methodological and theoretical contribution is made to the human sciences.

Achievements and Limitations

By now a view of the re-education process and the psycho-educator's role in favouring it has been presented. But what about concrete achievements or limits?

Most of the work accomplished to date has been carried out with boys and girls of eight to eighteen years of age, of normal intelligence, with severe behaviour or personality problems, including delinquency. The bulk of the experience consisted of treatment in residential centres, with a significant part of it in school settings. Some work has also been carried out in psychiatric hospitals. For the last two or three years psycho-educators have begun to work in community centres, prisons and therapeutic group homes.

In the area of activity or milieu programming several thousand person-hours have been invested by psycho-educators in the preparation of individualised didactic materials or group projects. Professional expertise has also been developed in participant observation of behaviour, case-reviewing (which includes the planning of preventive or corrective action) and in a relatively wide array of intervention techniques. I will not here delve into the very controversial issue of 'rates of success' except to mention that a few follow-up studies were conducted during the last decade.

A longitudinal study of one institution was also carried out in the last five years by a group of criminologists of the University of Montreal, the results of which are beginning to be reported.[4] The overall tendency of these studies is rather favourable especially those studying the social climate in organisations that really apply the psycho-educational model. By and large it has had lasting positive influence on the social adaptation of the two main categories of young people with whom psycho-educators have worked in various settings.

A presentation of the psycho-educational approach to re-education would be incomplete without recognising its potential weaknesses or limitations. Let us try to draw a list of them, here presented tentatively and with full acknowledgement that ingenuity coupled with dedication may well push them back ever further.

1. The psycho-educational model is labour intensive, hence costly. Founder team members accepted working 60 to 70 hours a week at

minimal wage, but as professionalisation and institutionalisation progressed with the acquisition of academic degrees and the development of a network of centres, salaries to psycho-educators have markedly increased.

2. Because of its reliance on psychodynamic development as a function of maladjusted youngsters living through long-term experiences with highly trained personnel, it becomes vulnerable to competing models that claim, quite often erroneously, to achieve quicker results.

3. The very success of the model may lead to cheap imitations, converting a theoretically grounded discipline into gimmicks.

4. Psycho-education has obtained considerable success with delinquent adolescents or children with severe behaviour problems but its concepts and methods remain to be tried systematically with such clienteles as the very young, the physically or mentally handicapped, adult offenders or mental patients.

5. Finally, an internal threat appears on close examination much more dangerous than it looks from a distance, namely the reification of programmes. By this is meant that programmes which were evolved from careful analysis of behaviour and personality of youngsters tend to be considered as values in themselves. Then efforts are made to have children conform to programmes rather than make reverse adjustments. Reification of programmes leads directly to conformism instead of personality development, a pitfall most re-educators want to avoid.

In terms of adaptability of psycho-education practices to the United Kingdom context a few trials have been made for the last two years which allow us to entertain high hopes: a training course given by University of Montreal teaching staff at the Richmond Fellowship is now in its second year and, through numerous exchanges with first-line workers engaged in various institutions of this country, it seems that psycho-education does have characteristics that are cross-cultural. So it is our fervent hope that intense exchange of knowledge and experience occurs between re-education specialists on both sides of the Atlantic.

For this to occur there are prerequisites. The first one is strong support by a major re-education organisation. The second is formal recognition of training by a British university in order that educators who go through higher-level training have access to a career where they can apply their skills with support by the wider society. The third is help by government and union officials so that psycho-educators whose role requires a combination of functions previously fulfilled as separate by teachers, social workers and psychologists, may be given a relatively wide margin of freedom to experiment new ways and means of joint re-education. The fourth is of course financial means, but I rest assured that, given the first three conditions, that resource will be forthcoming.

Notes

1. E.H. Erikson, *Childhood and Society* (Norton, New York, 1964).
2. J. Guindon, *Le Processus de rééducation du jeune délinquant par l'actualisation des forces du moi* (Centre de recherche en relations humaines, Montreal, 1969). See also her chapter 'The Psycho-Educateur Training Program', in W.C. Morse *et al.*, *Training Teachers for the Emotionally Disturbed* (University of Michigan, Michigan, 1973); also 'The Psycho-Educateur Model', document du travail no. 54 (School of Psycho-Education, University of Montreal), May 1977.
3. G. Gendreau, *L'Intervention psycho-éducative, solution ou défi?* (Editions Fleurus, Paris, 1978).
4. See for example the series of reports on a 1973–8 longitudinal study of Boscoville, a psycho-educational re-education centre for juvenile delinquents, by Marc Leblanc and his colleagues at the Groupe de recherche sur l'inadaption juvénile, available at the Department of Criminology, University of Montreal.

11 ASPECTS OF WORKING WITH FAMILIES IN A RICHMOND FELLOWSHIP HOSTEL (UK)

Michael Kelly

The Setting

Highlands is a Richmond Fellowship specialist unit for families who present a variety of problems. The hostel is a converted mansion situated in its own grounds with half an acre of garden in the Gidea Park area of Romford, Essex. It has been functioning as a family unit since 1970. Each family has its own bedroom with a separate sleeping area for the children, except for some one-parent families where the child(ren) may share a bedroom with the parent. The remainder of the house is shared by all the families, with a communal kitchen, dining-room and sitting-room. The house can accommodate up to five families at any one time, ideally three two-parent families and two one-parent. A playroom adjoins the house and a playgroup for the younger children is run here each morning from 9.00 a.m. to 12.00 noon, Monday to Friday, during the school terms with children also attending from the local community. The older children attend the schools in the neighbourhood. The practical day-to-day aspects of running the house are shared by all and each weekday morning there is a structured work programme of cleaning, cooking etc. Families share a communal meal at 1.00 p.m. each day but cater for themselves for the other meals. The therapeutic programme consists of weekly group meetings of all the families and staff; parents and staff individual, marital and family therapy sessions; play sessions for parents and children; practical meetings to look at areas of household management.

The Staff

There is a team of five full-time staff (Warden, Deputy Warden, Senior Assistant Warden, Assistant Warden and Trainee Scholar) who work together to provide both practical support and therapy to the families. They have particular families to work with but share information as a team through weekly discussion of each family's progress. One staff member does on-call duty each evening. Staff are trained in individual, group and family work through attendance at the organisation's own in-service training programme, and subsequently at outside training institutes. Additional support and guidance is provided by the supervisor who visits the unit weekly and serves both a middle-management and clinical/training function. He heads a bi-weekly family therapy workshop and acts as live-supervisor to some of the family therapy sessions. There is a house psychiatrist who visits bi-weekly and meets with staff for case discussion, diagnosis and assessment.

A playgroup leader and her assistant run a playgroup in the house. They work therapeutically but non-interpretatively with the young children both from the hostel and neighbourhood and attempt to establish relationships between the respective mothers through coffee mornings, jumble sales and informal chats at the beginning and end of sessions. When a family with a baby is resident, the health visitor from the local clinic visits regularly to offer practical advice and help. The hostel provides placements for CQSW students and students from the Richmond Fellowship College Human Relations Course, as well as volunteers from overseas.

The Families

The unit has had the experience of working with 54 families since its inception in 1970. They have presented a variety of problems ranging from psychiatric disorder in one or both parents to a basic lack of parenting skills. A common feature is that parents and children may have been separated for anything up to a year before being referred, either through hospitalisation of parent or removal of children into care following neglect or abuse. Highlands, therefore, provides an opportunity for the family to rebuild. Families in crisis are also referred and a placement at the unit can prevent a break-up of the family, or if separation is envisaged, an opportunity to work this through in a constructive manner. The majority of the single-parent families are mothers with either babies or young children, who lack basic mothering skills or have serious management problems. These mothers usually suffer from depression and are socially isolated. While referrals are made from all over the country, the majority are from the London area. Families stay for periods up to eighteen months and their progress is reviewed every three months. This involves examination of the goals set by the family at the initial interview both by the staff member responsible for working most closely with the family and the rest of the community. A written report is sent to the referring authority which is responsible for financing the family's stay and guaranteeing rehousing when the family leaves.

The family living at the hostel is usually two-generational, parents and children, but if it is felt that there is someone else in the family's network who may be crucial to change in the system then such a person or persons, e.g. grandparents or ex-cohabitee, would be invited to the hostel for consultation or therapy.

Some Recurring Group Processes

Comings and Goings. The arrival of a new family to the unit usually poses a threat to the families already living there in terms of their position and role in the community at that time and their relationship to staff (similar to the arrival of a new baby into a family). Feelings of being pushed out and unwanted come to the surface, reflecting early childhood experiences in the family of origin, and leading at times to acting-out behaviour to gain attention. The new family may even express a wish to leave. Careful preparation is important and our thorough admissions procedure minimises the impact.

Leavings also evoke many feelings, e.g. a deep sense of loss akin to the loss of the primary object, particularly when the person who is leaving is a significant staff member, or if the family which is leaving has had a good experience at the hostel; feelings of omnipotence, self-blame and guilt and a wish to make reparation; survival fears and realisation that one will be alone with one's family again.

Sub-groupings and Pairings. These occur regularly across family lines and can lead to intense boundary fears, e.g. two wives may find that they get along better together than with their own husbands. Displays of vulnerable feelings are often treated with more tolerance and respect by members of another family than by one's own. The mothers and fathers often use themselves as parental substitutes to children other than their own, displaying quite warm and affectionate feelings, even though they may be defective as parents in their own family. Cross-family alliances are also formed to counter loneliness and isolation.

Flight. It is common for a family member to 'flee' from unhappy relationships and difficult situations in their own family into finding substitute relationships within the community. The community can serve as a kind of extended family network where individual family members can go either for support or escape, in an attempt to substitute for, or dilute pathological relationships in, their own family.

Projection processes in the individual locate unacceptable feelings outside the person. These are then perceived as external threats, which are countered by defensive responses. Similarly, *family projection processes* operate as a defensive manoeuvre to avoid facing up to problems in one's own family system. Problems can be projected onto the existing structure, staff group or another family. At the beginning of a family's stay the parents fear blame most and to counter this develop a rigid system of denial, projection or withdrawal, but as they begin to trust the community, defences are lowered and the feelings of guilt, blame, helplessness and failure can be shared.

The wish to avoid looking at weaknesses, or recognising collective responsibility is also manifested in *scapegoating*, that is, the location of problems in one individual or family. Scapegoating usually focuses on the 'craziest', i.e. the person displaying the most bizarre behaviour; the most 'attention seeking', i.e. the family that is experienced at taking up most staff time; the parent who decides to have the child fostered.

Arising from encounters between families is *envy* of a supposedly more advantaged family, which may respond with a mixture of fear of envy (for various reasons), and pleasure at being envied. Lack of male support in single-parent family can lead to intense feelings of envy, jealousy and rivalry towards the wife in a two-parent family, who to counter these attacks may devalue her husband as non-supportive and claim their sexual relationship to be non-existent. Single staff too are frequently envied for their freedom from the constant demands and burdens of parenting.

A strong wish to nurture may be evoked by the presence of a baby in the community. This reaction is frequently met with in the mothers with older children, who, because of their own early deprivation, find it difficult to control or deny their children anything and who probably have had their happiest relationships with them when – as babies – they were totally independent. Another feature, springing from early loss, is the expectation that the child should be mother to the parent and behave like an adult.

Temporary Loss of the Parental Role. The behaviour of family members is often different inside and outside their own family setting. When parents are relieved temporarily of having to care for their children, they sometimes regress to earlier stages of development, e.g. behaving like adolescents, or they experience a loss of sense of identity without the parent role. The sense of relief that ensues, following the departure of the children to the playgroup or school, is often accompanied by a fear that they will henceforth forget their children.

Children tend to *act out conflicts* occurring between their parents. Individual therapeutic work with the child is invariably ineffective, and the disturbance needs to be understood and addressed as a function of the family interaction.

Approaches and Techniques

Recently, some of the interventive work in the unit has been influenced by the structural/strategic approaches of Minuchin and Haley, with use made of prescription and paradox to effect change in the family system.[1] The psychoanalytic model can be usefully combined with these although the treatment interventions used which arise from this approach are aimed more at the individual than the actual family system. Transference distortions inevitably develop in a situation which can become highly charged emotionally because of the intensity of living closely together, and it is found that these can only be worked through successfully by use of an interpretative approach either in a one-to-one or a group context.

A major difficulty for staff is objectivity and a recurring pitfall is being sucked into the family system through overidentification with, for example, child against parent or parent against parent. There is opportunity for looking at staff counter-transference problems in weekly staff dynamic sessions; through use of live supervision of individual family sessions and working in co-therapy pairs where one member can pick up the 'blind spots' of the other. Because of the very low sense of self-esteem of parents and the expectation of being blamed, staff have to look for ways of intervening which are not experienced as a 'put down' and which permit a positive relationship with staff to be established. We find that 'relabelling' or 'reframing' as a technique is useful in this regard, e.g. a mother who knows no other way to control her child (or her anger) and who beats her child may be reassured that she is doing this because she loves her child and wishes her child to obey her. This needs to be accompanied by an exploration of other ways to control children (and impulses). Modelling, of course, is another useful, effective and non-threatening way of bringing about change and is used to the best advantage in the living, day-to-day situation of the house.

Monitoring tasks is another effective means of creating change in family relationships. Parents who are overinvolved with their children by being overcontrolling and can only see negative behaviour in their children may be asked to look for examples of good behaviour and give children a positive reward each time they are good. This helps to create a healthy distancing between parents and children, and leads to children learning to take more responsibility for the control of their own behaviour.

Parents are responsibile for the care and management of their children – staff are available to help parents but not to assume direct responsibility. They attempt to refrain from imposing controls in order not to be seen by the family to be assuming a parental role, although by definition they are often cast in this role, perhaps more as grandparents who are there in an advisory capacity. Staff see their primary task as helping to establish a milieu that is supportive and non-judgemental; every encouragement is given to the sharing of feelings and difficulties and testing of reality, so that family members can experiment with alternative and more rewarding ways of relating to each other.

In being supportive staff have to be careful that they are not infantilising parents by a process of perpetuating dependency needs and the balance would seem to lie somewhere between being neither too intrusive nor too remote. An important ingredient here is the ability to differentiate what are genuine maturational needs from those which are purely substitutive, and staff see it as their task to fulfil the former but to withstand and frustrate the latter. However, we have found that on the whole most requests for help spring from real developmental needs and our accepting and responding to these has resulted in greater participation in the therapeutic process. Bernstein, in the context of the patient/analyst relationship, states, 'With very young or very helpless patients we may find that they bring us a whole array of maturational needs which it is our obligation to fulfil . . . One of the major technical goals of treatment is gratification of maturational needs, for failure to gratify such needs inhibits the process of maturation and growth . . . Both gratification of maturational needs and frustration of substitutive needs are required. The one prepares a patient to be able to renounce the other.'[2]

Staff are perhaps most active in relation to the structure of the house programme, ensuring that families are clear about what is expected of them and that the structure is maintained. This is a most important factor since the majority of the families suffer from a lack of clear structure, without which little growth or change can occur. In upholding the structure we find that therapeutic processes will emerge of themselves, and, provided we ourselves do not become too central, the families will begin to help each other. Confrontation may be called for occasionally in a situation where there is clear neglect of parental responsibility and children may be at risk. Here too, however, families can serve as watchdogs to each other and staff can stay more in the background, making themselves available and ready to step in if needed. In the once-weekly, multi-family therapeutic group, staff play a fairly non-directive, facilitative role, allowing the families to challenge and confront each other, although at times staff may have to assume a more confrontative position because of a multi-family collusive defence system operating between the family. The group provides a safe setting each week for both intra-family and cross-family transferences to be explored so that a modification of distorted perceptions can occur and relationships can approximate more to reality. As a result, people are no longer seen primarily in terms of some significant past family figure.[3]

Leaving

Leaving is a primary consideration throughout the family's stay. Field social workers maintain contact by visiting at least every three months, and during the three months prior to leaving liaison with social workers and housing officers becomes particularly important. As we stated previously, practical arrangements have already been initiated, since no family is accepted without a written guarantee that it will be rehoused by the referring local authority. The quality of housing does not appear to influence the outcome in terms of family adjustment. After the family leaves, the social worker resumes the major helping role, although staff of the therapeutic community continue to help the family through the weaning process, by visiting at least twice within the first six months. All families are sent a follow-up questionnaire. When the therapeutic relationship is terminated, families frequently remain in contact with the community on a social basis. Separation and independence are found to be more successfully achieved in families who stay for a full year; two-parent families tend to adapt better to the loss of the community than do single parents. Those families whose leaving is planned manage as a rule to work through their dependency on the community.

Notes

1. L.S. Minuchin, *Families and Family Therapy* (Tavistock Publications, London, 1974); J. Haley, *Problem-solving Therapy* (Harper and Row, New York, 1978).
2. Bernstein, *The Fear of Compassion in Success Failure in Psychoanalysis and Psychotherapy*, edited by Benjamin Wolman (Collier Macmillan, London, 1972).
3. The following books and articles have proved useful in the writing of this chapter: A. Bentovim, 'Group Processes in a Day Centre for Pre-school Children and Parents', private circulation; M. Bowen, *Family Psychotherapy with Schizophrenia in the Hospital and in Private Practice in Intensive Family Therapy* (Harper and Row, New York, 1965); P. Casement, 'Group for the Advancement of Psychotherapy in Social Work', private circulation; E. Leichter and G.L. Schulman, 'Multi-family Group Therapy', in *Family Process*, vol. 13 (Nathan, New York, 1974); P.B. de Maré, *Perspectives in Group Psychotherapy* (Allen and Unwin, London, 1972); A.C.R. Skynner, *One Flesh, Separate Persons* (Constable, London, 1976); P. Watzlawick, J. Weakland and R. Fisch, *Change: Principles of Problem Formation and Problem Resolution* (Norton, New York, 1974). P. Watzlawick, J.H. Beavin and D.D. Jackson, *Pragmatics of Human Communication* (Norton, New York, 1967).

Part Two

THE STAFFING QUESTION

Love seeketh not itself to please,
Nor for itself hath any care;
But for another gives its ease,
And builds a Heaven in Hell's despair.

William Blake, 'The Clod and the Pebble', from *Songs of Experience*

EDITOR'S DISCUSSION

Staffing is the crucial ingredient by which the therapeutic community stands or falls. Various studies have illustrated the relationship of staff attitudes and conflicts to the progress of residents (clients/patients). Wing and Brown identified the more optimistic attitude of nursing staff as one of the social factors which correlated with clinical improvement in a group of chronic schizophrenics.[1] Conversely, Stanton and Schwartz documented in detail the disturbance arising among patients when covert disagreements persisted among staff.[2] Patients who became the focus of such disagreements were unable to tolerate mixed feelings towards the staff involved, and tended to split the two factions into good and bad – an overt expression of covert staff attitudes. Only when the staff members were able to face their conflict did the patients' disturbance subside. In cases where whole groups of staff were implicated in the disagreement, the disturbance was reflected in the total patient group.

Hence, it is not enough for staff to possess skills and personal qualities of a high order: they must also be self-aware, and capable of acknowledging their own reactions and interactions in the day-to-day situation. 'The only small problem', writes Thomas Barton in Chapter 14, 'is where such paragons are to be found.' And, he might have added, once found, how are they to be supported and trained in such a way that they can remain on the job?

Staff Selection

In the personal caring services, the reliability of paper qualifications in selection of staff has always to be treated with caution. In no field is this more problematic than in the therapeutic community, where no qualifying course which is both specific and generally recognised as yet exists. Previous professional experience may awaken staff's interest and provide a relevant discipline or framework. In the US, licensing authorities tend to value academic qualifications, especially in the case of senior staff, who are expected to have obtained a Master's degree in a relevant discipline, usually an MSW. It has been suggested that experience in a related profession, which imparts rigid role boundaries, such as nursing, may generate problems in adapting to a more flexible role. What are the criteria for selection?

Therapeutic communities commonly place their main emphasis in staff selection on motivation. It is frequently stated that staff are employed in order to help residents; gratification of basic emotional needs must therefore be met outside the community, and staff need to have established a viable personal life before being accepted. However, it is clear from interviews with the staff teams of two therapeutic communities that their motivation to join included elements of self-gratification, and that the opportunities for personal development, learning and belonging were important in enhancing the quality of their work. Motivation to take up the work was expressed variously as the wish

– to work at an intensive level
– to specialise in work in mental health
– to live and work within a community
– to work with groups
– to utilise my own interest in reflection and introspection
– to learn more about myself and others
– to fill in time usefully whilst planning a different career (the two staff members who gave this response were now into their fifth and sixth years of work)
– to live one's values in daily life
– to participate in a close-knit community life
– to see people as human beings instead of 'cases'
– to get to know and understand people.

Maturity is an attribute which is usually sought in staff, although hard to define and measure. It could perhaps be summarised as the ability to perceive one's own personal conflicts and resolve them; or if not resolvable, to contain them, rather than using others through whom or on whom to act them out. Although maturity is difficult to assess, applicants who are having significant problems in facing their own anxiety, or who lack the ability to combine sympathy with independence, can often be identified through a thorough selection process. Barton considers that staff who prove unsuitable have usually been accepted as the result of a skimped assessment; it appears however that Barton overestimates the potential accuracy of selection procedures. (From his account also, it may be conjectured that some potentially suitable candidates fail on the job through lack of friendly support, as perhaps was the case with 'Jane'. See Chapter 14.) The major test comes when the candidate is on the job; it is therefore the practice of the Richmond

Fellowship to regard the first six months of work as an integral part of the final stage of the selection process.

Nine out of ten applicants to the Fellowship are in fact selected out before embarking on the work. Selection follows a sequence of group interview, individual interview, and visits to at least two of the houses, following which reports are submitted from both the applicant and the staff team. If all these stages are satisfactory, a final interview completes the process. It often happens that the initial group interview shows up basic incompatibility; and a short personal interview, to communicate the decision and explore alternative employment, is the final step.

During the following six months, some of the major criteria which can be established are: whether or not the person has the stamina and commitment needed to sustain the upheavals inherent in this work; whether the person's outlook and way of operating are suited to work within the therapeutic community; whether the necessary degree of awareness of self and others, and the proper balance of tact and decisiveness, are present; and finally, whether he or she possesses the essential qualities of commonsense and practical application of ideas.

Common pitfalls for staff are described by Peter Hawkins in Chapter 13. It is unavoidable that staff at times reveal a particular weak spot, and this is acceptable so long as it is not excessive and so long as the staff member is open to acknowledging and working on it. Trainee staff, for example, often need help to recognise the twin pitfalls of overidentification and excessive distancing, one or the other of which frequently tends to seduce the newcomer. There will be times when staff suspect that there is not much to choose between their own mental state and that of the residents, and sometimes with reason! Thomas Barton cites staff members' fear of becoming psychotic as one of the reactions which is frequently experienced during the second to fourth months after beginning work. An obvious defence against this anxiety is to intensify the gulf between the sick and the well, so that the resident's disquieting communications may be discounted. On the other hand, inappropriate identification may lead to an uncritical acceptance of the resident's point of view.

The consumers, in their interviews, give some indication of those qualities and abilities which are experienced as helpful: good staff are perceived as 'warm and undogmatic', they 'help me to get in touch with my feelings', they offer encouragement and support – 'the indignant kind as well as the understanding or appreciative kind'. A staff team, asked to name the qualities which they felt essential for their job, spontaneously yielded the following: sensitivity, empathy, self-awareness, a sense of humour, intelligence, initiative and endurance! Perhaps the most useful guideline in selecting staff is that they should be the sort of people who can provide a model for residents: maintaining appropriate self-esteem, concern for others, perception and straightforwardness, and with a willingness to work at their own problems. Such guidance as staff can give must be authenticated from their own and/or society's collective experience of facing and working on problems, although not necessarily of reaching conclusions. The conference report of the proceedings of the Therapeutic Communities of America Planning Conference states: 'It is presumptuous to attempt to provide answers for problems which are not worked out in the lives of treatment personnel and society at large.'[3] Utopia indeed! Those who come for help need the assistance of *authentic individuals*, with whom they can review and put into perspective the problems of society at large. They need help to live in that society, and to make their contribution. If these criteria are met, staff will be able to act both as catalyst and model, and will be able to avoid collusion or displacement of problems, both of which can be catastrophic for the community or create major problems in the organisation. This area is especially sensitive in industrialised countries through employment protection legislation. It is important that staff working in this difficult field and in vulnerable positions are appropriately protected against arbitrary dismissal. At the same time most legislation fits industrial situations rather than those pertaining to a therapeutic community, which means that only gross misconduct or unsuitability gives grounds for requiring staff to leave their post. This makes good selection even more critical.

Conceptual Frameworks

Staff need to maintain high standards in an exacting job. What concepts can they usefully adopt to guide them?

Parenting is an emotive issue. Therapeutic communities usually maintain a strong resistance to having parental staff, in the sense of authoritarian or infantilising figures, as this conflicts with the avowed aim of enabling the resident to become autonomous. It has been pointed out by Barton that 'a halfway house is by definition a situation of dependence for the resident', and that staff need to counteract this tendency. However, it needs also to be recognised that some kind of parenting has been and will be sought by the resident until he is able to relinquish it, and that parenting can have a positive role to play. Many residents have already placed themselves, through breakdown, in institutions which provide the extreme of protective, authoritarian care. If compelled to leave hospital without the capacity to manage alone, and without support, they seek readmission through a relapse. The revolving-door syndrome is well known. Frank Ochberg, for example, states: 'Most of the [follow-up] studies show that 30 to 40 per cent of patients interviewed six months after release have been rehospitalised at some time during the interval between release and follow-up. For patients studied one year after release, the percentage increases to between 40 and 50 per cent; and for those studied at three to five years after release, 65 to 75 per cent have been rehospitalised' (Chapter 19). The revolving-door situation follows on the policy of discouraging long-term residence in institutions, whilst failing to compensate through relevant community facilities. Some degree of parenting is therefore indicated. For some people a permanent home may be necessary.

However, the concept of the therapeutic community includes where possible the goal of separation. 'Parenting' includes the concept of enabling maturation to occur; the parent assists the child to grow away from him by certain qualities of caring. First, the parent recognises necessary dependence, and assists separation only at the correct maturational stage. Premature 'weaning' results in precarious adult adjustment, and anxiety-governed behaviour. Suttie comments: 'In our culture in particular, the brusqueness of the cleanliness-training, the frequent and prolonged separation of mother and infant, and the mother's own intolerance of tenderness . . . bring about a precipitate "psychic parturition", attended by anxiety, acquisitiveness and aggressiveness which is reflected in our culture.'[4] Liedloff notes the same competitive and anxious adult behaviour, which attempts to compensate for what she terms 'deprivation of the in-arms experience'.[5] Gosling states:

> Essentially, the Fellowship gives people a chance to rethink their own position in relation to others, to what they are doing with their lives, to what kind of people they are, and in the process of rethinking to re-establish their own integrity, their own capacity to manage their own affairs. How does a therapeutic community or half way house approach this? I think for this task there are two important factors: One factor is that this therapeutic community has to be

> devoted to development, to change, to emancipation. At the same time, it has to be able to protect, to offer security, to hold, since development is, I think, impossible unless there is also a holding environment that allows change to take place. *Of course, you can see that what I am describing really is a home and parents.* What do you want parents to do? You certainly want them to be devoted to change, to development, particularly in their attitude towards their children. At the same time, you want of your parents that they shall provide such security for the child that he will not feel that the first time he opposes his parents he is out on the street, or that experiments he may attempt, innovations of his own, will invariably lead to failure, and lead to punishment as well. There must be some feeling that the old ways will be available if needed, while new ways are being invented.[6]

At a level appropriate for adults, therefore, staff need to provide restitution in the form of emotional security.

It is equally important, however, that staff are alert to signs of readiness to progress and meet them with a prompt response, and not with overprotectiveness or possessiveness. In addition, staff replicate the role of parents in relation to individual residents by increasingly presenting their own reality needs and boundaries. The mother is tired when she returns from shopping; the child will have to wait for his story until she has had a cup of tea. The child has to experience frustration and anger with his idealised parent: the experience which many residents have found too painful to tolerate, and which they therefore deal with by denying their love and/or their hate. Staff in the therapeutic community are ideally placed to reactivate the problem and they therefore become the recipients of dependent behaviour at an infantile level. Not only do they offer understanding and acceptance; they are also part of the environment with which residents contend in their struggle for maturity. The intention in establishing the first Richmond Fellowship house was to share it on an egalitarian basis with people in need. It was the element of being 'in need' which forced the original concept to be modified. The founder realised that she was in danger of being manipulated into the role of the overindulgent parent who is dominated by the child's demands; in response, she began to define the qualities needed by staff in order to activate the strengths of residents. 'The role of the staff is a particularly difficult one, in that he is both the social worker and part of the environment through which the resident needs to come to terms with his problems; the person to whom and about whom many complaints of residents are made' (Jansen, Chapter 15).

It is a mark of maturity in a staff member that he is reasonably comfortable in the midst of this tension, which is never resolved. *Staff are not required to enter a win-or-lose battle in which they or the residents must suffer defeat.* Confrontations over issues of daily life are frequent, and constitute much of the learning material within the therapeutic community. Fee-collecting is an example of an activity which regularly elicits emotional reactions – sometimes as virulent as the citizen's hatred of the taxman! Some of the ingredients in this explosive mixture may be: the requirement on the resident to give when he feels like withholding or receiving; his ability in this situation to exercise power over the authorities; his feeling that the money is a vital part of him which it is persecutory of staff to demand; his wish that care should not be conditional on payments. Whatever the problems, staff and resident are confronted by an external reality: not only that the community needs money in order to survive, but that the resident needs to accept that he must contribute to the cost of his own upkeep, and must therefore be enabled to deal with this aspect of reality. It is essential, not only that the issue is eventually resolved, but that something is learned from it; perhaps the resident learns a little about the origins of his behaviour, in addition to coming to terms with adult obligations. In the process, too, staff learn the skills of motivating and, in a sense, *enticing* people to participate in life again.

The function of staff in providing *a model of social behaviour* has been referred to in Chapter 9 in relation to adolescence, but many residents have reached adulthood without acquiring social skills. In addition, they have lacked adequate opportunities in the past to learn how to reconcile internal and external realities; to communicate their own needs appropriately whilst respecting the needs of others. Staff therefore provide a model of how to display emotions, form opinions and arrive at decisions; they also demonstrate that a healthy relationship may not always be the same as a happy or comfortable one, but that a healthy relationship can contain safely many different aspects. Thus, Mary, a staff member responsible for supervising a long-stay house, stated: 'I see it as part of my job to act as a role model for the residents, by being as open as possible with them. If I disagree, I say so straightforwardly, and I encourage the residents to do the same.' It is important to remember that the impact of role-modelling is dependent on the containing relationship. This same staff member was able to express disapproval effectively: 'One resident was refusing to do any of his cleaning chores. I eventually wrote him a note, threatening Notice if he didn't improve. This step had an effect, and the resident is now rather more responsible in looking after himself.' The threat was undoubtedly constructive *because* it was made within the context of a caring relationship.

Staff not infrequently find themselves in situations of uncertainty and indecision, which will usually need to be contained within the staff group. On some occasions, however, it may be appropriate to involve residents in staff differences, when this may be used as a model for learning. Two situations are discussed here. The first is felt to be legitimate material for sharing with the residents in the community; the second is considered to be illegitimate.

Situation A

Morning housework, shared by all unemployed residents and by staff on duty, had finished, and the 'coffee group' was in progress. It centred on Claire, who had failed either to go to her job or to report for household duties. Several residents and four staff were present, including the Warden. Claire was still in her dressing-gown; she looked pale, resentful and withdrawn. Tommy was also present, a resident who had likewise failed several times to report for housework, and was now on a 'contract' to comply; if he broke the contract, he would have to leave the community. Tommy was militantly of the opinion that Claire should receive the same treatment as himself. The staff were split in their views; the incident was later discussed with one staff member.

Interviewer The staff present held differing opinions. Could you say why you were split?

Staff We had seen different aspects of Claire's behaviour. For instance, the Warden knew that, since Claire had been resident here for a year, she was aware of the community's requirements. This was the latest of several such actions by her. It was felt that her *manner* of opting out was manipulative: she tried to make it appear that she was in fact at work. This was seen as a damaging way of handling her anger and depression, which will not help her to manage when she leaves, and so it was important for staff and community not to collude.

On the other hand, Claire felt unwell, and some staff felt that household duties should take account of this, and she should be given light work. Another staff member pointed out the difference between Claire and Tommy: Claire has a regular job which she has done consistently, until recently. However, Tommy's feelings also had to be considered: we were concerned that he would feel discriminated against if Claire was 'let off'. In fact, it is made clear that individuals are different, and can have different needs in the same circumstances. It would be easier for the staff if everyone was treated exactly the same, but that isn't our idea of adult relationships!

Two preceding events are relevant to this incident, which we also had to keep in mind. The household duties had not been carried out properly in recent weeks, and staff intervened by putting the whole house on an agreement to co-operate. So it's an issue that people are feeling strongly about, and no one wants the new sense of co-operation to be sabotaged. Then, Claire was upset and angry that another resident had left recently, and this had affected her own behaviour.

There was no consensus. Eventually it was agreed that Claire would be put on a contract if it happened again. It was felt that to force the issue at this point would result in her leaving, which at this stage would be particularly damaging for her.

Interviewer How did you feel about exploring your indecision and differences in an open meeting?

Staff Sometimes it can be helpful for residents to know that we do not see a simple answer, so long as it doesn't happen all the time! It's important that this happens in the context of a stable staff team, which residents know cannot easily be manipulated or split. In a confused situation it would be even more confusing if staff were to deny their mixed feelings. Residents need to learn with us that it's all right to stay with uncomfortable feelings such as confusion, rather than taking refuge in an arbitrary decision.

Situation B

This is the situation described by Thomas Barton in Chapter 14. For the sake of ease of comparison it is here quoted in shorter form.

> Jane has been a staff member for four months. She is beginning to leave her work unfinished for the next staff shift to do. She slams doors and responds to instructions from the director with mumbled angry comments . . . Rage contorts her face as she denies being angry.
>
> Incidents of physical violence begin to occur among house residents, leading to three evictions in two weeks, and staff meetings become entirely focused on Jane, who grows more sarcastic and generally insulting to staff and residents. At one

> Monday night house meeting, residents ask what is wrong, perceiving problems among staff. They are told. Jane, still 'not angry', attacks the director in the meeting for discussing her 'in front of these kind of people'. At that point, in the middle of the meeting, without consultation, all remaining staff decide Jane has to leave, and staff and tenants tell her how angry they are at her talk of residents as 'these kind of people'.

Both situations present staff disagreement openly expressed in an open meeting, and therefore, superficially, both conform to the principle of 'open communication'; the issue of legitimacy requires clarification. Both the substance of the disagreement and the motivation for its expression in the open meeting are relevant here. Therapeutic communities exist in order to help residents to deal with reality, as represented by the community programme; staff are employed to facilitate the task of the community, and not to seek the community's aid for staff disfunction. Situation A shows the community engaged in its proper area of concern, that is, in exploration of the problems of a resident in coming to terms with reality. Staff in this context may legitimately demonstrate that it is not necessary to find a black-and-white solution, that different viewpoints may coexist, and that it is sometimes necessary to tolerate uncertainty until an avenue can be found. Situation *B* moves into the area of staff dysfunction, which is not the problem for which the community was established. There may, indeed, be occasions when staff as a team may decide to present an area of disagreement for open discussion, in order to gauge the residents' point of view, or to validate residents' perceptions, or as learning material. The situation centring on Jane however, is presented to the residents without her consent, and by default. Staff have been attempting to resolve the problem for several weeks, and it is their failure to do so which allows the issue to explode in a community meeting; only at this point are staff able to make the decision that they can no longer work with Jane. Residents are left with the responsibility and possibly the guilt for having triggered the staff's anger, and precipitated the decision which staff had until then been unable to face. 'Open communication' must not be the rationale for staff to abdicate responsibility for solving their own problems!

The *educational role* of staff has been emphasised by Peter Hawkins in Chapter 13. Education is here defined not as a receptive experience on the part of the resident, but as a joint venture between residents and staff in exploring human behaviour. Its 'course material' is provided by the everyday incidents of community life, and learning is a process of experience, feedback and reflection in which personal patterns of interaction become recognisable. Staff may also, in some circumstances, fulfil a more directly instructional role, in explicitly teaching social and practical skills (see Chapter 10); and this may be necessary not only for adolescents, but for adults whose range of experience may have been extremely circumscribed in the past. In addition, many residents have suffered emotional and physical 'atrophy' and attempt to maintain the status quo by manoeuvres and attitudes designed to make staff feel guilty if they entertain expectations of residents' participation in a reasonable work programme. The collusive staff reaction can be seen in a demoralised household where the most obvious tasks needed to enhance the quality of life are ignored. In a house where staff are sufficiently independent there will be a healthy range of activities, covering most of the working day, and resulting in initiatives of various kinds with the accompanying rewards of self-esteem and the confidence to extend oneself further.

Whilst residents' regression can have a profound effect on a household, it is ultimately the level of staff skills which sets the tone and overcomes (or succumbs to) the 'force of gravity' exercised by residents. In this, as in other aspects of their role, staff will need training, supervision and support in order to sustain the demands of the work.

Training

It is increasingly being recognised, in practice as well as in theory, that residential social workers need to acquire skills through appropriate training. The key statement on this subject was undoubtedly the Discussion Document, 'Training for Residential Work' (the Allen Report), which was issued by CCETSW in 1973. Covering the broad spectrum of residential work in the UK, the report began by summarising the current situation in the approximately 11,000 residential centres identified, and it drew attention to the 'worrying figure' of 62 per cent of staff (out of those for whom information was available) who lacked any form of qualification or training. The report set high standards for residential care – that is to say, high in relation to the standards frequently obtaining. It pointed out that residents need to be recognised as complete human beings; that they need to be considered and respected as individuals; that they should be enabled to exercise the maximum independence; and that they should participate with staff in determining their own goals and contributing to residential life.

> Because many who come to be residents in institutions have not been able, whether through misfortune or waywardness, to establish their own dignity and worth in the outside world, there is a strong pressure on institutions to regard their residents as failures, as people capable of receiving but not of giving, and therefore as people less deserving than the rest of us. We explicitly reject this view of the residential institution as the last resort for social failures . . . In our view, good residential care involves a collaboration between residents and staff, to establish their capacities and needs, and to define the objectives of work. This process of definition and goal-setting requires continuing reassessment . . . *This view of residential care as a dynamic process, has direct implications for training.* [Our italics.]

In order to achieve the enlightened standards implied in this statement, training of a level equal to that of field social work would be required (said the report), and there would be a need to develop suitable residential placements for students. Moreover, learning would need to be ongoing, and it was incumbent on employers to recognise and provide for this need.

Much of what was said in the Allen Report is applicable also to training for staff in therapeutic communities, with the additional need to help staff to acquire skills for a specifically therapeutic and rehabilitative task. The development of such training on a wide scale is as yet in its infancy, and therefore it may be of interest to describe the Richmond Fellowship training programme, which has been developed over the past twenty years, concurrently with the development of the organisation.

The two-year in-service training, some or all of which is obligatory for all staff in the Fellowship communities, is basically a day-release programme, and comprises an introductory first year, and an advanced second year. It employs a variety of teaching methods and covers all aspects of work in a therapeutic community. There is an emphasis on the use of material from community life as course material, and on the application of course learning to work in the community: thus, for instance, both years provide training in management skills, and the second year includes sessions in creative group work, enabling staff to rehearse facilitating techniques which have direct application to group work. Both years also provide an experiential group in which members gain first-hand experience and interpretation of group processes, within the context of a peer group. The value of experiential learning is as yet not widely acknowledged within social work, although it forms the basis for psychoanalytic training and for most forms of training in psychotherapy. It would seem evident, however, that in an area of work where the staff's sensitivity and personal qualities are of crucial significance, this form of training is appropriate in enabling staff to gain awareness of self and others. Similar methods in formal training schemes appear to be seldom used, although experiential learning in groups has proliferated amongst the various alternative therapies of the 'growth movement'.

A recent addition to the courses available at the Richmond Fellowship college is the training in psycho-education in which staff learn to distinguish discrete developmental abilities, and to plan individual programmes in detail, as well as acquiring skills in group work, and a range of practical skills (see Chapter 10).

Why Professional Staff?

The preceding discussion of staff selection, role definition and training presumes that a position has been reached on the prior issue: who enables the community to be therapeutic? Is this the function of a professional worker? Or is the professional *per se*, in this context, anti-therapeutic?

Several of the contributors to this book have questioned the appropriateness of professionalism, the most extreme stance being adopted by Hans Huessy in Chapter 24. He poses the crucial dilemma: how is it possible to provide the essential element of human caring, that is, a 24-hour, seven-day-a-week commitment, in a context which is not that of kith or kin? As he remarks, true caring cannot be purchased by salaries, and it is his thesis that greater professionalism brings greater demands for professional privileges, which lead to distancing from the client. The solution which he proposes is a kind of 'national service' for all youth, in a caring situation. Thomas Barton (Chapter 14) tends towards a similar conclusion, in his dictate that staff members work for only one year: both practitioners are pessimistic about the possibility of obtaining the required commitment from staff over an extended period. Elisabeth Shoenberg (Chapter 2) regrets the need for professional carers, and reminds us that much of what is now termed 'therapy' is the universal human capacity to care: neighbourliness, or brotherly love.

Yet the consequences of non-professionalism must also be examined. The therapeutic community is dedicated to fostering personal growth and adjustment. In attempting this, the community adopts particular principles of functioning, which have been stated by Hoffman in Chapter 3 as: recognition of the therapeutic potential of all members; articulation of the community's value system; open communication; participatory decision-making; role diffusion amongst staff; and integration of techniques of treatment and rehabilitation. These principles require an ability on the part of staff to relinquish traditional role barriers, and it might therefore be assumed that non-professionals would be more easily able to meet this requirement. In practice it appears problematic for most new staff to find the balance between adhering to their role and repudiating role barriers; and Barton, for instance, comments that staff are just beginning to feel comfortable in their role when it is time for them to leave. At that point, skills have been acquired which are of benefit to the residents; a turnover of staff which does not permit these skills to be reinforced, utilised and conceptualised may be said to exploit the residents, as guinea-pigs for staff learning. Experienced staff are not only an essential resource for the residents; they are the transmitters of culture and means of learning for new staff.

The problem of obtaining an ongoing commitment must then be addressed. Is it possible that commitment may be combined with growing professionalism, that is, with growing appreciation of and competence in the task? Many staff have demonstrated already that ideals of service usually result in a wish to improve their understanding and competence. The experience and training in the therapeutic community provides a valuable preparation for many spheres of service, a fact which is well appreciated by many agencies. Yet, just as the profession of psychotherapist is a career in its own right, it is essential that a number of competent practitioners will see the task of working in a therapeutic community as a worthwhile career, in order that therapeutic communities can be fully and expertly staffed. Perhaps a crucial element in this context is the role of the community, or network of communities, in providing a framework, support, stimulus and status for staff, so that the task of assuring the community's survival and standards of service does not rest with one or two individuals. Staff support and supervision are therefore issues of management.

Management

The Role of the Staff Supervisor

The issue of staff management is not usually thought to be as appealing as that of training. It is in part restrictive and demanding, as well as nurturing and supportive; in fact, it evokes in staff the mixed feelings which staff tend to arouse in residents. It is not a cosy area.

It is intended here simply to concentrate on the role of management towards field staff. It has already been stated that management responsibility has two components: supervision and support. In the Richmond Fellowship, these functions are the direct responsibility of six staff supervisors, who carry a 'case load' each of three to five therapeutic communities, which are visited every two weeks. The supervisors spend time with the staff group, and have a one-to-one session with the Warden; in these meetings, every aspect of the community is scrutinised. The supervisor is trained and skilled in group and individual counselling, and therefore equipped to act as a technical consultant; in addition, he or she is able to advise the Warden on staff and staffing problems, and on the resources of the organisation. At the same time, it is the supervisor who is the key figure in transmitting to field staff the standards and policy of the organisation, and ensuring that these are appreciated and adhered to; or, if there are strong grounds for change, ensuring that this is appraised and agreed by management. It is sometimes suggested that supervisory and supportive functions make for an uneasy combination; and it is certainly a common response to mixed feelings to attempt to separate the recipients of those feelings. As has been mentioned, however, staff in the communities are expected to combine both accepting and confronting roles, and it is therefore felt to be appropriate that the staff supervisor models the management of these two aspects of authority. The boundaries and valid claims of different areas have to be clarified: in particular, the issue of what is owed to oneself and what to other people. Time, money, activities, needs, feelings and relationships have to be managed. Staff are role models for residents; their ability to manage the community is enhanced and stimulated by the example of the supervisor.

Dynamics of Staff Anxiety

Inevitably staff will also, in this anxiety-provoking work, need help to manage their anxiety, that is, to acknowledge it and to contain it within the proper bounds. It is understandable that staff, who are under constant bombardment from residents to concede limits and to allow the sick solution to prevail, will at times seek escape from the pressures. Various defensive strategies will be employed, and it is these which present the greatest challenge to the understanding and skill of the staff supervisor.

For some staff, the only way to cope is to create distance, that is, to practise deliberate toughness and non-involvement, and perhaps to live physically apart from the troubled scene. More frequently, staff attempt to evade the pressures by lowering their expectations of residents which are then rationalised as being unjustified or in need of revision. In this situation it is nearly unavoidable that pressure, similar to that placed on field staff by residents, will be placed on supervisory staff to lower their expectations of field staff. As an additional means of seeking relief from their strenuous role, staff may also seek the role of patient in relation to supervisory staff, who are expected to assume the role of therapist. There is indeed a legitimate place for the expression and examination of feelings, which will be intense in relation to stress experienced on the job; however, this should not be permitted to become divorced from issues directly relating to the task. The misplaced efforts of field staff to meet residents' dependency *demands* (as against their *needs*) lead inevitably to exhaustion, resentment, and the wish to experience an uncritical acceptance from their seniors. The resulting onslaught of 'basic assumption dependency' on the visiting supervisor can be overwhelming, and will certainly illuminate areas of uncertainty and diffidence in the supervisor, which in turn compound the insecurity of the staff. In such a climate, the supervisor can become disabled for the tasks of clarification, critical appraisal, direction and teaching, which are the only offerings actually of assistance to staff in their desperate search for a liferaft, compass and oars!

Middle-management Problems

Although the existence of pressures to compromise over standards is discussed with new staff, and their ability to resist is carefully assessed, this naturally does not obliterate either the force of the pressures or the tendency to succumb. The visiting supervisor tends therefore to be seen with considerable ambivalence, and his or her total function as appraiser is denied; the 'bad' functions (criticism and inspection) are split off from the 'good' functions (support, understanding, advice, praise). In time, the next level of seniority (whether middle or senior) will be subject to corresponding pressures, and may to a greater or lesser extent be driven to collude with field staff and become split from management, or alternatively, in order to avoid painful involvement, become distant or 'tough' in relation to those supervised. If the middle manager resists collusion, the picture may be complicated by other significant figures (neighbourhood committees, external consultants) who may become embroiled in the staff/management relationship. It is essential that external consultants and advisers do not reinforce defensive tactics, and are able to perceive the risk of being used as an alternative management.

It is easy to see how a split-off middle manager takes on all the desirable aspects of an organisation, leaving his or her colleagues or seniors to carry the projection of the 'bad' parts, which then become a caricature of authority. This is particularly so in the case of the chief manager of an organisation who, by virtue of being least accessible and carrying most authority, becomes the recipient of the most intense and least integrated feelings. At one and the same time, staff wish to perceive the chief manager as a friend and colleague, and also as a safe figure on whom to test out destructive phantasies. It is inevitable that staff will have the greatest difficulty over accepting their ambivalence towards the leader, who is the target for intense frustrated dependency needs. The difficulty can be either compounded or clarified by middle-management staff, through their ability and willingness to mediate and exact organisational needs and requirements, and thus to accept a share of the negative emotional content of staff responses.

Middle management tends to experience such phenomena as an unfair extra burden. It is part of the education of middle and senior management to recognise that dealing with collusion and splitting is part of their task. The more perceptive, autonomous, stable and consistent a middle-management team becomes, the more it will provide the secure environment needed by staff, and the less will be the desire to test out the boundaries. Obviously staff equally require a coherent philosophy, and reasons why certain practices are required or encouraged, others prohibited or discouraged. Moreover, both staff and residents need the experience and the satisfaction of debate: of being able to pursue arguments for or against whatever the therapeutic community or organisation stands for, and of being a potential contributor to policy. (That having been said, it is important that those who join an enterprise are in the main agreed with its tenets so that an excessive amount of time and energy are not expended in debate designed to change the project in the direction of an individual or sub-group.)

The Case for the Organisation

The wisdom of developing an organisation of therapeutic communities, as the Richmond Fellowship has done, is sometimes questioned. Perhaps this is because some losses are inevitable: loss of informality of functioning, and loss of face-to-face contact with every other member. Despite this, however, it has been found that there remains equal and often greater scope for individual creativity, initiative and responsibility. Experience has shown that complaints about organisational restrictions are likely to be a displaced response to inadequacy on the job.

More important, it has been found that the advantages for the users of the service outweigh any disadvantages. An organisation can offer a range of services, thus providing the most appropriate care for residents, and a range of training opportunities for staff; it can amass a body of knowledge and expertise which can be transmitted to new staff, thus obviating the need for unnecessary experimentation; it can provide the means for planned innovation within a relatively stable framework; and it can stimulate and raise standards of work, through comparison of standards and results in the various communities.

Notes

1. J.K. Wing and G.W. Brown, *Institutionalism and Schizophrenia: a Comparative Study of Three Mental Hospitals, 1960–1968* (Cambridge University Press, Cambridge, 1970).
2. A.H. Stanton and M.S. Schwartz, *The Mental Hospital* (Basic Books, New York, 1954).
3. G. De Leon and G.M. Beschner (eds.), *Proceedings of the Therapeutic Communities of America Planning Conference* (US Department of Health, Education and Welfare, 1976).
4. I. Suttie, *Origins of Love and Hate* (Routledge and Kegan Paul, London, 1935).
5. J. Liedloff, *The Continuum Concept* (Duckworth, London, 1975).
6. Address given by Dr Robert Gosling at the Annual General Meeting of the Richmond Fellowship, 1969, printed in the Richmond Fellowship Report for that year.

12 THE CONSUMER'S PERSPECTIVE (UK)

O the mind, mind has mountains; cliffs of fall
Frightful, sheer, no-man-fathomed. Hold them cheap
May who ne'er hung there.

Gerard Manley Hopkins, Sonnet 41

The opinion of the consumer, authentic and unconcerned with proving a theory, is the acid test of existing provision. Five people who are or have been resident in a Richmond Fellowship community agreed to give their views: Janet and Gillian addressed the 1973 conference, and the others spoke individually to the interviewer.

The residents were selected on the basis of being the first to volunteer in different diagnostic categories and/or age ranges. The very fact of volunteering one's views is liable to weight the sample of residents in favour of those with positive experience of the organisation, and with the ability to be articulate. These accounts are therefore not intended as a basis for generalisation or as a complete range of views. Apart from the fact that about ten per cent of the Fellowship's residents fail, by such criteria as ability to maintain themselves outside hospital, hold gainful employment and engage in a satisfactory social life, doubtless a larger number would be found to be ambivalent or sceptical about their experience in the organisation. Nevertheless, the residents' views have their own validity. They enable attention to be focused on what is actually being provided and achieved, as against what is planned and hoped for; and in the history of mental health care we can observe that there has frequently been a very great difference between the two. If methods of community care are to be meaningful, apart from simply replacing obsolete methods and settings, their value must lie in their sensitivity to individual needs, despite the necessity for theorising and large-scale planning.

Bruce (Interviewed in London, 1978)

Bruce, who is a resident of a central London Fellowship house, is thirty-nine years old – an enormous Australian with a pronounced stutter and a rich sense of humour. In common with many others, Bruce dealt with family problems by putting a vast physical distance between himself and his parents. His childhood experience was of a cold, formal environment in which nurturing was rationed rather than lovingly bestowed: 'like a scene from Oliver Twist'. *In order to find a home, he had to leave. In spite of his self-deprecation, his account is very coherent.*

My parents were both first-generation settlers, their parents having emigrated from Scotland and England. My father kept a shop in a city, where the social climate was formal and restrictive. I was the first child and was followed by three sisters.

At the age of four years I developed a stutter, following a tonsillectomy during which, I am told, I was unsympathetically handled by the hospital staff. I was taken to see a child psychologist, who considered that I had not developed a normal identification with my father; this was because my mother tried to shield me from him and keep us apart. I shared very little with my father, and he seemed largely absent from my life, but my mother was chillingly real. Her face seemed to me like a Gorgon. Trying to crack the mask became my goal, and I had an insane desire to please her; insane, because the task was impossible. My mother's perception of me was distorted by her own needs, and she thought that I ought to rescue her from her unhappy life.

At the age of ten, my family moved to a remote country area, and I was sent to boarding-school, which I disliked. One day when I was fourteen my father apparently said he was going out 'for a while', went into the outside toilet, and shot himself.

It took years for me to lose hope of a satisfying relationship with my mother, but gradually I became emotionally frozen, and I was unable to concentrate on academic work. I failed at art school, managed to pass my School Certificate, and failed university entrance. I moved to another city in order to get away from the Gorgon, and earned my living at clerical work, which was below my potential. I gained entry finally to university, but dropped out after one year. At the age of twenty-eight I got on the plane to London.

There, I imagined hospitable landladies who would look like pink-and-white milkmaids! Instead, I found a grey, unfamiliar city. I got a bedsitter, and as I spent many hours alone there, repressed memories and feelings began to emerge. I had violent headaches, and was afraid I was going mad. I went to several people for help, even to the office of an Englishman I had once met in Australia. Striding into the vestibule, I announced in ringing tones, 'I'm mad! I'm mad!' To which, with typical British aplomb, he replied, 'Won't you come in and have a cup of tea?'

I went to a London teaching hospital, which I found unsympathetic to my problems. The Samaritans provided a valuable crisis service, but gave inappropriate longer-term counselling; in the end, it was an intuitive Church Army officer who gave me the support I needed. Then one day I reached a crisis point: I looked at the gas oven in my room and thought, 'I can't stand any more.' I can't explain what happened next, except by describing my physical sensations: it felt like a giant toad belching twice – uurrrp, uuurrrp! – and it was as if an object forced itself up and out through the top of my head. Then it was all over. Suddenly I realised that my mind was clear and I could think.

That was the turning point, but only the beginning of years of working on my difficulties. I was by then euphoric and in need of care. I went to a psychiatric department and they arranged for me to go into a large mental hospital, where I spent nine months. On my discharge in 1968 I was referred to the Richmond Fellowship, and went to stay in one of the longer-term houses where there is no great pressure to leave. I stayed five years, and worked meanwhile as a bookkeeper. I tried leaving to live in a hostel for young people in London, but nearly broke down again: this stage coincided with the death of two people close to me, which reactivated all my fears. I had to return to the Richmond Fellowship, in a terrible state. I am now about to leave with a group of other residents, to share in a cluster-housing scheme.

The community in which I now live is in a Victorian house in central London. There is room for thirteen people of working age, living in three flats above communal rooms. There are no resident staff. The Warden visits every weekday and she sees everyone who wishes for individual counselling. She also comes to the weekly community meeting, which is attended by everyone as a condition of residence. The other conditions are payment of rent and non-violence. The fees are £35 per week and residents contribute out of their income, and most receive local authority grants.

My most important experience of living at the Fellowship has been of finding an emotional home. I feel part of a warm, caring group in which I have become more aware of my own feelings, difficulties and capabilities, and where I am developing greater emotional maturity. Specifically, I have found through relating to the Warden and some of the women residents, that my relationships with women can be based on mutual understanding rather than mutual phantasy. Understanding the other person tends to dispel fear. The job of creating this climate of understanding falls first and foremost on the staff. It is vital that they should be suitable people; and in my opinion, that means that above all they should be warm people who are free of dogmatic attitudes.

Understanding and acceptance are slowly altering my attitude towards myself. Since my earliest days, I have been conditioned to an expectation of failure; now I am learning that there is the possibility of change.

My most obvious problem, to other people, is my stutter, which can be a barrier to social relationships. It becomes more troublesome when I talk about my family. I also think that I use it to infantilise myself, and so lessen the expectations which others might have of me. I have tried various forms of therapy and am now working with a behaviour therapist who is helping me to gain confidence and learn to relax.

The stutter is really a manifestation of tension, which stems from anxiety, and also resistance. My experience with my mother has made me extremely anxious about whether my efforts at communication, especially with women, will be successful, and so I often defeat my own efforts through trying too hard. On the other hand I recognise that a part of me feels punitive towards my mother, and doesn't want to talk: why try so hard when she can never be pleased? This aspect of myself I experience as an onlooker who taunts me: 'Go on, make a mess of things!'

For seven years I was employed as a bookkeeper, a post which was below my potential capacity, but which aroused in me undue anxiety. I have now left that job, as it was unsatisfying to me, and I have yet to establish a career. I therefore greatly value the secure environment and social network which I have established through living at the Fellowship. I am looking forward to moving into group housing which will be a transitional step towards independence; I am trying now to take every opportunity of 'retribalising' myself and becoming a part of society again.

Diane (Interviewed in Exeter, 1978)

Diane comes from a large working-class family in the Midlands. Her mother has been married three times and has had three separate families. Diane is one of three girls born to the middle husband. The family life was very rough and disturbed, her mother was violent, her parents were unable to cope with so many children and nearly all of them were taken into care at some stage of their lives. Diane herself was in care from the age of two years and can remember almost nothing of life at home. However, she has had fairly regular contact with members of her family during her growing years; but she does not want to continue doing so. She feels she cannot trust any of them and does not like the people her sisters mix with. So she has more or less made the decision to have no more to do with them. There was a discrepancy between the totally negative way Diane saw herself in her earlier homes and her positive aspects appreciated by others. She always saw herself as dim, and played the role (at times consciously) of the stupid child or tomboy, constantly getting into trouble. At one time she was part of a gang engaged in removing slates from roofs and making them into spears, for the purpose of attacking other children. On the other hand, she revealed to others both intelligence and imagination. She enjoyed writing and spent much time at school composing plays and short stories, particularly about pop groups. She also found an interest in drama and a considerable talent for mimicry, and she has already been interviewed on local radio. She is keen to follow up this interest and hopes to go on a drama course.

I have lived in many different kinds of homes. I was fostered a number of times, but never found a happy foster home. One foster mother in particular was very unpleasant, someone who spoilt any fun and was always down on me. I took to trying people out by playing the tomboy and becoming a rebel. In addition to several periods with foster parents I was in several children's homes, and at last I arrived at Countessthorpe, a large children's home in the Midlands, where I stayed until I was about twelve years old. This was the happiest time of my childhood. I got on particularly well with one of the house-mothers and still keep in touch with her, although 'Auntie Joan', as she is called, is now confined to a wheelchair, and this upsets me and makes it hard to visit her.

Then Countessthorpe was closed for a house to be built on the site, and I was moved to yet another children's home nearby which was really awful. The Warden was a terrible character, a large fat woman who was very bossy and made trouble amongst the children by having favourites. I was definitely not a favourite! I couldn't take that kind of regime and finished up by having a fight with a male member of staff who had a reputation for violence. He started the fight, but I didn't make an official complaint because my word would never have been believed against his. My main objection to the children's home was the lack of freedom, and being constantly told what to do and what not to do. We were allowed to do little jobs around the house, but twelve-year-olds want more responsibility and should be able to live in a freer, more relaxed atmosphere.

At the age of fifteen I was transferred from the home to an assessment centre. This gave me more freedom, though still not all that much. We were allowed out on our own, provided that we said where we were going. We were allowed to smoke and answer the telephone. The task of the assessment centre was to see what we were like and to decide where we would go next. At the end of six months I was offered two alternatives. One was a local authority hostel for girls; the other was a Richmond Fellowship house for adolescents.

My first choice was the girls' hostel. This was because I didn't like the label of 'Mental Aftercare and Rehabilitation'. I had always connected mental illness with dimness and mongolism, and I had always seen myself as dim. I felt I couldn't tell my friends that I was going to live with nutters. But then I decided I preferred the idea of a mixed hostel, so I came to Exeter for interview, and I was surprised that the other residents were ordinary intelligent people. I have been living here now for four months.

Certain parts of my life in this Fellowship house are particularly important to me. For instance, the freedom. At first I found this frightening, but now I have got used to the advantages it can bring. I have my own possessions and look after them, and I can call them my own. I can come and go as I please without having to tell people the whole time what I am doing next. I take an active part in the work groups and most of all I enjoy being chairperson of the house meeting and finding that I can get people to join in and use the meeting to get things done.

The three things I most want from being here are: first, to work. Too many residents want to spend time loafing around. This is a waste of time and it's bad for them. I'm waiting for news about my application for the drama course, and in the meantime I am taking part in the house programme. Then, I want to learn responsibility and achieve independence, and I think I can do it now that I have been chairperson. But I also need the space which the house is giving me to help me to discover more about myself.

Christopher (Interviewed in London, 1978)

Christopher is aged twenty-five; a tall, dark-haired young man with a round, youthful face, and glasses. He is resident at one of the Richmond Fellowship communities in a West London suburb. When first interviewed he had been in the community for one month; the second interview took place during his seventh month of residence. The following is an amalgamation of the two. Christopher was asked to give his views on living in the community, and to provide some personal background as a context for the reader.

Christopher I was born in Canada, in Toronto. My father was a Polish motor mechanic, and my mother English, and they had emigrated to Canada from England. I was their only child. When I was five years old, we moved back to England. I wasn't told the reason at the time, but my mother later explained that my father had become very ill. He had a heart disease, and died when I was six. I don't remember much about him, but the memories I have are pleasant.

I was educated at Christ's Hospital [a public, i.e. independent, school] from the age of ten. It was quite strict there and I was beaten several times for trivial misdemeanours. I haven't lived at home very much. From boarding-school I went to teacher-training college where I lived in a hall of residence for the first year, only going home for the holidays. But I left during the second year of my course, without qualifying. I went back to Canada.

Interviewer Did you visit the place where you used to live?

Christopher Yes, I did. I suppose that was partly why I went. I went to look at the outside of the house, and it seemed familiar, but I didn't ask to go inside.

Interviewer What did you do in Canada?

Christopher I did a few casual jobs, drank a lot, and smoked pot. Then I had my first breakdown, and spent two months in hospital in Vancouver. I then came home to live with my mother, but we don't get on. She does show emotion, but in ways that I dislike. When I was at school, she was loving towards me only if I could show that I had made progress. She turns to me when she is upset, but I don't sympathise with many of the things that upset her: for instance, she cried when an Asian family moved in next door. That sort of thing makes me sick. She doesn't understand my difficulties, either. I tried a few jobs, but each time I began to think that people were criticising me, and so I left. My mother nagged me about this.

Interviewer Didn't you have friends to turn to?

Christopher I don't have very many friends, and those I have tend to be socially isolated or outcasts – for instance, my two closest friends in Canada were both illegal immigrants! I have difficulty in approaching girls because I'm afraid I'll be rejected. I've been in hospital several times because of nervous breakdowns. I spent two months in hospital in Vancouver. After returning to England, I spent six months in Northwick Park Hospital, two weeks in Shenley, and two months in Wembley Hospital. It was there that the social worker recommended me to come to the Richmond Fellowship: the only alternative offered was hostels of the doss-house type! No other hospital had tried to arrange aftercare for me. There is not enough follow-up in most hospitals; one day they suddenly tell you you're better, and you are not prepared for life outside.

Interviewer How was the idea of this step put to you, and what did you think of it?

Christopher I was pleased to hear that there was somewhere I could go where I would be supported and understood. At first, however, I said no. But then I panicked at the idea of going home again, without a job, and I decided to apply. I came here first on a very short visit, which didn't give me much idea of the place. Then I came for the formal interview, met other residents, and was told how it runs: that everyone joins in the housework, and has a responsibility to help one another. I thought it was a very good idea. Funnily enough, although I didn't know the term 'therapeutic community', I had already got some vague idea in my mind of what I needed, and this was it.

Interviewer What do you think of it, now that you're here?

Christopher I think it's very good. I used to have a lot of extra-ordinary phantasies, but I have them to a much lesser extent now. The staff help me to get in touch with my feelings, and I am able to relate to other people more.

Interviewer Any complaints?

Christopher Well, I don't agree with the compulsory hour which we all have to spend with our counsellor each week – an individual counselling session. Sometimes you don't have anything to say, but you still have to go. Then, I think £13.50 per week is a lot to contribute out of one's Supplementary Benefit . It only leaves £4 for personal expenses, and it's even harder on the women, because they need more clothes.

Interviewer May I ask how living here has altered your relationship with your mother, if at all?

Christopher It's much better now, because we don't see so much of each other. She used to phone me every night when I first came, and I used to spend each alternate weekend at home. But now we've cut down the contact. I phone her once a week, and I visit her on alternate weekends, for one meal only.

Interviewer Do you feel, here in the community, that people criticise you, as you have felt in the past?

Christopher I occasionally have paranoid feelings, but these soon pass.

Interviewer Do you worry at all that you may be stigmatised because this community is known to be for ex-psychiatric patients?

Christopher No, that doesn't worry me at all. Finding work worries me. I haven't worked whilst I've been here, except for one day at a very unsuitable job. But I want to find work now. The trouble is, most employers are not willing to take on people who have had psychiatric trouble, so one feels one has to tell lies about the past when one goes to an interview.

Interviewer You've spent a lot of time away from home in the past. How do you feel about leaving this community, which is now your home?

Christopher I'm glad that there is a follow-up scheme. This community is getting a flatlet house so that several residents will be able to move in as a group and live communally, and they will continue to get some support from the staff here. I think it's very important, and I would like to move on there after I leave.

Janet (Address to the Richmond Fellowship Conference, 1973)

At the age of one-and-a-half years I was taken into care as my mother was an alcoholic and she was divorced from her husband and I was in care in one place or another until I was sixteen. At the age of sixteen I went to a job in Exeter where I was very lonely and at the age of seventeen I became pregnant and had to have the baby adopted as the father did not want to know. This started off a serious drinking problem; I worked for fourteen hours a day to help me get a bottle of whisky which I consumed and perhaps sometimes over. Due to all this I started breaking down physically and mentally and I was admitted into Exvale Hospital, Exeter, where I was given treatment which did not really help me. I became violent, hitting at windows, hitting staff if they wanted to lock me up. I smuggled drink into the locked ward and altogether my behaviour was very bad so they could not put up with this any longer. I was transferred to Broadmoor Hospital, Berkshire. This was a very dismal place and I saw many people locked up for many weeks on end and I wondered why I was taken to such a place. I had never ever been in a criminal law court and I had never been in trouble with the police but that was where I ended up. I thought my life was ended and I became frightened and introvert and often thought that the end was near. After about a year being in that hospital I contracted bronchial pneumonia and nearly died, but after about a year I began to pick myself up and they decided that it was time to be taken back to Exvale Hospital once more, so back I went. My aftercare there consisted of eleven days in the hospital and then after eleven days I was put on St David's Station to go to London where I was to end up to be with my mother. I was very frightened so I consumed three double scotches on the station, so by the time I got on the train I was all right, I was not frightened any more so I continued drinking. By the end of the journey I was about to get off the train and it was still moving and I nearly fell out, but this man helped me – his name was Jim – and he is now my husband. Well I eventually got to my destination but it proved unsuitable so I had to go back into Broadmoor once more and Jim had to work very hard for a long time to get the hospital to let me out. This time they thought of a halfway house so they decided to send me to Trelawn, the Fellowship's house for alcoholics. I went there but I did not find it agreeable to me and I speak only for myself; the other residents liked what went on. There was too much talk on alcoholism and psychoanalysing their own problems which I thought was very dangerous, and so I had a drink slip and I was warned that if I did it again I would have to go. The pressures became too much for me so I drank and I drank, and this time I really did have to go, but a very nice warden called Bernard who is not here today, and I am very sorry to hear that, saw what position I was in, so he decided that another Richmond Fellowship house would suit me and this was Rutland House in Oxford. Well I got there and I found it a totally different atmosphere; the people were younger, they had various different problems. The staff and the residents gave me great encouragement and I had a great deal of support there, the indignant kind as well as the understanding or appreciative kind. I got a good job and I kept it and when things got difficult I managed to work it out instead of to drink. I began to think of myself differently and other people began to see me differently – I don't know which came first – and we all began to feel we had a future after all. In the end I left to get married and I have now been married for nearly three months and I am very happy. May I end just by saying that people who come out of mental hospitals usually are very very frightened and they have to start again where they left off and there is a great need for these hostels because if it helped me then it can help a lot of other people.

Gillian (Address to the Richmond Fellowship Conference, 1973)

I started drinking at the age of twenty-eight. I think I knew very soon what was happening to me, almost from the time I started – that I was drinking for the effects rather than just drinking socially, as I had done before. I was a medical student, and my ex-husband was a doctor, and there were plenty of text books around the house that I never looked at, because I didn't want to know the prognosis. I thought that would be too frightening, and it has indeed proved extremely difficult to give up alcohol.

I had three small children when I first started drinking; the eldest was five and the youngest eighteen months old. My marriage was going wrong, and I would say that the drinking was not the cause, but that it simply precipitated the break-up. I separated from my husband, and although he knew I was drinking, he never mentioned it, except to say when he left me that if I continued drinking he would take the children. He did trust me at that stage. I kept the children with me for another two years, and continued to drink. I tried to stop, but never managed to abstain for long, and in 1970 I asked for help from the Bethlem Royal Hospital; I just said that I wanted tablets. They wanted me to come into hospital for two months and I said, 'You don't understand, I can't leave the children or he would take them.' But I did go in, thinking that my environment was wrong, and that once I decided I wanted to stop drinking, and saw someone about it, then I would be able to stop. It did not prove as easy as that.

It has been a very slow process really, I think that it was very hard to know what one had to change in one's life. At the age of nineteen I knew that there was something wrong with me. I had had psychological tests which showed that I was very withdrawn and isolated, and I was very ashamed of the test results at the time. I never told anybody, and just stored them away, and thought that I would have to manage as I was. And when I went into hospital I still thought, 'I have to stop drinking, but I have got to manage to cope with my personality as it is now.' The hospital said that it was going to be a very painful process because it is not easy to understand yourself. It's all very well to say that – try it! You feel like leaving, because in a way there is a great pressure on you in a psychiatric hospital, even when you are voluntary – but unless you make necessary changes in yourself you should not leave, and in a sense you are also unable to do so. Nobody is actually holding you there: you are a prisoner almost of your inner self, and of the problems for which you are receiving treatment; in a way, a prisoner of the conflict between how you are and the progress you think you should make.

In the end I did leave and I started work (having learned to type in hospital), but I was drinking and so lost my job very quickly. This led me to make several suicide attempts, and I could never ask for help in an adult way. I have been back in hospital four times in the last three years, and each time my confidence went lower and lower, till by the end I felt totally unable to face life. I went into Warlingham Park Hospital last year. That was my last hospital admission, and I hope my final one, and there I really gave in altogether. It was a very disciplined treatment in some respects, for instance, we were not allowed out for about six weeks, and I found that I became very scared. When I did go out I used to drink and not tell anybody, because I still felt in need of help and didn't want to be discharged. I really was drinking continuously by that stage without even telling people, and that was the difference; when I first had treatment I used to tell people, because I wanted to ask for help.

I didn't really want to go to the Fellowship's home for alcoholics, Trelawn. I thought, 'What difference is that going to make?' I had already tried another Fellowship house on leaving hospital the third time, and that had proved a failure. I said at this stage that I did not want to be with alcoholics, but I finally went, and to my surprise I found that my attitude changed completely, as I found that other alcoholics could understand and help me more than other people were able to. My family, for instance, were sympathetic to my problem, but they believed me when I assured them that I was able to get over it straight away, and when I found that I couldn't, they did not know how to cope. I think that this is one way in which other alcoholics have been a great help to me, that is, they don't put me under enormous pressure – 'What's going to go wrong now?' – when I look depressed, and if I look happy they don't think I have had a drink, whereas my family would get very worried still.

Trelawn was an enormous help to me in another way, since by this time the gap between being in a psychiatric hospital and the outside world had become enormous. On my first time in hospital, I was allowed home at the weekend and every night if I wished, and the difference between the two worlds was not very great, but by my fourth hospitalisation I felt that I was getting institutionalised and frightened of the world. For that reason, I have mixed feelings about hospital treatment. All the hospitals, although I let them down a lot, have really helped me each time. But I do sometimes wonder if it was necessary to have been so completely cut off from my everyday life, and if there had been some possibility of having my children with me, whether things need have drifted so badly apart.

I don't really know how to say Trelawn has helped. These things are hard. People are given a lot of personal responsibility and freedom there. I know other hostels for alcoholics where people feel as if they are in a prison: they have to come in at certain times, they are not allowed to do things for themselves, and are not allowed to have personal freedom, which we do have in Trelawn. There are only two basic rules, one of which is that we don't drink, and the other that we attend the house meeting once a week. We don't wrap each other up in cotton wool, but there is a lot of understanding of when a person feels lonely, even if it is not put into words, and a lot of support just by joking, and also by talking seriously if you want to, which people do from time to time! The staff have also given me enormous help and encouragement.

As a result of my improvement, I have been able to get a lot closer to my family again. By the time I left hospital the second time, I hardly wanted to see my children, because I felt so terrible about it. They really had been my whole life, in fact it could be said that they had been too much my life. I had always believed in a mother being a mother, and I really could not forgive myself for what had happened. I still don't find our meetings very easy, but we have been able to see each other much more frequently, and my ex-husband, who by my second hospitalisation did not trust me at all, is now beginning to trust me again. For example, on Tuesday he rang me up saying that my eldest daughter was having her tonsils out, and I said, right, I would come up, and he said, 'Shall I tell her, then?' Now a year ago he wouldn't have said, 'Shall I tell her?' because a year ago he wouldn't have known whether I could keep to that arrangement or not, and that's the kind of difference that is happening. He is slowly getting his trust back, and this is something that I feel does take a very long time.

I think perhaps the treatment of alcoholics also takes a long time, and I have seen it in myself and amongst my own friends. When I get depressed because I have had a slip, I say to myself, 'Well okay, it's been eighteen months, and I haven't had a drink: don't let's make too much of one slip, because however serious it is, I have at least managed to stay sober for eighteen months, which is more than I have achieved before.' I think that some people also need longer than a year of rehabilitation, although for myself I think that one year is going to be quite enough. I feel quite differently about everything now, and I am ready to set up an independent life, but for those people who have hardly known any other way of life than the alcoholic one, I think an enormous amount of encouragement and aftercare is needed. With this in mind, I think that communal flats and communities where people take total responsibility for themselves are a good idea. There are difficult times in Trelawn, for example, when there are changes of staff, but we feel that we are taking quite a lot of the burden, and I think in fact that we get a kick out of it. We imagine that we depend on the staff ultimately, but in reality I think that after a certain stage it is possible for people in these communities to learn to look after themselves.

13 BETWEEN SCYLLA AND CHARYBDIS: STAFF TRAINING IN THERAPEUTIC COMMUNITIES (UK)

Peter Hawkins

A staff member in a halfway house therapeutic community has to be a jack of all trades – somebody who can be equally at home sorting out the finances as leading groups; who can organise decorating and gardening as well as counsel residents who are working through difficult and painful feelings; and who can turn his attention to a group of psychiatrists at one moment, an overdosing crisis the next, and then perhaps a phone call about a blocked sewerage system! So what sort of person does this work demand? The job is very different from that of the traditional therapist who has learnt a professional discipline which gives a firm structure within which to work, a distance from his clients, and who can leave his work and go home at the end of the day. The Richmond Fellowship staff member has to be somebody who can be therapeutic not only in his personality and his professional discipline, but in his daily living.

In recent years there has been much consensus in research on successful therapeutic milieus and therapists' attitudes and personalities. Yallom[1] came to the conclusion that the personality of the therapist was more important than the therapeutic discipline he practised; and that the important traits for a therapist were insight, accurate empathy and non-possessive warmth. Carl Rogers[2] emphasised the importance of the therapist or counsellor being able to face problems, to be congruent in his own personality, to have an unconditional positive regard and empathetic understanding of his clients and an ability to demonstrate and communicate these to the client.

More recent research by Tom Caine[3] of University College Hospital London, showed that there was a high correlation between staff and clients who functioned well in a therapeutic community milieu, and a high capacity for divergent thinking. Certainly the experience of St Charles House, the Richmond Fellowship training house in London, has borne out this research. We have found that convergent thinkers, who tend to have black-and-white beliefs about what is right and wrong, find it hard to cope with the complex and paradoxical situations that living in a therapeutic community involves.

A therapeutic community is a milieu with a guiding principle which governs all individuals, both staff and residents, who live and work in it. This principle is, learning through shared experience, observation, experiment and feedback. Just as Sheldon Kopp and Sydney Jouard[4] have pointed out that the individual therapist at best shares his own experience of incompleteness and struggle, so therapeutic community workers, at best, demonstrate their own attempts at endorsing the therapeutic community ideals of commitment to self-scrutiny, authenticity, relatedness and responsibility.

Residents and staff need to aim for the same ideals, if they are going to work towards maximising the learning within the community. These are:

1. An ability to be open to different points of view, to varying emotions, to new ways of operating, and to be responsive to others, intellectually and emotionally.
2. An ability to treat each situation as new (without however ignoring past experience). To avoid stereotyped responses and set answers which tend to label and confirm set patterns of behaviour.
3. An ability to be personally involved while at the same time to be objective. To remain committed to, but not trapped by, the inter-relationships of the community.
4. To have, in the words of Antonio Gramsci, 'optimism of the will, but pessimism of the intellect'. To be able to maintain and demonstrate a faith in human change against both personal and group negativity, while at the same time not becoming dependent on concrete signs of growth and success, either in oneself or, for staff, in one's clients.

In addition, the staff need the ability to recharge their batteries. In America many articles have been written on the nature of 'burn-out' in residential social work.[5] Some exceptional staff can recharge internally, but most staff need friends, relations, good holidays and interests outside the work which can help them renew their energy.

These ideals are not intended as a blueprint for what a staff member should be but as a means of providing a direction to be aimed for – and the process of keeping these goals clearly in mind can help to clarify the pitfalls that one must avoid in order to achieve the balance that leads to learning.

The most common pitfall that a staff member encounters in his career is *submergence*. The symptoms are easy to identify: the staff member stops reading books or writing letters; he becomes unable to objectify his experience in case conferences or supervision; he finds it difficult to set limits, say no to resident requests or to protect his off-duty hours. Several times at St Charles House I have encountered staff members in supervision who were extremely overtired and yet felt that they were so indispensable that they had to carry on doing vast amounts of overtime – and yet were very resistant to giving time to standing back and reflecting on the effectiveness of what they were doing. Occasionally a whole staff team is swept into submergence, and the community stumbles from crisis to crisis, with little awareness of the processes operating. The community feels as though it is in an uncontrollable whirlpool of actions and emotions. The perspective is all foreground with no background, and there is little or no long-term planning. Residents will often start to miss parts of the community programme and external commitments, and their newly established ability to order their lives will be undermined.

A related pitfall is *overidentification*, either in the sense of being unable to separate other people's difficulties from one's own intra-psychic dynamics, or investing one's own success, failure and validation in the success or failure of the residents. Anthony Storr[6] has found in his work with creative artists, that one of the strongest causes of breakdown is their overidentification with their work, be it a painting or a novel. Similarly it is important for a staff member to avoid being overdependent on his particular residents making significant behavioural changes in order for him to feel validated in his work.

Some staff have to be weaned from a dependence on their 'good' self-image of being always loving and accepting, and need support to be confronting and limit-setting in their work with residents. They need to be able to allow residents and sometimes even other staff to be angry and hating towards them, and still stand firm when necessary. Staff can get into a position where they are emotionally feeding off the life of the community, where they have to be the 'good guy' in order to win the admiration and friendship of the residents, in order to boost their own waning self-esteem. These staff need strong support in setting limits on their involvement with their clients, and in developing a life outside the community which will lessen their need for emotional support from their client group. It may also be that the staff member has reached this position through being isolated from and undersupported by the rest of the staff group.

Another problem concerns the failure to cope adequately with authority, both one's own and that of others. Trainees often find the paradox that they are members of the community, but also staff with authority and special responsibility, difficult to live with. This often leads to flight, either into democratic utopianism or into the defence of hiding behind the professional staff role. The former defence negates the authority and responsibilities vested in him as a staff member and lays claim to the belief that staff and residents are all equal; even to the extent of ignoring the obvious such as that staff are paid and residents pay. In training sessions on group work I have twice experienced a group of new staff attack the whole notion of being trained in group leadership and dogmatically cling to the opinion that all leadership is an imposition, and that staff members should just 'be' in groups! The latter defence, of overprofessionalism, negates the common humanity of staff and residents, distancing the residents both intellectually and emotionally.

Residents can similarly flee from authority issues into a denial of their own authority or into a refusal to acknowledge what authority the staff do and don't have.

Some of the apparent pitfalls of the therapeutic community milieu are also its strengths; for instance, as the staff members (or residents) become involved with the community, they often experience strong emotions within the community, which mirror emotions which as individuals they have never fully faced. This presents the challenge of keeping a balance between feeling overwhelmed by the emotion which is triggered, and fleeing from the feelings into rationalising and other distancing defences.

The programme of the therapeutic community, from counselling to community meetings, from daily-living encounters to small groups, must be so designed as to steer a course towards the ideal, while at the same time avoiding the Scylla and Charybdis of the pitfalls. The programme, in order to perform this task, must provide: constant feedback to the individual on how he is perceived by others; time and space to be able to retreat from involvement in the community and see it in perspective; a conceptual input so that the trainee/staff member is able to make sense of his work in terms of different intellectual frameworks; a grounding in basic practical and interpersonal skills, and last but not least a climate of challenging assumptions and of questioning attitudes. The structures must create a balance between experiential involvement and time for reflection aided by conceptual input.

The Richmond Fellowship has planned its staff training programme in two main areas: first, through on-the-job involvement in the ongoing life of the community, and particularly the staff team; and secondly, through the complementary training the Fellowship provides through its college. Thus a balance is created between learning through the immediacy of the particular community and learning through conceptual input and shared reflection at the college.

Within the house, the staff members' learning programme in some ways reflects that of the residents. For like the residents, they too have time set aside in the staff meetings to reflect upon their own dynamics in relation to their group of colleagues and the group with whom they are working. Where the resident has a weekly counselling session, the staff member has a weekly supervision session with either the Warden or Deputy Warden. This session not only provides an opportunity to oversee the administrative, counselling and group work that the staff member is doing, but also to explore the ways that each person is relating to and coping with the work. It also gives the opportunity for the staff member to explore how his own functioning may be affecting the work or how the work may be triggering off difficult areas of his own personality or emotional life. If it becomes obvious that a staff member is in need of therapy or ongoing counselling, he or she is expected to seek it in a different context.

Also built into the policy of the Fellowship is a six-monthly individual and team appraisal in each house where the strengths and weaknesses of staff during the past six months are reviewed, and individual and team goals for the next half-year agreed upon. The individual appraisals are done with the Warden or Deputy, but it is important that they are linked with an opportunity for the staff member to receive feedback from the whole staff team. We have found that this works best when structured in a way that encourages an opportunity both for positive and negative feedback, and when shared in a way that recognises that each person's feedback is their individual experience and perception, rather than a verdict.

The weekly staff meetings also provide space for systematic reflection. Each week there is a review of the current position of each resident in the house, as seen in the context of that resident's long-term and short-term goals, and at regular intervals each resident is reviewed in greater depth through the presentation of a more detailed case study by his or her counsellor. There is also a weekly review of the areas of administration, each of which is allocated to a particular staff member.

After group and community meetings there is a staff post-group, where the staff are encouraged to look at the processes they have just been involved in and how they related to them. Some attention is given to reviewing how the staff members in the group worked together and what can be learnt from this.

The learning process is augmented by the regular visit for a whole day every two weeks of the house supervisor. The supervisor, who also has an inspectorate function, is a member of the Richmond Fellowship middle management, and combines an awareness of the overall task of the organisation with professional expertise in the management of therapeutic communities. The supervisor normally covers five communities, and is thus able to bring a wider perspective to what is happening within each individual house, to question group attitudes and assumptions and challenge group collusion. In some of the specialised communities such as those for ex-drug-users or whole families, the necessary learning opportunities are provided in part through regular sessions with a house consultant with particular expertise in the area of specialism.

Besides the training which is part of every Richmond Fellowship community, certain houses have been assigned a specific training role. St Charles House is the locus for the central part of the senior staff training. Staff are accepted who have either completed their basic training in the Richmond Fellowship and are in line for promotion, or who are newly arrived in the organisation but already have appropriate experience. Thus the training has to be flexible and geared to the learning needs of the individual trainee. This is done by the trainee appraising himself in all aspects of the work and also being appraised by the staff team, Warden and supervisor of the community from which he comes. From these parallel assessments, learning goals for the three-month training programme are drawn up in discussion with the training house staff. At the end of the training period the trainee writes a second self-appraisal, as well as receiving observations on his performance from his fellow trainees, the training house staff, and his particular supervisor, who will write an evaluation of his placement.

Constant feedback on performance of the various parts of the work is a central feature of the training, and various means have been developed at St Charles to further this process. Each trainee takes on one or two of the residents for counselling, and to enhance the learning from this, the trainee is required to tape-record several of the sessions; in conjunction with his supervisor he then analyses the contents of the interview. This exercise is supplemented by requiring each trainee to do a full case presentation to the staff team of one of his counsellees, and to explore the links between the counselling process, the resident's patterns in the house, and his or her life-themes.

As prospective senior staff, the trainees have in addition to develop their own skills in supervision, teaching, research, evaluation and planning, and so methods have been developed to promote learning in each of these areas. The trainees not only receive weekly supervision from a senior member of the St Charles staff, but also are supervised by and supervise a fellow trainee in a peer supervision system. The trainees are also required to carry out a research project which must include a practical, unexplored component, and discuss the application of the results. Trainees also lead one of the weekly learning seminars for the staff team.

Thus within the house a balance of action and reflection, involvement and detachment, support and confrontation is provided to guide staff through the difficulties outlined above and towards greater expertise. This is complemented by attendance at the two-year in-service training, which takes place one day per week, both at the college in Holland Park, London, and the two regional training centres in Bristol and Manchester. Learning opportunities are thus provided in three ways: first, by providing the necessary factual input on such subjects as residential management skills, administration, drugs and their side effects, psychiatric first-aid, human growth and development, and on elements of psychiatric practice; secondly, through experiential training, helping staff to develop personal skills in observing, listening, interviewing, counselling and group work; and thirdly, by giving the opportunity for staff to reflect upon their house experience in the light of case work seminars led by skilled practitioners, and to share ideas and their application between colleagues from many different houses.

Besides the day-release two-year courses, the college also provides short block courses, such as those in group dynamics and organisational perspectives. The latter gives the opportunity for staff to meet in seminars with headquarters staff and to look at key issues from an organisational rather than a house perspective.

The college courses provide essential opportunities for reflection, feedback and cognitive input related to the work, but therapeutic community training must always be centred in the community itself, since learning is the very function of the therapeutic community. It is important that training for staff in the community is not something that happens on the periphery, for as I have tried to show, it is integrally linked with the life and learning of the whole community.

Nor should learning stop at trainee staff, for above all it is important that the trainers and senior staff remain learners as well. It is so easy for ways of working to become an unquestioned and unthinking tradition. There must always be a constant reworking of the approach. There has to be a sense of constant rebirth, constant research and an awareness of what is going on and why.

Notes

1. I.D. Yallom, *The Theory and Practice of Group Psychotherapy* (Basic Books, New York, 1970).
2. C. Rogers, *On Becoming a Person* (Houghton Mifflin, New York, 1961), Ch. 3.
3. As reported at the MIND/ATC Conference, 'The Changing Forms of Therapeutic Communities and Implications for Staff Support', 10–12 June 1975.
4. S. Kopp, *If You Meet the Buddha on the Road, Kill Him* (Sheldon Press, Palo Alto, California, 1972); S. Jouard, *The Transparent Self* (Van Nostrand, New York, 1964).
5. See for example 'Symposium: Stress and Burn-out in Child Care', *Childcare Quarterly*, vol. 6 (Summer 1977).
6. A. Storr, *The Dynamics of Creation* (Secker and Warburg, London, 1972).

14 SELECTION, TRAINING AND SUPERVISION OF MENTAL HEALTH HALFWAY HOUSE STAFF (USA)

Thomas F. Barton

This chapter deals with methods of staff recruitment, selection, training and supervision for a residential rehabilitation division of a community mental health centre, comprising two halfway houses for psychiatric patients, with a total of twenty-one residents and three full-time staff members, supervised by a Director of Residential Rehabilitation.

Although the residential rehabilitation programme in this instance is part of a larger operation, a community mental health centre, the methods involved are applicable to similar facilities, whether or not part of a larger programme, and consideration of the way they are handled here may be useful to others in the field.

There are differences between halfway houses attached to a larger programme, and free-standing facilities, those differences (fewer financial resources and absence of an associated day-programme of social and vocational rehabilitation work) generally operating to the disadvantage of entirely independent facilities. Yet the problems of finding suitable staff, interviewing them, training them and supervising them exist within any setting.

Indeed, administrative staff of an internationally organised chain of halfway houses for psychiatric patients, the Richmond Fellowship, have expressed the view that adequate staffing in the US is one of most serious problems they face in day-to-day operations, a product of larger financial difficulties,[1] experienced in a culture where staff value themselves largely in terms of their salary.

Staffing

There are three line staff positions in the division of residential rehabilitation. One of the two halfway houses in the programme serves also as the location of the programme office and staff apartment. When on their work shifts, staff members stay overnight in this apartment.

The position is formally called Rehabilitation Counsellor and pays over $13,000 yearly. Membership in the hospital workers' union is automatic after 90 days' probation. There are many associated medical, dental and school benefits. Full tuition is paid for course work at any university in the area, at either undergraduate or graduate level, provided the course work is pertinent to the job. The high pay and benefits are a strong incentive for new staff to retain their jobs.

The only educational requirement is a high school diploma. Informal requirements are exacting and will be discussed below. The job is formally limited to one year, although at times has been extended to as much as two years. New staff understand this limit, and it is included in their hiring letter, along with a stipulation that vacation time (20 days per year) may not be taken until the end of the first year, to avoid burdening other staff with extra duty, since the house must be staffed at all times after 4.00 p.m.

The time limit on job duration is imposed to prevent the development of an 'institutionalised' staff, and to attract the kind of individuals wanted for the position: men and women interested in intensive work with the severely emotionally ill in a situation maximising teaching and practice as a step in upward mobility in the mental health field.

Each counsellor works a different shift: Friday at 11.00 a.m. to Monday night at 10.30 p.m.; Saturday at noon to Tuesday night at 10.30 p.m.; Monday 2.00 p.m. to 10.30 p.m. and Tuesday 2.00 p.m. to Friday noon. It should be noted that there is always an overlap when staff coming on duty and those leaving work together, facilitating continuity and communication of events during the leaving members' shift. The director is present from 2.00 to 10.30 p.m. Monday, from 10.00 a.m. to 7.00 p.m. Tuesday, and 9.00 a.m. to 4.00 p.m. Wednesday, Thursday and Friday. As the director has other duties at the mental health centre across the street, this means in practice being present the hours indicated Monday, from 4.00 p.m. to 7.00 p.m. Tuesday, and intermittently during the rest of the week.

As can be noted, all staff and the director are present from 2.00 p.m. to 10.30 p.m. on Monday. Monday is the *only* day *all* staff are present at the halfway house, involved in discussing residents' problems, staff problems with residents and each other, interviewing prospective new residents, and participating in the house meeting Monday night, followed by discussion and evaluation of the house meeting and staff functioning.

Staff Work

The main work of staff on duty is to attend the evening coffee hours, from 6.00 to 10.30 p.m. every day except Monday in the first-floor social room. All members of both halfway houses are invited. Attendance is voluntary except in instances of a resident withdrawing into his or her room completely, whereupon attendance for one hour three times weekly may be required. The atmosphere is informal, and the emphasis is on encouraging residents to relate to staff and each other in socially appropriate ways and discuss problems frankly and openly. Residents are limited to one year and staff begin to help residents prepare to leave as soon as they arrive, by refusing to become 'mothers' or 'fathers' to them.

The basic assumptions upon which staff work are:

1. Despite mental hospital diagnosis, usually some label of 'schizophrenia', residents are neither fragile, nor made out of glass, and can and must be treated as responsible adults during their year of residence.
2. Staff are not there to help residents, take care of residents, or meet residents' needs, but to provide a milieu where residents learn to do these things for themselves. Infantilisation is the worst possible form of interaction.
3. Unless limits are set, and meant, residents are quite correct in perceiving staff as uncaring. Failure to pay rent, use of illegal drugs, any act of violence against another person or the house, and repeated failure to attend day programmes are cause for eviction, and there are no exceptions to this, for any reason.
4. High expectations tend to encourage maximum performance and change.
5. Residents are encouraged to express feelings directly and openly, especially anger, which many residents have been taught or believe is the same as being 'crazy'. A staff member who is 'nice' and 'helpful' all the time, or even most of the time, is a disaster for the house, and ineffective as a role model and object for venting resident anger. There is no contradiction between anger and real caring. Indeed, they are inseparable.
6. A halfway house is by definition a situation of dependence for the resident, and the staff must make every effort to counteract that by fostering self-confidence and independence. It may be much less comfortable for a staff member to respond to a helpless plea of 'What should I do today?' from a resident with 'Why are you asking me?' and face the rage produced by such a response than to come up with half a dozen infantilising suggestions, but staff are not being

paid to be pathogenic.

7. Defeat, retreat into hopelessness, and failure are unacceptable. The worst disservice a staff member can do a resident is accept a self-definition by that resident of being a 'hopeless case', unable to change, even if the alternative is eviction from the house.

Coffee hour is the main arena where these battles are fought out, with questions of dependence versus independence and testing of limits at the centre of them. This is the most important work the staff member does. There are moments of warmth and feelings of affection as well, which have real meaning for both staff and residents because they grow out of mutual respect, anger honestly expressed, and the clear and repeated message that there are no 'mental patients' living here, only responsible adults who are in some cases residents and in other cases staff. Real warmth and affection can grow in no other ground. Without mutual respect and self-respect, there are only victims and executioners, acting out in an endless merry-go-round of passive aggressive hostilities, both residents *and* staff.

In addition to coffee hours, each counsellor meets with a sub-group of four to six residents for one and a half hours one evening a week to discuss a definite number of house chores, including rotating cooking responsibilities, for which each sub-group is responsible; problems in getting along between members of the sub-group may also be discussed. Counsellors understand they may never act as therapists or quasi-therapists providing individual counselling to residents. Residents may not enter the staff apartment, except briefly on business such as paying rent, and counsellors may not enter residents' rooms, except briefly on business such as making repairs or at morning rounds. There are no private relationships of any kind between counsellors and residents. Residents who wish such relationships are referred to outside psychotherapy or counselling.

Finally, counsellors are instructed to respect privacy and handle issues involving residents with their full knowledge. No information is offered to or accepted from other mental health workers, family members and so forth, about what the resident is or is not doing, how the resident is or is not behaving and so forth, short of a drastic crisis, and in any crisis situation the resident is given a full report of what house staff and any other person has said about him or her. Staff refuse to hear any complaints about residents from another resident unless the man or woman complained about is present, and make it clear that anything told to one staff member is shared with all staff members.

During the day hours of the week, residents must be out attending vocational or social rehabilitation programmes, school or work if they have jobs. During those hours on the weekend, residents generally do whatever they please, without staff involvement. The day hours find staff handling administrative details, paperwork, sometimes going to school themselves, or doing whatever *they* please. On weekdays the staff member on duty at 9.00 a.m. makes 'rounds' to make sure every resident is out of the house attending a programme. Generally there are *no* acceptable reasons for being in at rounds. Residents who claim physical illness must be out to a doctor being treated for it.

To summarise, in addition to understanding and being able to act on the above, the staff members must:

- be open and honest about their own thoughts and feelings, in an appropriate way
- be unafraid of expressing their own anger when appropriate
- be able to set consistent limits and mean it
- be able to recognise and deal with their own acting-out and so serve as role models for residents
- accept limits on them set by the director
- be comfortable working with initiative and personal responsibility, and without much direct supervision
- understand that they are not hired to be therapists with a zeal to cure, like physicians of old with a zeal to bleed. They are primarily role models in handling life-problems: people whose problems are not so different from those of the 'schizophrenic' residents; who have had to deal seriously with the question of their own sanity and can work through their own fear of being 'crazy'; who are not problem-free or afraid to face their own problems, but who communicate the conviction at a thought and feeling level that change and growth are possible, if an individual decides to work for it, *and that they experience this as no less true for themselves as for those with whom they work.*

The only small problem, of course, is where such paragons are to be found.

Recruitment

The problems of recruitment begin *before* a vacancy occurs. Any unfilled staff job doubles the workload on other staff, who must stay at the house extra days to meet the requirement that at least one staff member be available at all times for crisis intervention. There is compensation in 'time and a half' for such overtime, but no compensation for the deprivation of time-off needed for rest away from the house (staff members maintain their own apartments, and *may not stay at the house on off-shift time*), the exhaustion and resentment that build rapidly during such periods of extra work, and the general decline in ability to function.

This means there must be a clear, set time agreed upon between the director and leaving staff member well in advance of termination. At least eight weeks are needed, and ten whenever possible. This period also helps the departing staff member deal with difficult feelings about separation from what has been a very intense work experience, a period of working through, which is not less important for staff and residents being 'abandoned' by the leaving staff member.

The largest source of job applicants is advertisement in the Sunday 'help wanted' section of newspapers. Notices can be sent to graduate schools of counselling, psychology and social work. Leads may come from personal contacts staff may have with other professionals working in the field, either privately or at institutions. An employment agency specialising in social work and mental health can be utilised.

Advertisements emphasise excellent pay and benefits, intensive training in a prestigious facility, and hard work, and invite applicants to send a résumé. The fact that staff must live-in part time is mentioned.

Neither treatment for emotional illness, nor past psychiatric hospitalisation is a bar to employment; indeed, in an individual successfully coping with emotional problems, such experiences constitute an asset.

Several other lessons have been learned in the course of recruitment:

1. Educational level of the applicant is largely irrelevant. There has been no correlation between staff members' educational attainment (MA, MSW, BA or high school diploma) or field of study (sociology, psychology, pastoral counselling or social work) and their ability to do the job. What has made the difference, for example, has more to do with the emotional health of the staff member than the professional education which overlays it: a staff member with an MA proved unable to deal with her own anger and had to leave the job, and a high school graduate worked out successfully. There does appear to be positive correlation between ability to handle the job and current participation

in individual psychotherapy outside working hours, principally having to do with insight gained into intrapsychic process through such experience, and used as an outside source of relief from job tensions. It is recognised that given two persons of equal health and ability, an education in psychodynamics may be useful and an asset in a staff member possessing it, provided that the staff member has been able to transfer information learned in classroom settings to real experience.

2. Beyond providing a phone number to call for an opening discussion and in a few cases indications of personal instability ruling out follow-up, résumés give little help in assessing whether someone is a possible staff member. They may be helpful in an interview itself suggesting topics for discussion, but the qualities already described which are needed in a successful worker are personal, while résumés tend to describe education and experience in formal, routinised ways.

Typically, one serious possibility may be found for every twenty-five to thirty applicants. To be sure of alternatives in case a serious prospect does not work out during pre-hiring explorations, the interviewing should not stop with the first possibility.

In a programme where interactions are extensive and intense, staff must work closely and well together. A new staff member must be acceptable to each remaining staff member as well as to the director, or the group will fail to work as a team and havoc result in the house, with residents acting out inter-staff hostilities and problems. All staff must be fully involved in selecting the new member, and any staff member has the right to reject a candidate, although this is less true for the leaving staff member.

Lastly, individual pathology in a job candidate is more likely to occur when the candidate is under constant observation by the whole staff, and the observation can be confirmed by more than one staff member. For example, candidate Bob may relate very well to both male staff members, but show unmistakable hostility to the females. Or candidate Carol may be charming, warm, and friendly with the director, but obliquely cold to other staff, showing tendencies to identify with authority and reject peers. Both would be trouble. Candidate Joe may appear depressed to staff member Bill, who is leaving, but the rest of the staff may disagree, and Bill who would have rejected this candidate if seeing him alone, may find his impending departure has left *him* depressed, and he has projected this onto his replacement, whom he is unlikely to love in any case. In another instance, a leaving staff member, who had done his job very well, admitted that he so resented his having to leave when his year was up that he found himself strongly recommending the hiring of someone he thought would be ineffective, just to 'get even'.

Given the dangers of interviews by less than full staff, and the shortage of time, a group screening process has been adopted. Up to one dozen job applicants are invited to the house for coffee, and told about the programme. This is presented as being helpful to them in deciding whether they wish to pursue their application, which is in fact true. Since they are together as a group, staff do not ask them personal questions, but experience has shown that up to 80 per cent can be weeded out, and the serious prospects asked back for the valuable individual interviews on Monday.

The Individual Interview

The director leads the interview, asking for information about the applicant's education, work history, experience with the emotionally ill including immediate family members, personal experience with emotional illness, goals, ways of handling anger, ability to set limits, understanding of being 'helpful', and other general topics. While the director and staff engage in this conversation, close attention is paid to the applicant's interactions with those present. Sufficient to ensure rejection as a job candidate would be the following:

'I don't get angry.'
'I have no personal problems myself.'
'When I get angry I just walk away and cool off.'
'I've *always* gotten along with my mother and/or father.'
'I think telling sick people what to do is bad for them' or 'good for them.'
'I think what people like this need is lots and lots of loving care.'
'I never have sexual feelings about people I work with.'
'I never have problems getting along with people I work with.'

Also looked for are denial of depression, denial of anger, lack of sense of humour, secretiveness about self, defensiveness about own personality characteristics, lack of assertiveness, inability to answer a direct question directly and directing answers only to staff, only to director, or only to one sex present, tendency to leave sentences uncompleted, seductiveness toward director or staff, lack of personal grooming, and strong expressions of need for much 'direction' or 'supervision'.

It is obvious that every human being has problems in some of these areas. The question is whether there is denial of them, and whether one or more are present to a gross degree. And when all the words are exhausted, there is, most important, the feeling that staff have about the applicant and the feeling the applicant has about him or herself and the staff that either leads to a 'no' or a 'yes'.

A candidate surviving the initial interview is asked to spend a Sunday and Monday at the facility, sleeping over in the staff apartment. During this period the candidate experiences the house and the residents, sees what staff do, and is in turn observed by the residents and on-duty staff. Unfavourable indicators are: clinging to staff, fear of or hostility to residents as a group, marked tendencies to private discussions with residents, seductiveness with residents, interactions with residents which foster dependence, and antipathy of residents to the prospective staff member, usually expressed as distant formal politeness.

During this weekend, the candidate is invited to read the daily log kept by staff, and also papers about the house; a general description of its dynamics and functioning, on setting limits, on the importance of clear communication of expectations, and on group work. There is a chance for discussion with staff and the director, and the candidate can see how the activities and house dynamics discussed in the papers are put into practice by staff.

Following the Monday night meetings, the candidate is told what the staff think of his or her interactions, and, if the response has been positive, formally offered the position. Staff pay considerable and careful attention to the reaction and comments of the residents as well, who, having experienced emotional difficulties, and recognising the damage that can be done by pathogenic staff, have a considerable investment in seeing good staff hired, and a high degree of perceptiveness of potential staff problems.

Staff Training

Training has already begun before formal hiring. The new staff member has experienced the kind of direct confrontation in the job interview that marks interaction between staff and residents, has been told what the working assumptions of staff are, as outlined at the beginning of this chapter, and seen those principles in action during the weekend trial visit.

Orientation to social and vocational rehabilitation programmes that residents attend during the day is important. A resident talking in evening coffee hour about problems with programmes at the mental health centre or vocational rehabilitation might as well be discussing life on Mars for all the house staff know about it. Unless house staff have visited and participated in the day programmes they remain mere words, and hinder staff ability to discuss them intelligently.

Similarly there is much talk of life in the hospital before the resident came to the halfway house. Staff who have never experienced life in a mental hospital may wonder whether talk of beatings by hospital staff, stealing of patients' food, favouritism, sexual abuses of patients and irrational and incompetent hospital personnel, represents reality or some exotic form of paranoia. A few days on a locked ward at a nearby mental hospital would also have a highly educational function, although possibly be more difficult to arrange.

At most, this would cost two to three working days for each new staff member, and should be delayed until the second month of work, when the new staff member is not overwhelmed with learning the routine of the house itself.

Beginning Work

When the new worker takes over the weekday shift, the first four working days at the house may begin on a weekend shift, working with another staff member before beginning work alone Tuesday night, Wednesday and Thursday. When the weekend staff member is new, there is another staff member already working the weekend as a matter of course.

As can be seen, formal training is quite limited. This is possible because the facility has a distinct theoretical point of view, a way of putting that viewpoint into practice in interaction with residents, role models for the new staff member in the director and other staff, high morale, and high expectations for residents and staff. Just as new residents are quickly absorbed into the life of the house and its atmosphere of positive change, growth and success, the new staff member is absorbed into it as well, and usually becomes a successfully functioning member of a closely integrated staff team.

The way, however, is neither smooth nor strewn with flowers.

Staff Supervision

Examples

Mary has been working at the house, on the weekday shift, for three weeks. She feels less confused, has learned how to take the rents, do the petty cash, fill out the productivity forms, met some of the people at the mental health centre across the street where most residents go for their day programmes, learned the names of the various residents, begun to form an impression of most and a relationship with some, and understands how things are supposed to operate. She can set limits, does not allow herself to become involved in doing things for residents they can do for themselves, can usually tell people when she is angry with them and why. She is not forming private relationships with residents, and when they try tells them she will talk with them in coffee hour but not privately. She feels she is learning the job, and getting favourable comments from other staff members and the director. There is just one problem: Joe. A resident. He seems to make a point of coming to coffee hour on her shift, making endless complaints about the house, the way it runs, her role and her work. She is beginning to dread walking into the social room and finding him there. She can't keep from thinking about how irritating he is. She begins to avoid interactions with him, and other staff notice this. So do a few other residents, who begin relating to her as Joe has done.

Whoever has noticed the problem gives her a chance to raise it in the Monday staff meeting. If she doesn't, other staff will, without hesitation, as it introduces a disequilibrium into the house and throws the work of setting limits with Joe on to the two other staff members, who have their hands full as it is and their own problems to deal with. Mary is asked what is going on. If she denies a problem, her actual behaviour is pointed out to her. With respect, but firmly, she is told she must deal with it.

She is invited to discuss it openly and frankly, and it is pointed out to her that denying she is in trouble will be more of a threat to her job than openly acknowledging it and trying to understand why this particular resident is getting to her. She doesn't have to be perfect, she *does* have to be honest. The discussion often leads to the staff member associating the resident with some particularly hated and loved relative, and expressing fear of rage towards both the resident and the relative; fear of losing control.

Mary is told that how she works through the intrapsychic reasons for the problem is up to her. She may discuss it with a therapist or a close friend, but staff are neither. She is also told that she has every right to be angry with the way Joe is interacting with her and to tell him so, in four-letter words if necessary, but she *must* choose between dealing with him and what he is doing, and what she is doing, or leaving, because otherwise the job will become unbearable for her and other staff. It is clear that she can discuss in future staff meetings how this problem is working out, that it will not be pushed under the rug, that other staff recognise it is difficult and may take some time to work out, and that what is not acceptable or appropriate for a staff member is acting out the problem rather than confronting it.

Bill has been a new staff member for two months. Other staff members begin to notice that on days he has rounds, he has let a resident, Arlene, stay in bed repeatedly despite 'bullshit' excuses on her part. Other women in her apartment are also beginning to stay in. The director has noticed Bill relating to Arlene in a flirtatious way in coffee hour. The director tells Bill what she has noticed, tells him to stop it, and tells him to warn Arlene of suspension the next time she is in at rounds. She tells Bill he has been around long enough to know what to do about problems of this kind: deal with them.

Jane has been a staff member for four months. She is beginning to leave her work unfinished for the next staff shift to do. She slams doors and responds to instructions from the director with mumbled angry comments, but when confronted in staff meetings by the director and other staff, says she is not angry with the director, the director is angry with her. Other staff notice her seductiveness towards male tenants in coffee hour, which she also denies, accusing other staff of 'picking on me'. In staff meetings, it becomes increasingly obvious she often says what she believes others want her to say, rather than what she thinks and feels. When this is pointed out, she says, 'OK, I'll say whatever you want me to say.' Rage contorts her face as she denies being angry.

Incidents of physical violence begin to occur among house residents, leading to three evictions in two weeks, and staff meetings become entirely focused on Jane, who grows more sarcastic and generally insulting to staff and residents. At one Monday night house meeting, residents ask what is wrong, perceiving problems among staff. They are told. Jane, still 'not angry', attacks the director in the meeting for discussing her 'in front of these kind of people'. At that point, in the middle of the meeting, without consultation, all remaining staff decide Jane has to leave, and staff and tenants tell her how angry they are at her talk of residents as 'these kind of people'. The following hour of verbally expressed rage at her behaviour leads to her resignation from staff the next day. Jane was an example of 'hiring by exhaustion' discussed above.

Mark, a new staff member, has come to his turn to cook Monday dinner for the house. In a helpless voice he asks the director how to cook the dinner and what he should cook. The director says bluntly and firmly, 'That's up to you, what are you asking me for?' Mark, furious, decides what to cook and how to cook it. The next time a resident asks him the same kind of helpless, dependent question he gets from Mark the same kind of blunt, non-infantilising, infuriating reply.

The Director

The director provides the same kind of interaction with staff as desired between staff and residents, and this is taught by direct example in living interactions rather than in lectures. The list of operating assumptions used by staff in interacting with residents is the same for interactions between the director and staff.

The director is not around too much. More than twenty hours weekly physical presence in the house begins to diminish staff sense of self-responsibility and is harmful. Supervision relies heavily on peer pressure and training by other staff. This is not a job one walks away from at 5.00 p.m. What a new staff member fails to deal with on shift awaits the staff member coming on the next shift, usually in the form of resident acting-out, sometimes in the middle of the night, requiring crisis intervention. Consequently, staff make it very clear to their new associates what is expected, indeed demanded. A new staff member who cannot set reasonable limits, or sets them but can't make them stick, causes trouble for residents and other staff, throws the functioning of the whole house off balance, and is the subject of immediate and intense peer pressure to 'shape up or ship out'.

The role of the director, in summary, is to serve as a role model for staff, to communicate that staff will have great freedom in their individual application of the operating assumptions of the house, and that they will make decisions and take action along those lines as they see fit with as little direct instruction as possible; to let staff know that their input into decisions is necessary and valuable, and, when issues arise requiring the director's intervention, to let staff know that after staff comment, the director is indeed making the decision and that staff *must* carry it out.

Other activities by the director tending to build good staff morale include:

1. Avoiding undercutting of staff authority. If staff member Bob tells resident Ronald he can't play his stereo at 5.00 a.m. and Ronald gives him an argument, Bob knows if Ronald refuses to turn it down, he has full authority to warn him of immediate suspension or eviction from the house. He does not have to phone the director to ask permission to do this, nor would he expect for one second that the director would intervene in such a situation to bypass him and set the limit with Ronald. Bob is expected to handle the problem himself, on his own authority. If he loses that by invoking higher authority, he is useless as a staff member and will be correctly perceived as powerless by the residents.
2. Handling the unpleasant decisions when necessary. If a resident must be evicted, for example for repeatedly failing to attend programmes, and the director knows there will be a strong reaction from family or other professionals involved, the decision is *not* passed along to staff, letting them take the heat later. What the director evades, avoids, or tries to escape handling, the staff will treat similarly. Many confrontations in a facility of this kind are unpleasant; emotional illness is not pretty. But a director who hides behind staff will produce staff who hide behind each other.
3. The same applies to staff problems. Tensions between staff perceived by the director require discussion, not an attitude that if one doesn't discuss them, maybe they will go away. Frankness and openness about these kind of problems require the director to be no less open to being 'called' on irrational acting-out with staff and residents as the staff members being supervised. If staff meetings fail to show criticism of the director from time to time, it is a clear signal of submerged problems between director and staff. If a director handles critical comments by hiding behind 'authority', staff also learn to handle criticisms of their work by residents in the same way, and an unhealthy milieu results. To function well and maintain a healthy milieu, director and staff must work together as a team in an atmosphere of mutual respect and trust, recognising that anger and criticism are parts of mature relationships, and that personal and interpersonal problems are solvable when handled openly and frankly.

Staff Meetings

Issues that arise during staff meetings that staff and director should be prepared to face include:

1. Working with the practised patient who recites endless 'history'.
2. Problems around setting limits with residents, and how to respond to testing of limits. Avoiding inconsistent responses from staff as a whole or individual staff members. Problems arising when residents attempt to play staff off against each other.
3. Dealing with residents who relate to staff in excruciatingly dependent and infantile ways and/or who refuse to take responsibility for their own growth and development.
4. Residents who appear to be in trouble: withdrawing into their rooms, failing to attend rehabilitation programmes, interacting only in hateful or hostile ways with other residents and staff, showing overt signs of psychotic behaviour.
5. Staff members who have been 'gotten to' by a resident and are experiencing embroilment in feelings of murderous rage, fear, loathing and/or sexual fascination with that resident, and may or may not be fully aware of their loss of perspective. This is sometimes verbalised as 'being driven crazy by' the resident,[2] or incessant talking about the resident.
6. Feelings of the same kind between staff members, to the extent they begin to be acted out and interfere with ongoing work.
7. Staff member's fear of becoming psychotic, usually experienced between the second and fourth month of work.

Many others could be listed, but these tend to show faithful regularity.

The form of the meeting is simple. The director names a resident and asks for any comments on problems, continuing until the entire list of residents is completed. This is followed by a call for discussion of inter-staff problems.

In addition to doing the practical work needed to keep the house going, the Monday staff discussions also serve as role models for sub-group meetings led by staff members in the absence of the director, and to some extent for those parts of the evening coffee hour where serious discussions or problems arise.

Supervision must also take into account the different stages of development of individual staff, just as staff as a whole take account of those stages in following the course of a resident through the house programme.

While the length of the stages varies, depending on the integration and ability of the individual staff member, a similar pattern tends to recur.

Confusion and Good Behaviour. The new staff member does not fully understand what the job is or how to do it, relying heavily on other staff and following their motions and example. There is an earnest desire to please, to do well, and to get through the probationary period without being fired. The director is frequently regarded as a terrifying mother-father figure who becomes angry for incomprehensible reasons, cruelly evicts helpless 'mental patients' who don't pay their rent or who smoke dope in the house, and yells at staff members and residents. Somehow, though, other staff members seem to know what they are doing, or at least act like it, so maybe there is hope for the new staff member as well.

Testing. The new staff member is managing the day-to-day work, has established relationships with other staff and residents, has survived coffee hours without collapse or major disaster, no longer expects to hear from the director and other staff when something is done well, and is increasingly getting 'hassles' from the residents, who are beginning to test the new staff member's ability to set and enforce limits and acknowledge emotional weak spots. Frustration and anger begin to grow, and the staff member begins to 'hassle' other staff and, more cautiously, the director, in the same way residents are treating the new staff member. Things start getting personal as the new staff member acts out with staff the difficulties that are being experienced in relations with residents and *their* acting-out. At some point, the new staff member and the director yell at each other, find they have both survived and that neither is a doormat, and begin to trust and respect each other. The same usually occurs between new and old staff, and between new staff and residents. This was the point where Jane, discussed above, failed, unable openly to test her ability to express and survive anger.

Intimacy. Going from bad mother-father and nasty sisters or brothers, the new staff member experiences a period of syrupy warmth for other staff and the director. Partly a result of relief that accumulated anger has been expressed, and partly a nostalgic phantasy of having at last found a perfect family, the new staff member has not yet realised that the staff is not *really* a family, and far from perfect. The phantasy soon dissolves as hassles continue, but from it the new staff member emerges with a sense that other staff are usually, if not always, rational and sensible, capable of being trusted with discussion of one's difficulties at work, and really committed to helping each other and residents function as responsible adults.

Autonomy. The staff member has a sense of knowing what to do, how to handle most situations, and is comfortable with making innovations in house routine and activities. Setting and enforcing limits with residents is no longer a struggle, and feelings of pride in work, self-confidence, and developing skills predominate. Other staff and the director are seen more as human beings and less as phantasied family members, and the relationship shifts to that of extremely close and valued colleagues. A new staff member has probably come along, and now the ex-new staff member becomes in turn a role model, teacher by example, and hassler.

Separation. Just at the flowering of abilities, the staff member realises that there are about three months left. This chilling thought is at first ignored, pushed away, denied. But *sic transit gloria mundi.* It is impossible to ignore. Residents begin to ask when he is leaving. Other staff and the director begin to discuss when to run want ads. Residents interact more heavily with staff who are not leaving, beginning to prepare themselves for the difficulties of separating from the departing figure. Depression and morbid gloom may fill the departing staff member as he wonders how he will survive 'out there', just as residents whose year is up face leaving with fear and anxiety. Rage against remaining staff is not unknown either, along with a conviction that the entire facility will collapse into rubble with his departure.

At this point, the director and remaining staff also have feelings about the separation to deal with, and discussion of those feelings in staff meetings is helpful if not dwelt on endlessly. One objective is to do as much as possible to minimise regression of the staff member before actual departure, which can show itself both as a return to the low-level functioning of the first weeks of work, and in acting out in interactions with residents, failing to set and enforce limits, losing rent money and petty cash, breaking house dishes and equipment by clumsy accidents, and myriad other indications of separation anxiety. Not all staff carry on to these extremes, and many handle separation in a mature way, but it is wise to be ready for anything.

And that, after all, is what the staff of a halfway house have been learning to do since the day they step through the door for the first time.

Notes

1. Conversations by the writer with Richmond Fellowship personnel, New York, 1974.
2. See H. Searles, 'The Effort to Drive the Other Person Crazy', in *Collected Papers on Schizophrenia and Related Subjects* (International University Press, New York, 1965), Ch. 8.

15 THE HOSTEL AS A THERAPEUTIC COMMUNITY AND THE IMPLICATIONS FOR TRAINING (UK)

Elly Jansen (Transcript)

The basic question, 'what are hostels for?' has not proved a very comfortable question, and in honesty we have had to answer that many hostels exist to fulfil the demands of the 1959 Mental Health Act without really trying; and that some exist because trying was given preference to planning, or planning was undertaken without reference to the needs and what could be found out about *whom hostels are for*.

This question must be examined, repeatedly and at length. It is obvious that

- we have to come closer to a definition of realistic aims of hostels and a discovery of which patients may benefit from what kind of hostel, and how they may be selected or identified
- we have to look at the problem of staffing, the recruitment, training and support of staff, their status, conditions and job satisfaction, and to recognise what is lacking
- we cannot escape looking at the relationship between the hostel and other agencies, especially the hospital – the referring and treating agency – in order that mutually the best use may be made of the facilities provided
- we need to establish who should pay the cost and how available funds can be used to a greater advantage.

If no steps are taken to examine these issues, enthusiasm to provide hostels will be as defeating as is indifference. And it is indeed not easy to discover the facts. For a start, there is little written on the subject, and what is written is usually in the form of an idealistic, sedate account of tidy, well-behaved communities where all the contingencies are taken care of, but where problems do not interfere, apart from such simple ones as, for example, finding suitable staff – or suitable residents! Having lived for over ten years in therapeutic communities of one kind or another, many of the descriptions and expectations given appear to me to be strangely out of touch. The nature of the community interaction, the transaction, the philosophy, the underlying assumptions of a community, are not often described.

Maybe the doers are not writers. It is clear that as a rule the writers are not doers.

A few surveys have been undertaken by, for example, Robert Apte, who covered 25 short-stay hostels, and by Dr Temple Phillips and Dr Alison Campbell, who covered respectively local authority hostel provision over the whole country and that of Lancashire County Council.[1] From the various surveys, contradictory conclusions emerge: Dr Orwin says in *The Lancet* that 'hostels for patients not requiring the full services of the Mental Hospital have unfortunately not been forthcoming in anything like the number required'.[2] Phillips says that 'many hostels in the provinces are *underoccupied*'. Apte says, 'If there is no waiting list, the [hostel] services are known and vacancies exist, it can be assumed that there is insufficient demand within that geographical area.'[3] But can this be assumed? The answers to Phillips's questionnaire gave such reasons for underoccupancy as 'reticence of mental hospitals in referring suitable cases'; 'lack of understanding of the true function of the hostel on the part of the hospital staff'; 'lack of enthusiasm on the part of the hospital staff'; 'lack of enthusiasm on the part of the consultant'. In 1968 the Richmond Fellowship sent out a questionnaire to hospitals on policies in prevention and aftercare, the response to which conveyed a strong wish for the provision of further hostels. A typical reply reads: 'A great need exists for such accommodation and should such become available great use would be made of it by this hospital. I live in hope!' It has been implied that without much guidance a revolution could take place which would make central and local government health services, so far hardly connected, collaborate to the full in planning an efficient aftercare service and financial policy. Is that not expecting too much? If grants are made available from central finance, conditions for detailed plans and policy need to be attached based on what has already been learned in the field. The strains of bad planning and haphazard intake land on staff who have to cope with the results, which may be fatal to the long-term usefulness of the hostel.

How does the law of supply and demand operate in the hostel field, and anyway, who is making the demand? Usually not the patient or his family! The hospital, as has been suggested, may for reasons of covert rivalry or lack of time or initiative, not make the demand. Or the supply may not be considered to come up to scratch – which may indeed be the case! Figures stare us in the face, pronouncements are made on the basis of them, and these are acted upon, but where is the forum in which an appraisal can be made? There is always one criterion to fall back on: finance! What costs much money is bad, what costs little is better. The country needs to economise and the economies are clearly indicated; but are they? The divisiveness of our welfare state has been highlighted, resulting, for example, in the pressure to keep people in hospital because their keep would have to come from a different administrative pocket if they were to live in a halfway house. Orwin comments: 'As these hostels would be substituting for Mental Hospital beds, Local Authorities may understandably be reluctant to subsidise the running down of the mental hospitals.' She says – and I think rightly – that 'This highlights one of the weaknesses of the Mental Health Act, 1959', but not for the reason which she then gives, that 'prophylaxis and after-care are specifically delegated to local authorities which lack the resources to fulfil them'.[4] She implies that the hospital possesses the resources for community care and should continue statutory responsibility, a point of view which would go against the spirit and insight of the Mental Health Act. This control of the clinician over the hostel staff appears to be tacitly supported by Dr York Moore, who felt that hostel staff should not be supplied with the available information in written form. The rationale for this is to achieve flexibility and quick admissions: but this can be achieved in spite of supplying the necessary records. It is true that so far the community has not developed the necessary expertise, nor can it as long as there is a parochial spirit in financing hostel facilities, research and training. The lack of coordinated administration and financing may well be costing the country money, as well as impairing the lives of people! Although so much is at stake, there appears to be no concerted effort to establish a consistent policy in this field. The point at question is whether sufficient and reasoned pressure can be put on the ministry to look at its financial policy and give it an overhaul.

But what about the use of our existing hostels? What are they for? Who are they for? What right expectations can we have of them? How can we use them best? What do we demand of staff, and do we, in a variation of St Augustine's words, 'grant them the things which we require'? Many patients can live without causing undue strains within the community and are kept in hospital or are discharged without sufficient support to find their feet. The hostel is more likely to be utilised for the chronic patient about which the hospital staff feel guilty or specially concerned, rather than for those who could use the hostel to prevent possible relapse. Both need the halfway house. The relatives of the mentally ill often cannot or should not have to cope. Those who are spared this problem in their family are not as a rule eager to introduce someone who may kindle their private fears or who may pose a real problem or create an invasion of family life through manipulation, dependency or withdrawal. A halfway house is not just needed on the patients' side; the community at large also needs a halfway house if it is to come to terms with both internal fears and external behaviour problems, often displayed as much in society at large as in 'sick' people. The community needs the halfway house to overcome reluctance for involvement and to understand and accept their solidarity with 'the patient': the mad or sad or bad within.

Having excused the community from *full* reponsibility for the ex-patient, the question arises – who will carry the can? The staffless house naturally presents itself as a godsend. The difficulties in finding the additional funds for staff salaries, as well as the right kind of staff, have no doubt contributed to this idea, as well as the more positive reason of realising the appropriateness of this solution for a certain kind of patient (or the unacknowledged punitive wish to let them take it out on one another). Dr Clark from Newport appears to be very sanguine about the advantages of the group home without staff. He says: 'The experiment of establishing these homes has been so successful that my committee have accepted my proposal not to proceed with the original plan to construct two [30-bedded] hostels.' The question is, what is his criterion of success? One-fifth of the population of 50 returned to hospital since the inception of the scheme in 1962; three-fifths of the patients are still in the homes; of the remaining one-fifth, two died and eight left and managed independently. How satisfactory is that success rate and, moreover, what happened to those who did not fit into the scheme? In the summary Dr Clark gives, the criterion appears to be strongly that of economy, i.e. the project is successful financially. No doubt the staffless homes, as well as the boarding-out schemes, are a necessary and useful part of community care, but the staffed hostel is more likely to be the obvious halfway measure between living independently and requiring the services of the mental hospital; the fellow patient or the average family is not usually in a position to provide skilled support.

The pertinent question is whether staff can function at a level where they can provide this skilled support and not lapse into a custodial or merely parental role. It is often taken for granted that a patient leaves hospital when he is 'well' again, but this may mean that he is no longer in the same acute state of pain or disease. He or she has not necessarily gained any understanding of the factors which made for a breakdown or found more satisfactory ways of relating. But even when this is the case, it is at the time when a person is undertaking responsibilities again that he will specially need skilled support. Great skills are required from the Warden: the ability to help in the assessment and selection of the most suitable residents, to create a helpful social atmosphere, to gauge when people are ready for work and help find the appropriate job, to encourage useful contacts in and with the community at large. Also the Warden's so-called 'practical support' over against the social worker's 'skilled case-work' support is a dichotomy which the problems of the job do not justify. The weekly group meeting where problems of the house come into the open, would be ideally conducted by the Warden, who at other times needs to be the expert where the management and the functioning of the community is concerned. The Warden has a major responsibility in training auxiliary staff, and the whole staff team need to learn to understand and cope, to acquire the appropriate skills and techniques as they are the team who in the daily living with the residents have to provide the necessary conditions to make the therapeutic community a possibility. This is not to say that the social worker has not a very important role to play in supporting the Warden, exploring the task with him and enabling him to contain the manifold problems, and helping him to gain skill and confidence as a manager of a therapeutic community. This need showed up particularly strongly in discussion with staff of halfway houses in America who were working in isolation and felt that they were groping in the dark and lacking informed support.

What are the conditions for a therapeutic community? The term 'therapeutic community' has been borrowed from certain mental hospitals which, although usually expecting staff to set the boundaries and carry final responsibility, rely to a large extent on the potential of members of the patient group to help one another and to explore difficulties in relationships together. The difference from the mental hospital approach lies mainly in the presence of reality demands of the halfway house which as a social unit has more potential for normalcy and the discouragement of excessive exploration of childhood problems and of sickness and symptoms, which tends to be more prominent in the protected treatment situation. It is often thought that the 'enlightenment' of the halfway house consists of being very permissive and in fully accepting acting-out, and aggressive or regressive behaviour, and that it is repressive to discourage or check this form of self-expression. The staff can collude with these 'progressive' expectations and with the residents' demands, which, if unmet, will make the staff unpopular (and to be unpopular we all wish to avoid). To be the therapist (i.e. to closet oneself with one resident and to be accepting), to be nurse or parent-figure, is often a much more desirable role than that of someone concerned with what a fellow member of the community is doing with himself and towards others, and whether he is working towards the goal of rehabilitation.

Rules are often seen in terms of regimentation and as overlooking the rights and needs of individuals. Yet the staff have to learn, and it often takes them a long time, that it is quite essential to have certain expectations, and that the programme of rehabilitation, of adaptation to independent life, requires a structure, but a reasoned one; also that community life may require certain measures which are not necessarily in the direct interest of every individual all the time, e.g. the question of routine. It is not surprising that the exercising of responsibility, which the patient has given up by virtue of his breakdown, is the very issue over which the main fights will be fought, often in a roundabout fashion, by manipulative acts, which corner and threaten staff and make life uncomfortable. To keep the issues clear and maintain a firm and consistent position, staff will need a great deal of support, of opportunity to compare notes with others in the same sphere of work, and of learning from those who are thoroughly conversant with the problems.

The staff have to be very aware not only of what is going on within the individual, but also of what the group is doing. They have to be at the same time accepting of infantile needs which manifest themselves, but also able to discourage unhelpful acting-out such as finding scape-goats or monopolising staff time. The challenge to the staff will not necessarily be to 'take matters in hand', but to enable the group to mobilise their own abilities, to recognise and resolve these difficulties, and to treat the individual as a grown-up and respect him as a person, with his own point of view and rights of decision-making.

The role of the staff member is a particularly difficult one in that he is both the social worker and part of the environment through which the resident needs to come to terms with his problems, the person to whom and about whom many complaints of residents are made. He lives 'on the job' and is expected to do without traditional barriers which might prevent encounter, yet he needs to maintain a necessary distance and insist on his own rights and needs. It takes a good deal of maturity, and for many staff the necessity to contain conflicts whilst working through and thinking out the issues, before they can cope with this dual role and live reasonably comfortably in the community.

In addition to coping with their role in community relationships, staff need to learn to run a household. The house itself is part of the environment, and the requirements of running a halfway house form a useful opportunity to involve residents in realistic work and responsibility and teach them necessary household skills. Dr Knight of Hertfordshire County Council has emphasised the need to plan purpose-built hostels to meet a variety of purposes so that new understanding of the needs would not render the buildings 'white elephants'. Such caution is no doubt commendable but one might go further in defining the purpose of the hostel, and it might be found, for instance, that to purpose-build is defeating the purpose of rehabilitation. There is no doubt that labour-saving devices and good physical standards are a necessary requirement but these should not be too far removed from the conditions to which the residents will have to adapt. The best aftercare may therefore well be effected in an adapted family house accommodating a group, at once sufficiently small and large (e.g. between twelve and twenty) to allow each member to participate in the domestic running and maintenance, and in planning and implementing decorating schemes and other changes.

If the work of the hostel is genuinely going to be the concern of the wider community, and real integration is to take place, the staff need to initiate and further neighbourhood participation, and cope with fears of patronage, rejection or invasion on the side of the residents, and fears of embarrassment on the part of the neighbours. Much is made of the resistance by local residents to having hostels in their area, but in our experience this is a matter of approach. The official letter preceding planning permission is virtually an invitation to raise objections. What needs to be got across, and which we have found is responded to, is the right of people to live in that area, and their need to be made welcome. Staff who have undertaken the visiting have invariably found the neighbourhood willing to help with the setting up of the house, and to participate in the life of the community, in spite of the problematic nature of the work, and fears and phantasies which have to be overcome. In this respect the

Richmond Fellowship may well be at an advantage in its demonstrable need for practical help from the neighbourhood, through which, nearly imperceptibly, integration and education comes about.

It may appear that to undertake this work *ein Herrenvolk* (supermen) are needed; where can the above-described specialist be found? Some feel that the obvious choice is the mental nurse. Orwin says, 'An indirect advantage [of the hostel] would be the provision of an outlet for senior mental nurses from the Mental Hospital . . . who often have a special liking for their long-stay patients.'[5] Mountney suggests that 'Hospital experience may well be a counter-indication for this work.' This is perhaps borne out by Apte who states that 56 per cent of long-stay hostel residents were people who were able to leave the hostel and live independently, but no plans were being made for them.[6] Hostels as well as hospitals can encourage dependency and allow patients to become static, and unnecessarily take up permanent residence, often in very comfortable surroundings, for which they do not carry any responsibility, and to the detriment of themselves and the ratepayer. The keynote must be fostering independence, and the mental nurse of the traditional hospital will need a thorough re-orientation when working in the hostel. The same goes for a social worker, albeit to a lesser extent, in that the focus of the social work training often still lies in the person-to-person counselling or case-work relationship – the areas of group work and community work not being covered, nor allowing for the recognition of a 'total' environment relationship. It may be said that the trained person is unlikely to collude to the same extent as the untrained person, but our experience in the selection of staff is that salient factors are the personal qualities of staff and their motivation, which are augmented by the training and experience they receive on the job and in service. It will not be easy to provide a full-time training as the Williams Committee suggested which is as effective as in-service training, and the latter will always remain necessary.

The personality of the staff needs to be taken into account where the appointment for a specific hostel is concerned. It is often quietly assumed that all hostels need 'a certain type' of staff, but although there may be people who could cope with almost any type of halfway house provision, others can make a much better contribution in one sphere rather than another. It has been pointed out that it is important to differentiate hostels and plan them for specific categories of problems or for certain groups of people. This differentiation has been a development in the Fellowship, which has taken place quite naturally. In ordinary life a certain amount of social selection takes place and we have made provision for this within the Fellowship. Another development which came about pragmatically was the differentiation between the longer-stay and shorter-stay hostels. If a society or local authority runs a considerable number of hostels, much more experimentation can be undertaken. In addition, instead of having to refuse a resident because he does not fit into the nearest hostel at a particular time, he can be accepted in another one, especially in an area such as London where many hostels are needed. In making special provision for adolescents, for students, for mothers with young children, for people with addiction problems and so on, an organisation is able to make the best provision for a particular kind of patient, not least because it provides opportunities for staff to use their specific interests and ability to a larger extent. Staff can be given a training placement in one hostel, and be given an appointment in another, where they may best be able to work with the community and the staff team. Whilst staff are scarce countrywide, the Fellowship has no problems in attracting applicants, presumably because of the appeal of the more specialised work, the level at which it can be conducted and, above all, the training facilities available.

It has become accepted that the therapeutic community approach is a major factor in getting residents functioning again. It is not always recognised that staff also need a body of peers with whom to explore and compare difficulties, preferably with the help of a consultant, who can assist them in their task and is able to clarify the issues. Although training schemes have been in existence since the Fellowship started in 1959, it was only during the following three years that, in consultation with the Tavistock Clinic, a systematic training programme was planned and established. From the problems encountered in running hostels, it has emerged that staff training needs to take place in four main areas: there is a clear need for academic training in the field of development and social psychology and psychiatric theory; the staff need seminars in which they can bring their practical problems in case work and group work to the fore; they need the opportunity to experience and understand some of the characteristics of groups as well as their own reactions by participating in study groups; and they require general acquaintance with the practical details of the work, such as household management, keeping records, administration and first-aid. The training needs also to aim at the development of a businesslike attitude on the part of the staff, and particularly the Warden, in regard to his employers. The problems with which staff have to cope are often such that they in turn may wish to act out and attach their feelings to inappropriate issues, particularly in relation to the parent body who leaves them to carry the can, and expects them to tolerate pain. To recognise the issues and distinguish the wheat from the chaff, and to make representation in an appropriate manner, should be an object of the training. Whilst there is an ongoing task of evaluation, it has so far appeared that in principle the model is an appropriate one, helping staff to gain skill and confidence, and to use the scope of the work within the existing structure to a greater advantage.

Notes

1. R. Apte, 'The Transitional Hostel in the Rehabilitation of the Mentally Ill' in G. McLachlan (ed.), *Problems and Progress in Medical Care* (Oxford University Press, London, 1966); T. Phillips, 'Hostels for the Mentally Disordered', *The Medical Officer* (1966); A. Campbell, 'Characteristics of 352 residents and 119 ex-residents of 14 Lancashire C.C. hostels for mentally disordered adults', *The Medical Officer* (5 January 1968), p. 3.
2. *The Lancet*, 20 March 1965.
3. Apte, 'Transitional Hostel', p. 168.
4. *The Lancet*, 20 March 1965.
5. Ibid.
6. Apte, 'Transitional Hostel', pp. 178–9.

16 THE TRAINING OF HALFWAY HOUSE STAFF (UK)

Maryann C. Phillips

The contradictions and paradoxes of the halfway house create special problems and challenges. On the one hand it is more protective, nurturant and accepting than many other social units in an open society. On the other hand the halfway house makes explicit some limits, requirements and standards which would not be viable as explicit restrictions on behaviour in other adult groups. For example, rules may prohibit addictive drug-taking or sexual behaviour within the house, or require that the resident seek and find employment. He is expected to have a high level of personal commitment to the house as shown by his attendance and participation in group meetings.

Similarly the halfway house staff member is allowed in some respects greater freedom and flexibility than would be the case in a job in other organisations. At the same time, his personality, values, attitudes and behaviour are assessed as relevant aspects of his suitability for this work. In another kind of job such an assessment would be considered irrelevant, indeed an invasion of his privacy. He is expected to demonstrate considerable personal involvement and commitment to the work as well.

In this chapter I wish to explore the extent to which these same contradictions may occur within a training programme for halfway house staff; to suggest ways in which the structure and methods of the training programme serve as an important model for staff in their relationships with residents in the house; and to describe a new course in the Richmond Fellowship training programme which may provide an alternative to some of the discussed contradictions. I have not lived in a halfway house as either staff or resident, and so my comments are drawn from my work as tutor on the Richmond Fellowship training programme. I was for several years an outside consultant to group dynamics sessions and application groups; I am presently Field Skills Convenor and seminar leader. I am also a member of the Richmond Fellowship training subcommittee, and have been involved in recent revisions of the training programme.

The Richmond Fellowship provides its own training for staff in the absence of outside courses which address themselves to the comprehensive teaching of the skills and knowledge in this field.

Courses are held at the Fellowship college one day a week for six 10-week terms over two years. This is initiated by an intensive one-week course, and augmented over the two years by two-day workshops. The major part of training is, of course, in-house. House groups, staff meetings, informal communication, supervisory sessions, and the experience of the work itself are an integral and continuing part of the staff member's working life. In this chapter, I shall address myself to the central training programme only.

The sessions of the central training programme include such seminars as human growth and development, elements of psychiatric practice, field skills, residential management skills, case and group work, group dynamics sessions, sociology etc.

The Goals of the Training Programme

These might be grouped as follows:

Training

To bring each staff member up to a minimum standard of working as defined and required by the employing organisation. Purposes include:
– to convey information
– to communicate and maintain the organisation's values
– to enhance skills and teach new ones necessary for the work.

Education

To encourage and inspire each staff member to reach his own maximum capacity for work. Purposes include:
– to excite intellectual curiosity
– to stimulate personal growth
– to encourage flexibility and openness to new ideas
– to provide some conceptual frameworks for the practical work.

Management

To give support to staff, maintain open communication in the organisation, and encourage effective and smooth functioning. Purposes include:
– to give support to staff
– to help staff maintain a perspective on the more enveloping aspects of residential work
– to provide a common basis for discussion among staff
– to enhance co-operation and communication.

In many respects these goals overlap. However in some important respects they are contradictory or even mutually exclusive. Can one both maintain the organisation's values and encourage openness to new ideas? How does one stimulate and challenge individuals, yet give the group a common basis for discussion? Put succinctly, what happens when the organisation as employer conflicts with the organisation as educator? To illustrate some of these problems I want to discuss the group dynamics sessions which form part of the Richmond Fellowship training and to raise issues regarding assessment of staff as part of a general training programme.

Group Dynamics Sessions

The inclusion of group dynamics sessions in the Richmond Fellowship training programme highlights one area of conflict: under what condition is it necessary, wise, ethical, or beneficial to require staff to participate in training events which are designed to engage people personally and liable to lead to anxiety and exposure? That the Fellowship should deem it necessary to provide training in group processes is not surprising, as the halfway houses work on the group/ therapeutic community model. As in other types of caring professions, some interpersonal skills can be learned only through experiential techniques. There are precedents from fields like psychoanalysis, where the patient role is a prerequisite for the analyst role, and social work where personal supervision precedes independent case work.

Richmond Fellowship training frequently begins with a one-week orientation course on the Leicester-Tavistock model of small group, large group and inter-group events. There are small group sessions weekly thereafter for three terms over the two years. Three aspects of these group dynamics sessions raise particular issues: First, attendance is compulsory (as for all other training events); secondly, members of a group are colleagues in the training programme and sometimes house colleagues as well; and thirdly, while some group consultants are brought in from other institutions, some consultants in the one-week course may be drawn from among the Richmond Fellowship full-time staff whose primary duties are managerial within the organisation.

Disadvantages

How does one stimulate curiosity and personal growth under a required attendance rule? How does one encourage openness and communication among staff in the presence of a consultant who is an employer-manager outside the group sessions? Can group explorations of authority and leadership be safely tested in the group with the consultant in such a dual role? To what extent does the group dynamics experience of interpretative learning about unconscious group processes provide members with an inappropriate model in the co-operative work required in the house situation? The extent and power of these 'double-binds' raise serious questions about the inclusion of such sessions in the training programme. One alternative is to send staff to outside agencies for the group dynamics training. A second alternative is to take full account of the conflicts inherent in the situation and where possible to use them as part of the learning situation. Where such conflicts cannot be avoided and cannot effectively be used for learning, protective steps must be built into the training session itself.

Advantages

I want to argue here that the second alternative is feasible and arguably is essential as part of the training for halfway house work. The double-bind conflicts are just a sample of the kind the halfway house embodies as its working milieu: halfway nurturant and protective, halfway restrictive and demanding. The challenge lies in the paradox.

The parallels between his own experience of the group dynamics sessions and the resident's experience of the house can provide valuable perspective and empathic understanding for the staff member. But the parallels need to be drawn clearly and repeatedly in the training. This can be done via application seminars. In the Richmond Fellowship, these occur at mid-term and end of term. Lectures also provide important conceptual material which can be used to understand the experiential elements of training. It is my experience that much of the value of experiential techniques can be lost or misapplied if there are not systematic attempts to conceptualise the experiences and apply them to the work situation. In application seminars, staff are asked to present in detail some recent group meeting in the house. The group, with the help of the seminar leader, then analyses the events of the group meeting in group dynamics terms, referring to relevant experiences in their group dynamics sessions. To illustrate: a staff member reports that in a recent house meeting one resident remained silent and was ignored by the group. The staff member is concerned about how he could have understood what was happening and encouraged participation. The application group could try to think of a similar occurrence when a member was silent in their group dynamics sessions. How did they experience it? What was happening in group terms to maintain the silence? Did other members perceive the silent member as he perceived himself? Can any of this be used to understand what was happening in the house meeting? If so, what are the implications for encouraging participation of silent members?

Staff more typically understand a resident's behaviour in intra-psychic terms; group process analysis is perhaps less intuitively easy and more complex. The application seminar can provide an important link in showing how group dynamics analysis can illuminate house functioning. We have usually had the same person as group dynamics consultant and as application seminar leader. This has two advantages: the references to group events are shared by everyone, and the shift of role by the consultant to seminar leader helps provide a model more congenial to work in the house. Some of this application work can also be done in case and group work seminars where the primary focus is on the house.

The Training Programme as Model

Perhaps most important of all, in considering the issues raised by the group dynamics sessions, is the model which the training programme provides for the staff. The tutors, consultants and managers of a training course can and do provide models for imitation and inspiration for the staff in training. If the trainers can manage their own role conflicts, avoid unwarranted personal invasions into staff privacy, and maintain reasonable levels of expectation about staff performance in training, they can provide helpful models for staff who have to face similar problems in their work with residents in the house. Nevertheless, the model cannot be used in its entirety and staff under pressure may at times press for the provision of training methods or models which would be more immediately and completely applicable. Such methods exist and are being included in training, but there are not many readily useable models.

Staff Assessment – Part of Training?

As an employer, the halfway house organisation has the right, and an obligation to residents, to demand minimum standards of performance from its staff. It has been suggested that some of this evaluation could be included as part of the training programme, either by examination or tutor assessment.

Advantages

1. Some material is easily examinable, such as psychiatric classification, drugs, first-aid etc. There is no easily available means on the job of knowing a staff member's competence in these areas unless he is called on to use them.
2. Minimum standards can be made explicit by the organisation through the assessment procedures.
3. The burden of evaluation for the supervisory staff is shared by the trainers. The co-operative and supportive functions of the supervisor may at times conflict with his evaluative function and make him less objective.
4. Assessment can provide an incentive for staff to learn.
5. The employer may wish to evaluate the training work of staff for which he is paying a wage.

Disadvantages

1. Performance in training which may or may not be rewarded by the employer may induce compliance rather than internalisation or utilisation of the material.
2. Evaluation may arouse anxiety which, if excessive, inhibits learning.
3. Evaluation may arouse hostility which undermines the trainer's function (unless he can use it to model responses to such attitudes).
4. Many of the skills included in training and necessary for work in the house are not examinable by traditional means.

The Richmond Fellowship training course normally includes a limited assessment scheme in its training programme; evaluation is mainly on job performance. There is an attendance requirement, since the organisation pays staff for their time at training. The most obvious disadvantage of this scheme is the relative lack of an incentive to study or write projects outside the training sessions. This is not surprising given the demanding nature of the work, but it is frustrating to tutors and poses special problems when no outside work can be required or expected. When such requirements have been set, a different problem has arisen in that tutors failed to follow up staff or to notify the employer about unfulfilled requirements.

The Training Programme as Model

It is interesting to speculate to what extent the staff are responding to training as residents respond to staff in the house. Residents, it would seem, are often reluctant or unable to show enthusiasm beyond the call of duty to expectations and encouragements of staff. The inability or unwillingness of some staff to show their enthusiasm for training by outside study might be understood partially in this light. The kinds of demands trainers make, and their response to staff participation in training, may offer a model for staff *vis-à-vis* residents in the house setting.

Specific aspects of the RF in-service training programme have been designed to address some of the problems discussed above.

Field Skill Seminars

This seminar occupies one session of the weekly training over five terms. Its purpose is to enhance fundamental skills of observation and interpersonal communication. The method is experiential, but is not interpretative (as in group dynamics), nor didactic (as in conventional seminars), nor directly house-related (as in case and group work). The four topic areas include observation, role play, interperson and group communication, and teaching others.

Observation

Goals include sharpening observational skills, distinguishing between observation, inference and interpretation, comparison and sharing of observations with others, consideration of ethical issues in observation studies, analysis of the role of the observer and practice at communicating observations.

Role Play

Goals include increasing one's awareness of another's experience, awareness of one's own role and the power of role induction by others, and practice in alternative modes of responding.

Interperson and Group Communication

Goals include further practice of observational skills in participant situations, attending to cues which initiate, facilitate, disrupt and end communication, comparison of two-person and larger group interactions, increasing awareness and flexibility in communication, practice at different kinds of role interactions.

Teaching Others

An opportunity for staff to consider and try out techniques which might help residents with interpersonal skills, e.g. job interviews; includes special consideration of the role of teacher or learner.

The seminar is designed so that some event occurs during the session and is then discussed by the group. For example, in observation the group members all went to the kitchen, made a three-minute observation, wrote notes, then compared and discussed their observations in a seminar. In role play a flat-sharing situation where a new sharer was needed was acted out and discussed. In interperson and group communication members tried out greeting behaviours and explored the varying impact of different procedures and roles. In teaching others some members take on the role of teachers, others of residents, in a situation where the resident wants and needs help preparing for a job interview.

Advantages

1. Sessions are not very anxiety-producing or evasive. Each member is put in ordinary but trivial situations; the application to personal and work behaviour is obvious but is left for private consideration.
2. Material for discussion is commonplace, but real and frequently encountered. A place in training where 'normal' concerns are primary in relationship terms.
3. Seminars are lively and enjoyable, events are shared, no outside preparation is required.

Disadvantages

1. Adequate tutorial staffing is hard to obtain; a seminar leader is best prepared by himself having been a member of such a seminar.
2. Expensive to run: groups need to be small (about eight) and audio-visual equipment is an advantage.
3. Staff may find it embarrassing to role-play.

There are many other issues concerning training of halfway house staff which could be raised. Is training best carried out by the employing organisation or by an outside organisation? How far should training be aimed at social work in general and how far at the residential situation only? To what extent do specific training sessions perform the necessary function of putting in perspective the in-service training which takes place the whole time in an innovative therapeutic community? How important is the professional qualification to staff?

How much and what kind of staff participation should occur in planning a training programme? To what extent could one reasonably and beneficially use staff as training tutors for their colleagues?

The contradictions of the employer as trainer provide a challenge. Decisions regarding training reflect and can directly affect the success of the halfway house ideal. The challenge lies in the paradox which is inherent in the therapeutic community situation.

17 A SPIRITUAL PERSPECTIVE (UK)

Anthony Bloom (Transcript)

Editor's Introduction

> . . . our heart is not quiet until it rests in Thee.
>
> St Augustine, Confessions, I, i.

In this section concerned with service to one's fellow men, it was felt appropriate to conclude with an address by Archbishop Anthony, despite the fact that, as he remarks, the spiritual is of a different order from the psychological: 'There is a breach of continuity.'

The idea of completeness and perfection is universally entertained in the sense of seeking after something which has not yet been attained, but which is somehow familiar: 'As the hart panteth after the water brooks, so panteth my soul after thee, O God. My soul thirsteth for God, for the living God: when shall I come and appear before God?' (Psalm 42). The origins of this experience are open to interpretation. The religious idea of a nurturing, enfolding deity is strongly linked by emotion and imagery with the parent as perceived by the child: 'Thou didst make me hope when I was upon my mother's breasts – I was cast upon thee from the womb' (Psalm 22). Is the longing for God a manifestation of insecurity? And if so, is this insecurity no more than a reflection or a consequence of man's universal life-situation; or is it a pathological state, giving rise to the desire to regress to an infantile state of dependence? Or is perhaps the infant's experience of contentment itself a reflection of man's relationship with the divine? In our struggle for enlightenment, probably most of us do not progress beyond the comprehension of the six-year-old in the following conversation:

'Who made the person who made the person who made God?'

'That has always puzzled *me*! God was always there.'

'I can't understand what eternal means: I keep thinking of it, because when I keep thinking of things I understand them. But I don't understand how anything can be eternal.'

'I have never understood it either; I don't think anyone has.'

'Thank you for saying *that*!' (emphatically and with great relief).

The spiritual perspective raises the question also: what are the springs of motivation for service to one's fellow men? Psychoanalysis has revealed the many egocentric realities which may lie behind a mask of altruism, and the individual distortions which can occur in the performance of duty – just as it has illuminated the repressed or denied positive qualities which may underlie ruthlessness. Religious motivation itself has been frequently interpreted as a rationalisation for more infantile and self-seeking ends. What is the nature of this surrender and devotion to a higher cause? Is it a wish to relinquish responsibility or a cover for masochism? Can it be an adult commitment, a relationship within which the person may find wholeness?

Commitment to God has not always been felt to be an easy path, and the demands of the sacrificial life have been met with resistance:

> I fled Him down the nights and down the days;
> I fled Him down the arches of the years;
> I fled Him down the labyrinthine ways
> Of my own mind; and in the midst of tears
> I hid from Him . . .
>
> (Francis Thompson, 'The Hound of Heaven')

Yet the sacrifice of self can lead to a joyful transformation, and there remain compelling examples of people who have lived a life of service, without the sense of reluctant or partial giving, and without superiority or separateness from those served. The perception of the good of others as one's own, can lead to a reconciliation of potentially conflicting needs, and render irrelevant the concept of sacrifice.

In terms of human suffering, also, the spiritual dimension intrudes on our rationality. There is a dimension in mental suffering (as there is in ecstacy) which would be neglected if the question of man's spiritual nature were not considered. The issues of individual value, and of the purpose of human existence, are issues which 'puzzle the will' and call for acknowledgement. It may be that the individual, whether well or sick, will derive great comfort from his certitude that God has willed him, and that whatever the vicissitudes of his life, there is a life hereafter of pure joy – of unity with the divine. He may however conclude that human values do not require the context of eternity in order to invest them with meaning; and will say, with Anna Freud, 'Another life? Whatever for?!' This also requires faith of a kind, and maturity: to be capable of accepting mortality, and unity with the physical world. It may be that one must resign oneself, or choose, to live without finding or adopting any belief as to man's ultimate destiny – 'the undiscovered country from whose bourn/ No traveller returns.' In whatever direction one is compelled or resolved to go, it is necessary to recognise the dilemma, in order to come to terms with man's basic insecurity – *sic transit gloria mundi.*

A Spiritual Perspective

When we speak of the spiritual needs of people residing in a halfway house or a hospital, we have a tendency, and a wrong one, to think that only the people who are in our charge have spiritual needs. As long as we assume that all *our* needs are fulfilled, we are on safe ground and do not need to acknowledge our own problems. This is a mistake which I feel we must correct at once. The people who are in charge of others should be helped spiritually, possibly even more than the others, because they are at the giving end, and one cannot give without being replenished. One can give only when one receives, and this is something which is not always understood by staff in caring situations. Staff usually consider that they are in a position to give 'as if in no need' – or very little need – of receiving, and that they must *always* be in a position to share.

The second point that I would like to underline is that when we speak of the spiritual needs either of staff or patients, we should be aware that the life of the spirit is not simply an outcome of the psychological and cannot be achieved simply by creating psychologically 'integrated' people. There are people who are psychologically unbalanced and who have a deep and real spiritual life, and there are people who are perfectly adjusted but who have little spiritual life. There is a breach of continuity between the psychological and the spiritual. The spiritual stands in its own right and should be considered as such.

The third point, however, is that as regards being aware of our own spiritual life or that of other people, we can perceive it only to the extent that it is reflected in our minds, or has an effect on our bodies – because all activities, both of our psyche and of our spirit, are mirrored in our physical condition. This is something which I wish to bring to your attention, but on which I will not elaborate, that when something is happening in the realm of the spirit, there will be repercussions on the psychological level – and conversely, we must be aware that some psychological experiences may be reflections or echoes of what is occurring elsewhere.

I would like to give you an example of what I mean. A number of years ago a woman was sent to me by one of the Anglican religious communities. She had come as a novice. She seemed to be extraordinarily disturbed, and had been sent to a psychiatrist, who did something which happens very rarely. He said, 'This is a thing which I do not understand; it is not a psychological disturbance – it is a spiritual problem.' He showed thereby more insight than I have usually seen. Because I am a physician by profession, and had worked for some time in a mental home in France, this woman was sent to me. She began to tell me her story, and I stopped her after five sentences, and said, 'Don't go on. I will read it out for you in the works of an ascetic of the sixth century', and I read to her what she had described and the answer to it, which was nonsense in the realm of psychological readjustment, but was relevant on the level of a spiritual problem, and which proved to be the answer to this woman. This is simply to indicate that there is such a thing as a spiritual realm, and that there are approaches to it which are different from the psychological.

Although we may spontaneously encounter the life of the spirit, in ourselves or in others, we have no access to it in the sense that we cannot induce it; it is not something which we can create in people or for people. The life of the spirit is basically – whether you are a Christian or whether you have some other approach – a communion, a communication, with the divine. This cannot be engineered by human techniques, so that if we speak of the spiritual needs of people, staff or patients, we must realise that this is a sphere which is out of our control. It is that aspect which is God's 'own' territory. But there is a great deal which we can do on the human level to help people to become aware of, and responsive to, their spiritual selves. May I single out a certain number of things which I think belong partly to the psychological realm and partly to the spiritual, more to give food for thought than to provide answers.

If there is a spiritual realm, then at the root of things there is the very notion of man's destiny; it is a logical conclusion that a person does not simply exist between the narrow limits of birth and death, but there is a meaning and a future to his existence. This is the first thing which belongs to the realm of the spirit, because from the point of view of empirical observation, one can speak of a purpose or a vocation within the limits of earthly life, but not beyond it. It is by assuming that there is a spiritual dimension that one can speak of a destiny that goes beyond death. Now many people would be helped if they had an awareness that there is a vaster scale to their existence, and a vaster destiny, and not alone a life that for some is made of torment, breakdown, suffering, perplexity and death. I am not speaking of creating an illusion that there is a destiny in order to help people psychologically, but if you do believe that there is such a thing as a destiny, this should be brought into the awareness of people.

Together with this notion of destiny, there come two other notions: that of meaning and that of value. We live in a world in which everything has a concrete meaning or use, as far as our material environment is concerned. Things have a meaning, words have a meaning, advertising has a meaning. There are, however, one or two things for which there is no obvious meaning, not because they are 'optional extras', but because they cannot be resolved in empirical terms: life and death, suffering, love, beauty, art, things that cannot be assigned a meaning without a philosophical or spiritual frame of reference. So that on the human level, when we want to help people spiritually, we will have to meet face to face with the problem of meaning, and see whether things like death, suffering, duty, love, have a meaning for us – because we can obviously convey no meaning other than that which we have already discovered for ourselves.

Then, may I say something about the notion of value. There are different scales of value. There are those which are adjusted to the empirical situation, to the world of matter and the short compass of life between birth and death. If there is a spiritual level, then we may discover a quite different scale of values. This is not simply to say that we will put God first, and that then the world will take on a different set of priorities. It affects in a very direct way one person who matters supremely to each of us, that is, I myself. Where do I belong in the scale of values? Am I the absolute centre of things? Am I the aim and criterion of things? Have I the rights that a predatory animal has, or are there other scales? There can be a scale of, say, neighbourliness, a social scale of concern for my neighbour, in which my neighbour may loom very big or very small. He may be just a friendly acquaintance, he may be the object of *all* my concern – and no one has greater love than he who lays down his life for his neighbour – or he may be somewhere in between, and present therefore, a sort of balance between my rights and my duties. But there may be yet another scale, in which we discover a God who is not simply a creator, the originator of all things, but who is Love and who places us in a situation in which on the one hand, whether we are a failure or a success, whether we are good or evil, we are *loved*; and on the other hand we are *challenged*, whether we are a failure or a success, to make a success of the one thing which is possible for everyone: love. This alters everything: it means a totally new structuring of the scale of values, not simply in terms of priorities, but by which the lowest, the meanest, the most insignificant, the one who has failed totally, can discover that he has absolute significance and absolute possibilities.

And on the therapeutic level (which is not the aim of the exercise but still a valuable outcome), that discovery has great importance, because to be certain of having an absolute value, even in the face of social failure, may be a turning point in a person's recovery. One of the things that we have to rethink is the notion of success and failure, which is one of the great plagues of our society. On the spiritual scale of values, we discover that success, failure, even collapse, make no difference to being loved. There is then a sense in which a collapse on any level – illness, or mental breakdown, bankruptcy or any form of failure – is an event which can be exploited, in the best sense of the word, to achieve something constructive. In the normal way, we spend most of our lives living in an artificial way, with reference to the people who look at us, who are aware of us, who judge us, who appraise us; then suddenly, with the collapse, there comes the moment of truth. We are free – free from this kind of judgement, free to be seen and valued for the person that we are, and not for our achievements.

Let me take an example from another realm, that of psychology. I remember when I was a prison chaplain, a man said to me, 'It was such a blessing for me to be found out.' Knowing that 'found out' meant he was in prison did not make his statement obvious to me, so I said, 'What do you mean?' He said, 'You know, I was a professional thief. I tried to put my life right, but whenever I made an attempt, people began to taunt me, and say, "What's wrong with you? You're changing." And so I could never do it. The day the police got me, I could begin to change according to my desire, because everyone knew I was a thief. So I could change without being discovered as a thief.' This applies both to physical and psychological illness to a great extent. One comes to a point where one is beyond judgement because one is implicitly 'written off', or because compassion enters where judgement reigned. And this is the moment where one can begin to rethink things with honesty, and with the liberty to act in a totally new way.

Now if as I said before we are at 'the giving end', what can we give to the person who has reached this state of breakdown, in whatever way? There are two things that we can give: first, what we already possess, not by hearsay but with the certainty of our own experience; and secondly, something which is beyond our experience, but which we recognise as being beyond us, and can present to others with the truthfulness which goes with humility and which consists of saying, 'Of this I have no personal experience, but others have, and you seem to be a person capable of receiving this message which I personally have not been able to receive or make use of.' One can give what one hasn't got, provided that one has the honesty to present it as such to the other person.

Then, from a practical point of view, the way in which we approach the person in need will vary with what we are, what the other person is, and also, not least, with the specific tenets of his and my faith. Two Christians meeting on these terms may find their common ground in the Gospel. But if I meet a Buddhist, a humanist or an atheist, I cannot force my creed upon him. I can share with him all that I have, but I must be careful to respect his attitudes. And that means, if you wish to relate this to the setting of the halfway house, or the consulting-room, or the study or drawing-room in which you see people, there will be a great variety of approaches and a variety in what you may and may not do on moral grounds.

I said that we must be careful about the notions of giving and receiving, and what I mean is this. I spend my life seeing people in interviews about their problems. I spent fifteen years of my life as a physician and twenty-five years up till now as a priest, so the situation is one which I know very well. What is 'giving help'? You may imagine, and the patient may imagine, that he comes with a question and you are there to give an answer. Well for one thing you know perfectly well that you have not always got an answer to give, but even when you have, what are you receiving in exchange? You give compassion and a listening ear, and possibly technical advice. What is the other one, the person who has come to you giving? Something which is immeasurably more significant and precious in terms of humanity: he gives you his confidence. He comes to you with a readiness to reveal himself, to let you in, to allow you to see things which he is afraid of seeing. He is prepared to be more open with you than he is with himself, and this which he brings to you is a gift much more important in human terms than the kind of advice you can give him. I think that this is something which should be conveyed to the person who comes with a spiritual need, that he who is receiving is also giving, and that you the giver are able to receive something of great value from him.

The first problem in the realm of truth always consists in facing one's own self and, so often, when we look at ourselves we are afraid to see what we may discover. But if we remember that we belong to a world of twilight, a world where good and evil are intermingled, a world where the light shines and, although never quenched also never is fully received, if we remember that we are called to be co-workers with God in order to build out of this twilight the full brightness of a divine Kingdom, then the discovery in ourselves of what is inadequate or what is contrary or alien to the Kingdom, or what is unworthy, not only of God but also of ourselves, would be a joy, because it is only when we see evil that we can overcome it. Here, cowardice has no place; it is daring that matters. It is one of the most daring things a man can do – to stand face to face with himself and with surrounding reality, and face it squarely and face it calmly. This requires a basic faith which is so immensely important and which we must teach ourselves and others in order to acquire moral, mental and physical wholeness. This faith is complex, because it is rooted in an experience of God or in an act of supreme daring; that daring is one of the characteristics which we very often lack. There is arrogance in us, there is a sense of adventure, there is readiness to experiment, hoping that things will turn out right, but there is very little of this daring that allows us to risk all of ourselves on something which we believe is worth the risk, and to risk not in order to win, but simply because it was right to do so. William the Conqueror said, 'There is no need to hope in order to undertake, there is no need to succeed in order to persevere.'

We are a community and no one lives for himself, no one perishes for himself. Each of us is not only responsible but decisive in the destiny of others, but this community is both help and hindrance. When we speak of people who are mentally unstable or disturbed, we must remember the meaning of community. How many people would not be in the state in which they are now if they had been simply loved; if instead of being mechanically cared for, they had been loved and cared for personally and humanly. How many people break down because, at best, they are superfluous, because there is no place for them in life, because, more probably, they are in the way of others. If we could only accept that we are called upon to give to everyone around us the certitude that he is willed by God, and that our vocation is to manifest to every creature of God this basic relationship of love, which exists between Him and every creature, how many people would respond and say there is hope and there is life. There is not only a future, but even a present in which I can struggle, not through which I can struggle, but within which I can struggle building a divine Kingdom.

In our work among people who are unsettled we must aim at giving back to society people whose faith is an act of creative trust, people who in an act of creative trust are prepared to dare and to risk their own selves to face the truth of what they are and what their vocation is in a world of tension. This is why it is so immensely important to have places where people can be helped and why there must be places of training for staff where a way can be found, a way not yet clear to us, towards which we are groping, to readjust a person to a situation of tension and not to a situation of false equilibrium. We must build such places, we must gather and train such staff, we must, with all the energy of mind and person, support that kind of work in order to make it possible for anyone, however frail, to acquire the kind of frailty which does not lead to defeat, but leads to the fulfilment of God's word: 'My power is made manifest in weakness.'

Part Three

POLITICS AND PLANNING

A tree as great as a man's embrace springs from a small shoot;
A terrace nine stories high begins with a pile of earth;
A journey of a thousand miles starts under one's feet.

Tao Te Ching 64

EDITOR'S DISCUSSION

Community mental health care, including residential care, is declared policy, and is legislated for, notably in the UK and the USA; yet over a period of approximately twenty years the gap between policy and provision has not been bridged.[1] What are the obstacles which stand in the way of implementing the policies, and how can they be overcome?

This section attempts, first, to review a number of problems in the community mental health field which are common to the developed countries of the world. They are problems which arise from past and current attitudes to mental disturbance and from the cumbersome machinery of existing systems, which tend to act like 'black holes' to consume all measures for change. Secondly, the policies and legislation of certain of the progressive countries are examined, with the aim of clarifying to what extent these have effected changes in the system.

Obstacles to Implementation of Policy: General Considerations

Funding

Among the many problems which stand in the way of community care, the reluctance of governments to fund their programmes is of primary concern. As is stated by Norman Fowler (Chapter 20): 'For the government, of course, the chief priorities are those of expenditure.' He adds that the opposition is, however, well placed to make a serious study of issues on their merits, and to plan programmes; the flaw being that, when the opposition becomes government, its priorities change. What then motivates governments to adopt humanitarian programmes which they are at best ambivalent in nurturing? An analysis in terms of political systems is offered by Scull.[2] Scull argues cogently that progressive measures in mental health, which had long been advocated, were finally accepted because they seemed to accord with budgetary needs arising from changing social and political realities. The need for capitalism to provide welfare services for the labour force, and the rising costs of that provision, have diverted an increasing percentage of the Gross National Product to expenditure on social services: in the UK, it rose from 10.9 per cent in 1937 to 24.9 per cent in 1973;

and in the US, from 9 per cent in 1955 to 15 per cent in 1969. Rising expenditure on welfare in the community, combined with other factors such as the rise in costs of equipping, maintaining and staffing institutions, and the increase in the dependent, aged population have rendered institutional care uneconomic for all groups, including the mentally ill.

The lobby for community care, which as Scull shows was already vocal in the nineteenth century, has therefore at last been able to obtain a willing ear, but not the necessary funds. 'In the circumstances, it is scarcely surprising to learn that decarceration in practice has displayed remarkably little resemblance to liberal rhetoric on the subject. Indeed, the primary value of that rhetoric . . . seems to have been its usefulness as ideological camouflage, allowing economy to masquerade as benevolence, and neglect as tolerance.'[3] This statement is substantiated by accounts of community projects (see Chapters 23 and 25) and it is indisputable that the policy of decarceration has often resulted in neglect of the client. However, Scull's political analysis ignores the possibility that governments may also reflect the *humane* concerns of society, and there are signs that the dangers of the new policies have been recognised; with what effect, remains to be demonstrated. The British government stated in 1975: 'Our aim is not the closure or rundown of the mental hospitals as such; but rather to replace them with a local and better range of facilities. It will not normally be possible for a mental hospital to be closed until the full range of facilities . . . has been provided throughout its catchment area, and has shown itself capable of providing for newly arising patients a comprehensive service independent of the mental hospital. Moreover, even then, it will not be possible to close the hospital until it is no longer required for the long stay patients admitted to its care before the local services came into operation.'[4] The proof of good faith regarding these policies will come when governments demonstrate that they are prepared to enforce and facilitate the necessary expenditure.

The Legacy of the Mental Hospitals

It has already been noted that the large mental hospitals form the focus of unrest regarding care of the psychiatric patient. Enlightened policy is committed to reduction of the institutional population, and a gradual phasing-out of the institutions. In 1961, for example, the then Minister of Health for England and Wales, Enoch Powell, declared his government's intention to reduce the bed numbers by approximately

50 per cent (75,000) by 1976.

The large psychiatric hospitals, however, far from being redundant, still play an essential part in mental health care. For example, the total psychiatric in-patient population in England and Wales has indeed fallen: from 140,162 (0.31 per cent of the population) in 1960, to 92,467 (0.19 per cent) in 1975. The number of admissions however has risen: from 114,552 in 1960 to 186,081 in 1975. Of these, only a small number form the 'new long-stay', the psycho-geriatric schizophrenics and the severely mentally impaired and multiply handicapped. The great majority are discharged within six months back into the community (the discharge figure for England and Wales for 1975 was 175,786) and may present the hospital with a 'disposal problem'. They include many for whom provision is lacking, since their care does not offer identifiable benefits to society, viz. the confused and disturbed elderly, the chronically mentally disabled who need staffed accommodation, and those with severe personality disorders. Other categories of patients who may also need, and benefit from, supportive residential care are those who have a good prognosis following a neurotic or psychotic breakdown. Hospitals therefore must ensure that the patient's needs are thoroughly reviewed, if they are not to substantiate the criticism of one of the consumers that 'there is not enough follow-up in most hospitals; one day they suddenly tell you you're better, and you are not prepared for life outside' (Christopher in Chapter 12).

There are varying accounts of the extent to which hospitals make this review, and with what results. Kathleen Jones[5] comments that, following the Hospital Plan of 1962, many different estimates were given as to the number of in-patients who were no longer in need of a hospital bed. She points out that the estimates were influenced by local and by subjective factors: the extent of active rehabilitation undertaken by the hospital; the adequacy of community facilities; the doctor's judgement of the clinical and social factors involved. In addition, several writers (for example, Elisabeth Shoenberg in Chapter 2) have drawn attention to the 'mutual selection process' by which staff gradually accumulate patients whom they have an investment in keeping. This is a tendency to which staff need to be alert, as the desire to leaven the hospital population of elderly and severely disabled may well lead to failure to pursue community options wholeheartedly. However, it must equally be recognised that many clinical staff are in sympathy with the aim of early discharge, but are reluctant to discharge the patient into a community ill-equipped to cope. In order to overcome these problems, hospitals need to scrutinise fully the reasons for admission and prolonged stay, and vigorously exploit and encourage the further development of community facilities; some clinical teams have already made important contributions in this area.

Sainsbury and Grad have fully documented their work in Chichester, in which discharges to an area with a community service (Chichester) were compared with discharges to the control area (Salisbury) over a two-year period.[6] In this example, community care is provided by the hospital service, and so is a clinical rather than a social service. It was found that the availability of a community care service increased the number of psychiatric referrals, but reduced the number of admissions (62 per cent of patients were treated entirely in the community in the research area, as compared with 41 per cent in the control area). Additionally, length of stay in hospital was reduced, the mean duration of stay being 29 weeks in the research area as compared with 42 weeks in the control area – a difference which was significantly affected by community psychiatric support given to an elderly senile population living in boarding-houses. Those patients who were admitted tended to be those whose behaviour presented severe social problems, or where social support was lacking. Discharge arrangements were found to be dependent on social as well as clinical factors, and the study looked carefully at the burden experienced by families of patients who remained in, or were discharged back into, the community. On the whole, the community psychiatric service was able to support families adequately; but it provided inadequate family support in the case of neurotic and depressive patients of working age. With this group, the research area fared worse than the control area, and the results correlated with a lack of social work support compared with the control area. In some cases an increase in stress was noticed in other members of the family. It appears likely from the account that some of the adults in this group would have been able to benefit from a residential therapeutic community, but this was not available as an option.

Flexibility of movement between various types of care was emphasised as central to a community-orientated psychiatric service. 'Hospital discharge in a community service therefore becomes a less significant event in the course of treatment, and the decision whether a patient is now ready for the critical step of leaving hospital less important than that of deciding which of available facilities is the most appropriate one in which to accommodate the patient at any particular point in his illness.'[7]

In Camberwell, London, J.K. Wing and his colleagues have documented the progress made in developing a local, community-orientated psychiatric service. It is emphasised[8] that an idealistic attempt to transfer patients wholesale from hospital into the community was not envisaged; instead, the emphasis was on shifting psychiatric assessment and care into the centre of population, and on reducing new admissions to a minimum through the use of community facilities. The problem of mental disorder was to be viewed and treated in its context: 'One has to be aware of those who contribute to the patient's illness or who are put at risk by it.'[9] In the first years of the project observations were made which are of direct relevance to therapeutic communities.[10]

1. It was found that the number of admissions to hospital in the Camberwell area increased between 1965 and 1979, in line with the national trend but at a higher rate (17 per cent for this period). Of the diagnostic categories, the one which contributed most to the rise was that of personality disorder, with an increasing ratio of in-patient to out-patient treatment. This finding was of concern to the team, since 'the value of a medically oriented setting for the treatment of this type of patient has been questioned. A subgroup of patients in this sample was studied more intensively, and the conclusion was reached that greater provision of day-care and short-term hostel accommodation might well have obviated the need for admission in half the cases.' However, there was no local authority hostel for the adult mentally ill – nor, it appears, any voluntarily run hostel catering for the area – in Camberwell at that time.

2. The team studied a number of admissions retrospectively, and considered that out of 50 patients admitted, 17 could have been helped by use of alternative resources (although five of these would have needed intensive help).[11] Case summaries were given of all twelve patients who were thought most able to be helped by alternatives to hospitalisation, and of these, the team suggested that two would appropriately have been referred to a hostel: Case 4 (a single, socially isolated girl who wanted hostel accommodation) and Case 7 (a divorced man, suffering from paranoid schizophrenia, and living uneasily with his parents). In addition, it appears from the account that Case 10 (a single woman, who was thought to have developed paranoid ideas and was socially isolated, although supported by her landlady) may well have been another patient who would have benefited from the social and personal support of a therapeutic community suited to her particular problems. The three

patients identified were without a spouse, socially isolated, and either motivated to accept residential care or with symptomatology which made independent life difficult to sustain.

3. The discharge needs of 62 long-stay patients (over six months in hospital) were studied, and a mixed group of 17 patients were found to be in need of a hostel with medical and nursing supervision. Common factors in this group were socially troublesome or self-destructive behaviour, or frequent psychotic episodes.[12] In addition, the aftercare needs of a group of 72 chronically psychotic patients were studied. It was found that at least 9, and possibly another 16, were in need of hostels or other sheltered accommodation, as part of the services essential to maintain them in the community.

A picture emerges of a wide range of appropriate candidates for hostels run as therapeutic communities. They range from the motivated and minimally disturbed, to behaviour-disordered people who primarily need the opportunity to internalise more mature attitudes and form stable relationships, and the chronically psychotic who would, in hospital, soon become the new 'institutionalised patients'.

Various projects in the United States in recent years have also probed the necessity for hospitalisation, and alternatives to in-patient care. Training in Community Living (TCL) was designed in relation to the chronically disabled psychotic patient, and was an attempt to provide an adequate treatment programme in the community. Essentials of the programme were identified as: ensuring that the patient could obtain material resources; equipping him with coping skills; motivating him to persevere; helping him to disengage from pathological dependent relationships; and providing a support system which would take the initiative in contacting the patient if he was suspected to be in need or had lost contact with the staff. All patients in the sample were accepted for the programme, whether or not they had family support. If possible, they were referred to the programme at the point of psychiatric assessment; where hospitalisation was necessary (in cases of severe psychosis, or for protection against suicide/homicide) the programme was instituted on discharge. The research subjects and the control group, who were treated conventionally in hospital, were assessed at four, eight and twelve months following the beginning of treatment. At each point the subjects revealed less symptomatology, and greater self-esteem and satisfaction with their life, and the burden on families was reduced.[13]

A very different model of alternative treatment was evolved, also for those suffering from a psychotic disorder. The treatment centre,

Soteria House, set out 'to provide a homelike alternative for schizophrenics who would otherwise have been hospitalised', and emphasis was placed on Soteria's non-medical orientation, which would reduce the likelihood of residents developing a 'mental patient' identity and enhance psycho-social functioning. The admission criteria were fairly detailed: experimental subjects and controls were those diagnosed schizophrenic, who were in adolescence or early adulthood, in need of hospitalisation, to all intents and purposes single, and had had no more than one previous hospital admission, of no more than two weeks' duration. The patients thus selected were admitted either to Soteria House or, in the case of the control group, to the community mental health centre's in-patient service, where the treatment setting was two locked wards of 30 beds each.

The treatment for the control group consisted of an active programme of evaluation by means of physical and psychological tests, history-taking and observation, combined with chemotherapy in order to suppress psychotic symptoms and disordered behaviour. The aim of the programme was to evaluate the patients as speedily as possible, and to discharge them back into the community after the shortest possible stay. The Soteria programme differed markedly on three measures: staff attitudes towards this diagnostic group; treatment methods; and timespan. Staff were concerned primarily to understand the psychotic experience and to validate the person in the psychotic state. This attitude had consequences for treatment: there was no attempt to suppress symptoms or restrict unusual behaviour (unless dangerous), and phenothiazines were not normally used during the first six weeks. Thereafter, some medication was given if the patient's condition warranted it. 17 per cent of subjects received medication, as against 100 per cent of the controls. The patient was expected to stay in the therapeutic setting for long enough to benefit from interaction with the community, rather than moving on after initial improvement. Length of stay at Soteria was around 24 weeks, as against three weeks on the ward. After four years of operating the project, some results were identifiable. The most significant findings were that the experimental group fared *as well as* the controls regarding reduction of symptoms, adjustment in the community after discharge and readmission rates. Moreover, it was felt that the Soteria patients were at an advantage in their social functioning, in that they did not acquire the identity of mental patient: 'Ex-Soteria patients are not interacting with their environment in a way that makes them look like back-ward patients . . . They are actively engaged in living – they have not had their passion suppressed or taken away.'[14]

In pursuance of the intentions of the Community Mental Health Centers Act of 1963, numerous other clinical teams in the United States have embarked on valuable although less radical programmes in community psychiatry, involving a more critical approach to hospitalisation and use of more flexible arrangements for treatment.[15]

There is now general recognition, based on numerous controlled studies, that treatment and care in the community can be both practicable and preferable to hospitalisation, which should be reserved for situations in which 24-hour medical and nursing care is needed, and/or where secure provision is needed in order to protect the person from suicidal or other violent acts. In other circumstances than these, hospitalisation tends to misuse expensive resources by overprovision, produce a self-repeating situation in which the patient is readmitted because he or she was previously admitted, and reinforce the tendency of dependent people to assume the 'sick role'. As pointed out by Wing and Hailey, amongst other writers, there is a strong possibility in many cases that, if hospitalisation is the only avenue for obtaining relief from stress, the person will develop a permanent adaptation to the sick role; whereas transitional facilities allow relief whilst enabling the person to continue to fulfil, at least to some degree, their social roles.

The challenge that now appears to confront the hospital service is to implement these findings and repeat the research programmes on a wider scale, above all using the facilities that can be provided by informed *social* rather than medical agencies. Whilst medical facilities are an essential part of the range of psychiatric facilities needed, for many people clinical treatment is minimal, routine or inappropriate; further, it has been argued that the (proper) use of authority in medical settings is no longer appropriate to the therapeutic relationship which should motivate the ex-patient to integrate and socialise.[16] The medical model and some considerations in developing alternatives are discussed below.

The Medical Model

The bricks and mortar of the large mental institutions are a powerful reminder of the dominant model influencing the understanding and treatment of mental disorders today: that is, the medical model. Any attempt to bring mental health care into the community must take the strength of the medical viewpoint into account, must decide how far (if at all) this model is of value, and what kinds of approach may otherwise be adopted. The formulation of a decisive and informed policy is, however, bound to be seriously affected by the ongoing debate on the nature of mental disturbance, and the related disputes over treatment, on which psychiatric opinion is deeply divided.

As many writers have pointed out, the advent of the phenothiazine drugs in the mid-1950s reinforced the medical model, which has retained its dominance in state treatment programmes both in the UK and in the USA. On the other hand, the cost of medication is a constant cause of concern. In England, the National Health Service drugs bill has been growing at the rate of five per cent per annum, and is projected to continue at the same rate unless economies are exercised.[17] In 1976 the NHS drugs bill totalled £450 millions[18] and of this a large percentage must have been allocated to psychiatric drugs; however, the breakdown of expenditure was not known to the DHSS at the time of writing. Prescriptions for psychotropic drugs increased by 19 per cent from 1965–70, and by 7.8 per cent from 1970–5 (47 million prescriptions in 1970, 50.9 million in 1975).

In addition, the contribution of drugs to treatment of mental illness is beginning to be more closely examined, and may perhaps now result in greater recognition being accorded to other factors. The most extreme stance is adopted by some schools of thought who see drug therapy as ethically unacceptable, requiring the urgent development of alternative methods of help. 'If one sees man as a machine, and despair as a manifestation of this machine going wrong, then it is not illogical to choose mechanistic means in order to eliminate the alleged malfunction . . . However, if one sees man as a sentient being, capable of change and choice as to his personal relationships and social organisation, then it is illogical to take a cavalier attitude towards a treatment which can lead a person to be less capable of feeling, choosing, or changing.'[20]

Other writers, whilst allowing that drug treatment can have enabling effects, have redressed the balance in favour of a combination of clinical and social measures acting together to bring about changes in the pattern of hospitalisation. Scull examines the studies on the decline in numbers of mental hospital patients, and concludes that other factors had already initiated this trend, in advance of 'the drug revolution': 'National figures on mental hospital populations, when taken by themselves, may be a seriously misleading guide to when the deinstitutionalisation process actually began. For they tend to mask the earlier changes at the local level, and to obscure the degree to which the fall in overall numbers, when it did come, represented a continuation rather than a departure from pre-existing trends.' The role of rehabilitation techniques as well as drug therapy in reversing the rising bed-occupancy in mental hospitals was also noted by Wing and Brown.[21] The White Paper, *Better Services for the Mentally Ill*, states: 'The discovery of the phenothiazines . . . was important, but one should not underestimate the significance of other developments: changes in staff attitudes; the introduction of non-physical approaches to treatment; the development of social security and other forms of support outside hospital.'[22] This more balanced perspective is greatly to be welcomed, since over-reliance on drug therapy is itself an obstacle to an objective exploration and evaluation of the underlying problems. Not only does it consume finances which might otherwise be diverted to community care facilities; it also tends to label the problems as medical, and in doing so may lower the impetus of professionals, patients and the general public alike to recognise their common humanity.

The medical model is not however reliant on drug therapy for its supremacy: it is maintained primarily by a strong emotional investment on the part of both layman and professional. The definition offered by Hoffman and Singer gives indications for the strength of its appeal: 'First, the patient is sick and neither he nor any other person has any responsibility for his sickness. Second, the doctor is an absolute authority who confers the sick role and who assumes the responsibility for treating the patient for his sickness. Third, the role of the patient is to submit to the treatment. Fourth, the immediate alleviation of suffering takes precedence over candor. Fifth, the prestige and authority . . . of the doctor must be preserved at all costs. To this end, a united front must be presented to patients at all times.'[23] Accepting this as an extreme but fundamentally accurate definition, the rewards are clear: for the patient and those close to him, relief from responsibility for the past, present and future; and for the doctor, an indispensable and unambiguous function.

The rewards of relinquishing these roles are not so clear, and are attended by the insecurity which is inevitable during periods of change, so that the collusive attachment to the medical model is not surprising. Shoenberg comments in Chapter 2 on staff's reluctance to discharge patients, on the rationalised grounds that medical expertise is still necessary for 'therapy' – in other words, that progress cannot take place elsewhere. 'We keep people until working through their problems – psychotherapy – becomes a way of life.' A psychoanalyst writes: 'When progress is slow, may this be due in part to the worker's own unconscious feelings? Perhaps we suffer a certain pain ourselves in letting the client go – similar to that which a parent feels when an adolescent son or daughter no longer wants his help. A client may sense these feelings so keenly that he is unable to tell us about his decreasing need for us.'[24]

The need to be needed is a problem with which those in the helping professions are familiar, but one which persists, particularly in times of job scarcity. Changing from a system of rigid role-definition to a flexible democratic approach has in itself been found to threaten many staff. A much greater threat is presented when medically trained staff are asked to share 'their' patients with, or relinquish them to, those with less specialised or no training. It is perhaps hard for staff who prize their training and expertise to give sufficient weight to the characteristics which have been found to be essential in a helper, and which cannot be created by training: however, various studies have given convincing evidence of their contribution to the helper's effectiveness. (For a review of some of the salient studies, see Chapter 13.)

An empathetic understanding of the patient's need is not *necessarily* conferred on the professional through training; nor is it confined to the professional. Recognition of this fact has enabled some imaginative schemes to take root: for instance the student volunteer scheme, originating at Harvard in 1954, which enabled university students to work with deteriorated psychotic patients at the Metropolitan State Hospital, Waltham, Massachusetts. Some resentment was initially aroused amongst ward attendants concerning the influx of young people who were not concerned with routine: 'The attendants wanted to keep a ward quiet; the students, to disturb it. The attendants saw the patients' needs as new furniture and clothing; the students, as friendship and love.' The problem (which is here oversimplified) was overcome gradually, partly by exchange of tasks so that each could appreciate the aims and difficulties of the other.

If the professional helper has an investment in adhering to the medical model, as great and sometimes greater is the investment of the disturbed person, and of those who form his social context. Wing and Brown have pointed out that certain patients are already predisposed to become institutionalised at the time of admission to hospital. They include isolated people, passive, dependent personalities and those who find social intercourse difficult. 'Thus there may be, for various reasons, a state of susceptibility to institutionalism which is present when the individual first enters the segregated community, so that, at its most extreme, a person may show dependence on the institution, and apathy about leaving, very shortly after admission.'[25] Nor is it merely the very disabled person who experiences dependency and wishes to relinquish personal responsibility. These are attitudes characteristic of people, however well functioning, in both individual and group transactions, and as such are well documented (for instance, in the writings of W.R. Bion).

It seems that the disturbed person does not have any confidence that either he or those around him can contain his anxiety; and his view is frequently shared by society. Dependence on the expert is linked with the fear of personal and social disintegration. In addition, the patient's deviance threatens society's view of itself as a humane system, since deviance is seen as a form of criticism or rejection of that society. It is a consequence of abandoning the medical model that society is forced to question whether the inadequacy lies only in the deviant, or whether perhaps it is shared by other individuals, or is inherent in the social system.

The process of self-examination is difficult and painful. Nevertheless, beginnings have been made. The feminist movement, in particular, has looked at the part played in women's mental disturbance by social conditioning, in view of the greater susceptibility of women to some forms of disturbance.[26] The contribution of the women's movement in this area has been to identify the social pressures which in reality place a special burden upon women, and to work to alleviate them; at the same time it recognises the psychological problems to which women are especially vulnerable by reason of their conditioning, and offers help to resolve them. It is also emphasised that these are problems characteristic of a particular era and section of society, and therefore are not the result solely of individual pathology. Some of the areas in which social change is needed, in response to women's situation, are identified by Brown and Harris in their recent study of depressed women in Camberwell. Depression was found to correlate with loss of the mother before the age of eleven years, in combination with current social stressors, including: the number of children at home under fourteen years old; lack of work outside the home; lack of someone in whom to confide; low social class; and major role or situational changes.[27] Studies such as these highlight the extent to which clinical measures are often taken in default of an appropriate social response, which would require a more costly personal involvement by others.

Some factors influencing the current adherence to the medical model as an approach to mental health care have been discussed. What are the effects of reliance on the model? Two major consequences may be distinguished: the high cost of provision, and the social stigma attaching to the care services.

Cost of Provision. It has been widely acknowledged that care under the medical umbrella is in general more costly than non-medical care. Comparative costings, however, are hard to establish, and it may be that, when all expenditure is taken into account, costs for those in need of intensive multidisciplinary help may be on a par. At a workshop on psychiatric rehabilitation, held at the National Council of Community Mental Health Centers Annual Meeting in Denver, Colorado, in 1976, the group which studied this question concluded: 'It is possibly a myth to believe that community residential care is *necessarily* cheaper than hospital care, and this should not be the basis on which community care is provided. Community care should be provided because at a given time it is the appropriate service and not because it is cheaper . . . Of course, in the long run, people who can live a full life and become wage earners and tax-payers will constitute an economic advantage.'

On available figures, however, basic residential care is certainly less costly where extraneous medical provision and personnel are excluded. In the UK the estimated average weekly cost of a resident in a local authority hostel for the adult mentally ill is given as £41.60; that for an in-patient in a mental illness hospital is £81.[28] For the US, figures vary from state to state. For the State of Massachusetts, costs per patient per annum (pre-1973), were given as follows: mental hospitals – $10,307; conventional halfway houses – $3,000-4,000. Costs per patient per day in the State of Hawaii for 1977 were given as: state hospital – $80 ($29,200 per annum); Community Residential Intervention Program for Adults – $30-31 ($10,950-11,315 per annum); conventional halfway house – $16 ($5,840 per annum).[29]

Despite lower costs, however, most community care programmes at present are faced with a dilemma: either they must operate within the medical services, or they are not eligible for the necessary funds. In the US, for instance, health insurance schemes usually make third-party payments only to medically directed programmes.[30] Funding by local state governments for community-based projects is notoriously erratic, both in the UK and US, so that care for the individual rests largely on the random factor of his place of residence.

The problem faced by private insurance and by local government is that of assessing the credibility and competence of schemes which are not medically based, and hence therapeutic communities, in conjunction with government departments, need to define standards of provision and practice. In this area, the body of expertise built up by organisations such as the Phoenix houses and the Richmond Fellowship can be of value in helping to establish standards of provision for a range of models, and appropriate criteria for accreditation of staff.

Social Stigma. Establishment of community programmes within the medical services leads, by association, to the definition of people receiving help as 'patients' with a 'diagnosis'. To the extent that this may deter from obtaining help those people who are still living independently, it creates an anomaly by which only those already in a clinical setting are referred to the community facility. The paramedical image thus created is inimical to the spirit of the therapeutic community, which approaches the person in terms of his adjustment to his life-situation rather than by emphasising a pathological condition which requires treatment.

It is of course necessary that criteria for financial support in the community are established on an agreed basis, and at present it appears that a medical assessment will continue to be required by funding authorities. However, it is encouraging that a proportion of applicants are coming forward for admission to therapeutic communities who have not previously been hospitalised or who have had minimal exposure to hospital life. It is also recognised that the assessment need not be made by a psychiatrist, and the Richmond Fellowship accepts referrals from general practitioners, therapists and probation officers.

Social Integration

The acceptance of disturbed people within the community poses questions and uncertainties which many people feel ill-equipped to resolve. In this respect, agencies providing community care need therefore to perform an educative function for the public. The medical model, whilst attempting to gain acceptance for the mentally ill, has also done them a disservice in promulgating a confused concept of 'acceptance'. It is not easy, even for the experienced worker, to find the balance, on the one hand, between caring and tolerating, whilst at the same time encouraging mature behaviour and use of autonomy. Residential communities, in their interaction with the neighbourhood, are well placed to disseminate information and encourage enquiry, as has already been achieved by the Richmond Fellowship and Phoenix communities. Initial establishment in a neighbourhood is probably the most delicate stage of integration, and this may depend on winning over or defeating one or two key objectors. The Richmond Fellowship as a matter of policy informs the neighbours personally of its intention to establish a community, and seeks support of a personal, neighbourly kind. In only a few cases has this approach met with opposition, and in each instance in which the case was legally contested, the judgement given was in favour of the Fellowship. In one case (New Jersey, USA) the threat of recourse to legal action was sufficient to overcome opposition. In Brisbane, Australia, and earlier in Liverpool, England, legal action was taken in order that no precedent for rejection should be set. The case of Liverpool was noteworthy as the only example to date of a Richmond Fellowship project being resisted in a residential area in Britain. The main objector was a local doctor, who opposed the plans on grounds of safety to local residents, and as a result of his activity, the local authority refused planning permission (zoning). An appeal was made to the Department of the Environment, who were able to, and did, override the local decision. Once the project was under way, the objector became reconciled to it, as his initial fears were not substantiated.

A study of the Phoenix House programme at Prospect Place, Brooklyn, has also demonstrated that fears may initially be high, but can be substantially diminished once the project is operational. Initially there was opposition locally, on the grounds that property values would be adversely affected; in this instance an influential local man, who happened to be a real-estate broker, was instrumental in reassuring other local residents. One year after the community had been established, a survey was carried out into the attitudes of local residents, and 64 per cent replied that they did not consider property values to have been affected. Other responses, on the issues of safety of the public, and increased drug use in the neighbourhood, were equally favourable. It was noted however that general acceptance did not indicate a close acquaintance with and understanding of, the programme and of the Phoenix House residents, although residents in the programme felt that they were accepted in the neighbourhood.[31] It seems that, in order for neighbours to progress beyond a superficial acceptance and acquaintance, it is necessary for positive steps to be taken in introducing them to the community, and offering them a defined role: such as, for example, the local committees and friends' groups which are set up in conjunction with the Richmond

Fellowship communities.

Therapeutic Communities in the Community Mental Health Spectrum

Problems discussed so far have been concerned with the shift from medical, institution-based care, to care provided in the community, not necessarily under medical direction. In some measure, community facilities are already being provided, but it is apparent that the therapeutic community is not among those most favoured by the planners, although it has given ample evidence of its value.

The questions then arise: why is the therapeutic community failing to compete successfully with other forms of community mental health care? What can be done to demonstrate the need for this specific provision?

The word 'compete' is used advisedly, since not all types of facility which are recommended can in fact receive support. As long as mental health care remains a low-priority area, and as long as legislation lacks the means of enforcement, it is inevitable that different interests will compete in the race for resources. The therapeutic community has so far not achieved a good track-record.

One reason perhaps lies in the multitude of facilities which are recommended, many of which can cut costs by utilising existing premises (for instance, clinics) and existing staff (for instance, community psychiatric nurses and social workers). It is also increasingly usual for the concepts developed in therapeutic communities to be utilised, and sometimes mimicked, in piecemeal or modified forms in other, more easily funded, facilities. The wide spectrum envisaged for example by the US Joint Commission Report included: day hospitals, night hospitals, aftercare clinics, public health nursing services, foster family care, rehabilitation centres and ex-patient groups. It should be noted incidentally that the night hospital is cited as an equivalent to the halfway house, since 'it functions in essentially the same way'! In the UK community mental health facilities include day hospitals, psychiatric day centres, work centres, ex-patients' clubs, group homes, and individual support in the home setting by medical or social work staff.

A second factor inhibiting the therapeutic community movement is the vested interest of the professions which traditionally have had the task of 'treating' and nursing the mentally ill. In many countries where there is no public system of medical care, the medical professions have not been resourceful in identifying a new role in which to deploy their expertise. Their livelihood is therefore perceived as dependent on existing medical institutions, a view not entirely without basis, since doctors are not *per se* effective psychotherapists, and as has been emphasised by Balint, training in psychotherapy is of a different nature from medical training.[32] The therapeutic community as a non-medical residential resource presents an appropriate alternative to hospital care, and thereby a threat to hospital staffs, who nevertheless pay lip-service to the need for transitional living-facilities. Mendel and Allen identify 'professional comfort, economic forces, and social and cultural resistances' as central to the continuing hegemony of hospitals.[33] (In countries where public medical systems exist, financial problems of a different nature intrude, since the patient is not accompanied in his transfer from hospital to community by transferable funds.)

Thirdly, the therapeutic community faces difficulties of legitimisation, in seeking acceptance amongst essential sources of support. Not only is the therapeutic community a relatively new and unfamiliar concept; it also by its nature as an alternative social environment appeals to romanticism, with the potential both for adventure and escape. Unless leadership is disciplined, the tolerance of extreme behaviours will lead to doubts being cast on the movement as a whole. There is a tendency displayed by some individuals in this field to pursue an isolationist course which leads to lack of comparison and standardisation, and accordingly lack of confidence from those who can provide professional and financial sanctions. Even where standards are recognised to be high, governments and insurance agencies have a bias toward the high-cost hospital rather than the low-cost halfway house which can reach a much larger client group. Not only do high-cost facilities attract an irrational respect but they also produce higher 'spin-offs'; in addition they can afford high-cost grant-writers through which the status quo is maintained. Bardach has pointed out that bureaucracies have little interest in assessing innovative ventures, and prefer to exercise control by stringent licensing regulations, which serve to inhibit positive developments. He points out that hospitals present fewer problems of control, and their contribution can be more easily, although not necessarily more accurately, evaluated.[34] Legitimisation therefore requires a co-operative effort from the therapeutic community movement.

There also exists a scarcity of suitable personnel, because of the diffidence and lack of awareness amongst policy makers regarding the specific expertise required. This expertise can only be provided through training programmes designed to prepare staff for the specific conditions of this work. In spite of its relative enlightenment the 1959

Mental Health Act (UK) failed to grasp the need for a new approach in training to accompany a move to the community. In other countries also, there is no systematic approach to the creation of skills. No major breakthrough for this type of intervention can be expected until governments and the professions not only recognise the need for specialised training of carefully selected personnel, but act on that recognition.

Alternative facilities, financial obstacles, vested interests and prejudice hide the need for residential care. That the need does exist, is shown by the rapid occupation of most halfway houses as soon as they are set up. Such evidence however does not convince authorities of the particular contribution of halfway houses, and therefore more specific determinants of the need must be sought. Who are the people who become resident in therapeutic communities, and what were their previous living circumstances? What previous help did they seek or receive, and why did it prove inadequate? How and why did they apply to the therapeutic community, and with what intentions and hopes – and with what outcome?

Some indications may be obtained from figures available on the Richmond Fellowship. In the year 1977–8 the Richmond Fellowship (UK) cared for a total of 752 residents (329 women and 423 men). This figure includes eleven children who were admitted with their parents. The diagnostic groups were: 19 per cent neurosis, 42 per cent psychosis and 39 per cent personality disorder. These figures include those whose presenting problem was drug or alcohol addiction. The overwhelming majority (654) were single (including eleven children), and of the remaining 98, only 13 still had a spouse. It is suggested that a very large number of those in need of such care lack family roles which are appropriate to their adult status: a suggestion borne out by an examination of the records of 400 ex-residents of the Richmond Fellowship, which was carried out in 1974 as a preliminary to designing a research project. Of the 400 subjects, 340 were single, 48 were separated, widowed or divorced, and 12 were married. In terms of previous hospitalisation, 51 had not been hospitalised, 123 had one hospital admission, 71 had two admissions, 64 had three admissions, 88 had between four and nine admissions, and three had 'very many' admissions. Allowing for changes in individual circumstances and in willingness to be referred to an after-care facility, it would appear that those who had between four and nine hospital admissions, or very many admissions (total number 91) took an unduly long time to reach referral channels. It is, however, encouraging that 51 (12 per cent) had not been hospitalised; it is a regrettable consequence of the cutbacks in public expenditure that applicants have increasingly been obliged to prove their need by becoming hospitalised in order to qualify for funding.

A number of surveys and studies have given indications as to the population for whom community residential facilities are needed. The Camberwell Register suggested certain vulnerable and/or suitable patient groups as candidates for hostel care (personality disorder, chronic psychotic, younger well-motivated single people). In a pilot study conducted in 1973 by Ryan and Hewett for the MRC Social Psychiatry Unit, the potential 'new long-stay' were identified as in need of long-term supportive residential care.[35] 76 elderly and socially isolated residents were interviewed, living in ten hostels in London and South-East England. Of these, nearly four-fifths were diagnosed schizophrenic, and three-quarters had never married. The age-group was predominantly middle-aged and elderly. The hostels were of two kinds, long-stay and transitional, and residents in the two kinds of facility varied somewhat in certain respects. Nevertheless 'what both groups had in common was a high degree of social isolation, combined with a long stay in their present environment'. In terms of preventing return to hospital, the hostels proved to have a good record: 52 per cent of residents had remained in their hostel between one and five years, and a further 19 per cent for over five years. Social isolation however continued to be a problem.

It would appear that social isolation and lack of appropriate familial roles are common factors preceding breakdown, and that these are not necessarily ameliorated by residential care 'in the community'. The positive efforts of the therapeutic community to engage residents in relationships, and to establish links with the surrounding community, therefore appear essential if any substantial improvement is to occur in residents' social functioning and gratification.

The need for research into users of the service, and the service itself, is acknowledged to be a high priority, but the methodological and funding problems would seem to be deterrents. It is however essential that research should be much more widely undertaken in future, in view of its crucial role in the development and wider acceptance of the therapeutic community.

In the interests of evaluating the specific contribution of the community-based therapeutic community, internal studies must be accompanied by probing the extent of the need in the wider community. There is, however, no legitimised method of establishing need; in addition, distinctions are rarely made regarding the *forms* of community provision which are indicated. Recommendations usually refer to a range of community mental health facilities, which compete with one another for support.

In so far as attempts have been made to estimate the specific need for therapeutic communities, this has been *either*
– on the basis of the psychiatric hospital population *or*
– on the basis of the incidence of mental disturbance in the population *or*
– on the basis of testing the need by means of pilot projects.

It would appear, from the experience of the Richmond Fellowship in seeking government support, that the first two are the methods most favoured by statutory authorities, which normally require statistical evidence as the basis for comprehensive schemes. The concept of piecemeal provision which can be evaluated and proceed by stages is less familiar to governments, but is more congenial to the ethos of voluntary bodies. The respective standpoints are illustrated in the following debate between representatives of the Richmond Fellowship and the Commissioner of the State of Rhode Island, USA, where active government interest exists in providing community mental health care.

Commissioner In this State, for example, we have just under a million population – I think it's about 980,000. We have a State hospital that has right now about 1,270 psychiatric patients . . . Now, take that 1,270 – I would say that our hospital population should really be more like 500 for this State.

Interviewer And you would set the number of facilities you need entirely by the population of the hospital? You wouldn't think that there are people living *in the community* who are being deprived of a reasonable way back to normal living – that is, a therapeutic community?

Commissioner I am sure. But I would first want to take care of the hospital population because *that is such a demanding one financially*. If we could establish the appropriateness of that facility . . . then we could talk about outreach programmes . . . So I would rather we do some study before we begin to build.

The attitude of caution on the part of governments, and particularly the concentration on reduction of expenditure, are evident in this extract; this is the more noteworthy in this example since the state referred to has shown itself to be exceptionally progressive and generous. (Rhode Island is in some respects well supplied with community facilities. For instance, as at 1977 there were: for drug addicts, one group home (20 places) and one country estate (105 places); for alcoholics, ten residential facilities (119 places); for the mentally retarded, eleven group homes (130 places) and several shared apartments (60 places). Numerically, the least adequate provision was for the mentally ill – for whom two Richmond Fellowship houses had been established with 100 per cent government funding.)

Policy and Legislation: An Overview

Some major obstacles to implementation of mental health programmes have been reviewed:
- economic considerations
- the legacy of the mental hospitals and their changing role
- the dominance of medical concepts
- problems of stigma and social integration
- specifically, the need to define the role of the therapeutic community in the spectrum of community mental health services.

To date, these problems have greatly retarded the implementation, and blunted the impact, of policy and legislation. In addition, policy and legislation are to some extent themselves problematic, in that clear directives and means of enablement and enforcement are not built in, and these issues are here examined in relation to three of the developed countries.

The USA

The United States is one of the few nations which, besides Great Britain, is positively committed to the principle of care in the community. Legislation in the US, as in Britain, received a major impetus for revision, and for incorporation of progressive ideas, from experiences and data obtained during the Second World War. Subsequently, reports of the nation's state of mental health aroused public concern, notably through the work of Albert Deutsch recorded in his book, *The Mentally*

Ill in America.[36] In 1946 the National Mental Health Act recognised mental illness as a major public health problem, and in 1948 Congress appropriated the necessary funds: the National Institute of Mental Health (NIMH) was established in 1949 to administer the recommended programmes. The Mental Health Study Act 1955 called for a nation-wide survey of the problem; the study was sponsored by the Joint Commission on Mental Health and Illness, and its findings in 1960 were recorded in *Action for Mental Health*. The subsequent action taken by President John F. Kennedy in appointing a task force is well known, and is reviewed briefly in the Introduction to this book. The recommendations made by the task force were embodied in the Mental Retardation Facilities and Community Mental Health Centers Construction (CMHC) Act 1963, which has subsequently been several times amended.

For the purposes of the therapeutic community, the amendment of direct interest is the Special Health Revenue Sharing Act (Title III), the CMHC amendments of 1975. 'Title III extensively revises the original CMHC Act . . . It expands the number of services CMHCs must provide in order to be eligible for federal support, from five to twelve essential services.'[37] Among the services added were *follow-up care for discharged patients, and transitional living programmes in communities for former hospital patients.* As at 1977, 570 CMHCs were fully operational. Within two years of receiving the initial grant the twelve essential services were to be available. Therefore 570 catchment areas should have had access to a transitional living programme. This was not the case by 1979 and even today provision in most areas of the US is poor and sporadic.

Legislative and administrative machinery for community care, including residential care, was thus gradually established, culminating in the CMHC Act 1963. A national policy of deinstitutionalisation was affirmed, and a structure created which was intended to provide working links between the complex systems of health care at federal, state and city/county levels. Yet the implementation of policy has continued to arouse concern, and many of the criticisms were summarised in the report to the Congress submitted in January 1977 by the Comptroller General of the US. Entitled, 'Returning the Mentally Disabled to the Community: Government Needs to Do More', the report attempted a detailed evaluation of progress since 1963, and of the impact made by federal policies and programmes. It gave a broad definition of the extent and nature of the problem: 'The Department of Health, Education and Welfare estimates that about 10 per cent of our population, or about twenty million people, has some form of mental illness, which is defined as an affliction resulting in a disturbance in behaviour, feeling, thinking or judgment to such an extent that a person requires care and treatment.' (In 1978 the official estimate was 15 per cent.) Of the estimated twenty million, over half a million (2.5 per cent) as at 1963 were being treated in public mental hospitals. A decade later, the in-patient population had fallen by over half, to 249,000. As in Britain, however, the fall in the mental hospital population has been accompanied by a disturbing rise in the number of readmissions, many of which are felt to be admissions in default of suitable community provision. The readmission rate rose from 47 per cent of admissions in 1969 to 54 per cent of admissions in 1972.

Various studies have attempted to estimate the number of avoidable admissions: for instance, a study by the Massachusetts State Department of Mental Health in 1973 found that between 50 per cent and 75 per cent of admissions could have been avoided if community care had been adequate. The committee responsible for producing the report to the Congress found, in the course of its investigations, that data from one public mental hospital in Maryland suggested that 70 per cent of admissions in 1974 were necessary because of lack of community facilities. Other assessments support the proposition that between one-half to three-quarters of patients admitted to mental hospitals are not strictly in need of institutional medical care, and it is widely recognised that the policy of deinstitutionalisation has not been accompanied by adequate community provision. In some states, indeed, the policy of deinstitutionalisation has been used blatantly as an opportunity to run down the large hospitals, with disregard for the outcome in terms of patient welfare: California, for instance, under the Republican Governor Reagan, has carried through a drastic programme of decarceration in advance of the availability of sufficient community facilities. On paper adequate plans were made, in the form of 90 per cent matching funds to be provided by the state government for all approved facilities; in reality, however, the problem of overcoming resistance amongst the city and county authorities has not been solved, and the take-up of funds has been relatively low. For example, a city as large as Los Angeles is practically devoid of residential care facilities for the emotionally or mentally disturbed. In the San Francisco region a few facilities exist, but the large majority of discharges found their way to substandard and deteriorating boarding-houses – many in the San José area, which has become a ghetto for ex-mental patients.

Many of the patients discharged through such administrative manoeuvres are the chronically sick and institutionalised, who are severely handicapped in their ability to adapt and fend for themselves. The question of what happens to these patients, in particular, has exercised the concern and endeavours of several bodies in recent years, and it has become apparent that the majority of ex-patients enter the so-called 'extended-care' placement system, whereby people are accommodated in privately run nursing homes. A survey conducted by the National Center for Health Statistics in 1974 showed an increase nationally of 48 per cent in the mentally disabled (including subnormal) population in nursing homes since 1969, from 607,400 to 899,500. Of this total 200,300 (about 22 per cent) were mentally ill, excluding the senile. The NIMH has found that nursing homes are the largest single locus of care for the mentally ill: in 1974 nursing homes consumed 29.3 per cent of estimated total direct care costs, whilst the public mental hospitals consumed 22.8 per cent. Yet the responsibility assumed by the nursing homes, and by the licensing authorities, appears to be in no way commensurate with the significant numbers of residents who are dependent on this provision. As with any system of scattered, privately run and profit-making enterprises which fulfil a vital social function, the tendency is for the facilities to be used without the stringent inspection and monitoring which should be recognised as essential. Kohen and Paul found that rehospitalisation rates in such placements ranged from 30 per cent to over 50 per cent within a period of under two years. They note that rehabilitation goals and methods are frequently absent: 'Professional follow-ups [of patients in] extended-care placements are notably lacking. However, when follow-up has occurred, a complete absence of rehabilitation programming has been found' and, not surprisingly, declines rather than improvements in functioning. They quote Koltuv and Neff in their thesis that the result of the deinstitutionalisation policy has too often been 'moving the locus in which (the emotionally disturbed) vegetates and experiences personal misery from the custodial hospital to the community'.[38]

The report to Congress is similarly critical of the standards maintained by the nursing homes. It contains such comments on the result of its investigations as: 'In general, the homes offered very few services other than custodial care . . . For the most part, the residents were just sitting, watching television, or lying on their beds.' 'A typical day for a mentally ill person in a nursing home was sleeping, eating, watching television, smoking cigarettes, sitting in groups in the largest room, or looking out of the window.' Yet, as pointed out by Kohen and Paul, the need to accommodate large numbers of chronic patients who are still accumulating in the state mental hospitals indicates *an even greater role for extended-care placements in the future.* Kohen and Paul conclude by making detailed recommendations for the redirection of efforts and resources in nursing homes towards the goal of rehabilitation, rather than the current incentives to concentrate on administration and physical care – which in any case are often subordinate to maximising the profit margin. The profit motive in mental health services, and particularly the nursing home world, has been well documented and was declared a 'national disgrace'.[39]

Other community facilities suffer similarly from privatised, unstandardised and unmotivated programmes. The report in its review of group homes, foster-care homes, halfway houses, bed and breakfast facilities and 'welfare' hotels, comments: 'Many were placed into decent, comfortable settings, and were provided with a range of services to meet their needs. Others, however, were placed into overcrowded, substandard, and dirty facilities without provision being made for needed services. The only service provided to many mentally ill persons released to the community was medication.' 'In several instances programming was limited to activities such as sitting and doing nothing, or watching television.' Shands (Chapter 23) and Jansen (Chapter 25) have also given graphic descriptions of the conditions frequently prevailing.

The Therapeutic Community

What part, then, has the therapeutic community played in community care developments? Procedural problems of introducing new forms of provision are more intractable in the US than in Britain, and progress towards establishing the therapeutic community has been slower and more sporadic. Within the therapeutic community movement, the more pressing social problems of alcoholism and drug addiction have attracted more consistent and committed government support than the cause of the mentally ill. In 1963 Raush and Raush were able to identify 40 halfway houses.[40] In 1973 a survey conducted under the auspices of NIMH found 209 facilities primarily for psychiatric patients, with an 85 per cent occupancy of 6,003 residents (*three per cent of the number of mentally ill accommodated in nursing homes*). Over one-quarter of the residents were accommodated in halfway houses having 50 beds or more, which must have adverse implications for the quality of rehabilitation. The halfway houses provided a range of counselling, vocational/educational and recreational services. The age range of 42 per cent of the residents was 25 to 44 years; 75 per cent came direct from mental hospital. The majority stayed for periods ranging from five months to two years; on discharge, 41 per cent went to live in independent situations, and 15 per cent returned to mental hospital.[41]

Some progress had evidently taken place during the decade 1963 to 1973, although insignificant in terms of the potential clientele, and it is of interest to review some of the salient developments during that period. The work of one of the earliest foundations, Spring Lake Ranch, is expounded by Michael Wells in Chapter 4. This rural community, operating on an increasingly progressive basis, is centred on a work programme essential to the ranch, which thus provides the focus and unifying force for the residents. The necessity to participate as a working member of the community in creative tasks, provides a stimulus for residents to exercise previously undiscovered strengths, and to obtain satisfaction thereby. The Phoenix House programme for drug addicts (see Chapter 6) was initiated in 1967, and has continued to develop its philosophy and methods, and expand its operations. The director of the Richmond Fellowship first sought to explore developments in the US in 1967, and recognised that, far from providing well-established models which could be applied in the UK, fragmentation of effort was then impeding individuals and agencies. Requests were received from schools of psychiatry for assistance in establishing an equivalent Fellowship network in the US; it then became an objective of the Fellowship to extend its services to the US and to unite with other therapeutic communities in facilitating developments. The first Richmond Fellowship halfway house was opened in Washington DC in 1969. The work has subsequently expanded, and communities founded by the Fellowship now operate in Washington DC, Maryland, New York, Rhode Island and New Jersey.

It has been found that the establishment of a coherent system of halfway houses presents obstacles which arise peculiarly from American attitudes and procedures. Administrative regulations involved in the establishment of therapeutic communities are daunting in their complexity (see Chapters 18, 23 and 25). Parochialism is more evident than in the UK in the desire of a regional branch to evade organisational obligations after the initial advice and resources have been obtained from the parent body, and there is a reluctance to think on a national rather than a local scale. The annual report of the Richmond Fellowship 1977–8 states: 'In the toil or panic of trying to survive, halfway houses tend to live by the day, to scatter and work in isolation, instead of building up a programme of joint learning, standard-setting and approaches to insurance, the government and the community. This crisis-oriented approach results in the benefits of therapeutic communities not becoming sufficiently visible and accepted, and the lack of planning and investing in overall organisation in the end comes to roost on the individual projects which have limited impact.' The problem of establishing an organisational structure is exacerbated by the anomalies created through variations in legislation from state to state, which create difficulties in bringing the organisation under one, non-profit-making corporation. The relationship 'by contract' between separate corporations (as against parts of one single corporation) leaves room for breach of contract or of 'gentleman's agreements', for which the unpalatable remedy is recourse to law. Isolationist thinking, amongst other problems, was found to be still a major and widespread deterrent to provision in the US when a study tour was undertaken in 1977 by the editor of this book and her husband on behalf of the Richmond Fellowship. Unco-ordinated and restrictive planning and licensing requirements, varying from state to state, were often a deterrent. Political expediency was also a major factor as was noted in New York: 'Political considerations are unashamedly acknowledged as uppermost, and the only way . . . to get systematic work undertaken would seem to be either on the basis of extreme wealth and philanthropy combined with extreme tenacity or . . . of feeding in to ruthless exploitation. The latter takes place to some extent in the provision of large proprietary welfare hotels.'[42] Single-room occupancy hotels (SROs) are the major depository for New York City's rejects, paid for by welfare departments who make token requirements of these dilapidated slums – whilst they set unreasonably high standards for halfway houses.[43]

In the District of Columbia the reputation of CMHCs was found to be poor. In addition, DC had failed to honour its obligation to sustain projects which had been initiated by or subsidised by federal funding, by making up the annually decreasing grants with state funds. This resulted in closure of projects which had made an important contribution; for example, the Albert Deutsch Center was closed down in the early 1970s; in 1978 the partial closure followed of the Richmond Fellowship Model and Training Unit, which was the first Richmond Fellowship therapeutic community to be established in the US, and had been operational for ten years. The problems of obtaining state co-operation in establishing and maintaining community projects are noted also by the report to the Congress. In its comments on NIMH the report notes that this agency, although responsible for providing leadership at the national level for the care and treatment of the mentally ill, has failed to establish acceptable forms and standards of community care, that the NIMH itself does not possess the necessary resources, and that it has been unable to obtain the necessary co-operation from other agencies. In addition, the federal government has contributed to the failure to implement plans: 'The Nixon Administration impounded millions of dollars, voted by Congress to finance Mental Health Centers . . . the Administration's sentiments [were] that the comprehensive community mental health centers had fully proved their worth and that the State should now assume the burden of financing.'[44]

The need for united action by agencies concerned with the therapeutic community has long been evident, and is a primary target for achieving improved facilities, both qualitatively and quantitatively. A step in this direction was taken in 1976 when, following the Fellowship's international conference, a National Council of Community Residences was formed with the aim of bringing organisations together in order to promote united action to establish standards of accreditation and licensing, to facilitate zoning and to lobby for funding. The problems which the council will need to overcome are the symptoms of the 'American Ailment' – the desire for kudos and control at the expense of collective action in a situation of governmental chaos.

The report to the Congress made recommendations directed specifically at the numerous government departments involved in deinstitutionalisation programmes, and included the crucial recommendation that a single federal committee be constituted, with overall responsibility to oversee all federal efforts towards deinstitutionalisation of the mentally disabled. This would include the goal of enabling all patients to exercise their right to be treated in 'the least restrictive setting appropriate to their needs'. It was recommended that Congress amend legislation so that funding for outpatient mental health coverage under Medicaid would become more widely available. More appropriate methods of funding state programmes were also suggested.

The report of the Comptroller General, although couched in moderate and innocuous terms, amounts to a massive indictment of the federal, state and local governments for paying lip service to the goal of deinstitutionalisation and not developing any clear, comprehensive, and systematic strategy for effective action: 'absence of an effective management system for clearly defining objectives, roles, responsibilities [and] actions to be taken . . . lack of a systematic way to finance deinstitutionalisation . . . lack of criteria or standards for defining adequate or acceptable community placement . . . appropriate to the needs of persons with . . . mental disability.' The theme of all the recommendations is perhaps summarised thus: 'We recommend that the Secretary of HEW . . . *Designate the problems identified in this report as areas of national significance* and direct that some of the Department's discretionary funds be used to develop and test solutions.'

The President's Commission on Mental Health was authorised by President Carter early in 1977 and presented its report in 1978. The Commission found that 'the foundation exists for reaching the goal of making high-quality public and mental health services available at reasonable cost to all who need them'. It proposed that the strategy for reaching this goal should be developed and implemented by 'partnership' between the Federal Government with State and local government and between the private and public sectors of health care. Insofar as the private sector includes profit-making and profit-orientated agencies and professions, the proposals are in difficulty from the beginning. As with Medicaid and Medicare, public funds will be absorbed at maximum speed by the various bureaucratic systems if not by the highly-paid professions, leaving only scraps to nourish the client-group and to remunerate those directly involved in providing 24-hour care.

The Report to the President was outspoken about the 'deplorably inadequate' existing provision. It states: 'In assessing mental health care in 1978 we have been struck by the inconsistencies that exist between what we know should be done and what we do'. This is in keeping with the condition of sinful man in general, and with the social planning of American society in particular!

> Time and again we have learned – from testimony, from inquiries, and from the reports of special task panels – of people with chronic mental disabilities who have been released from hospitals but who do not have the basic necessities of life. They lack adequate food, clothing, or shelter. We have heard of woefully inadequate follow-up mental health and general medical care. And we have seen evidence that half the people released from large mental hospitals are being readmitted within a year of discharge. While not every individual can be treated within the community, many of the re-admissions to State hospitals could have been avoided if comprehensive assistance had existed within their communities.

And again:

> A basic premise of the movement toward community-based services was that care would be provided in halfway houses, family and group homes, private hospitals and offices, residential centers, foster care settings, and community mental health centers. Social and human services were to have been integrated with more formal mental health care, resulting in a complete range of services.
>
> In the few communities that had this broad range of services, many patients made effective transitions from State hospitals to the community. The majority of communities, however, did not have the necessary services, were not given proper assistance to develop them, or enough time to prepare to receive returning patients.

The reception of returning patients raises the problem of stigma and public resistance which needs to be addressed. This has already been referred to, but is particularly pertinent to the situation in the US, where the majority of the population in state mental hospitals has traditionally been detained compulsorily, and where public involvement has been minimal. In recent years, judicial hearings and the reports of the media have contributed to a recognition of the civil rights of the mental patient: as of June 1975 there were one hundred completed or pending court cases in the US affecting the rights of the mentally disabled, and this activity has undoubtedly been a factor in arousing the public conscience (although it has by no means consistently contributed to making appropriate provision for the plaintiffs). Rosalynn Carter commented: 'Stigma is a problem in getting people into treatment in the first place; it is a problem during treatment; and it is a problem in trying to get a patient reinvolved in the community.'[45] The Joint Commission on Mental Illness and Health reported in 1960 that 'unlike physical illness, mental illness tends to disturb and repel people rather than evoke their sympathy and desire to help.' The President's Commission reported in 1978 that 'This Commission does not know how to end discrimination.' It cited a reminder 'that almost all Americans encounter [mental health] problems, either themselves, or in their families, or among their neighbours and friends . . . that none of us is immune from mental illness or emotional problems, and that the fear, the anxiety, and even the anger we feel about people who suffer these problems may merely reflect some of our own deepest fears and anxieties.'

(Report to the President from the President's Commission on Mental Health, Washington, 1978, page 57.)

The 1978 President's Commission on Mental Health, although not sufficiently wide and thorough in scope, was enlightened in outlook and specific in many of its recommendations. Especially the emphasis given to the need for staff training and public education as well as for Mental Health dollars was a step forward. The new Mental Health Systems Act which is now (1979) before the legislature is designed to address some of the problems discussed. However, commissions and legislation have come to be seen as designed in the main to ward off public attack. Any new legislation, therefore, will need to be incisive and thorough if it is to restore confidence in official policy.

Australia

1. *The Extent and Nature of the Problem*

Interest in a vigorous restructuring of Australia's health services on a community-based system effected some changes during the early 1970s. Concern with the quality of health care found official expression in 1971, when the Senate Standing Committee of Health and Welfare rashly stated: 'The enjoyment of the highest attainable standard of health is a fundamental right of every citizen.'[46] Amongst the areas of concern, the needs of the mentally ill and mentally handicapped were specifically recognised. In 1973, it was estimated that 'about two per cent of the population have some serious mental illness or handicap, and an additional six per cent suffer from significant psychological disorder. Large numbers have co-existing emotional and physical disorder.'[47] Facilities for care of the mentally ill, however, had long been recognised as stagnant and lacking in imagination. The Callan Park Inquiry (NSW) reported in 1961:

> Callan Park is heir to a tradition that you place patients in one mould; that you gear therapy to a system of locked wards; that you do not give patients good food because it will not be appreciated; that you do not clothe them well because they will wet their clothes and dirty them and spill food on them; a tradition that you do not put doors on bathrooms or WC's because some patients will use these places as a means of suicide or to indulge in indecent acts; that you disallow privacy in their sleeping accommodation because they cannot be overseen; a tradition that you refuse them

liberty because a man might seduce a woman patient, run away or do some other harm.[48]

Prior to the adoption of community care as a national priority, developments in mental health care had already tended to parallel those in the United States and in Britain. For instance, an account of developments occurs in Reports Nos. 79/1 and 79/3 of the Health Commission of NSW Division of Health Services Research. From the early 1930s, it became legally possible for state mental hospitals to treat voluntary patients, and by 1975, voluntary admissions to mental hospitals in NSW represented 77 per cent of total admissions. From the end of the Second World War, resources began to be directed towards prevention of hospitalisation, and reduction of the mental hospital population. Efforts were made towards providing more local and flexible treatment facilities, and in line with the national trend, the first psychiatric unit in a general hospital in NSW was opened in 1964 (Prince Henry Hospital). From 1960 a combination of factors, paralleled by those in the UK and the USA, brought about a sharp decrease in the numbers of the mental hospital population: for example, in NSW the psychiatric population declined by over 50 per cent, from 3.0 persons per 1,000 population in 1965, to 1.2 persons per 1,000 in 1978.

This trend may be illustrated also by reference to statistics published by the Mental Health Authority of the State of Victoria. In 1966, the number of persons treated within the Authority's services (including the mentally handicapped) was 28,354, of whom 11,849 were in-patients, and 8,973 were first referrals. Five years later, in 1971, the number of persons treated was 31,484, of whom 9,086 were in-patients, and 10,863 were first referrals. It will be noted that, in line with trends in other developed countries, the number of persons treated, and of first referrals, rose, whilst the number of patients treated on an in-patient basis decreased. Over twice as many first referrals were accepted for out-patient as for in-patient treatment; the highest proportion of first referrals, especially to out-patient clinics, was represented by psychoneuroses, 'transient situational trait disturbances', personality disorders and alcoholism (in males). Of the total number of 30,066 referred in 1971, 16.3 per cent were mentally retarded or brain damaged, 83.7 per cent being mentally disordered.

By far the majority of the total numbers treated were in the categories separated/divorced/single/widowed (although some disorders showed a lower incidence amongst the widowed than amongst the married). It is to be noted that out of a total of 26,355 patients in treatment during the year (excluding the mentally retarded) 64 per cent constituted re-referrals, including a small number readmitted from trial leave. This figure should perhaps be seen in relation to the average length of stay of those discharged from residential hospital care (*excluding* the mentally retarded) in 1971, which was approximately nine months for both men and women. Of *all categories* of patients in residence on 1st January 1971, 27.7 per cent of men, and 26.2 per cent of women, had been in hospital for less than one year. In 1976 the number of persons treated was 33,111, of whom 8,664 were in-patients and 10,314 were first referrals. Of 35,194 admissions, 24,200 (69 per cent) were readmissions. 27.6 per cent of men and 27.3 per cent of women had been in hospital for less than one year. It would appear that measures to avoid institutionalising patients with acute and/or mild disorders were not being complemented by adequate facilities in the community, leading inevitably to a high rate of readmission.

2. *Measures Towards Community Care*

It was in 1973 that nationwide concern regarding community care found more formal expression, through studies and programmes initiated by the Department of Health of the Commonwealth Government. In May of that year, the then Minister of Health, Dr D.N. Everingham, issued a Press Statement giving the policy decision of the Cabinet to assist the States with their expenditure on community mental health, alcoholism and drug dependency, and recommending that the emphasis be on education, prevention and rehabilitation. It was hoped thereby to reduce the costs of institutional care. The sums proposed were $7.5 m. in 1973/4 and 1974/5, for the above-mentioned services.

In June 1973, the Interim Committee of the National Hospitals and Health Services Commission submitted its first Report to the Minister, entitled, 'A Community Health Programme for Australia'. The Interim Committee had as its brief the task of recommending capital and operating funds payable from Federal Government for health care delivery systems, arising from the national policy of regionalisation and modernisation of hospitals, and the development of community-based and preventive programmes. The Report emphasised that primary care was the key component of the community health programme, and articulated the need for co-ordination between the different services and disciplines, and for support to general practitioners. It recommended that government should reimburse to the States 75 per cent of capital costs and 90 per cent of operating costs for approved programmes, and that these subsidies should be available for both block grant to States and specific grant-aided schemes. Subsequently, the Community Health Programme supported a wide range of initiatives, including comprehensive community health services; community mental health services; community based alcohol and drug assessment, treatment and rehabilitation services; health education; community geriatric services; community rehabilitation services; domiciliary and home nursing services; staff training programmes; women's health services; youth and adolescent services; and migrant health. In addition, the Programme made some smaller inroads into the following 'special needs areas' of health care – Aboriginal health; family planning services; and occupational health.

In October 1973, Parliament debated the Mental Health and Related Services Assistance Bill, which was to implement the policy announced by Dr Everingham earlier that year. Government would provide assistance towards the capital costs of community facilities for the mentally ill and handicapped, and for alcoholics and drug addicts. Grants would also be available towards operating costs. *It was envisaged that the funding would enable an expansion of hostel and halfway house accommodation for the chronically mentally disabled and for those suffering from social handicap.* The Bill provided for allocations of up to $7.5 m. for the years 1973/4 and 1974/5, after which services would be integrated in the Community Health Programme. The Bill became law and came into effect in November 1973, replacing the States Grants (Mental Health Institutions) Act. It provided the proposed financial assistance up to 1975, as stated above.

The Interim Committee issued further recommendations in November 1973, in its Report entitled, 'A Medical Rehabilitation Programme for Australia'. The Report made it clear that the term 'disability' included psychiatric disability; it also stated the need to increase staffing in line with the programme recommendations, and suggested various avenues by which staff could be trained in rehabilitation, including support to 'those institutions which provide programmes for trainee specialists in Rehabilitation (Medicine) and related fields.' It was again recommended that the Commonwealth Government's contribution towards the expenditure of eligible organisations should be 75 per cent of capital costs and 90 per cent of operating costs. It was estimated that expenditure totalling $50 m. would be needed for the Programme over the following three years. The recommendations of the Interim Committee included the requirement that *high quality rehabilitation services be made available to all who need them.* In December 1973, the Interim Committee issued its second Report on the Medical Rehabilitation Programme for Australia, emphasising the urgent need for resources, and drawing attention to the need to ensure that certain groups of handicapped people – the geriatric, the psychiatric and the severely subnormal – should not be submerged in the organisation of regional services. In 1974, the Handicapped Persons Assistance Act was passed. Amongst its main provisions were the allocation of subsidies to eligible organisations providing training with associated accommodation.

3. *Voluntary Agencies*

Government policy and legislation heralded the possibility of an expansion of voluntary specialist agencies, in coordination with State services.

Despite the previous lack of Federal Government support for community work, a range of organisations in the area of mental health had been able to take root. A Government Working Party, set up in 1977, identified fifty agencies falling within the broad definition of prevention, care and rehabilitation, but excluding the problems of mental retardation, and alcohol and drug abuse, and excluding the work of religious organisations. Of these agencies, 21 gave evidence to the Working Party, which was given the task of examining the contribution of voluntary agencies, and the implications for future government funding. The Working Party, under the Chairmanship of Dr L. Drew (Senior Adviser in Alcohol and Drug Dependence, the Commonwealth Department of Health), reported in February 1979.[49] It concluded that, in general, voluntary agencies worked to a very satisfactory standard, and should be regarded as having a vital role to play in fostering mental health. It recommended that funding by the Government should be at a level equal to that of funding for the State-run services, and should be secure.

Voluntary agencies associated with mental health display the variety which is characteristic also of the voluntary movement in Britain, in terms of scale, philosophy and focus. Prominent amongst schemes to assist the mentally disturbed is the self-help organisation GROW (formerly RECOVERY), established in Sydney in 1957 as a response to what was viewed as the inadequacy and breakdown of traditional social support systems, for those going through a period of distress and disorganisation. Based on small groups which meet for mutual education, GROW recorded the existence of 300 groups and seven administrative/community centres in Australia in 1977, and it had initiated activities in other countries including the USA. It aims through face-to-face encounter to assist individuals to achieve greater maturity, and to enable society to resume its traditional caring role.[50]

Agencies specialising in the problems of those addicted to drugs or alcohol include *Buoyancy*, established in 1967 in the State of Victoria, to provide crisis-intervention and a communal living facility for drug abusers; and *The Way Back Committee*, founded in 1972 to provide communities for those dependent on drugs or alcohol. An interstate crisis service is provided by *Lifeline*, the telephone counselling service, which was started in Sydney in the early 'sixties by the Rev. Dr Alan Walker. The self-help movement has manifested itself in numerous local groups, notably arising from concern for the social problems of women and of the migrant population.

4. *Residential Resources*

Amongst the achievements of the voluntary sector, however, as amongst the State-run services, therapeutic residential care is barely represented. Hostels for the adult mentally disordered have tended to concentrate on the geriatric chronically disabled, on a long-term custodial basis. For example, in Western Australia, a significant growth in community facilities for the mentally ill was reported, and in 1976 there were 25 private hostels in the metropolitan area, catering for 600 patients; *but* most of these were chronic patients with little hope of gaining independence. (In Ellis, A.S., 'Non-Institutionalisation of West Australian Mental Health Services', Community Health Bulletin No. 5 (Oct.–Dec. 1976), pp. 13–15.) In the State of Victoria, eight hostels provided 150 places in 1976 *but* provision was largely for the chronic patient.[51] South Australia was proud to provide, in 1977, over 500 halfway-house beds, *but* these were found to be occupied almost exclusively by geriatric burnt-out schizophrenics. The low staffing ratio was totally inadequate to activate these residents, who could have received more individual assistance in hospital (Editor's observation). However humanely instigated, 'community care' in these circumstances is clearly organised in order to cut costs, rather than to improve the quality of life for the mentally ill.

Two distinct problems have therefore to be addressed: the dearth of residential rehabilitation programmes for mentally-disturbed adults who are not chronically sick or disabled; and the tendency of environments for the chronically sick to become stagnant and lose sight of rehabilitative goals. The latter problem was highlighted by a survey carried out under the auspices of the Federal Government's Commission of Inquiry into Poverty, in which the circumstances of 175 discharged psychiatric patients were investigated.[52] All of the patients had left hospital at least six months previously. It was possible to trace and interview 98 of the sample; some basic information was obtained on the rest. As a group, the sample was characterised by: a high proportion of more chronic and sick patients; a high proportion (78.9 per cent) of single people; a high proportion having a history of previous admissions (47.4 per cent had more than four previous admissions); and high mobility. It was found that 56.5 per cent had gone on discharge to a different address to that from which they were admitted; and that the proportion who had to seek new accommodation tended to increase with length of stay in hospital. Thus, of those hospitalised for up to 28 days, 48.8 per cent went to different accommodation on discharge, compared with 55.2 per cent of those hospitalised for between 1 to 11 months, and 80.8 per cent of those hospitalised for one year or more.

The quality of housing left much to be desired. Of the 98 patients interviewed, 57 were found to be living in private homes (with family or friends), and 41 in specialised housing. Of the latter, 10 were in boarding houses, 19 in nursing homes, and 12 in institutions. The researchers arrived at two conclusions which are of significance to those engaged in planning for residential after-care.

First, no type of accommodation was found to be both suitable and adequate for the task of supporting those patients who no longer needed a nursing environment. Families and friends were on the whole unable to cope without undue strain on relationships; and boarding houses were rated as mostly providing a low standard of accommodation, dictated by the need to make profits. They tended to attract the most chronic patients, and yielded the highest rate of readmission to hospital. The researchers concluded that a more supportive type of accommodation was needed: 'There is in the community a need for a type of supervised accommodation resembling the current boarding-house provision, but with a wide range of services provided on the premises.' Needs specially identified were: supervision of medication, counselling on day-to-day problems, and assistance with problems of social integration.

Secondly, it was felt on the basis of the survey that the need for supportive accommodation for the more disabled patient was not a bottomless pit. Out of the 98 people interviewed, 21.4 per cent were thought to be in need of such provision. The researchers noted: 'If this is representative of the need for this type of accommodation in the whole population of discharges in New South Wales, then the community problem of supplying this kind of accommodation at an adequate level is a relatively small one.'

The above survey related to long-term supportive facilities, for those chronically disabled by mental illness. The absence of shorter-term residential therapeutic communities with more ambitious goals, for those able to benefit, had also become a target of criticism, and a focus for action. Run-down boarding-houses were usually the only facility which State and patients could afford, and the extent to which this solution was adopted had become a national scandal. The government was ready to act, and this opening was welcomed by the Richmond Fellowship. In 1973, a programme was launched in order to establish halfway houses on the model operational in the UK. By 1977, four Fellowship houses were in existence, in Brisbane, Sydney, Melbourne, and Perth, and work was in progress to extend the programme to Canberra and Adelaide. The establishment of a network of residential therapeutic communities, providing a continuum of care, was recognised by the government as an essential aspect of community provision on a national scale.

5. *Effects of Federal Policy and Funding*

The new measures introduced by the Australian Government in 1973, in support of its major health programmes (the Community Health Programme and the Medical Rehabilitation Programme), meant that approved facilities might become eligible to receive finance towards both capital and operating costs, through the assistance of the Department of Health towards State programmes and subsidies. The implementation of the assisted programmes has indeed proved of value to voluntary as well as State services, although some problems have become evident.

It is clear, for example, that government departments are reluctant to fund operating expenditure (on which the stability of services depends); this is attributable to the fact partly that the costs are recurring, and partly that they do not provide visible monuments to governmental concern. Problems have also been encountered as a result of split departmental responsibility (as is the case in the UK and in the USA).

The Federal Government's Department of Social Security provides 50 per cent of staffing costs for approved residential facilities; the other 50 per cent cannot usually be met from the contribution of residents, and therefore each facility is dependent on finding the balance from other sources. In the case of minimally-staffed facilities, this percentage may represent a small figure, but in the case of a full-scale therapeutic community the staffing costs may be as much as $50,000 per annum. Admittedly, State Departments of Health may, at their discretion, make supplementary grants to psychiatric halfway houses, of which a percentage may be reimbursed by Federal Government, under the provisions of the Community Health Programme. Serious objections have been raised to this arrangement. In the first place, the State Departments of Health do not consider that the Federal contribution is adequate. Furthermore, it is seen as irrational that funding for hostel staffs should be the responsibility of the Department of Social Security, whilst operational subsidies fall under the Department of Health. In addition, funding from two Departments leads to more haphazard funding, less security of income, and less systematic provision.

Despite flaws, however, the initiatives of the Labour Government have borne fruit. Without its encouragement and assistance, for example, the Richmond Fellowship project could not have been established or developed with such rapidity. Subsequently, during 1976 a total of 34 'approved projects' were accepted for assistance in the category hostel/halfway house/group home, and in 1977/8, eleven projects were assisted in this category, from three States.[53] Such developments make it imperative that support for community projects be maintained. However, following the fall of the Labour Government in 1975, the trend has been to curtail expenditure. A Task Force was set up in 1976 to study Coordination in Welfare and Health; it recommended that 26 Commonwealth Health and Welfare programmes and benefits *including the Community Health Programme* should be transferred to the States, which would assume responsibility for administration and programme delivery.[54] This proposal has been vigorously opposed by voluntary bodies, as it would undoubtedly be a retrograde step in achieving the national quantity and quality of community care which were originally envisaged.

The concern of the Australian Commonwealth Government, shown in the early 1970s, for the many patients who were discharged from hospitals without appropriate community provision, was not to last. The government's vigorous measures were short-lived, and its generous financing policy aborted, bringing to a halt any consistent provision in the field of community care, and especially in terms of therapeutic communities. Federal Community Health grants for capital expenditure decreased from $14.114 m. in 1976/7 to $10.411 m. in 1977/8 and to $5.880 m. in 1978/9. Grants for recurrent expenditure decreased from $56.874 m. in 1977/8 to $45.420 m. in 1978/9.

Unless there is a wholehearted reversal of present policy, the run-down boarding-house will for many years to come be the mecca of enlightened care to which a Liberal Australian Government has committed the mentally distressed of the '80s.

A Study of Developments in England and Wales

Report of The Royal Commission

The fundamental changes in the concepts of mental health and ill health, to which the Report of the Royal Commission on the Law Relating to Mental Illness and Mental Deficiency, published in 1957, gave expression, were rooted in a growing recognition of the relationship between behaviour and environment. This development paved the way for a shift of emphasis from hospital care to community care as part of the process towards providing a comprehensive, integrated mental health service capable of dealing with people in all stages and degrees of need. It also facilitated a change of the hospital's role from almost wholly custodial to that of an increasingly curative or therapeutic nature, partly through the extension of the criteria for informal voluntary admissions.

By recommending voluntary admission to and discharge from psychiatric hospitals of all who needed care, the commission not only initiated a more general application of advanced methods of treatment, but also facilitated the development of a fully integrated and comprehensive service in which hospitals and local authorities could play their distinct but complementary roles, defined on lines broadly the same as in relation to physical illness or disability.

The policy, which has become known as that of 'the open door', and which lays stress on the rehabilitative and therapeutic functions of the hospital, was enshrined by the commission in the statement that the 'aim of hospital treatment or training is to make the patient fit to return to life in the general community . . . At that stage the provision of residential care becomes the responsibility of the local authority.'[55]

Even before the Report of the Royal Commission and its legislative sequel, the Mental Health Act 1959, had taken effect, the repercussions of new forms of treatment were being reflected in hospital bed numbers and the number of hospital beds had fallen from 3.4 per 1,000 of population in 1954 to 3.1 per 1,000 by 1960.[56] The idea of the psychiatric hospital as a large custodial institution serving a diffuse and ill-defined catchment area, without links with the community, was giving way to the concept of small, treatment-intensive and community-based units serving defined catchment areas, thus facilitating the co-ordination of hospital and local authority services in the community, and with a large element of day and out-patient care. *The Hospital Plan for England and Wales 1962* further recognised the place of the short-stay psychiatric unit as a part of the general hospital and contemplated that many of the existing mental hospitals would have no place in the new pattern of service.

The Community Care Plan was published a year later. It promoted the case for community care for all but the most acutely disturbed patients. It comprised, in the words of Kathleen Jones, 'some glossy photographs, and 321 pages of detailed local authority returns on their future plans. Those who looked for a rationale of community care and a positive lead from central Government were disappointed.'[57] The government for its part rationalised its approach on grounds of lack of authority to enforce its recommendations. To some extent, however, its strategy of publishing comparative plans served as a stimulus to local authorities to formulate ambitious schemes. This result was not wholly beneficial in that, whilst encouraging local authorities to face the need, it also instigated inappropriate planning which was undertaken without the benefit of sufficient research and pertinent expertise. Local authorities also tended to overlook the advantages of working through organisations which had already blazed a trail, and thought in terms of purpose-built hostels, staffed in a manner which would obviate the need to rely on 'patient labour', an issue which had come under attack in the hospitals.

The implication for the hospital service of the change of emphasis towards community care is clearly shown in the statistics: National Health Service revenue expenditure on services for the mentally ill dropped from a share of 12.9 per cent in 1964/5 to 11.5 per cent in 1973/4. This must be due in part to the policy of closing or running down large, out-of-date hospitals with an increase in day-patient facilities – between 1954 and 1975 the number of in-patients in mental illness hospitals and units in England and Wales as at 31

December dropped from 152,197 to 92,467, while admissions rose from 114,552 in 1960 to 186,081 in 1975[58] and the number of new day-patients rose from 13,438 in 1965 to 36,383 in 1975.[59] There has been, in addition, a steady increase since 1964 in the proportion of patients discharged within a month of admission.[60] Reduction in expenditure on in-patient facilities has inevitably been offset by the need for greater expenditure on day and out-patient facilities.

Turning now to examine the role of local government in a comprehensive community-based service, the commission, after reviewing the very limited existing provision for community services for the mentally ill in general, and residential services in particular, recommended in Part V

- that there should be a general reorientation away from institutional care in its present form and towards community care, resulting in an expansion of local authority services, including the provision of residential accommodation for the mentally ill, severely subnormal and psychopathic patients, who for various reasons may need residential care but do not need or no longer need hospital in-patient care
- that the provision of community care for all types of mentally disordered patients should be made a positive duty of county and county borough councils.

The commission had pointed out that the statutory authority for the provision by local authorities of the community services contemplated was merely permissive in character.

The Sequel to the Mental Health Act 1959

In order to ascertain the extent to which the community-orientated service for the mentally ill recommended by the commission and embodied in the 1959 Mental Health Act has been realised in the 20 years that have elapsed, it is necessary to review

- legislative changes which have taken place
- the successive policy statements by central government on the priorities implicit in and the financial implications of a community-based service
- the practical effect of such changes and statements as reflected in the statistics which are available at the time of writing.

The picture which emerges reveals a substantial disparity between formal acceptance and practical realisation.

Legislative Changes

Section 21(1) of the National Assistance Act 1948 made it the duty of every local authority *inter alia* to provide 'residential accommodation for persons who, by reason of age, infirmity or any other circumstances are in need of care and attention which is not otherwise available to them'. The categoric nature of this requirement was largely watered down by the effect of subsection (8) of the same section, which relieved a local authority of an obligation to make any provision under this section in cases where it was '*authorised* or required' by another enactment to make such provision, as was done by section 28(1) of the National Health Service Act 1946, which merely empowered but did not require local (health) authorities, (unless directed by the minister) to 'make arrangements for the purpose of the prevention of illness, the care of persons suffering from illness or mental defectiveness, or the after-care of such persons'.

The Mental Health Act 1959, section 6(1), extended the provisions of section 28(1) of the 1946 Act to persons who are, or have been, suffering from mental disorder, and by section 6(2), included the provision of residential accommodation amongst the purposes for which arrangements were authorised or might be required to be made under section 28(1).

The powers of local authorities thus remained permissive unless the minister gave a directive under section 28(1) of the 1946 Act.

This position was not altered when section 12 of the Health Services and Public Health Act 1968 (now consolidated in section 21(1) of the National Health Service Act 1977) replaced section 28 of the National Health Service Act 1946, and the provision of residential accommodation for prevention and aftercare continued to be permissive, with the proviso, as before, that the minister could, by a direction, *require* such provision to be made.

In exercise of the powers vested in him by section 12(1) of the 1968 Act, the Secretary of State, by Local Authority Circular 19/74 dated 23 April 1974 *directed local authorities, "for the purpose of the prevention of mental disorder or in relation to persons who are, or have been, suffering from mental disorder . . . to provide residential accommodation* (including residential homes, hostels, group homes, minimum support facilities or other appropriate accommodation) for persons who are ordinarily resident within the area of the authority, and for persons in the authority's area who have no settled residence, and the care of persons for the time being resident in accommodation so provided.' Such direction replaced a former direction made under section 28 of the National Health Services Act 1946, but did not substantially affect the *implementation* of the duties placed upon local authorities.

Whilst the Secretary of State is vested with statutory powers to declare local authorities to be in default in relation to the carrying out of functions so imposed upon them, and to take steps to enforce the remedying of such default, including the transfer of such functions to himself (see section 57 of the National Health Service Act 1946) successive incumbents of that post have shown a marked reluctance to take any such step, despite officially acknowledging the poor record of local authorities generally in this vital respect. This reluctance may be illustrated by the fact that the then Secretary of State, David Ennals, addressing the Annual Conference of the National Association of Mental Health in July 1976, emphasised the need for public pressure on local authorities for the implementation of the shift to community care, thus, in effect, evading his own responsibility.

It is ironic in this context that the continued preference of successive governments for the indirect method of imposing duties upon local authorities by means of ministerial directives, as opposed to direct statutory obligations, could well be said to deprive the public of a potentially effective means of applying pressure, i.e. legal redress against the authorities enforceable in the Courts.

Government Policy Statements: Priorities and Finance

In para. 609 of its report, the Royal Commission made the assumption that 'a fair share of our national resources [would] be allocated in future to the mental health services both by the central government and by local authorities', and recognised that in many areas of these services there was a considerable amount of leeway to make up when compared with some other parts of the country's health and welfare services. The commission went on, in para. 610, to anticipate some reluctance on the part of certain local authorities to acknowledge their full responsibilities in the field of mental health, on account of the fact that almost the entire cost of local authorities' welfare services had to be met from rates raised by the authorities themselves.

Seebohm. However, impetus was given to local authority involvement through the report of the Seebohm Committee 1968 which recommended that social services departments should be formed and should assume full responsibility for mental health as part of the projected 'family service'. The report was critical of existing provision:

'despite the national commitment to "community care", and official plans to run down the number of mental hospital beds, [local authority expenditure] still represents a small fraction of total health expenditure for the mentally disordered. Although some local authorities have been remarkably successful in developing mental health services, there is a serious lack of staff, premises, money or public concern in other areas. The widespread belief that we have "community care" of the mentally disordered is, for many parts of the country, still a sad illusion and judging by published plans will remain so for years ahead.' With regard to *residential* care, the report considered that 'there must be more variety in the provision of residential care, an increase in the total quantity of provision, and an increase in its quality' and that 'there are two justifications for increasing the variety of residential care. First, since we do not know which are the most effective forms of care, it would be wrong to concentrate on only a limited range. Second, a greater variety would mean an ability to tap a greater pool of labour.' The Seebohm proposals were largely incorporated in the Social Services Act 1970 which 'replaced a number of fragmented specialisms with a confident generalism'.[61] It is unfortunate that the step which seemed progressive has not resulted in an equitable distribution of attention and resources.

The White Paper. The commission was more than justified in its fears that local authorities would in varying degrees fail to meet the challenge presented by the new Act, and was further justified in stressing the need to place a positive statutory duty upon them for that reason. This was confirmed by the review of developments in the mental health service, in the Government White Paper 'Better Services for the Mentally Ill' issued in October 1975. The White Paper was described in the foreword by the then Secretary of State for Social Services, Barbara Castle, as 'a long-term strategic document indicating the general direction in which we should move and the general background against which we should be taking decisions'. Since the general background and the necessary decisions were long since known and determined, the document was indeed long-term and strategic!

The White Paper sought to define the nature of mental illness, particularly in the light of changing concepts and sociological and scientific developments. It went on to examine developments in the services for the mentally ill, both in the decade prior to the enactment of the Mental Health Act in 1959 and subsequently, in order to ascertain to what extent the service envisaged by the Report of the Royal Commission had progressed. In para. 2.8 the White Paper acknowledged the fact that, while considerable progress had been made in implementing the 'open-door' policy from the hospital's viewpoint, there still remained a dearth of adequate supporting facilities in the community.

In para. 2.22 the following four broad policy objectives were identified as jointly forming the government's co-ordinated strategy to achieve the formation of an integrated, community-orientated service:

1. An expansion of local authority personal social services to provide residential, domiciliary, day care and social work support.
2. The relocation of the specialist services in local settings.
3. The establishment of the right organisational links between area social work teams and the social work staff in day centres and residential care, and between the multi-professional therapeutic teams and the primary care services.
4. A significant improvement in staffing to enable individual patient needs to be assessed and reviewed on a multi-professional basis and to provide for earlier intervention and preventive work.

As far as the first objective is concerned, the White Paper acknowledged that planning 'must take into account the prospects of securing the growing weight of expenditure that will be necessary on the part of the local authorities if we are to have any realistic hope of achieving the necessary shift towards the relevant community services'.

The remaining chapters of the White Paper examined the objectives both in the light of what had already been achieved and what remained to be achieved, identified the problems to be overcome and discussed the various elements of a comprehensive integrated and community-based service for the mentally ill. In para. 4.40, for example, it was generously concluded that while hostels for both short and long-term care and rehabilitation would numerically be a relatively small element in a comprehensive service, they were, nevertheless, a very important element.

In assessing the achievement in the 15 years since the passing of the Mental Health Act, the White Paper concluded that, while the horizons of the hospitals themselves had expanded into the community through the medium of increased out-patient attendances and day-centre facilities, non-hospital community resources were by and large still minimal. It conceded that the failure, 'for which central government as much as local government is responsible, to develop anything approaching adequate social services', was perhaps the greatest disappointment of the last 15 years.

Rather than announcing central government measures to remedy the resulting anomalies, the report rationalised the underprovision in terms of constraints imposed on local authorities by limited financial resources in the current economic climate.

It is in the context of the competing priorities confronting statutory authorities, both at central and local level, that the White Paper acknowledges the importance of the contribution of voluntary organisations in pioneering new developments and pledges continuing financial support for such voluntary activity as has relevance to the needs of the mentally ill. It was pointed out that, as at March 1974, voluntary organisations were providing nearly 30 per cent of the residential homes and hostels and 15 per cent of the day-centre places for the mentally ill and the view was expressed that while this proportion might fall as the expansion of local authority services took place, the voluntary sector would always have a unique and indispensable role to play, especially in the pioneering of new services.

The final chapter of the White Paper, entitled 'Progress Towards The New Service', briefly reviewed the difficulties and problems which had so far impeded progress towards an integrated service based on the philosophy of social rehabilitation, and concluded that for the same reasons it was likely to be many years before this pattern of services could be realised in practice throughout the country. Of the difficulties identified, financial resource constraints and the need to educate the community to accept its social and financial role in the rehabilitation of the mentally ill within the community were regarded as basic.

It acknowledged that continuing constraints on public expenditure were likely to be such that hard questions of priority would have to be faced over the entire spectrum of the health and social services, thus foreshadowing the consultative priorities document.

It was stressed in para. 11.16 that the national guidelines for health and local authority services based upon realistic resource assumptions would need to be translated into individual regional and area guidelines, and that for this purpose joint planning of health and local authority services was essential, such planning to take place through the medium of Joint Consultative Committees established under the National Health Service Reorganisation Act. A natural corollary of this development was the introduction of the DHSS Joint Financing Scheme in 1976, discussed below.

The problem raised by the administrative division in funding for treatment and aftercare between the National Health Service and local authorities has long been pointed out by bodies such as the Richmond Fellowship, which had thus far been ignored.

DHSS Planning Guidelines. The White Paper itself laid down planning guidelines for the three basic elements in an integrated district service for the mentally ill, i.e. psychiatric units in general hospitals, day centres and residential care facilities. The guidelines for hospitals suggested a minimum of 0.5 beds and 0.65 day-hospital places per 1,000 total population and those for day centres, 0.6 places per 1,000 population.

The department's *minimum* planning guidelines for residential care contemplated the provision of a range of accommodation, including hostels providing a relatively intensive programme of rehabilitation, staffed homes, small group homes and lodging schemes to meet a variety of short and long-term needs. The guideline level of provision for hostels suggested by the White Paper was 8 to 10 places per 200,000 population in areas of 'average need' and 10 to 12 places in areas of 'high need', while that for staffed homes and other long-stay accommodation was 30 places per 200,000 population in areas of 'average need' and 48 places for areas of 'higher need'.

Reduced to a smaller unit of population, 20,000, the suggested provision stands as follows:

		Area of average need	Area of high need
Short-term care		less than 1 (bed)	more than 1
Longer-term:	staffed	1	1.6
	unstaffed	2	2.4
Total		less than 4	more than 5

The suggested total for all types of residential provision for the mentally disturbed in the community is therefore between four and five places per 20,000 population, depending on the degree of need in the locality; and if staffed accommodation only is included, the suggested total is approximately two places per 20,000. The Richmond Fellowship would think it right to stress the distinction between staffed and unstaffed accommodation, as the degree of support and active work towards rehabilitation will inevitably be greatly affected by the participation of staff.

The Fellowship would further question the adequacy of the guidelines to meet the need. If it is remembered that one person in every 10, i.e. 400 people in every 4,000 can at some time in their lives be expected to suffer a mental breakdown, it may reasonably be estimated that at least *one* of that 400 is at any one time in need of staffed residential care.

The extent of provision indicated by the guidelines then begins to look sparse, and it appears realistic to consider that one staffed place would be the minimal provision for a population of 2,000, (10 staffed places for a population of 20,000): *a fivefold increase over the guidelines.*

The tentative and general character of these guidelines was stressed and they were stated to be subject to revision in the light of further experience and research. Whatever their objective accuracy, they serve as useful yardsticks to measure the achievements of both central and local government in the implementation of the department's proposals as embodied in the White Paper.

Annual Reviews. In para. 11.14 of the White Paper it was stated that a system of annual reviews over the whole field of health and social services had been set up by the DHSS to monitor developments in each sector and their financial and manpower resource implications, with the prime object of assisting decision-making on priorities and objectives over the following ten years.

The Consultative Document. The first annual review of the health and social services was published in 1976 by the DHSS in the form of a consultative document entitled *Priorities for Health and Personal Social Services in England.* It described itself as the first attempt 'to establish rational and systematic priorities throughout the health and personal social services', an exercise complicated and at the same time rendered more urgent by the need to restrain growth in public expenditure, as had been made apparent by the White Paper on Public Expenditure up to 1979/80, and by the fact that there existed areas in the field covered where past neglect had led to serious deficiencies. The document, by being consultative in nature, recognised that in a field of this complexity planning needed to be a co-operative enterprise in which both central and local government, the health authorities, professions and voluntary sector would take part.

While recognising the constraints imposed by the economic situation at the time, the document expressed the possibility of implementing two important aspects of government policy in the health services: the redistribution of resources in favour of deprived regions and areas, and the encouragement of joint planning between health and local authorities through the provision of special finance.

In the now familiar formula the document again highlighted the extent of unsatisfied need in the provision for the mentally ill as a major problem area, and designated services for the mentally ill as amongst those of first priority. It provided assessments of growth in current expenditure necessary to maintain the rate of progress towards the targets set out in the White Paper 'Better Services for the Mentally Ill', and the switch from hospital to community care implicit in the long-term strategies set out in that document. It recognised, as the White Paper had done, that local authority residential and day facilities, field work and domiciliary care fell far short of what was needed '*so that many patients stay unnecessarily in hospital or are discharged to unsatisfactory conditions in the community*'.[62]

In these services, in 1974, there were fewer than 4,000 residential places and only just over 5,000 day places, against an estimated national requirement of 12,000 and 30,000 places respectively. The document proposed in the period to 1979/80, increased *capital* programmes of £4 million a year for day centres and £3 million a year for residential accommodation, to yield an additional 1,200 and 350 places a year respectively. The growth rate in *current* expenditure on residential care was to be seven per cent annually, which is less than the annual inflation rate and results in a nil growth rate. On this basis it was estimated that the guidelines laid down in the White Paper would be achieved *over a 25-year period. This means that essential community services are, for many at least, a whole generation away.*

A number of ways in which faster growth could be achieved by local authorities were outlined, *including fuller use of places in the hostels of voluntary associations, 'some of which are at present underoccupied as a result of authorities seeking to reduce their financial commitment'* – and the importance of close contact between health and social services departments and voluntary organisations was stressed. It seemed possible that the submissions and recommendations of voluntary bodies such as the Richmond Fellowship had been heeded.

The Way Forward. In September 1977 the government continued what the Secretary of State, David Ennals, chose to call 'the debate' on priorities opened by the 1976 consultative document, by publishing a further review under the title *The Way Forward*. Therein lip service continued to be paid to the importance of adjusting the balance of care to a community-based service for the mentally ill, embracing a full range of facilities including community hospitals, hostels, day hospitals, residential homes, day centres and domiciliary support. Some adjustment was made in the departmental guidelines for residential care, particularly between the various categories, the range for the mental illness group being reflected as 19 to 30 places per 100,000 population.

One of the main aims of departmental planning continued to be identified as the remedying 'of past neglect of services, particularly those for the mentally ill'. The document envisaged that some increased resources would be available to local authorities 'supplemented by steadily increasing contributions by health authorities to the cost of jointly planned social services activities'.

White Paper: 'Review of the Mental Health Act 1959'. This long-awaited document, which had been foreshadowed by a consultative document on the same subject in August 1976, appeared in September 1978. It was rightly condemned in the press for being too cautious and conservative, and for merely 'tinkering with the detail of the Act', thus losing a major opportunity for laying down a legal framework for a progressive community-based mental health service with adequate and rationally based financing arrangements.

The White Paper, almost without exception, confines its attention to the limits set by the Act itself and examines various aspects of the mentally ill patient largely in the context of the hospital, dealing with compulsory admission, admission procedures, offender patients, safeguards for patients and staff, patients' rights and ancillary matters. Chapter 1 does examine the definition of mental disorder in the Act, but it is only in Chapter 4, 'Guardianship and Compulsory Powers in the Community', that any attention is given to the care and rehabilitation of the mentally ill in the broad sense. There is some discussion of the proposal made by the National Association for Mental Health (MIND), the Royal College of Psychiatrists and the Butler Committee, that more use should be made of guardianship as an alternative to detention in hospital, as well as of the suggestion that it would be possible to discharge some patients from hospital earlier, or avert hospitalisation, if there were powers for compulsory supervision or aftercare following discharge: the proposed *essential powers*. Under this option a social services authority would, for example, have specific powers to require residence in a specified place (a therapeutic community?) or to require attendance at specified places for treatment, occupation or training. The British Association of Social Workers has proposed a new type of compulsory order, to be designated 'community care order', which would parallel and provide an alternative to compulsory hospital powers, and under which social services departments would have a responsibility to care for, and to control, persons subject to the order.

Whilst inviting views on the three main options or combinations thereof, the White Paper drew attention to certain objections to the introduction of compulsory powers outside hospital, including, significantly, the fact that the number of people whom the powers might benefit seemed likely to be limited, as their use would depend upon the ability of social services staff to take on the work and responsibilities involved, not only by reason of lack of suitable experience and training, but also economic factors. In para. 4.13 the point was made that changes in the nature of compulsory powers should be in keeping with the building up of local networks of health and social services 'with the emphasis on the community-based patterns of care and after-care' contemplated by the 'Better Services' White Paper.

Certainly, a system of compulsory powers in the community involving community care orders, will be largely ineffective in the absence of a fully adequate community care and aftercare service throughout the country. The introduction of such a system at this stage would not only lead to discrimination in favour of those clients who are fortunate enough to reside in areas where the government guidelines for residential provision have been met, but could also have harmful consequences for those upon whom care orders are made, by reason of inadequate or inappropriate facilities and lack of trained staff.

The Achievements of Legislation and Policy

The co-operative efforts of central government, local government and the voluntary sector are essential in order that progress may be made in accordance with policy. Any attempt to look critically at achievements must therefore assess the total contribution of these three participants, and the relationships between them. It is, however, first necessary to review the progress made towards policy targets, in terms of expenditure and of provision: what do official statistics reveal the present level of attainment to be?

What the Figures Say

Comparative tables of actual expenditure in 1975/6, and of projected expenditure for 1979/80, have indicated reasonably close approximation to the programme estimate of expenditure in the consultative document for the mental health sector as a whole. However, the projected increase in local authority expenditure per head of population on residential facilities for the mentally ill in the five years from 1975/6 to 1979/80 was from 8p to 10p, whilst the cost per occupied place was expected to rise from £920 to £980 – 6.5 per cent. It is hard to reconcile these figures with the effective growth rate in expenditure of seven per cent *annually*, contemplated by the consultative document – a rate already in peril from the ravages of inflation.

Targets for service delivery were contained in the White Paper, in which the DHSS guidelines were expressed as the *minimum* requirement for areas of average and high need. In the DHSS guidelines for planning in 1978/9 issued by the department on 20 March (LAC(78)6), it was stated that the number of residential places for the mentally ill was, according to the statistics available, in line with the guidelines as revised in *The Way Forward.* The Secretary of State, replying to a question in the House of Commons on 13 June 1978, stated in support of this contention that:

> According to local authority returns, the number of places available to local authorities at 31st March, 1976, was about 4,700. 'The Way Forward' envisaged an increase to some 5,500 places by 1980. The number of places available at 31st March, 1977, according to the latest figure, was about 5,300.[63]

It is clear from the following reply to another question in the House on the same day that the statistics included not only local authorities' own facilities but also and rightly those made available to them by other organisations, such as voluntary associations, on whom, in fact, much of the financial burden still falls:

> **Mr. Moyle**: The number of places in England available in local

authority residential accommodation for adult mentally ill people at 31st March in the years 1974 to 1977 was as follows:

1974	3,628
1975	4,496
1976	4,685
1977	5,299[64]

The figures quoted include places made available to local authorities by other organisations.

Neither the questioner nor the respondent refers to the important factor of whether such facilities are staffed or not.

To see these figures in true perspective it needs also to be noted that at 31 March 1977, of 108 authorities in England, only *31* authorities (29 per cent) had met the guideline planning ratio for residential places for the adult mentally ill suggested in 'Better Services for the Mentally Ill' as a *minimum* for areas of 'average need'. At the same date eleven out of 108 authorities (ten per cent) did not record *any* residential provision for the adult mentally ill.[65]

Undoubtedly a major factor at the root of overall underprovision is to be found in central government's relative inability to enforce policies and patterns of spending at local government level. While welcoming certain developments evidenced by *The Way Forward*, the National Association for Mental Health document, *A Small Step Forward*, described it as a major disappointment, in that it highlighted central government's inability to influence local decision-making. It therefore urged the DHSS to address itself to the task of developing working relationships with local government and health authorities, so as to provide a more effective sequel to policy statements. Amongst the strategies recommended by the National Association for Mental Health were earmarked funds for local authorities, tightening up the legal framework in which mental health services to the community are provided, and addressing itself to the basic need to set and achieve qualitative standards of treatment and rehabilitation. The latter two recommendations would need to be carefully applied as they could create a new set of problems. New projects under *present* legislation are rarely attempted. The lesson learned from other developed countries is that good initiatives may be stifled by over-restrictive legislation. The demand for qualitative standards begs the question of how quality of service is to be interpreted. Whilst guidance is certainly needed and certain requirements can and must be made of all who provide services, there needs to be considerable flexibility in practice. The department could certainly take a much greater lead by initiating and financing evaluation and research in this field. Another important aspect of setting standards is the need for specialist training for the staff of these services. Since 1959 the Fellowship has pointed out the omission in the Mental Health Act of provision for training, and it is still the only organisation to provide a full-scale and relevant in-service training for people working in residential mental health facilities.

The harsh reality is that while, during the period under review, economic necessity has dictated restrictions on public expenditure, many local authorities have made capital and other expenditure on personal social services the target for savings, *in disregard of* the priorities spelt out in the g vernment policy documents already discussed. This is illustrated by the fact that the total figures for *capital* projects approved were £20 million in 1976/7, and £29 million in 1977/8, compared with capital expenditure assumptions of £68 million and £46 million respectively. These cutbacks were far in excess of what the government had anticipated, presumably not just out of sheer negligence in planning, but to avoid the subsequent outlay in running costs.

Cutbacks have similarly been effected in payment of maintenance for individual residents in psychiatric aftercare facilities. In some areas the criteria of eligibility for aid have been applied with increasing stringency, whilst in other cases the criteria have been changed, so that people presenting 'management problems' may take precedence over those who are most able to benefit. Some local authorities have introduced a quota system of grant allocation, so that applicants who are acknowledged to be both in need and eligible for assistance, cannot be accepted, or must endure long waiting periods. Various instances have been noted recently by the Richmond Fellowship: for example, a quota system is in operation by the Royal Borough of Kensington and Chelsea, who sponsor a maximum of seven residents for places in a 24-bedded hostel (established in the borough at its own request). Three suitable applicants are, at the time of writing, unable to take up the vacancies which have been offered, as the quota is full. As at January 1979, a total of 17 applicants who had been accepted for places in Richmond Fellowship houses in the UK were unable to take up their vacancy because the grant from the relevant local authority was not available. *As a result of the unavailability of grants, many social workers cease to refer clients, so that the magnitude of the need is increasingly hidden.* An analysis of the effects of the system is contained in a Research Report, 'Accommodation Needs of the Mentally Ill'.[66]

The quota system does not substantiate the hopes of David Crompton (Chapter 21) that the mentally ill were to be accorded the same level of care as children in need: 'the ascertainment of need of an individual, followed by the seeking of an appropriate placement, whether in a local authority home or, alternatively, in a unit run by a voluntary organisation.' Instead, those in need must fit the provision – a procrustean bed of extreme frustration and deprivation. If the quota system is defensible, may one propose that it be applied consistently towards all who are referred for residential placement, including the grossly disturbed and the convicted offender? It needs to be acknowledged that the disturbed or isolated adult may at some stage be as vulnerable and deserving of care as an infant; the recognition of his or her helplessness, and provision for that condition, is a necessary step towards enabling the adult to achieve autonomy.

The Voluntary Agency

The information given by the Secretary of State clearly indicates that DHSS targets could not be approached without the contribution of the voluntary sector. The extent of the voluntary contribution is illustrated in recent figures for residential places for the adult mentally ill: as at 31 March 1976 the total number of places available to local authorities in England and Wales was 5,100. Of these, 2,913 were provided by the local authorities (57 per cent), and 2,187 (43 per cent) by voluntary and private bodies.

In considering the relationship of voluntary agencies to government policy, two questions need to be posed. First, is it desirable that a large part of the responsibility for implementing government policy should rest with the voluntary sector? And if so, what is the proper degree of support which voluntary agencies should expect from local and central government?

The Wolfenden Report, *The Future of Voluntary Organisations*,[67] has drawn attention to the wide spectrum of activities and interests that are the province of voluntary effort. It is not surprising therefore that inappropriate generalisations are sometimes applied to this field, particularly regarding such issues as professionalism and professional standards, organisational stability, and efficiency; and the publication of the report stimulated a number of such criticisms. It was commented that voluntary organisations might not always be strong and flexible enough to survive and change in response to changing needs; queries were raised regarding systems of lay involvement in casework decisions and the disbursement of funds; and criticisms were made concerning the lack of accountability which sometimes mars the work of the voluntary sector.

All of these criticisms can at one time or another be applied to some voluntary bodies; but there are many bodies with excellent records of, for example, stability, relevance to need, and professional standards. There are also of course many instances in which local authority services themselves incur censure for those very shortcomings; and the work of professional staff is similarly, in the local authority, constrained by the surveillance of largely non-professional councillors. As in all areas of personal service, there is no foolproof system, although a degree of evaluation, monitoring, inspection and accountability can and must be built in. Let it not be said, however, that the justification for the voluntary organisation is that its services may be no worse than those of government bodies!

The Wolfenden Report identifies four major areas in which the voluntary organisation has a role to play. One is that of pressure group or advocate/adviser. The others are in the field of service delivery, that is, as the pioneer of new services in their experimental stage; as provider of complementary, additional or alternative services, offering a choice or enhanced quality of provision to the consumer; and as sole provider of a service. In each of these areas it is likely that the voluntary agency may choose to represent a minority interest – minority, that is, in terms of its popular appeal, although not necessarily numerically (for example alcoholics, the mentally ill, the recidivist offender), and the validity of such representation has been debated by local authorities. On the one hand it is felt by some local authorities that they have not been given a mandate by the ratepayer to make provision for unpopular causes – and 'unpopular' carries the connotation 'undeserving', in that help for these groups is considered wasteful as it does not offer identifiable gains to society. Other local authorities feel that instead of abdicating 'in favour' of voluntary bodies, it is the duty of the *statutory* bodies to make provision in the most demanding and least supported fields. Whilst commendable, such a development seems unlikely to be tolerated on any large scale. Historically, pioneering projects have been initiated by individual reformers and agencies which have not been accountable to the public nor constrained by public opinion; as David Crompton points out in Chapter 21, 'In some spheres of activity the local authorities are cautious to commence a service, for example with drug addicts and alcoholics . . . In other areas of work the statutory authorities have almost completely taken over responsibility, and some people may say that this suggests that the type of problem has now become socially acceptable'. Public accountability means that hostels managed entirely by local authorities are more likely to carry the requirement that their goals be clearly identifiable and justifiable to the public, and that they conform to accepted social standards and values. Crompton, in his suggested range of provisions, identifies possible goals as: long-term support of chronic patients in the community; treatment of young people with behaviour disorders; rehabilitation for work of young, well-motivated adults; and minimally supportive long-term housing. These goals, with the exception of the first, are of direct benefit to society as a whole as well as to the individual, and are therefore justifiable and explicable to the public. Other goals however may be less easily explicable, but no less important. The process of rehabilitation will ideally include opportunities for resolution of conflict and maturation, but in the context of local authority provision it may not be possible to articulate these goals, or even to address them. They are nevertheless of major importance to the consumer, and constitute a large part of the aims and job satisfaction of residential staff.

At the other extreme, there is much evidence to suggest that governments tend to act also on the basis of guilt rather than of reason and social utility. Both in the United Kingdom and the United States there are instances of undue emphasis on returning the institutionalised, chronic patient to an unwelcoming and unprepared society at the expense of devoting resources to the prevention of further institutionalisation. The duty exists to provide a reasoned system of priorities and so far as possible appropriate care for people of all age-groups and diagnostic categories, rather than to give an inappropriate emotional response; and it is in meeting a variety of kinds and degrees of need that the voluntary agency has an essential role to play, by reason of its specialist interest and expertise.

As significant as the *role* of the voluntary agency is its *mode of operation.* Two specific assets attach to the voluntary agency: the first is its *flexibility* which derives from responsible use of its independent status; the second is its *reliance on individual initiatives and involvement*, both of its own personnel and of the community. The creative opportunities of non-bureaucratic voluntary organisations can profoundly influence the calibre of staff attracted, thus enriching the quality of the service.

The flexibility of the voluntary agency is of benefit not only in its choice of target but in its methods of work. The Richmond Fellowship, for example, was able, at a time when residential care was largely institutional in pattern, to implement practices which would encourage personal responsibility and a sense of individual worth: choice of room decoration, joint planning of communal areas, participation in planning the house programme and, above all, the validation of the individual's contribution. The use of residential staff as individual and group counsellors was an innovation which, in the early days of the Richmond Fellowship, evoked criticism based on spurious distinctions between 'treatment' and 'rehabilitation'. In the present climate such distinctions are generally recognised to be inappropriate, although there is still a great dearth of training courses which will assist residential staff to develop the necessary therapeutic skills.

As a corollary of being relatively independent of government, the voluntary agency is more dependent on its own personnel, and on the neighbourhood and society at large, and this pool of voluntary strength constitutes a resource which is frequently underestimated by statutory bodies. Morale and co-operation may be greatly enhanced by the fact that a scheme is local, that it is dependent on local resources and goodwill for its survival, and that it is influenced by, and can in turn influence, the neighbourhood. Even the inability of most voluntary agencies to attract substantial government funds is not a wholly negative factor: financial dependency, to a reasonable degree, enhances the mutual involvement of the organisation and the community (although a point may be reached at which financial hardship becomes detrimental). On balance the reliance of the organisation on neighbourhood support makes for close involvement, and allows the voluntary agency to exploit its unique strength: enabling the potential power and goodwill of citizens to be actualised through response to a real need, and in this process achieving the goal of integration.

Government Support for the Voluntary Sector

It appears, then, that the voluntary sector has a role to play, especially in providing for specific areas of need and developing specialist skills. At the present time, also, the volume of services needed is heavily dependent on the contribution from voluntary sources.

Despite these considerations, however, financial support from government is pitifully inadequate. It is clear from the evidence that many local authorities neither make their own provision nor provide aid to voluntary bodies, and the deteriorating economic climate has led to the cutbacks in maintenance payments already mentioned. In addition, central government through the DHSS fails to recognise the need of service organisations for support, although giving substantial assistance to pressure groups. The justification for this discrimination appears to be that the clients of service organisations are sponsored financially by local authorities. This approach clearly ignores the needs of service organisations for the financing of new projects, the cost of research vital to adequate forward planning, the provision of consultation and public information, and the burden of central administration and staff training. The effects of government *laissez-faire* are twofold: inhibited growth of services, and inflated charges for residents in existing establishments, leading inevitably in turn to a quantitative reduction in local authority usage, and further spiralling costs. The joint financing scheme, discussed below, has not so far revealed itself in practice as an effective vehicle for providing vital central government funding.

The Joint Financing Scheme

The major contribution by the government towards a shift to a community-based mental health service, with the accent on rehabilitation, has undoubtedly been the joint financing scheme introduced in 1976. This was a necessary corollary of joint planning by health and local authorities towards a community-orientated service, for the purposes of which joint care planning teams had already been set up.

Joint financing proposals were first announced in the consultative document, which stressed their relevance to the development of effective services for the mentally ill and proposed the allocation of funds rising from £8 million in 1976 to £27 million by 1979/80. An increase to £40 million in 1980/1 was subsequently announced. Joint planning and joint financing between health and local authorities were 'recommended' in Circular HC (76) 18 issued by the DHSS in March 1976, as part of the government's overall strategy of developing community-based services for, *inter alia*, the mentally ill. Joint financing was described as being in essence designed 'to allow the limited and controlled use of resources available to health authorities for the purpose of *supporting selected projects for which local authorities bear the prime responsibility*'. The criterion by which it was suggested an Area Health Authority should use the money allocated to it from National Health Service funds, was that the project was in the interests of the National Health Service and *could be expected to make a better contribution in terms of total care than if directly applied to health services.*

The scheme was modified in several important aspects when Circular LAC (77) 10 replaced the original circular in May 1977, specific provision being made then for assistance with revenue spending even in respect of capital projects not originally financed under the scheme, *and for assistance to voluntary organisations, either with the object of helping to get a project established or to prevent its abandonment.*

Doubts as to whether the government's joint financing/planning strategy would encourage local authorities to create community facilities were expressed by the Royal College of Psychiatrists in its comments on the consultative document, and the college said that it would prefer to see the provision of community facilities as *a mandatory obligation* on local authorities.[68]

It cannot be denied that, in principle, joint planning and the joint financing proposals are a significant step towards the rationalisation of public expenditure on integrated health and social services, but it remains to be seen to what extent their potential will be realised. The inherent weakness of the proposals which has been revealed so far is that they are exclusively permissive in character, and no allocation can be made under the scheme without the active participation of the local authority concerned. Not only is there no positive duty imposed on any of the authorities concerned to resort to the scheme, but there is also *no overall central machinery to monitor the application of funds to ensure that planning and financial allocation accord with the priorities identified in the consultative document* and other policy statements. Area Health Authorities are required to notify the Minister of Health of details of projects selected for joint financing *only* if the project requires capital expenditure exceeding £50,000. As a result the government could certainly be accused of irresponsibility in relying too heavily on joint planning and financing to bring about the desired aim of achieving comprehensive and integrated services.

That joint financing is essential to the government's planning seems clear from *The Way Forward*, where it is said: 'Some increased resources will be available also to the local authorities, supplemented by steadily increasing contributions by health authorities to the cost of jointly planned social service activities. This will provide a sound base from which further expansion can take place.'[69] While one would have expected local authorities to have welcomed joint planning and financing as a means of escaping the full weight of constraints imposed by the present state of the economy, in fact they have been in many instances deterred by the obligation, under the scheme, to assume full financial responsibility for any project financed thereunder after a period of five years, and the 'tapering-off' of contributions by health authorities towards revenue spending in the intervening years. Circular LAC (77) 10 expressly states that the objective in all cases will be for the local authority to assume full financial responsibility as soon as possible.

The following figures reflect the proportions of the total joint finance allocations spent for the years and on the services specified, and clearly indicate a marked imbalance between allocations to services for the mentally ill and handicapped on the one hand and other services on the other hand. They indicate also a marked degree of unequal treatment between the mentally handicapped and the mentally ill, which does not appear to be justified by the assessments of relative need contained in the various official statements:

Joint financing expenditure		Services for the mentally handicapped per cent	Services for the mentally ill per cent
1976–77:	Capital	16	5
	Revenue	4	1
1977–78:	Capital	18	6
	Revenue	9	3

Source: Hansard, vol. 951, no. 131, col. 436

It may be of significance to note that Mr Moyle, in furnishing these figures in Parliament, was unable to give information about joint finance sums provided to voluntary organisations, although he was asked to do so.

The extent to which monies allocated under the scheme were actually expended showed progressive increase over the first two years. Of the £8 million made available in 1976–7, £4¼ million was taken up, whilst of the £21 million made available in 1977–8, approximately £19½ million is estimated to have been taken up.[70] In 1976–7 two-thirds of expenditure was on capital projects, but this diminished in 1977–8 to rather less than 50 per cent.

Whilst increasing resources to the funds made available in terms of the scheme appears on the face of it to be impressive, it does not necessarily follow that the objectives of the scheme, i.e. to provide additional sources of financing for local authority community health programmes in accordance with the priorities spelt out by central government, are being realised. The application of the scheme appears in fact to be distorted by the respective needs, in the existing economic climate, of the health authorities on the one hand, and the local authorities on the other.

The figures cited by Peter Townsend showed that the bulk of expenditure was accounted for by two client groups – the elderly and the mentally handicapped. He identified two crucial problems: the first, that planning was being carried out in relation to types of client group rather than type or severity of need, and the second, that client groups were being artificially segregated from life in the ordinary community, by providing an alternative form of *institution* for those who would previously have been cared for within the hospital system. From the point of view of the hospital service, he commented that Area Health Authorities have tended to prefer capital schemes because these imply long-term alleviation of the rising costs of hospital provision.

The 'tailing off' provision already referred to has clearly also distorted the approach of local authorities. In a special report by Gregg Kelly published in *Social Work Today* and drawn from a survey by the British Association of Social Workers, it was stated that 'the sting in the tail for the local authorities is that . . . "the objective in all cases will be for the local authority to assume full financial responsibility as soon as possible" '. The report concluded that 'because of its failure to guarantee local authorities the resources to meet the revenue commitments when area health authorities' contributions tail off, the structure of joint financing has not encouraged the growth of community care projects. Because of their "no growth" situation and because of predictions of growth of only around two per cent in the foreseeable future, social services departments have been forced to steer away from projects with extensive long-term revenue consequences.'[71] This tendency clearly favours long-stay minimum support projects, as opposed to those involving intensive care and support having rehabilitation of the client as their object. For similar reasons a rash of what the report calls 'Father Christmas' schemes have been fostered, having no ongoing revenue expenditure implications, such as the provision of fittings, furniture and decoration for all kinds of institutions, minibuses and so on.

The experience of one voluntary organisation, the Richmond Fellowship (which campaigned for a joint funding scheme in the early 1960s), may be cited to illustrate the workings and shortcomings of the present scheme, at least in so far as it affects similar bodies. In an effort to obtain revenue assistance under the scheme, to support those of its halfway houses threatened by low occupancy as a result primarily of inadequate local authority grant support for its residents, the Fellowship made formal approaches to the Area Health and local authorities for all the areas in which the houses were located. Of fifteen such applications made, only two were successful, both the Devon Area Health Authority and the Cheshire Area Health Authority agreeing to sponsor a specified number of residents at the houses in Exeter and Chester respectively. In this way the local authorities concerned, which lent their full support to the applications, were enabled to increase the number of referrals made beyond that which their own finances permitted.

All other applications, although submitted promptly, were either unsuccessful or consideration thereof was deferred, the reasons given in the former case including

– that all allocations were already committed
– that the Fellowship's proposals were not among those given priority for the limited funds available.

One London borough (Camden) stated that joint funding, in view of its tapering nature, did not appear appropriate for the maintenance of residents at the house concerned, and suggested that the Fellowship consider seeking approval of an increase in its residents' fee structure, and also attempt to obtain a greater central government grant from the DHSS! The first suggestion, even if successful, would obviously be self-defeating as it would result in fewer residents being able to be sponsored by local authorities with already restricted social services budgets. The second suggestion completes the vicious circle, as central government has always adopted the view that the sponsoring of residents is the responsibility of local authorities, and apparently acts on the assumption that overhead costs for the promotion of the work generally are a low priority.

Conclusion

Whatever changes emanate from recent policies, one is led to the inescapable conclusion, after so many brave words in the form of official pronouncements, and the dexterous juggling of figures that we have witnessed, that the conception of an adequate, community-based service for the mentally ill after twenty years remains bitterly remote from reality.

Be this as it may, such judgement is, of course, open to attack on the grounds that it gives insufficient credit for what progress there has been in a very unfavourable economic climate. In weighing up the facts that are available, it is necessary to bear in mind that the validity of the assumptions underlying the government's guidelines remains unproven, and upon those guidelines the government's case rests as far as the local authority's share of the burden is concerned. Much research is needed in the whole field of mental illness, not only for the purpose of testing the validity of the guidelines, but also in order to establish degrees and kinds of needs, both geographic and diagnostic as well as in terms of age-grouping, and, finally, to make some assessment of the kind of residential care that can assist each particular group, and how and through which body such care can most effectively be provided.

If Britain is to have an adequate comprehensive service within the lifetime of those who suffer or who are now at risk, the urgency of the task demands recognition. Inflation may for ever be called upon to justify deferred or cancelled provision, but human need cannot be ignored without danger to society. In the words of Margaret Mead: 'If we select for first consideration the most vulnerable amongst us . . . then our whole culture is humanised . . . Our values as individuals, our success as a society, can be measured by compassion for the vulnerable.'

Notes

1. See Department of Health and Social Security (DHSS), *Action for Mental Health*; *The Way Forward* (1977); Government White Paper, 'Better Services for the Mentally Ill', Cmnd. 6233 (1975).
2. A.T. Scull, *Decarceration: Community Treatment and the Deviant – A Radical View* (Prentice-Hall, Spectrum Books, 1977).
3. Ibid.
4. Government, 'Better Services'.
5. K. Jones, *A History of the Mental Health Services* (Routledge and Kegan Paul, London, 1972).
6. Summarised in Sainsbury's paper 'Selecting the Patient: The In-patient for Discharge' given at the Conference on Psychiatric Care in the Community, Royal Society of Health, London, 1968.
7. Ibid.
8. D. Bennett, 'The Camberwell District Psychiatric Services 1964–1974: The Provision of Alternatives to Mental Health Hospital Care' in L.I. Stein and M.A. Test (eds.), *Alternatives to Mental Hospital Treatment* (Plenum Press, Wisconsin, 1978).
9. Ibid.
10. J.K. Wing and A.M. Hailey, *Evaluating a Community Psychiatric Service:*

The Camberwell Register 1964–71 (Oxford University Press, London, 1972).
11. Ibid., p. 211.
12. Ibid., p. 241.
13. See Stein and Test, *Alternatives*.
14. L.R. Mosher and A.Z. Menn, 'Lowered Barriers in the Community: The Soteria Model' in L.I. Stein and M.A. Test (eds.), *Alternatives to Mental Hospital Treatment* (Plenum Press, Wisconsin, 1978).
15. See for example, Glasscote *et al.*, *Partial Hospitalisation for the Mentally Ill – A Study of Programs and Problems* (Joint Information Service, Washington, DC, 1969).
16. See I. Hoffman and P.R. Singer, 'The Incompatibility of the Medical Model and the Therapeutic Community', *Social Science and Medicine*, vol. 2, no. 6 (April 1977), pp. 425–31.
17. DHSS, *Priorities for Health.*
18. DHSS, *The Way Forward.*
19. These figures are for England and Wales. See PSSC/Central Health Services Council, *Collaboration in Community Care* (HMSO, London, 1978).
20. J. Berke, *The Butterfly Man* (Hutchinson & Co., London, 1977).
21. J.K. Wing and G.W. Brown, *Institutionalism and Schizophrenia: A Comparative Study of Three Mental Hospitals, 1960–1968* (Cambridge University Press, Cambridge, 1970).
22. Government, 'Better Services'.
23. Hoffman and Singer, 'Incompatibility of Medical Model'.
24. J. Richards, 'Whose Need?', *Social Work Today* (March 1973).
25. Wing and Brown, *Institutionalism*.
26. See for example the 1970–1 survey by the Office for Population Censuses and Surveys, quoted in 'Better Services'. It was found that twice as many women as men were diagnosed by their GPs as suffering from anxiety or depressive neurosis.
27. G.W. Brown and T. Harris, *Social Origins of Depression: a Study of Psychiatric Disorder in Women* (Tavistock, London, 1978).
28. See *Social Work Today* (June 1978).
29. C. Chien and J.O. Cole, 'Landlord-supervised Co-operative Apartments: A New Modality for Community-based Treatment', *American Journal of Psychiatry*, vol. 130, no. 2 (February 1973), pp. 156–9.
30. E. Jansen, 'A Contemporary Myth Maintained by Common Consent', unpublished paper presented to the 6th World Conference of Psychiatry, Honolulu, 1977.
31. G. Nash, 'Community Response to a Narcotic Treatment Facility: The Case of Prospect Place' in G. De Leon (ed.), *Phoenix House: Studies in a Therapeutic Community 1968–73* (MSS Information Corporation, New York, 1974).
32. M. Balint, *The Doctor, his Patient and the Illness* (Pitman Medical Press, London, 1964).
33. W.M. Mendel and R.E. Allen,'Rescue and Rehabilitation', in L.I. Stein and M.A. Test (eds.), *Alternatives to Mental Hospital Treatment* (Plenum Press, New York and London, 1978).
34. E. Bardach, 'Upgrading the Quality of Residential Care for the Long-term Mentally Ill in the Community: An Alternative to Licensing', unpublished article, King's View Foundation, 1974.
35. P. Ryan and S. Hewett, 'A Pilot Study of Hostels for the Mentally Ill', *Social Work Today* (March 1976).
36. A. Deutsch, *The Mentally Ill in America* (Columbia University Press, New York, 1949).

37. US Department of Health, Education and Welfare Directory, 1977.
38. W. Kohen and G.L. Paul, 'Current Trends and Recommended Changes in the Extended-care Placement of Mental Patients', *The Schizophrenia Bulletin* (University of Illinois, n.d.).
39. E.A. Hefferin, 'Rehabilitation in Nursing Home Situations', *Journal of American Geriatric Society*, vol. 16 (1968), pp. 296–312; R. Reich, 'Care of the Chronically Mentally Ill – A National Disgrace', *American Journal of Psychiatry*, vol. 130 (1973), pp. 911–12.
40. J.L. Raush and C.L. Raush, *The Halfway House Movement: A Search for Sanity* (Appleton-Century-Crofts, New York, 1968).
41. L.D. Ozarin and M.J. Witkin, *Halfway Houses for the Mentally Ill and Alcoholics* (NIMH, 1973).
42. Unpublished preliminary report on Community Alternatives written for the German Marshall Memorial Fund.
43. Licensing of Transitional Groupliving Facilities is now undertaken by the Department of Mental Hygiene in New York State.
44. M. Greenblatt, 'The Revolution in Mental Health – US Style' in M. Beiser, R. Krell, T. Lin and M.H. Miller (eds.), *Today's Priorities in Mental Health: Knowing and Doing* (Symposium Specialists, Miami, 1978).
45. Keynote Address given by Rosalynn Carter at the Vancouver Congress for the World Federation for Mental Health, published in Beiser *et al.* (eds.), *Today's Priorities.*
46. Report of the Senate Standing Committee on Health and Welfare, 'Mentally and Physically Handicapped Persons in Australia' (1971).
47. Report from the National Hospitals and Health Services Commission Interim Committee, 'A Community Health Programme for Australia' (June 1973).
48. McClemens, *Report of the Honourable Mr Justice McClemens* (1961). Royal Commissioner appointed to inquire into certain matters affecting Callan Park Mental Hospital, Government Printer, Sydney.
49. Commonwealth Department of Health, Canberra, 'A Report on Voluntary Activity in the Field of Mental Health' (1979).
50. C.B. Keogh, *'GROW', Australia's Community Mental Health Movement and the Start of a World Mental Health Community* (GROW Publications, 1977).
51. *Victorian Yearbook 1977* and Report of the Mental Health Authority of the State of Victoria for the year ending 31 December 1976.
52. Anne D. Liddy and Margaret L. Basser (September 1974), 'A Survey of Conditions of Ex-patients of a Psychiatric Hospital', in *Poverty and Mental Illness* (The Australian Government Publishing Service, Canberra, 1977).
53. Commonwealth Department of Health, Director General's Report, 1975/6 and 1977/8. Currently approximately 822 projects, including over 90 women's refuges, are funded under the Programme.
54. 'The Report of the Task Force on Co-ordination in Welfare and Health' (The Bailey Report) (The Australian Government Publishing Service, Canberra, 1976).
55. Report of the Royal Commission on the Law Relating to Mental Illness and Mental Deficiency (HMSO, London, 1957), para. 603.
56. Government, 'Better Services'.
57. Jones, *Mental Health Services*, p. 326.
58. Figures supplied by the DHSS.
59. DHSS Annual Report, 1975.
60. DHSS In-patient statistics for the Mental Health Enquiry for England.
61. Jones, *Mental Health Services*, p. 332.
62. DHSS, *Priorities for Health*, para. 8.3.

63. *Hansard*, vol. 951, no. 131, col. 438.
64. Ibid., col. 437.
65. Ibid., cols. 436–7.
66. Research Report, Principal Research Officer, Social Services Department of the Royal Borough of Kensington and Chelsea, 'Accommodation Needs of the Mentally Ill' (May 1979).
67. *The Future of Voluntary Organisations – Report of the Wolfenden Committee* (Croom Helm, London, 1978).
68. *British Journal of Psychiatry* (August 1976).
69. DHSS, *The Way Forward*, para. 1.6.
70. P. Townsend, 'A Review of Joint Financing Schemes for the Disability Allowance'.
71. Gregg Kelly, *Social Work Today* (August 1978).

18 THE POLITICS OF THERAPEUTIC COMMUNITIES (USA)

Theodore Cooper (Transcript)

Innovative, creative and courageous action is required to address hazards to mental health. Such action is against the grain of convention and against the easy way to do things, yet consecutive administrations have approved the goal of de-institutionalisation as a major priority. In this context, the work of the Richmond Fellowship, in introducing a meaningful connection and distinction between medicine and sociology, is at the forefront of many of the problems encountered in the development of a National Health policy.

The roles of major components of the Health Service delivery system are rapidly changing and we are seeing a real effort toward community-based services in general. So far, however, we have been only partially successful in providing comprehensive community-based services. One of the reasons for this is political; as the saying goes: 'nobody dies of a lack of comprehensive services'. You die of something and that is a political reality that we have to live with. The ease with which money can be stirred up to support cancer research or heart disease research is being experienced overall. It is much easier to get money when you can go and talk about somebody who has died with a heart disease rather than about the need for community-based services. Nevertheless, the hospital population in the area of mental health constitutes a tremendous problem, particularly here in the United States. Despite all the dramatic progress in reducing the inappropriate institutionalisation it is quite clear that thousands remain confined in hospitals, nursing homes or other institutional settings because of a lack of adequate community alternatives. Many others have been discharged from these settings, and have been thrown back into the community only to develop a pattern of recidivism or worse, which results in a totally unsatisfactory human solution. We have to recognise that many people are beginning to look at these problems solely in terms of *judicial* solutions at the expense of therapeutic implications, and that worries me a great deal. Judicial intervention on behalf of the mentally disabled is an example. I could cite the Supreme Court decision of Donaldson versus O'Connor which established a right to freedom for thousands of non-dangerous individuals previously confined to institutions. The implementation of this decision presents very difficult problems. Another example: Nixon versus Weinberger held that the laws of the District of Columbia indicated that mentally ill persons had the right to suitable care and treatment in the least restrictive setting, appropriate to their needs, and directed us to make provision. Congress, on hearing about some of the outrageous conditions and settings, sent their investigative arm, the General Accounting Office (GAO), to find out how badly we were doing the job in many of these areas. The Senate Committee on Long-Term Care had just released a searching report on the role of nursing homes and boarding houses which cared for discharged mental patients. All these things indicate an increasing frustration and impatience with government performance. The problem here is that medical standards will begin to be set through a judicial mode if we cannot come up with a significant proposal for some therapeutic improvements, learning how to bring about social medicine with an interface between medicine and sociology in a responsible way.

The National Institute of Mental Health has, through its tradition of mental health service programmes, long been interested in developing a more coherent federal approach to the creation of community alternatives. The political officers in the department, myself included, have not always been as responsive as the National Institute of Mental Health would like us to be to some of their proposals, yet we have been very much impressed with their sensitivity to what the future needs are going to be in this area.

Public Law 94/63 required that three new services relating to the development of community support services should be provided: it required that there be screening and provision of community alternatives for people being considered for referral to public mental hospitals; it required follow-up services for catchment area residents being discharged from mental health facilities; and programmes of 'transitional halfway house services'. The service is either an alternative to initial institutionalisation or readmission, or it assists people in making the transition to the community. That is the halfway house concept we recognise. There is no other requirement, but it admits a wide variety of community alternatives in living arrangements that can make for this type of adjustment. There has been a lot of thinking within the programme about what it means to develop comprehensive community support systems as required in the law for mentally disabled adults, and to make for progress in this area. To facilitate this, a series of working conferences was held in 1975 that involved consumers, providers and the general public, with help from professions and government agency representatives.

Using this material and the study by the GAO as a framework, discussions are now under way in the department to identify administrative policy obstacles to developing support service systems, and to define workable strategies to address the issues. Major policy and economic issues have been identified, on which our ability to determine community alternatives depends. These are very important. There is a fragmentation and confusion of responsibility for community-based services at the federal, state and local level. We feel that a comprehensive community support system can be developed only through the combined efforts of health (in general), mental health, social service, housing, employment, income, maintenance and rehabilitation agencies. These all have their own regulations, all have their own staff. *When the community has to interact with that system they have a shotgun to deal with.*

There is a major need to set out in a comprehensive sense *where* the community can go for *what* kind of action. We need to define that, and we haven't done so yet. It is our commitment to try and make that kind of definition. We need it, furthermore, in order to untangle the unnecessary patchwork and the red tape involved in obtaining the kind of resources that are allegedly available, by professional action designed to merge a wide variety of community resources. This very variety of resources has often become a trigger problem in dealing with the people themselves. I think it is inappropriate when the administrative cost in dollars and also the time cost exceed a reasonable level of the effort of practitioners. We, within the department, will work at trying to redefine the system, at least as far as our own department goes, and we will make an effort with other departments to ensure that there is a clear pathway for people who need help for development of community service support systems in this area.

All this also underscores the lack of a systematic way to finance community-based services which I discussed with Elly Jansen some time ago. She and Frank Ochberg defined many areas where they tried to convince me that mental health is, in reality, 'out'. I did not need convincing. There are at the moment several areas with fantastic competition for the dollar in a wide variety of social programmes. In other words, even here in the US there are inadequate resources. When you reduce it to this particular community, for example Washington DC, there are totally inadequate resources for this kind of human activity. There seems to be a lack of commitment for a mainstream type of human service agency that deals with essential mental health needs. It is always easier to get glamorous public notice for *other* kinds of problems. But the human toll of emotional distress is even more tragic and is continuing, and it never attracts the same sense of urgency.

We need to find better ways to utilise currently available resources by methods that we can use to *change* our leverage on the reimbursement systems that we have. We had been considering changes in our regulations, so that the change would benefit packages that would allow more appropriate reimbursement for some of the areas in the ambulatory setting, and for certain kinds of adjustment problems. The difficulty here is expansion at a time when the escalation of costs in the health care system in total is running at an exorbitant rate that will not be tolerated. There is also a lack of health insurance. For many of these activities called halfway houses it is impossible to get the same kind of benefit that you can get for hospitals or nursing homes. If you want to convert to a more modern flexible system, your thinking has to go into how you propose that, how you set limits on it, how you prevent abuses of it. You are unfortunately working at a time when the abuses in the nursing home area are being seen. People are going to be tougher than they were when the first nursing home legislation came about.

It is not enough to say that your service is important or that you can produce results. You have to be thinking of a wide spectrum of management problems that will make it a saleable, durable and portable programme, besides its necessity; I don't think *that* is at issue. There are some people who have difficulty with the complex of sociological and philosophical problems involved with medicine. There is one thing that I have come to learn: that the health service of the American people is not a reflection of the performance of the acute medical care system. I now believe that the health status of the American people is a sociological phenomenon that results from cultural and economic issues, community settings, education and a whole range of factors that depend on *human dignity* as part of the status of human kind. To make *that* idea a saleable item in the competitive system of resources will require recruitment of leaders from all sections of the community, that is, to make this particular message a saleable, durable and affordable one in the *political* process.

19 GOVERNMENT POLICIES AND PROGRAMMES FOR THERAPEUTIC COMMUNITIES IN AMERICA: UNDYING DREAMS AND GRIM REALITIES (USA)

Frank M. Ochberg

This chapter will focus on America's experience in attempting to care for some of our most seriously handicapped citizens: those with major mental illness, and those whose mental impairment has brought with it additional social and vocational disabilities. I would like first to survey America's history in providing for these troubled people, as background for comments on the current situation. Second, I will provide examples of some community programmes which are working well in America. Finally, I will offer some thoughts about directions for future public policy.

The History of Therapeutic Communities in America

During colonial times in America, as in European countries, responsibility for the 'insane', as they were then called, was left to local communities. Typically, the solution was either to lock people up in local jails or 'poorhouses' or simply leave them to wander from town to town. A Philadelphia general hospital, opened in 1752, was one of the first to make specific provisions for the mentally ill. Twenty years later, the Commonwealth of Virginia opened the first mental hospital in the United States. This was followed by the New York Hospital in 1791.

At about this time, the cries of the French revolution – *Liberté, Egalité, Fraternité* – were heard also in French mental hospitals, the Bicêtre and the Salpêtrière. These cries encouraged Philippe Pinel to strike the chains from the mentally ill. The spirit of the times, the concern for one's fellow man, reached England, and later the United States. In England the York Retreat was established in 1796 under the leadership of the Quaker, William Tuke. Here, under Pinel's philosophy of 'moral treatment', patients were treated with respect and kindness, yet firmness, in an atmosphere which allowed them 'quiet time' before returning to open society. Regular patterns of work and relaxation were provided. Moral treatment was carried to

American shores by the Quaker clergyman, the Reverend Thomas Scattergood, who visited the York Retreat in 1797. This approach dominated mental hospitals in the United States during the first half of the nineteenth century.

During this same period, a small group of private and public mental hospitals was established in the United States. Between 1824 and 1836 mental hospitals were constructed in Kentucky, South Carolina, Ohio, Massachusetts and New York. These early hospitals, with their philosophy and practice of moral treatment, reported that about 90 per cent of those who entered were helped. It was said that just being admitted to the atmosphere of these 'therapeutic communities' would result in alleviation of the symptoms of madness.

The movement to establish 'asylums' or 'retreats' for the mentally ill received a major impetus through efforts of the renowned Dorothea Dix. Miss Dix had visited the jail at Cambridge, Massachusetts, one Sunday in 1841 to teach a Sunday School class for the prisoners. She was horrified at conditions there, and found that many of the inmates were mentally ill. Her outrage found expression in a formidable citizens' campaign that took her to every state of the Union, and in 1845 to England and Scotland. Many new mental hospitals were established in the United States, and conditions were bettered in those already existing. In 1855, in some part as a result of Dorothea Dix's efforts, Queen Victoria appointed a Royal Commission to inquire into the conditions of 'lunatic asylums' in Scotland. Conditions there were also improved.

But the secure and kindly world of the asylum and retreat was not to endure. Radical change occurred in the US in the mid-nineteenth century, following the great influx of impoverished immigrants from Europe. Not accepted by society at large, the newcomers were thought to include disproportionate numbers of mentally ill persons. As more and larger mental institutions were established, cultural differences between staff and patients became a factor. Pessimism grew as to whether mental illness was curable. Gradually moral treatment faded from the scene and was replaced by custodialism. Mental hospitals became depositories, not only for those with mental illness, but for large numbers of society's ineffective and unwanted, In terms of either 'therapeutic community' or 'treatment', little was available.

The bleak era of custodialism continued through the first half of the twentieth century. Only a wealthy few could afford private hospitals. Conditions in private facilities were better, but treatment still was limited. The larger number, the poor, went to state hospitals – usually with little hope of returning to society. By 1946 one hospital in New York State reached a patient population of 14,000. Hospitals with more than 5,000 patients were not uncommon throughout the United States.

Forces of change again began to stir at about this time in our history. The Second World War had helped to focus attention on the relationship of stress and environment to behaviour and mental breakdown. After the war sociologists turned their research skills to studying the effects of closed institutions on the behaviour of patients and staff. Professionals seeking alternative solutions studied mental health services in other countries. In 1945 Dr Karl Menninger and a group of prominent American psychiatrists toured psychiatric hospitals in Western Europe to see new developments. The Millbank Foundation in New York helped groups of hospital superintendents travel to Britain to study service programmes. American visitors to England were particularly impressed by the therapeutic communities which had been established in hospitals through the work of Dr Maxwell Jones and others. Upon returning to the United States, many superintendents attempted to introduce the therapeutic community concept into their own hospitals. Progress was difficult, partly because of the size and architecture of the existing institutions; yet some improvements were made.

By the mid-1950s discontent with the situation in the state mental hospitals in the United States was widespread. The resident population in these hospitals had soared to more than 550,000. Approximately two out of every five hospital beds in the country were located in state and county mental hospitals. Appalling conditions in some of these institutions were described in grim detail by a cavalcade of American writers who stirred the conscience of the country. Despite advances in research and innovations in treatment – notably the development of insulin and electroshock treatment in the 1930s and the introduction of psychotropic drugs in the 1950s – it was becoming painfully clear that our society was not providing an adequate or even humane system of services to care for our most sick and troubled citizens. This led a concerned Congress, in 1955, to establish the Joint Commission on Mental Illness and Health. The commission's mandate was to study the problem of mental illness in America and to make recommendations for a national mental health programme. The report of this commission, published five years later, gave expression to a vision of mental health care which had been gaining acceptance among mental health professionals and other leaders throughout the country – a vision of community-based mental health care accessible and responsive to the needs of all citizens.

Community mental health philosophy stems from a recognition of the negative effects of long-term institutional care. The ideal is to replace this with out-patient care and short periods of hospitalisation when necessary. If some form of institutional care *is* necessary, less radical alternatives such as partial hospitalisation, halfway houses and hostels are preferred. Wherever possible and appropriate, services and supports should be provided to sick or troubled people in their own homes and communities.

The report of the Joint Commission on Mental Illness and Health specifically attacked the philosophy of large state hospitals and proposed that these be converted into smaller, regional, intensive-care centres of no more than a thousand beds. It recommended emergency psychiatric services in the community to reduce the need for prolonged or repeated hospitalisation. In addition, the report envisioned a broad range of rehabilitative services which would be available both before, during and after hospitalisation. The commission proposed massive federal financial assistance for the care of mental patients, in the form of matching grants. Finally, the commission suggested that the federal government establish and maintain standards for the quality of care of the mentally ill in America.

President Kennedy, upon receiving the report, appointed a cabinet-level task force to develop specific proposals for a national action programme. The work of this task force culminated with the passage in 1963 of the Community Mental Health Centers Act. At the same time, a federally funded hospital improvement programme and hospital staff development programme were initiated, to improve the quality of care in the large state institutions during the transitional period as new community facilities were being developed.

Beyond the goal of replacing the state hospital system, the community mental health centres legislation embraced an even more ambitious dream – that of seeking out the causes of mental illness and mental retardation and attempting to eradicate them. In addition to programmes directed at specific known causes, the goal was to strengthen community, social welfare and educational programmes in order to eliminate or correct the harsh environmental conditions often associated with mental retardation and mental illness.

The National Institute of Mental Health was mandated to attempt to translate the dream into reality. The concept of geographic accessibility was addressed through formulation of geographic units called 'catchment areas' which would serve 75,000 to 200,000 persons. Community mental health centres were required to provide five services to be available as necessary to all catchment area residents. These five essential services include in-patient care, out-patient care, partial hospitalisation, 24-hour per day emergency services, and consultation and education. In addition to these, federal support could be provided for the following optional services: diagnostic, rehabilitative pre-care and aftercare, training, and research and evaluation.

Deinstitutionalisation and the Transition to Community Care

Today, twelve years after enactment of the initial community mental health legislation, only 590 of the planned 2,000 centres have been built, providing coverage to only 41 per cent of the catchment areas throughout the country. Economic recession, conflicts between the legislative and executive branches of the government, emphasis on revenue-sharing, block grants, regionalisation and expenditure control have impeded full achievement of the original intent of the community mental health legislation. Community Mental Health Centers Amendments, extending and expanding the centres programme, are presently under consideration by the Congress. In view of the current economic and political forces just mentioned, however, we are not certain of whether these amendments will receive final approval and adequate funding.

None the less, national statistics tell us that during the two decades since the joint commission began its work there has been a dramatic shift away from institutional care. During this period, the movement known as 'deinstitutionalisation' has gained great momentum throughout the country, with the resident population of public mental hospitals dropping from 550,000 in 1955 to less than 220,000 in 1975. During the same period, there has been a dramatic shift in the balance between in-patient and out-patient care for psychiatric problems. In 1955 in-patient care accounted for 77 per cent of all psychiatric episodes; by 1972 the in-patient care accounted for only 42 per cent. Thus, of people with mental health problems, fewer are being treated in hospitals. And their stays are briefer.

This shift away from institutions has resulted from a combination of interrelated influences. Improvements in treatment, availability of psychoactive drugs for symptom control, and development of community programmes have combined with growing emphasis in government and professional circles on community mental health philosophy. Perhaps even more importantly, landmark court decisions have been made recently, upholding the rights of the mentally disabled to active treatment and rehabilitation in the least restrictive alternative. Legal pressure for better care has combined with general inflation in the country to send the costs of mental hospitalisation soaring. In many instances, these combined pressures on state governments have resulted in administrative decisions to discharge large numbers of patients, thus transferring financial responsibility from state mental health departments to social welfare and medical assistance programmes, which receive substantial federal support.

Despite the reduction in resident population of public mental hospitals, however, the numbers of first admissions and readmissions have generally been increasing. And, with the larger turnover in the public system, we still have large numbers of people involved. National statistics show that during 1974, 448,000 people were discharged from state and county mental hospitals. During the same year, these hospitals served as the locus of in-patient care for 43 per cent of the total number of patients hospitalised for psychiatric problems. So, it is clear that the state and county hospitals are continuing to play a major role in delivery of mental health services.

We also know that persons treated in these public hospitals are especially in need of aftercare and community support services. When compared with people treated in private hospitals, we see that those treated in public hospitals have less education, less financial capacity, are older, more likely to have an alcoholic disorder or schizophrenia, and are more likely to have been there before, than patients treated in private hospitals. In fact, about 54 per cent of all clients admitted to state hospitals in 1974 had been there previously. Yet, when these people leave again, national statistics for 1969 (the most recent data available) indicated that such hospitals made no referrals for 38 per cent of the patients. Even when referrals were made (most frequently to out-patients psychiatric clinics) we do not know how many of these clients got to their destination.

The Fate of Patients 'in the Community'

So far it has not been possible to obtain national data on what is really happening to these public hospital clients after discharge. We do know that we now find much larger numbers of mentally impaired elderly people in nursing homes than we did a few years ago. Too often, these homes are substandard, without adequate supervision and therapy. In 1974 the total number of elderly nursing home residents with mental disorders or senility was 827,000. This number was more than *three times* the number in 1964. If discharged patients are not elderly or infirm, and if they lack meaningful family or social ties in the community, they are likely to be released to boarding-homes or old hotels, where they may remain socially isolated and unemployed.

Various follow-up studies of patients released under different circumstances show remarkably similar results as far as re-admissions are concerned. The studies differ considerably as to time span, location, types of institutions, and types of aftercare services provided. None the less, most of the studies show that 30 to 40 per cent of patients interviewed six months after release have been re-hospitalised at some time during the interval between release and follow-up. For patients studied one year after release, the percentage increases to between 40 and 50 per cent; and for those studied at three to five years after release, 65 to 75 per cent have been rehospitalised. Such studies have also shown that clients at highest risk of re-hospitalisation seem to be those who are unmarried, living with their parents or others in their family of origin, occupying a peripheral family position, and living in a non-intact family. These seem to be the clients most in need of supportive living arrangements and 'total-push' aftercare and follow-along services. Research has also shown that these are the clients who benefit most from such help. Yet these are the clients least able to avail themselves of the fragmented services which do exist.

Journalists who have investigated the situation recently have published alarming reports of human suffering caused by discharge of patients without adequate resources and commitment to care for them. One such report, from the American Federation of State, County and Municipal Employees, is entitled 'Out of their Beds and Into the Streets'. This report asks 'How to explain a national non-policy on mental health that releases mental patients into community facilities that don't exist and protects their right to treatment by denying them publicly provided health services?' The author argues that ' "deinstitutionalisation," a lofty idea, has become something very ugly – a cold methodology by which government washes its hands of direct responsibility for the well-being of its most dependent citizens.'

A *New York Times* editorial dated 8 April 1974 entitled 'Civil Liberty for What?' says, 'If there were anything that could be described as even reasonable aftercare for discharged mental patients, the civil libertarians would have a case. Certainly they have been right to condemn the failure of the huge State institutions to serve a purpose that is more than tranquilizing and custodial. But what kind of crusade is it to condemn sick and fearful people to shift for themselves in an often hostile world? What are needed are open halfway communities. The idea is neither novel nor utopian. It is just costly.'

Prompted in part by disturbing reports of this kind, the General Accounting Office (GAO), an arm of the Congress, has launched a major national policy study on deinstitutionalisation. GAO investigators are now in the process of interviewing hundreds of public officials to try to find out what is happening to formerly institutionalised people. Follow-up studies of a number of discharged clients are being done in the five states which have been selected for most intensive investigation. Although reports of the GAO study are not yet available, the fact that it is being done testifies to a growing recognition in our government that issues of aftercare, community support, and the need for truly therapeutic communities outside the hospital are becoming matters of urgent national concern.

Models of the Therapeutic Community that are Working in America

We recognise that the journalists and other concerned citizens who are sounding the alarm serve a vital function. None the less, their reports often fail to describe many programmes throughout the country which *are* providing both humane care and growth-oriented treatment to hundreds of our most seriously handicapped citizens. Many innovative aftercare projects have been developed and evaluated under grants from the National Institute of Mental Health, the Rehabilitation Services Administration, and other federal agencies. The successful models take many different forms, in a wide variety of settings. They have demonstrated repeatedly that even the 'back ward' or 'revolving door' patient *can* benefit from comprehensive aftercare and rehabilitation services. While some of these patients may require periodic or continuing supportive services or semi-sheltered environments in which to live and work for a long period of time, they definitely can participate productively in society.

In the United States, the halfway house is the best-known alternative living arrangement for mentally disabled individuals. We are fortunate that the Richmond Fellowship and other similar organisations have established a number of excellent halfway houses in some parts of the country. Although halfway houses exist in very small numbers and are unevenly distributed, they are growing. A 1973 survey by the Biometry Division of NIMH identified 290 halfway houses primarily for psychiatric patients and close to 600 for alcoholics. We know that 455,000 persons were discharged from public mental hospitals during 1973. If we conservatively estimate that halfway house services would be appropriate for one-quarter of these persons who would remain an average of six months, this would suggest that current halfway house resources are meeting at best only one third of the potential demand.

At present, halfway houses are operated under a variety of auspices: approximately 17 per cent are sponsored by state governments, 23 per cent are operated as proprietary facilities, and 60 per cent are under the auspices of private, non-profit agencies. Although these facilities may receive partial operational support from a wide variety of private and public sources, no national policy or programme exists to assist with start-up costs or to provide supportive services. Nor have national standards been developed to assure quality of care in such facilities. Some government officials who are beginning to grapple with issues of community alternatives have suggested a possible need for federal legislation in this area. The currently pending Community Mental Health Centers Amendments call upon centres to provide transitional halfway house services in the future. If these amendments are enacted and adequately funded, the centres should substantially assist in meeting the need for services of this kind.

In 1967 the NIMH helped fund a national study of halfway houses conducted by the Joint Information Service of the American Psychiatric Association. The study report, which reviewed the literature on the efficacy of halfway house services, states that the lowest reported rehospitalisation rate was 9 per cent and the highest 45 per cent. Comparisons are difficult, however, because the halfway houses were working wich clients with varying degress of disability and the basis for computation of rehospitalisation statistics was not uniform. Costs of services also varied, but in general it appears that residence in a halfway house costs about half as much per day as in state hospitals and a quarter or less of the cost in psychiatric units of general hospitals. In view of the fact that halfway houses to a large extent serve severely impaired people who might otherwise require hospitalisation, the report concluded that halfway houses could have an important future as alternatives to hospitalisation.

The family foster home represents another alternative. Used to a considerable extent in the United States for a number of years, the popularity of family foster homes seems to be growing with the reduction in state hospital populations. National statistics are not available at present. However, a few research and demonstration projects have studied foster care programmes in selected areas. One project in Washington State placed 540 dependent adults handicapped by age, physical, mental or emotional disabilities in family foster homes in the community. Placements were made over a three-year period. Costs per client ranged from $207 to $353 per month – much less than the state mental hospital (about $770) or a nursing home. Periodic assessment of clients' functioning indicated that most clients improved following their foster placement. As an added benefit, public assistance recipients were enabled to reduce their dependency by serving in some instances as family home sponsors.

A particularly innovative and promising foster care project was developed through an NIMH research and demonstration grant to the Missouri Institute of Psychiatry and the St Louis State Hospital. This project developed a US adaptation of the idea which has worked so well in Geel, Belgium. Two small Missouri towns, New Haven and Troy, were selected as foster communities for chronic patients who were prepared for discharge into the community. At the same time, the communities were prepared to receive the patients. Ultimately, the community took over the programme which successfully provided homes for a number of patients who had been hospitalised for long periods. Hospital staff remain available for supportive services as necessary. Evidence indicates that most of the patients have been integrated very successfully into an already existing social system.

A contrasting approach which also seems quite promising is the Lodge system originally developed and evaluated through an NIMH grant to the Palo Alto Veterans Administration Hospital in California. This approach creates an alternative social system which enables chronic patients to live and work in a semi-sheltered environment on a long-term basis. In the initial project, patients in the hospital first were organised into small cohesive groups, and were trained in decision-making and mutual support roles. Then the patients were transferred as a group to a former motel where they established, owned and operated a janitorial, maintenance and gardening service business. No live-in staff was provided; professionals served only as technical consultants. The Lodge succeeded in becoming self-sufficient and still exists, with some of its members having been on their own for more than five years. Follow-up studies with a control group of patients who received traditional follow-up care showed significant advantages of the Lodge system in both community stay and work status. Its demonstrated success encouraged a number of replications elsewhere in the country and about 24 such programmes existed as of mid-1974.

Another approach to an alternative social system has been developed as an outcome of the Alcoholics Anonymous organisation in the US. A small group of former alcoholics some years ago conceived the idea of a self-help community for people with alcohol and drug dependency problems. This evolved into the community in California now known as Synanon, which has grown to a population of about 1,600 with a number of satellite programmes. High standards of work performance and discipline are enforced for all who wish to join the community, and a 'game' which has some of the elements of confrontation therapy is used to release tension and to protect the community against undue authoritarianism. Although neither state nor federal government was involved in developing this community, its progress has been followed with growing interest. Synanon methods for rehabilitating youthful offenders have gained acceptance among many agencies in California. The State of California now contracts with Synanon to provide services for troubled young people. A growing number of people not afflicted with alcoholism or drug abuse are now beginning to take an interest in Synanon, with some of them moving there as 'lifestylers', living as peers with others in the community.

While these alternative types of therapeutic community outside the mainstream of society seem to be appropriate for some individuals and groups, most organised treatment and rehabilitation programmes in the United States have attempted to reintegrate mentally impaired or troubled individuals into the larger society. Programmes with this goal in mind have emphasised the necessity of finding ways to assist former patients deal with practical problems of living outside the hospital. A variety of approaches have been developed through which professional or paraprofessional mental health workers, ex-patients or volunteers can assist clients with daily living skills, social life, jobs and living arrangements. A philosophy of mutual and self-help can be applied in ex-patient clubs, senior citizens centres, day centres and other programmes, all of which work well in a wide range of settings.

One outstanding example of such an approach was developed through an NIMH grant to the Mendota Mental Health Institute in Madison, Wisconsin. Here a 'Program of Assertive Community Treatment' has been developed as an alternative to hospitalisation. The programme is staffed by former hospital employees who have been retrained to work with patients in their homes or at their jobs. Project staff are available round-the-clock to provide whatever help is needed. Clients being served include some who are highly symptomatic, chronic or severely dependent. It is impressive to see that even with such seriously handicapped clients, only eleven per cent of those in the community treatment programme have required hospitalisation, as contrasted with 89 per cent of the control group.

Other investigators have experimented with crisis intervention, hostel or home care programmes to avoid the necessity for hospitalisation. An NIMH sponsored project in California is experimenting with a community residence operated according to the philosophy of Cooper and Laing. This facility, serving as an alternative to hospitalisation for a small group of 'first-break' young schizophrenics, is showing promising results when compared with a group treated at a community mental health centre in-patient unit. This programme and other alternatives to hospitalisation offer some evidence of both short and long-term cost savings through avoidance of in-patient care.

A discussion of community-based rehabilitation programmes in America would not be complete without reference to the outstanding work of a small and scattered group of facilities known as psychosocial rehabilitation centres. A field study of such programmes was conducted by the Joint Information Services of the American Psychiatric Association in 1970, with the help of a grant from NIMH. This study attempted to identify facilities throughout the country which provided truly comprehensive community-based services to seriously handicapped former mental patients. In order to qualify as comprehensive, it was considered necessary that the programmes include services related to resocialisation, training, work and living arrangements.

As of 1970, only 13 such comprehensive programmes could be identified in the United States. Six of these programmes were studied in depth: Fountain House, New York; Council House, Pittsburgh;

Horizon House, Philadelphia; Thresholds, Chicago; Portals House, Los Angeles; and Hill House, Cleveland. These six centres offer models of community-based rehabilitation which have potential for replication and adaptation to a range of other settings. Research on some of the programmes has documented their effectiveness in meeting the needs of individuals with serious social and vocational disabilities.

One such centre, Fountain House in New York, has pioneered the development of a transitional employment programme whereby jobs are made available to the agency by local employers. Fountain House assures employers that jobs will be covered if clients are unable to work at any given time. Staff will fill in for clients if necessary. Clients are assigned to jobs on a rotating basis, for part-time work of about three months' duration. This variety of work experiences gives them a chance to gain confidence before finding permanent jobs. The residential programme at Fountain House rents apartments in various parts of New York to two or more clients for varying periods of time. The agency also offers extensive social and pre-vocational activities for clients who are thought of and referred to as 'members' of a social rehabilitation club. Research has shown that the Fountain House patients attain more suitable, regular employment than do patients who receive only counselling or referral to another service for help. A follow-up of experimental and control patients at 24 months also showed a significant difference between the two groups in re-hospitalisation rates.

Summary and Implications for Public Policy

It can be seen from this review that during America's relatively short history, we have attempted to provide for our mentally ill and marginal citizens in a variety of ways. Our public programmes have evolved from the 'moral treatment' approaches through the 'custodial era' of the early part of the twentieth century, towards the current emphasis on community mental health. During the past two decades, we have made substantial progress in translating the community mental health philosophy into effective services. Clearly, however, much remains to be done if we are to meet the urgent needs of our most severely disabled citizens who are now being found in larger numbers outside the hospital.

It is obvious that we have no shortage in America of models of therapeutic communities which have demonstrated their effectiveness.

A wide range of approaches has been developed, suitable for people with all types of mental impairments. These approaches can be replicated or adapted to an enormous range of settings. We have adequate research documenting the superiority of many of these community approaches over institutionalisation – both from the standpoint of client outcomes and in terms of costs. The major problem that must be faced in formulating future public policy is that such programmes have not been established on nearly a broad enough scale.

It must be recognised that in a pluralistic society such as that of the United States, there is no *single* mental health policy or system. We have a range of approaches to hospital and community care, both public and private. The public sector includes not only federal programmes, but also those of state and local governments. As the era of 'institutionalism' and 'custodialism' fades, we are faced with complex new challenges. The future roles of public and private hospitals, social welfare agencies, rehabilitation agencies, halfway houses, psychosocial rehabilitation centres, sheltered workshops and community mental health centres have not been clearly defined. Responsibilities for 'community care' are fragmented. Accountability is difficult to achieve.

It is obvious that there is no single simple solution to the current crisis in meeting the needs of our most disabled constituency. It is vitally important, however, that we find ways to make more effective use of the public resources – both human and financial – which are currently available for services to this group. Ways must be sought to transfer such resources from institutional to community settings, where the skills and commitment of thousands of hospital employees can be used for greater public good. Those responsible for administration of scarce public funds for mental health and rehabilitation services should give major emphasis to meeting the needs of the most seriously handicapped clients. Effective approaches to aftercare, transitional and rehabilitation services, and community support and maintenance programmes should have high priority in the use of public funds for research, demonstration, training and services. All of these efforts must grapple with ways to help troubled human beings deal with the practical problems of living.

In examining use of public funds in serving this group, it will be necessary to re-evaluate existing federal and state legislation, which in some instances seems to be bringing about results which are inconsistent with our current philosophy and goals. For example, while many federal laws set forth the principle of community-based care for the mentally disabled, the largest federal mental health funding at present goes into the Medicare and Medicaid programmes, which have a bias toward institutional care. Too often these federal and state dollars are financing the transfer of patients from their homes or state hospitals to substandard nursing homes being operated privately for profit.

Although home health and long-term social supports for the mentally disabled are not being adequately provided by existing public programmes, the potential does exist in a variety of legislation already on the books. Consumers and taxpayers are becoming aware that they should have a major voice in holding service providers and public officials accountable for making appropriate use of public funds. We must pay attention to consumers and other concerned citizens in our efforts to find better methods for assuring quality of care in a variety of non-institutional settings. In addition, consumer advocacy can help to assure that individual clients are referred to settings appropriate to their needs, and that fragmented resources from diverse agencies are integrated into more effective community programmes.

Conclusion

Although we in the United States have not yet developed a system of community care which fully meets the needs of our most seriously handicapped citizens, we have learned a great deal about what is necessary to achieve our goals. Despite the difficulties and complexities encountered in the effort to translate our ideals into reality, we continue to embrace the dream of community care for the mentally ill and disabled – a dream that can be realised through the commitment, concern and creativity of individuals and groups in every sector of society.

20 THE ROLE OF GOVERNMENT: A POLITICAL PERSPECTIVE (UK)

Norman Fowler

Anyone who comes to the Department of Health and Social Security is immediately struck by the enormous range of subjects covered. Problems concerned with the elderly living in retirement, and often in poverty; problems concerned with the young, the one million children of one-parent families, and the children in trouble. Then there are all the problems concerning the Health Service which currently are receiving so much publicity and so much attention. Decisions have to be made upon which priorities should be laid down and for the government, of course, the chief priorities are those of expenditure.

For the opposition the task is rather different. They must decide which areas demand priority in the form of serious study and research, and there is a clear difference between the functions of government and of opposition in this country. A government which sets up an inquiry or a committee is often accused of prevarication. The argument is that they have the means; why don't they simply get on with it? An opposition does not have the means to implement their policies. What it does have is that invaluable thing in politics, the time to prepare for governing. Thus the committees set up by opposition are of fundamental importance for future government policies.

There is perhaps an assumption that, with the 1959 Mental Health Act, with the running down of the large hospitals and the 'open door' policy, the problems are over. One is struck when reading Kathleen Jones's *A History of the Mental Health Services* how progress, at least in a governmental, legislative sense, has followed the publication of scandal. The reform movement in the early nineteenth century followed the scandal at York Asylum where the staff burnt down part of the building to hide the evidence of neglect. In the middle and late nineteenth century concern arose not only over ill treatment but wrongful detention, and indeed the Royal Commission of 1924 partly sprang from the concern that large numbers of people were wrongly being declared insane. Of course, the 1959 Act itself also had as its background the scandal of overcrowding, beds placed in corridors, crammed in wards no more than nine inches apart. Nor of course has England been alone in this kind of reaction, which has led to legislative progress. In 1961 the Joint Commission on Mental Illness and Health in the United States came to very much the same conclusion. The commission found that Americans were what they termed 'alarm-minded' and 'action-oriented', by which they meant that when confronted with a deplorable situation the public wanted to do something about it. As the commission commented, 'Our first inclination in practice appears to be to expose in muck-racking fashion the alarming conditions, enumerate the victims, and name the villains.' As they also pointed out, such an approach begs the fundamental and much more difficult question of what actually can be done.

The point is that it is much easier to get general public agreement to the proposition that this or that scandal or alarming situation should be brought to an end than to go to the next stage of the action necessary to remedy that situation properly. It seems to me that we in Britain are very much in that next crucial but much more difficult stage. The decision has been taken to reduce the number of hospital beds. According to the last report of the DHSS, the number of beds in mental illness hospitals is now down to 2.15 per 100,000 of the population compared with 2.84 in 1963. That statistic is perhaps not the most informative of government pieces of information. By itself it certainly does not in any way substantiate the general or partial assumption of many people that all is well – the ship is safely on course.

Perhaps here I could quote what was said in an adjournment debate in the House of Commons in 1975. This debate was quite hopeful in itself, because debates on mental health in the House of Commons are in fact relatively rare. The subject was raised by a Conservative MP, Cecil Parkinson, who has no fewer than five major hospitals with over 6,500 beds in his constituency of South Hertfordshire. As he pointed out, statistics can be misleading. One can upgrade half the wards in a hospital, claim a general improvement in occupation level and still leave half the hospital at a quite unacceptable level. He also pointed out that there are other strange anomalies which come to light; one of the hospitals in his constituency has been reducing the number of beds in line with government policy. A grateful government has responded by introducing the rule that any hospital with fewer than 1,000 beds cannot be allowed to have a Divisional Nursing Officer as its head nurse. The Chief Nursing Officer must be of a lower grade. Thus the career prospects of the hospital are set lower because they are implementing government policy. And of course I am conscious that there is a much more general and much wider effect, that is, the effect on the morale of staff in the existing hospitals which, staff are continually told, are to be run down.

The crucial question is this: what happens after that policy of run-down is implemented? You do not dispose of the problem simply by running down the mental hospitals. You certainly can transfer it, for example, into the criminal system, a new system which incidentally is also seeking to treat more and more people in the community. But if you are going to deal with the problem properly, then you must have the matching community facilities, and unhappily the evidence points to the fact that this is simply not the case today in this country. Let me take Cecil Parkinson's example again. The situation in Hertfordshire is that though the hospitals are becoming better places in which to treat the mentally ill, new places are simply not being found in the community itself. One result is that patients are now sleeping in a hospital which is due to be closed because there is literally nowhere else for them to go. In other words we have simply not followed through the implication of the policy that has been laid down by successive governments.

Nor indeed, it must be admitted, have we got too much of the basic information upon which to base policy decisions. The Richmond Fellowship itself has been in existence since 1959, and there have been invaluable developments by other voluntary organisations. Yet we have very little objective research to help us in our task, simply because *we have not been prepared to devote the resources to this purpose.* When we talk of resources, for once in this particular area we are not talking about the hundreds and hundreds of millions of pounds which are necessary in some other areas. Research is not in that category of expenditure. If I may underline here a pet pre-occupation of my own, it does seem to me strange just how much money we, as a nation, are prepared to spend with only an imperfect idea of what actually we are achieving or what actually we are hoping to achieve. It is not just a commentary upon the DHSS, it applies to other government departments in the social area as well. If you consider that the total running costs of the National Health Service hospitals in 1972–3 was almost £1,300 million then the amount devoted to current research and development of about £50 million for the whole area does look puny indeed. This again was touched upon by the Parliamentary Secretary when he replied to the 1975 debate. He told the House of Commons that two research projects, limited research projects, were already being undertaken; I am not altogether sure about the 'already', but one of these, it is true, does involve the evaluation of alternative forms of residential care.

What is true is that we do, nevertheless, in this situation have pointers forward. In particular we have the experience of halfway houses and hostels which have been in operation for some years now. Halfway houses such as those run by the Richmond Fellowship, the houses run by the Phoenix House Foundation and the kind of houses run by Tim Cook, tackling particularly the problem of alcoholism. That then is the base. It seems to me that the urgent question now is, 'How can government, any government, best help such organisations to make their contribution?' I cannot pretend to have any total or neat answers; what I can do is to try and mark out some of the lines of that enquiry.

Clearly one of the most important areas that we must consider is the area of finance. Every organisation that exists on voluntary contributions today faces a crisis. Inflation is having a quite devastating effect on voluntary organisations: on the one hand their costs are going up, and on the other hand the ability of donors to give is going down – a disastrous combination. We should always remember the interaction of general economic policy, or perhaps even the lack of general economic policy, on the problems under discussion. For not only is there inflation, but there is also the fundamental choice of priorities that any government must make. Of course, we have to decide for ourselves, and maybe every individual has to decide for himself, what those choices of priority should be and are. I can only say that it does not seem to me strange that, as a result of the present choice of priorities in which subsidies go to many people who can afford the money, we find that the areas which we are discussing are starved of funds. I remember that in my Home Office days, money for better prisons was not a notably popular cause among the public, nor indeed was even money for the probation service. Historically, the same has been true of mental health. No one pretends that provision in the mental health field has ever been generous, and when you add inflation to the problems of a service which is already subject to attacks of money starvation, then the situation can easily become critical.

But let us proceed on the assumption that we see some stability over the next few years. We then have the problem of how we finance these services. Now clearly I see the force of what has been argued by the Fellowship, namely the difficulty of a situation where public policy requires that the National Health Service finances the hospitals, but places on local authorities the responsibility of financing and providing the treatment facilities like the hostels and the halfway houses. I am also attracted by the argument that the success of this second stage is not only to the immeasurable benefit of the individual, it also makes sense in economic terms, in as much as it leads to long-term economy by the very nature of that success. I would also accept that there is a special responsibility upon me in that it is government policy which has, if you like, caused oppression.

The traditional answer has been that once central government takes over the purse strings, the management of local services would be removed effectively from local hands and would go to central government. If that is the case, it is argued, then community care itself will be undermined, if by community care we mean the development of a local caring community. And yet, against that, we have the evidence of the National Association of Mental Health in their October 1973 survey which showed that whilst most local authorities had made some improvement, 'The existing services in the community for mentally ill patients and former patients are still grossly inadequate.' The Association made it clear that they were blaming the government here as much as local authorities, perhaps rather more so.

It seems to me that there are a number of criteria that the government must meet. First it must clearly recognise the interdependence of the voluntary and the statutory organisations. Voluntary organisations today are being used to fill the gaps in the community provision. Enormous demands are being made currently on local authority social services departments. They simply cannot do all they should and they are having to ration their services according to priorities. The Local Authority Social Services Act of 1970 rightly set up a Social Services Department as recommended by Seebohm, but this has meant that, now there is a focal point at which social problems can be directed, the amount of work has proved vastly greater than was expected. In terms of work also the situation has been further aggravated by the Children and Young Persons Act and the Chronically Sick and Disabled Persons Act. *But I think that the government must also recognise that the voluntary organisations are doing more than filling a gap, that there is a positive and lasting role for them. By their very nature they are independent and thus more likely to experiment and to seek new ways forward. They have a flexibility which in this field it seems to me is of the utmost importance, and thus their work must be very clearly recognised.*

Secondly, there is the question of training and of standards generally. As David Clark said at the Richmond Fellowship Conference of 1973, most small homes and halfway houses are staffed by people who have been trained to do something very different; and as he also said, sometimes this works magnificently and sometimes it is a ghastly failure.

Thirdly, it does seem to me that the government must accept responsibility in the hostel and halfway house field. Whatever financial structure is used and is decided upon, whether direct support from the DHSS or the present system geared to local authorities, the DHSS must retain overall responsibility. What would be quite unacceptable is that treatment should depend upon the administrative pocket from which the finance comes.

These are some of the present problems; and then there are problems for the future. I go back to David Clark's comment in 1973: 'There are still a lot of people in psychiatric hospitals up and down the country who could be living in suitable, freer, smaller accommodation and many of them could move to a greater degree of independence, but they are going to be much more difficult to help and rehabilitate than the people of the 1950s.' There are also new ideas being advanced. One of the suggestions, from the Harperbury Hospital in Hertfordshire, is that some of these big hospitals themselves should be turned into village communities which provide sheltered accommodation, bungalows, hostels and houses; but then such projects would cost money, and money is in very short supply. One of the advantages of the big hospitals is that they do at least have the essential supply of land.

In summary, there are three essential tests, it seems to me, for the government White Paper which is now awaited: the role of the voluntary organisation, the provision of training facilities, and the role of government itself. There are, in addition, other points such as the vital area of the young and the particular problem of drug dependence. The American and British experience has not at all been the same, not least in the extent of the problem. Yet for some reason the subject of drugs in Britain attracts widespread public attention, about which I only complain in as much as it diverts from other equally serious problems like, for example, alcoholism. Periodically there is concern in the press also about alcohol. We see headlines like 'Council says Alcoholism is Britain's Worst Health Hazard' and the one expressing concern about young drinkers: 'Five Hours' Baby-sitting Buys a Bottle of Vodka.' But somehow that concern is never consistent or lasting. There seems to be a tacit acceptance in this country of the alcohol problem which is in no way justified by any of the statistics. In 1964 there were 23 male admissions per 100,000 of the population to mental illness hospitals on account of alocholism. In 1972 that figure had gone up to 35. The comparable figure for drug dependence was five. There are other problems in this area of care where young people are concerned. Let me give an example of the treatment of children. At Harperbury there is a children's section where 200 beds are set aside specifically for children. The only trouble is that at present two-thirds of those beds are occupied by adults. There is no possibility of transferring them from one section of the hospital to the other because the beds in the adult section are oversubscribed. On the other hand in the community there are many children who need the facilities and could be treated if there were only the space.

Again I cannot help but mention the urgent need in this country for more research. Figures are notoriously difficult to analyse. The latest statistics show that 'first admissions' fell by nearly six per cent between 1970 and 1972, but what does that mean? Does it mean that there are now fewer new cases in need of treatment? Are they being helped in some other way, and so appear in some other statement of statistics? Or are the needs of the patient who previously had treatment more pressing so that they receive priority? There is an urgent need for research which follows individual cases through the service.

I recently read one research finding which stuck in my mind. That was a research project in the United States, in which the public was asked to list in terms of acceptability 21 forms of disability. The mentally ill ranked 21st in that list. I'm not sure what the result would be if such a survey were carried out in Britain, but clearly there is in this country a great deal of misunderstanding to be broken down in this field. This misunderstanding is based upon a lack of appreciation that these are real problems which people face, and understanding often comes only when the family unit itself experiences that problem.

21 THE LOCAL AUTHORITY'S PERSPECTIVE (UK)

David F. Crompton

Some General Observations on the Nature of the Problem

Who Are the Needy?

As a director of social services, faced with a considerable range of demand of personal social services, it is vital to distinguish particular areas of need, to tackle the problem of providing the best possible service with the most likely chance of success. In focusing particularly upon the question of residential care for the mentally ill, the question I ask myself is 'Which mentally ill are we talking about and where does residential care fit in?'

I should make it clear that the social services function is essentially concerned with the social work and the social caring aspects, which very often will involve my department in preventative action geared towards diminishing the likelihood that an individual, or indeed a family, may become mentally ill through the stress and strain in a total family situation. This is in no way to deny that there may be organic aspects as regards mental illness and that certain individuals may well be predisposed towards a mental breakdown. In this sense any work which the social services department can carry out with the parents of younger children can be looked upon as preventative of mental illness. In the course of this activity it may well be that the social services department will provide some appropriate form of residential care for children and young persons.

However, in the context of this chapter, I think it will be useful to focus upon the needs of the younger mentally ill, or potentially ill, from the ages of seventeen or eighteen upwards and into the fifties. Once we enter the age range of sixty and above, I think it will be agreed that we are talking about the chronically mentally ill, those who are probably institutionalised through long periods in hospital, and finally the age range which is often categorised under the title of the 'elderly mentally infirm'. These latter issues are being dealt with largely in the programme for elderly persons' homes.

What Do They Need?

Much of the emphasis to date, following the Mental Health Act of

1959, has been upon the provision of residential accommodation for the younger mentally ill, following an acute breakdown and treatment in a mental hospital. In view of the deployment of the social services department in area teams of social workers, who are increasingly involved at the community level and orientated towards the prevention of family breakdown, it should fairly be assumed that a range of treatment options (in the form of social work intervention, home helps, holidays, short-term care and day care, in co-operation with the general practitioners and out-patient departments in psychiatric hospitals) will have already been tried before the need for residential care on the longer-term basis is established. Nevertheless, the team of people concerned in the community will undoubtedly, at some time or other, be faced with the need of the sick person for some kind of living accommodation away from the family. Similarly, as regards the rehabilitation of a person following a period of treatment in a hospital, a case conference will have made a decision, i.e. that the family itself is either not strong enough ever to cope or certainly cannot cope with immediate demands in terms of rehabilitation. Some kind of alternative group care is indicated which lies between, on the one hand, independent living in lodgings or a separate household and, on the other, the custodial or caring treatment situation to be found in a hospital ward. The use of the term 'halfway house' in itself implies a measure of selectivity in the first place and therapy geared towards the ultimate ability of the individual to become self-supporting. From this it follows that there may be degrees of ability in various individuals to make the grade, as it were, and we are therefore posed with the problem as to whether a halfway house can of itself cope with the whole range of differing ability, or whether there should be a variety of such residential units. A proportion of residents may well ultimately require a long-term supportive environment. Certain halfway houses will undoubtedly be used as a form of continuing assessment. Therefore, the halfway house must be seen as an integral part of the total team involving social work, the GP services, and the psychiatric consultative and nursing services, whether deployed in the community or in hospital.

What is the Size of This Problem?

In order to plan properly and to ensure that sufficient resources are made available, some measure of the actual numbers of people requiring such help has to be established. The very limited number of research surveys which have been carried out (mainly on the day-to-day experience of field social workers and their GP colleagues) show that the incidence of mental illness in modern urban society far exceeds the numbers of those who actually receive some kind of treatment or support from hospital, general practitioners or local authority services. Although approximately two per cent of the population may be receiving help at any one time, it has been suggested that possibly four times this amount could be identified. One of the results of integrating social work under the local authority social services department has been to bring into the open the fact that many mental health problems have sometimes been masked under some other category of work; for example, care of children, adolescent problems, multiple family problems, alcoholism or drugs. The more comprehensive approach of a family service can avoid a fragmented approach to the individual who formerly would be passed from one specialist to another.

Two important developments in the social services department should lead to a much deeper look at the needs and numbers of the mentally ill: namely the growth of the research and development function within the departments and the pressure from the DHSS on local authorities to produce and regularly review ten-year plans of development of services. Local authorities now have guidelines on the level of provision of all kinds of services over the whole range of responsibilities, and the regular publication of ten-year plans should in itself provide an incentive between authorities on a comparative basis. Within the individual local authorities the total plans which have to be produced must undoubtedly present a clearer picture of essential areas of development and form the basis of decision-making in terms of priority.

For example, in my own authority, a London borough with a population of approximately a quarter of a million (in an area of average need), allowing for our existing provision of residential care for the younger mentally ill (28 places), we shall have to provide at least another 44 places, assuming that other local authorities who already use our existing hostel will be able to transfer their residents or offer us places in units of their own. In fact, my authority has planned to provide about 60 additional places of various kinds in the ten-year period.

I am concerned, as I am sure a number of directors are, that the ministry at this point of time has deferred some decisions regarding capital works for the mentally handicapped and the mentally ill, presumably because local authorities have placed in their programmes more projects in the early years than can realistically be approved on economic terms. This immediately faces me with the possible option of speeding up the programme for the mentally ill by calling upon voluntary organisations to assist in the area.

As a matter of interest, the DHSS figures ((a) SBL 629, Table 1) show the following progress in local authority provision of residential places for the adult mentally ill:

Dec. 1967	Dec. 1968	Dec. 1969	Dec. 1970	Mar. 1972
1,508	1,717	1,634	1,753	2,016

This shows slow but gradually increasing provision, speeding up in recent years. These figures, of course, cover up the effective use of residential units, their turnover and success in rehabilitation. Of 174 local authorities in England and Wales some 50 appear to make no provision themselves (up to December 1972) ((b) IMTA figures). If we assumed an average of 50 places provided per local authority, 8,700 would be required. A modest suggestion, but a fourfold increase!

The Residential Care Role in the Local Authority

We can begin to see a clarification of the role of the residential unit as part of a programme of facilities in community care. Residential care is no longer only a question of custodial care, security or material welfare. Its purpose is one of prevention and/or rehabilitation, and within this context it has important close links with employment, education, social security, industrial training and occupational therapy. Similar developments in the professional practice of residential care can be seen where the staff of children's homes and those for the elderly and the physically handicapped are involved. Social services departments, through their integration, have already been able to facilitate the interchange of training and ideas between the various specialist residential workers, many of whom are beginning to identify common approaches in their work. This in turn is leading to a strengthening of the profession of residential social work, a call for equal opportunities of training and support, reasonable staffing levels and comparable status. This trend is likely to continue, particularly with the growing body of knowledge regarding group dynamics and community work, which is broadening the whole basis of social work generally, and leading away from overemphasis in the past upon individual case work. Progressive ideas on the development of the therapeutic community within hospitals and elsewhere are being translated into the community care field. Such ideas increasingly emphasise the important part which all members of residential staff have to play in the treatment programme besides stressing the absolute importance of involving the clients themselves in setting individual goals and at the same time participating in the total decision-making process within the residential unit.

As a result of these trends and the growing confidence and skill which the residential workers 'at the coalface' must inevitably gain, they are likely to become more vocal in defining the needs of the mentally ill and will inevitably press for a greater say in the evolving policies within the total systems, and they will begin to influence the appropriate distribution of resources. There is no doubt that these people will, through promotion, have an increasingly influential part to play in the total running of social services departments and the larger voluntary organisations.

The revenue costs of better staffing policies are likely to be high, and at the same time the satisfactory recruitment of growing numbers of people of the necessary calibre, in itself, is already bringing difficulties. Residential care, therefore, is not 'by any to be enterprised nor taken in hand, inadvisedly, lightly or wantonly . . . but reverently, discreetly, advisedly, soberly, and in the fear of God'; this applies equally to committees, managers and staff.

What are the Possible Limitations on Achieving Adequate Services?

A number of important factors have to be borne in mind but are not necessarily insuperable, dependent on the determination of those concerned with the provision of satisfactory services for the mentally ill to work together, and on a willingness to base declared aims upon the specific needs of particular communities, which implies a proper study of the facts at the local level and a serious attempt to measure the level of need.

Finance

The declared national social policy for health and social services is one of prevention and care in the community. This applies not only to the specific sphere of mental illness, but also the spheres of mental handicap, the chronically sick and disabled, child care, delinquency and the elderly. Long-term custodial care in hospitals or other institutions is no longer an objective. Community, medical, nursing and personal social services are to combine to provide appropriate facilities within the family home, local day centres or small, locally based, residential units. District general hospitals are to develop largely for the acute aspects of illnesses on the short-term basis. This will apply particularly to psychiatric illness, and over a fifteen to twenty-year period it is envisaged that the large specialist mental hospital will gradually run down. The feasibility of decanting large numbers of older, institutionalised patients from the mental hospitals must be looked at as a special aspect of the policy. It is perhaps not surprising that local authorities show apprehension at growing local expenditure on residential care and the transfer of cost from central taxation to the rates. However, with the reorganisation of the National Health Service, those medical and nursing services which now are financed from the rates will be transferred to central finance. It still has to be decided whether local authority social services departments will have to pay for the provision of medical or psychiatric advisers to their department.

There has always been a fair amount of misunderstanding in the public at large about who pays for health and social services. Although the National Health Service is often spoken of as being 'free', in the end it is the taxpayer or the ratepayer who pays for any services administered by the government. Schemes administered by local authorities are far more under the critical eye of the general public who receive their regular rate demands and the rating system is always, with some justification, a popular subject for attack in the local press. What is not usually pointed out is that approximately fifty per cent, on average, of the cost of the local authority services is met from the central government's rate support grant. Also, of course, the local authority is at liberty to charge the users of its services according to their ability to pay, although increasingly discretion is used as to whether a service shall be provided free or at a reduced rate.

With the emphasis on ten-year plans for the personal social services, central government is now laying emphasis upon the expected level of expenditure by local authorities. It is to be hoped that in collaboration with the local authority associations, the central government will find ways of better informing the ratepayers as to the funding of essential services, and perhaps devising more progressive methods of local revenue raising.

It has been suggested that the personal social services would be better funded in the same way as the National Health Service. However, should central government be held completely financially responsible, it is doubtful whether the management of the services would remain in the hands of local government. If this were to happen, I would suggest that there would be a serious undermining of the whole concept of community care services, if one interprets this as meaning the development of a caring community, locally based, geared towards the particular needs of individuals, families and neighbourhoods, over which the recipients themselves, both as clients and providers, could maintain some positive control. It does seem to me that much of the needed airing of the financing of the community care services at the local level could be very positively linked with the urgent need for a public relations exercise as to the purpose of all kinds of community care, and with a continuing social education function.

On the more practical here-and-now aspect of finance, local authorities are, I am sure, increasingly prepared to make grants to voluntary organisations and to pay for the care of residents on a per capita basis. There undoubtedly are delays and prevarications by some local authorities over individual case placements, although I would suggest that the integration of the social services department may have brought the position of the mentally ill more into line with the position which has applied for many years in the children's departments. The emphasis in the latter has been first of all the ascertainment of need of an individual, followed by the seeking of an appropriate placement, whether in a local authority home or alternatively in a unit run by a voluntary organisation. It is quite clear from the legislation that the *intention* is that the best interests of the client shall be served. Administrative financial responsibility should be dealt with after the client's needs in all cases.

At a time when there is need to expand the services and to encourage the maximum collaboration with the voluntary organisations, it is up to the local authorities themselves to come forward with imaginative ways of financing the voluntary sphere of activity. I was very interested to read, for example, in the Richmond Fellowship's annual report of a scheme whereby the local authority provided and maintained the fabric of the building, with the Fellowship staffing and managing the unit on a day-to-day basis. Similar arrangements have been tried elsewhere. A factor which must be borne in mind is that increasingly, voluntary organisations find it hard to sustain large-scale expansion of their services due to financial constraint, and in any event many voluntary organisations at the present time are increasingly dependent upon statutory funds by way of grants etc. Today, therefore, the interdependence of the voluntary and statutory services must be a foregone conclusion.

Financial considerations, bearing in mind the overall need for economic use of scarce resources, should not stand in the way of providing proper care and attention for the mentally ill. In my own authority, and I believe this applies in others, the standard charge to residents has been set at a realistic figure, well below the actual total cost to the authority, but not so low as to be a disincentive to the residents towards moving out into lodgings or other accommodation where they would have to be self-supporting ultimately.

Competing Demands and Unrealistic Expectations of a Local Authority

There is no doubt a situation regarding the personal services whereby pressure groups of different types of clients are increasingly vocal and demanding, both in the press, Parliament, and directly on the elected members of the social services department. One has only to think of the homeless, the elderly, the mentally handicapped and the chronically sick and disabled, to know what I mean. There is a very serious danger that 'he who shouts loudest' will get the most attention, and unfortunately some professional colleagues have tended to join in. There is a temptation on the part of some politically sensitive councillors to respond excessively in one direction or another, possibly with a mistaken eye on their election prospects.

To my mind the best safeguard for the interests of the less vocal, silent and possibly isolated persons in need lies in the first place with the professional staff, who must see as one of their functions the advocacy role in ensuring that these persons' interests are properly catered for. The research and development units also are increasingly slowing up the requirements of the less vocal, and the most important task of the director of social services is to convince the members of the social services committee as to the priorities which they need to follow in carrying out their statutory obligations. Certainly the task is made easier by being able to provide evidence in the form of hard data. Every opportunity needs to be given to committee members to visit model residential units where the needs of the client are clearly apparent, together with evidence of the activities which are producing results.

The work of the voluntary organisations for the mentally *handicapped* in sponsoring research and experimental projects is a good example of the power of hard data to change public opinion, regarding the prospects for individual development and responsiveness to a more favourable environment, and has led to the achievement of more positive forms of care and the corresponding resources required. Much positive progress in achieving adequate services for less fortunate members of society has in the past been inhibited by popular stereotypes of, for example, 'the idiot', 'the cripple' or 'the orphan'. There are similar stereotypes prevalent regarding 'the deviant' and 'the madman', and it is a major professional responsibility to bring to life the human being beneath the sweeping generalisation. Social workers are now expected to think primarily of the person and the total family situation; to assess properly the degree of need and the capacity of the individual and the family to cope or otherwise. No longer does the client have to be conveniently pigeonholed in order to receive a service, nor can he be rejected on the grounds of not fitting within a stereotype.

The social services department should not fall into the trap of merely providing service response on the prescription of some other agency, or an uncritical response to a client's demands. In many situations, of course, a crisis situation must of necessity be dealt with and a proper social assessment carried out subsequently with a view to making a longer-term plan. However, there are many situations of which there is knowledge in the early stages and the endeavour must be to make a proper appraisal of all factors with a view to preventing a crisis developing. The social worker's task in the social services department is therefore fourfold:

- to make a proper social assessment
- to act as a counsellor
- to make decisions as to the needs for various types of services
- to act as an advocate with outside authorities for the provision of benefits and services and alternatively within the local authority for an expansion of provision.

Who Shall Be Helped First?

One major obstacle to reducing the occupancy of mental hospital beds lies in the long-term patients who are now growing elderly, who have been in hospitals often up to forty years or more and are highly institutionalised. Certain local authorities, including my own, are taking a close look at such residents with a view to possible transfer to our elderly persons' homes. Indeed, such transfers are already taking place. Any determined effort by local authorities on this particular number of patients could well defer for many years to come any more positive approach regarding younger people.

Although I am very concerned at the danger of labelling categories of clients, for fear of overlooking their total needs as people and the family commitment that goes with this, there may be an argument, as the reorganised health and social services settle down, for beginning to think eventually of concentrating 'programme years' so that emphasis can be placed during those years on particular aspects of client need. To my mind there needs to be a fairly rapid advance in the initial years on a broad front of provision of all kinds, spreading resources according to the pattern of need revealed in different communities. This is the strongest argument I know for complete consultation between the statutory and voluntary spheres in order to decide who can best carry out what tasks.

Certainly in some spheres of activity the local authorities are cautious to commence a service, for example with drug addicts and alcoholics, and as a result there are large numbers of voluntary organisations willing to undertake the task. In other areas of work the statutory authorities have almost completely taken over responsibility and some people may say that this suggests that the type of problem has now become socially acceptable.

Community Reaction

As the community care services expand, so the social services department and the council will inevitably have to face the reaction of the local community to the consequences. All kinds of people who formerly were condemned to institutional life or an early demise are now expected to take their place living in the community, receiving education and training benefits, and needing to find some kind of employment or occupational niche. These include the mentally and physically handicapped, rehabilitated prisoners, unsupported mothers, problem families and increasing numbers of the mentally ill. It was put to me recently: 'I fully support the need for these people to have somewhere to live, providing it is not in my street.'

I sincerely hope that public antipathy is not so weighted against the mentally ill as it would appear from a United States study, which listed 21 forms of disability with the mentally ill rating as 21st in terms of acceptability. Mental illness ranked below alcoholics, ex-prisoners, epileptics and grossly physically handicapped persons. I heard of an example where a progressive voluntary organisation called a public meeting to discuss the setting up of a residential hostel for young workers. Local residents vehemently opposed this on the grounds that the area would be overrun by drug addicts, sexual deviants and alcoholics. Most of this is based upon a complete lack of understanding of the real problems which people can face. One rate-payer client said to me recently: 'It is not until you experience the problem in your own family that you feel strongly that the local authority should provide you with a service out of the rates.'

Where particular projects are planned, a great deal of care must be taken to ensure the co-operation of local residents, bearing in mind that the growing numbers of units will have to be accommodated somewhere within the community, and also, after the establishment of the unit, to encourage involvement of the local community in its activities as far as possible. Residential units placed in living communities should not only serve those in need, *but also act as a form of social education to the public at large* as to how coping with anxieties and problems can be achieved. Although I can sympathise very much with the 'asylum' concept as being vital as a refuge for a sick person away from the stresses and strains of everyday life, there is no doubt that the isolation of the mentally ill in large colonies away from the run of everyday life has contributed greatly to the readiness of the majority of people to deny that certain problems exist, and to be unwilling, therefore, to face the consequences in terms of helping to solve them. A major task of those engaged in community care should be to reverse this trend.

What Should the Priorities Now Be?

In order to achieve a fully comprehensive community care programme for the mentally ill, apart from providing adequate domiciliary, field work and day-care facilities, considerable emphasis has to be placed on the appropriate level and extent of residential care. One of the present weaknesses is that clients either have no choice or a one-choice alternative. What is required is a range of living accommodation along the following lines:

- for the long-term chronically sick requiring continual support falling short of hospital care
- intensive treatment units, particularly those for adolescents and younger persons with behaviour disorders
- short-term/medium-term rehabilitative units for younger persons orientated towards employment or sheltered workshops with the

hope of progression to:
- group homes under minimal supervision, possibly associated with the former hostel
- supervised lodgings
- sheltered housing
- normal housing provision.

Who exactly provides the various types of units to make up this range should depend on local negotiations between the statutory and voluntary authorities and the decision will depend on a number of factors, namely

- how quickly a voluntary organisation can take action
- finances as between the statutory and voluntary sphere
- whether the voluntary organisation is prepared to place a unit within a certain community
- whether certain specialised units would need to be developed to cover a region rather than a small local authority area.

Finally, in taking the broadest possible view of community care in general (and in this case as regards the mentally ill specifically), not only would I emphasise the urgent need for a partnership between the voluntary and the statutory authorities, but also would encourage every possible effort for community care to be seen as embracing the hospital rather than as being presented as an alternative to hospital care. The latter will depend almost entirely on the getting together of the various people concerned in providing and planning services, accepting that each has a unique contribution to make and being able to focus on the task in hand – the care of the mentally ill person.

Only in these ways can I see true development towards a caring community which fully acknowledges the common humanity of those who care and those who need care. Ultimately, in the last analysis, surely the two may be one and the same?

22 WORKING WITH GOVERNMENTS ON THE PROVISION OF THERAPEUTIC COMMUNITIES: A DUTCH PERSPECTIVE

M.A.J. Romme

In terms of future planning, the therapeutic community is important as an alternative to hospital care of the mentally ill, and as a model on which psychiatric hospitals may be organised. Its future will then depend on the experience and ideals of field workers, the organisational talents and skills of the directors of mental health care facilities and financial support given by the government. To my mind, the *most* important point is: will it be possible to make the therapeutic community an integrated part of all mental health care facilities, so that it works effectively because of its network of relations with the local community and its relations with the already existing mental health care facilities? This integration is important for the future development of the whole idea of the therapeutic community, because a therapeutic community within a society thinking along different lines will not be very effective. If in schools, in industries and in the whole complex of health care facilities, people are relating to each other in a totally different way from what is going on in the therapeutic community, the client will hardly profit from its efforts.

I stress this point of integration within the whole range of the mental health care facilities right from the start, because of its implications for the development of a new way of looking at health care that we see gradually developing in Holland amongst government bodies. This development is a gradual change from institutionalisation towards regional orientation. We are used to governments acting as control agents, and control is still exercised in the old-fashioned way by formulating general goals for health care and developing laws to guard these goals. This is not enough, however, as there is a considerable distortion when it reaches the local operation. Therefore a second weapon is used: financial control. This also fails, and a lot of regulations are formulated in relation to the quality of care as instruments of control. There are for example laws that link certain activities to certain professional groups, and there are norms formulated for the different institutions, such as number of beds related to space, number of staff, and safety regulations.

The trouble with the governmental control system is that it ends up in endless regulations without much guarantee for government control of the total health care system, because they are based on a number of misunderstandings. The first misunderstanding is that health care facilities are operating independently from each other. All the norms are linked to separate institutions, and this kind of institutionalisation leads in fact to the so-called 'patchwork quilt'. The second misunderstanding is that the primary task for the government is to control and that it is only a second priority to stimulate the right kind of facilities for the needs of the population. As far as the government does stimulate facilities, it is mostly only those facilities that may be called the more burdensome ones (like hospitals) that nobody likes to initiate, leaving the stimulation of the other facilities which are more likely to meet the needs of the population to private initiative.

The second misunderstanding goes hand in hand with a third problem. That is, that the input for government action and the feedback from the communities goes through political channels. This feedback may be too negative to change the primary task of the government from a controlling one into a stimulating one. We are now trying to take account of the fact that health care facilities do not operate independently from each other, and that flexibility of, or change within, a compartmentalised system is not possible because 'one man's gains are another man's losses'. If we want a more satisfactory mental health care system, we have to take as our starting point the health care needs in a circumscribed population, and bring the working units necessary to fulfil these needs together in one health care delivery system. Thus it is not necessary to make regulations per institution about how much money is spent, but in a regionalised health care delivery system a certain amount of money per head of the population is spent. The effort of distributing funds, and of debating on what the funds will be spent, should be left to the health care delivery systems in the region of operation.

A government should only help to deliver the tools necessary to distribute the financial support. Such help can be given by spending money on organisation experts and on experts in the area of information-gathering, because it is very important for government and existing services to know what are the health care needs in a particular region, and how services are best organised to meet these needs. A second government tool relating to this last item – to meet the needs of the population – is to stimulate evaluation activities of the health care delivery system. A third way in which the government can help, relating not only to the need for orientation about the health care needs but also to the evaluation of health care delivery, consists of stimulating the communication between health care professionals and consumers. Assessment of health care needs and evaluation of services depend not only on the thinking and experience of professionals, but, perhaps as important, on the thinking and experience of the consumers. To summarise briefly, there is a development in the role of the government: from control to communication with consumers; from institutionalisation to regionalisation; from finance per element of care to finance per head of population; from regulations per institution to feedback of health care needs and evaluation of health care delivery; and from centralisation of funding to decentralisation of distribution, according to findings in the field of action. This development probably does not sound too bad. The problem is that we do not start from scratch, so we have to be realistic and try to work out what has to be done to change gradually the existing pattern into a new one. Therefore, we see the Dutch government acting upon a White Paper (as it is called in England) produced in 1970 and renewed in 1974 by the two Secretaries of State, Dr Kruizinga in 1970 and Dr Hendrix in 1974.

A few steps taken so far by the Dutch government regarding mental health care are:

1. Stimulating a unified finance system for all mental health care facilities. Since 1968 the in-patient service is fully paid for as a result of 'The Law on the Special Costs of Illness' – alas, on a 'cost per bed per day' basis. It would be better, as we have said, to have a norm per head of population. Since 1971 the community psychiatric service – an extended preventative and aftercare service (or ambulatory psychiatric service as we call it) – is *fully paid for* under the same law on a budget system for the service, which is better than on an individual service basis, but not as good as on a 'per head of the population' basis. We are now developing a norm for the budget related to the population served. Since 1972 the day centres and the halfway houses (called institutes for evening and night care) have been *fully paid for* by the sick fund, alas, again on a 'per person per day' basis. From 1975 the child guidance clinics will be *fully paid for* under the law mentioned above, not as separate from the community psychiatric service but as an integrated service, with a budget being shared between those two provisions. In 1978 a new stimulus has been given to the development of alternatives to hospital care. A new law

is about to be passed in which halfway houses, day care centres, psychiatric hostels and other institutions that offer alternatives to hospital care, can become accredited facilities. This means that when a facility meets certain quality criteria it will be funded through 'The Law on the Special Costs of Illness'. This will stimulate existing facilities to meet the quality criteria. The number of beds and places in facilities that offer alternatives to hospital care will also be extended resulting from the plan for the coming years, that 3,000 beds in psychiatric hospitals will be replaced by beds or places in the above-mentioned facilities.

Next, as regards the development of a unified finance system for in-patient services, out-patient services and 'complementary' services (a term for halfway houses, day centres, etc.), we have seen another development:

2. The regional reorganisation of mental health in-patient services and out-patient services. The newly built in-patient services for psychiatric patients are limited to a maximum of 300 beds. Existing in-patient services have to reduce to this number of beds in two phases. The first phase requires the reduction to 600 beds. This is regulated by planning permission for renovation only on the condition of the reorganisation of the total number of beds. In every general hospital that has more than 200 beds the provision of a psychiatric ward of 20 to 40 beds is stimulated and complementary services as an alternative to mass hospital care are encouraged. Ambulatory services are being reorganised on a regionalised basis, which is at the moment the case in only three of the larger cities.
3. Support groups are stimulated to test and activate the interest of the consumers.
4. Relations between in-patient and out-patient services are being reorganised. For the time being, complementary services will be stimulated especially when organised by, or in relation to, the existing facilities for out-patient or in-patient services. This is based on the concept that it is more in line with a differentiated service programme when the complementary service (e.g. the therapeutic community) is linked to an ambulatory service.

In the Dutch perspective the halfway house therapeutic community is a complementary service. These communities will have to be integrated with all the other mental health care facilities and orientated not only towards their own methodology, but also towards meeting the needs of a geographically defined population and providing continuity of care which will make going back into society possible. The halfway house therapeutic community, when provided as part of the mental health care facilities, will be fully paid for in Holland from 1979 by 'The Law on the Special Costs of Illness', so long as it meets certain quality criteria.

The future perspective is part of the development of a new trend in the change from an institutionalised health care delivery system into a regionalised health care delivery system. The steps taken are:

1. The introduction of a unified finance system for all categories of facilities.
2. The reduction of the capacity of in-patient services per hospital to 300 beds orientated on a catchment area of about 300,000 inhabitants.
3. Stimulation of development of psychiatric wards in general hospitals and stimulation of complementary services as alternatives to 24-hour in-patient care.
4. Integration of ambulatory services into an organisation fit to provide a differentiated service programme for a catchment area of about 300,000 inhabitants.
5. Stimulation of interest groups for preventative mental health designed to stimulate the participation and feedback of the consumers.

This process is nearly completed and the way may now be clear for the next step, which will be the integration of in-patient and out-patient services, that are already provided on a regionalised basis. Working with governments can be very frustrating for various reasons: vested interest (possibly on either side); favouritism; blind spots; red-tape attitudes. It needs a 'long breath' (determination) and a long perspective, and involves considering how your needs can be fitted into the government's line of thinking. Working with governments however is also very promising. It results on a long-term basis in the stabilising of new effective mental health care facilities such as the therapeutic community.

23 COMMUNITY PSYCHIATRY IN THE METROPOLIS: NOTHING FOR EVERYONE (USA)

Harley Shands (Transcript)

Working in New York City is a great mental health exercise. If it is possible to tolerate living in the kinds of bewildering sets of restriction that one encounters in New York City, I think that one tends to be proofed against almost anything else. In the first place the British sold us a bill of goods. The idea of community psychiatry, the idea of establishing a localised area which constitutes some form of community and the idea of turning people out of mental hospitals onto the community resources is basically British. But in Britain there is a tradition for this, going back thousands of years. I understand it is changing a good deal, but until recently there was a very strong tendency for people to stay in the same place, for people to know who they were in terms of local identification. When you say 'community' in an established country like Britain, France or Spain, it means something. When you begin to get into the complexities of political organisation in New York City, you find that there is a series of health districts with certain definitions; there is a series of school districts with certain definitions; there is a series of water, gas and electricity districts; and in whatever context, you find that the city is broken up into districts. But none of the districts are the same. The health district is completely different from the school district. If there were any kind of tendency in New York to have a community, it is very difficult within these limitations.

What has happened over the last twelve to fifteen years in the district for which the West Side Community Mental Health Center is responsible is, for example, the building of the Lincoln Center for the Performing Arts, which came into a more or less established residential area and destroyed an enormous amount of it to put in the Lincoln Center buildings. That is a story that happens over and over again. Recently the authorities have been preoccupied with poverty, but up until recently they were preoccupied with development. One of the characteristic 'observables' has been that any form of progress usually requires tearing down and eliminating an enormous area. New York, Manhattan particularly, is very densely populated so that by the time you have knocked down two blocks full of housing, you have eliminated a substantial proportion of the community residents. What communities are increasingly resisting, with enthusiasm, is the fact that when you eliminate two or three blocks of apartment houses, you have eliminated the houses and the networks and the conditions of life that thousands of people are acquainted with. In order to improve the mental health of the community one knocks down houses sheltering a large proportion of the members of that community, who are thereafter left in bad mental health through losing their context.

The community mental health movement in many ways in the United States is a memorial to Kennedy. Kennedy was beginning to get into a lot of political trouble when he was assassinated, but he immediately got turned into a martyr because of his assassination. There were a number of programmes set up, of which the one that has affected us most closely is the community mental health business. It is an American characteristic that as soon as the problem comes into focus there is a gigantic programme of public relations which disseminates this information. There are committees and demonstrations, and politicians and everybody gets excited. Thus some kind of *ad hoc* programme has to cope with the problem but by the time that anything substantial might conceivably be done the attention has shifted to something else. In the very recent past an ambitious young member of the New York State Assembly masterminded a commission examining the excesses of the nursing home area. They focused primarily on one fellow who was an ex-rabbi. This guy had managed to milk twenty million dollars out of the nursing home business in the last fifteen years by exploiting the helpless aged. He is now in bad odour in the public press, but the prospect of any kind of major reorganisation of the nursing home programme on the basis of these exposés is not very good. The newspapers will veer off to something else.

The programme for people from mental hospitals again is an idea which began in Britain and was transferred to the United States. It was very gratefully accepted, I suspect, by the politicians, because what would be better than to get half the people out of the mental hospitals and put them somewhere else? What has seemed to me to be the reasonable expectation is that, if you discharge half the patients, you would reduce the budget. This is never achieved, but it gives politicians some kind of basis on which to recruit more votes. If I sound very cynical, it is because I have become very cynical in the course of the last eight or nine years in coping with the kinds of exploitations that are carried out in the name of mental health care in the metropolis. The name I have recently invented for New York City is Schizopolis. It seems to me that if you talk about schizophrenia, New York City is a beautiful example of schizopolis, because the same kind of rigidities and difficulties in coping with the discharge problem are there.

When I took the job at the Roosevelt Hospital in 1966, I took it primarily on the basis that it was a very small, local, elegant, delightful service. We have about forty in-patient beds, official capacity, and we run 105 to 110 per cent capacity because we generally have people in the so-called quiet rooms, so that makes us really fairly popular with the hospital administration. Another one of the complexities in this situation is that the cost of medical care in the United States is so high and rising so fantastically that the politicians constantly talk about the importance of getting people out of hospital beds, doing out-patient stuff and preventative stuff so that you do not have to have people in the beds. In the first place the American system of medical care consists of overlapping and competing bureaucracies. I suppose that the primary support for medical care in the vast majority of the working population is the Blue Cross, Blue Shield programme – private medical insurance. What you find there is the paradox that those programmes do not pay for out-patient care. So you get a tremendous effort to increase the out-patient care proportion of the medical delivery system which is 'free' – I mean, not paid for by insurance. If there is any evidence that the demand for hospital beds is falling the hospital administration goes into a collapse because they are already in very bad financial condition. As soon as there is any evidence that there is going to be less demand for insurance-paid medical services, it becomes a fiscal crisis within the hospital. The whole thing is the most unbelievable exercise in paradox that one has ever encountered.

When I took over this job, I was delighted that it was small and manageable. For a space of four years we doubled the budget every year, encouraged by the city and the state. The formula for the budget is one of the things that I am sure nobody in Britain can understand, and anybody with any sense in the United States cannot understand it either. To support our programme, the hospital supplied fifty per cent of the money and the city supplied the other fifty per cent. We establish a contract, for example, worth two million dollars. In order to get the money to run it, we have to send the city a cheque for a million dollars, whereupon they send us a cheque for two million dollars. I never really understood that, but that is the way it works.

Then the money does not belong to the city, it comes to the city from the state. The city has no other way of getting money other than through the state, except that in the United States there is another programme called Medicaid which supports the indigent and is in part federal money. There is a cut-off level which I think is now somewhere around $3,000 a year income, so that anybody who has less income than that can get medical care supported by Medicaid, particularly if they are on welfare. If you are on welfare, Medicaid is automatic. In order to operate this programme, we have to send in vouchers on Medicaid patients. The money that we get from the vouchers has to be then divided with the city. So we have to get the money in, process it, send half of it back to the city. If we don't do that, the state gets very angry because some of that money comes from the federal government, which reduces the costs of the state in supplying the money to the city to supply the money to us. There are all sorts of arguments over the formulas which we use to assess and establish these things. To me in many ways the most distressing thing about it is that the whole programme is one that absolutely makes dishonesty inevitable. You simply cannot do anything honest in this programme.

When we started, there were a lot of very idealistic and forward-looking programmes. For example, we had a number of people in school programmes counselling the teachers and working with the junior guidance programme in a variety of schools in the neighbourhood. Next thing we knew, the city destroyed the junior guidance programme – they just eliminated it – meanwhile eliminating those contracts. As the financial pressure built up, they began more and more to insist upon accountability, evaluations. As this continued, it became essentially impossible to do anything in the programme for which one could not submit a bill. Meanwhile, in the hospital there was a slow shift in the direction of putting more and more responsibility in the accounting department of the hospital rather than in the kind of crude accounting that we had previously done in the department and in the community mental health centre. As this happened, slowly all of the people who counted and registered the patients were absorbed by the accounting department and we lost contact with the funds and to a considerable extent with the patients. So the whole thing really has become an administrative nightmare.

What we have got out of this as probably the primary lesson is that we are pretty sure that anything that can be done with the kinds of extraordinarily disadvantaged and disabled people that we deal with really has to be done in terms of therapeutic communities – halfway houses and so on. When they dumped a lot of people out of the state hospitals, there were many people who had been in a state hospital for as long as fifteen or twenty years. They knew no other home; they had no other contact; their families had long since abandoned them, and all of a sudden somebody came around and said, 'You're free.' The patients said, 'Well, what the hell do I do now?' and people said, 'Well, we don't care about that because you have now been liberated. Instead of being incarcerated and taken advantage of and persecuted, as you have been for the last twenty years, you are now free.' This presented a tremendous crisis to a lot of these people and many of them wound up in what is called a 'welfare hotel' in New York City; 'single-room occupancies' is another name for them. These are very marginal hotels with tiny rooms that people live in sometimes for ten, fifteen, twenty or even thirty years. Their sole advantage is that the room and a modest amount of food cost just about as much as they get paid on welfare, and many of these people have lived in incredible states of squalor, distress and isolation, quite solidly for many years.

Here are a couple of episodes that stick in my mind and illustrate the kind of life that is in these hotels. In this area there is a particular brand of deviant, known as a collector. These tend to be senile old ladies who get shopping bags, go out and go through the garbage cans. Whatever they find in the garbage cans of value or interest to them, they put in the shopping bags and they come back and leave it in their room. There was one lady who had been doing this for many years to such an extent that her room was totally full, so that she couldn't even get into bed. So she slept in the bath-tub, but since this was a bath-tub that a number of people used, this produced some friction. This went on for a very long period of time until finally the lady died. When somebody decided to go through the bags, they discovered $230,000 worth of negotiable securities in the midst of this incredible collection. Another woman whom I remember acutely had a peculiar problem. She was very fat, but her obesity was such that she had a relatively thin thorax and then she spread out to unbelievable proportions. I have never seen such a figure in my life. She had an unfortunate habit of getting nervous and having diarrhoea. She lived about half a hall away from the bathroom. When at night she had a hurried call and rushed down the hall, she was so wide and the hall was so narrow that she would open the doors of everybody, thereby waking them up. They would come out and yell at her, whereupon she would become psychotic and after this went on for a while, she would have to be admitted to the hospital. Eventually she would go back home and things would be all right for a while. Then she would get nervous and the whole thing would start all over again. One of my associates had a brilliant idea. He said, 'Look, Harley, why don't we fix it up so that she has a room with a private bathroom?' and I do not think she has been back in the hospital since. This is the level of mental health care that we frequently find ourselves involved with.

Another aspect of New York City is that there are an incredible number of overlapping jurisdictions, because in any one of these projects you have workers from the Department of Social Services, from the Visiting Nurse Service, from the Roosevelt Hospital and from several other places. Each such organisation has its own territorial plan. An enormous amount of effort is involved in negotiating whose territory is which, whose job is it to do what, who has the privilege of taking care of a patient in this way, who has the duty of taking care of the patient in that way. In principle, in the brave new approach mandated by the original Community Mental Health Act, the community mental health centre is supposed to be the broker that integrates and negotiates between all of the agencies within the community. But we have enough trouble in our place negotiating between the in-patient department and the out-patient department and the day hospital and the community service and so on, so that we do not really have a lot of time left over to do the job of integration. In addition to that, we really do not have any power as far as integration is concerned. There is nothing that we can do to force any of those other people to co-operate with us in a way that they did not want to. So again and again one comes back to the point that this is a series of exercises in futility, except for the fact that in these welfare hotel projects, although their scope is very limited, we have remarkably successful teams.

One of the things that seems to me to be clear is that, in delivering mental health care in this kind of an operation, the very best trained professionals are nurses, one reason being that almost all of these people have medical diseases of one sort or another. There is a very high proportion of hypertensives, alcoholics, cirrhotic livers, diabetics and so on, so that they need a great deal of sensitivity to the general health programme as well as to the mental health programme. In my experience, nurses are probably the most efficient practitioners at doing this integrating job, although we have some social workers and an occasional clinical psychologist who do almost as superb a job as some of the nurses. As far as psychiatrists and physicians are concerned, they are essential for a variety of purposes, but they really are not suited to being primary deliverers. For one reason, in the United

States this kind of clientele and this kind of programme, with all the problems and discouragements that go along with it, had until very recently not been very attractive to psychiatrists because they could use their talents more pleasantly and profitably otherwise.

The welfare hotel is the area of greatest need and deprivation, yet projects are far less intensively staffed and manned than a halfway house. Even so, over a long period of time, we have had many of the same experiences that have been reported in halfway houses. For example, at the beginning, five or six years ago, there was a tremendous amount of input necessary to get a tenants' council going and get enough representatives out of the residents even to come to a tenants' council. Gradually over the years that has changed a good deal. Now it has got to the point which delights us, where the tenants' council meeting sometimes says to our personnel, 'Look, we don't need you. Why don't you just get out of here? We'd like to do this ourselves.' The programme that has worked most successfully in this one place is primarily a resocialisation programme – an attempt to get people to work with each other, to have some political input into the management of the hotel. One of the things that we have found to be enormously useful, more so than one would think from the expenditure, is something we call a job corps. This pays many of these people, who have no other occupation, a couple of bucks an hour to run errands or to take care of the switchboard – low-level jobs, very poorly paid. But since these people have no other income whatsoever, this makes a good deal of difference to them. Another ten bucks a month is quite a lot more than you expect it to be if you have nothing left over otherwise. So our experience has really been that this kind of semi-halfway house arrangement is by far the most efficient, most gratifying effort that we know. It takes enormous dedication on the part of the people. It is marginally supported at all times.

24 CARING, THE STEPCHILD OF OUR MEDICAL CARE SYSTEM (USA)

Hans R. Huessy

The topic of this chapter is treatment, care and caring. We do not question the need to pay for the professional treatment of chronic psychiatric patients. In fact, third-party payers will pay for many treatments which have never been proven beneficial. In addition, material care is well financed, as anyone in need is supplied with room and board. Difficulties arise, however, in financing the social framework which a chronic psychiatric patient needs in addition to professional treatment and material care. This necessary social framework consists of a group of people with whom the patient is in daily contact, and who respond to the patient with simple interpersonal concern for the patient as a fellow human being. When such concern exists between people it is called 'caring'. And while caring is a vital element in dealing with psychiatric illness, it is both strenuous as well as unmeasurable, and thus both more difficult to supply and finance than professional treatment or material care.

The healthy individual maintains and adds to his own caring matrix beginning with the family in which he grew up, and during a short illness his social matrix supports him. Psychiatric patients with chronic illness have lost their social matrix and have an inability to maintain their own social matrix; and therefore, either for a short period of time or for the rest of their lives, need a social matrix ready-made for them.

What makes up a social matrix? First, a group of people with whom we interact over long periods, our relatives, the people we live with like our family, room-mates, co-workers and people we play with. Within this social matrix occurs participation in common tasks and games, sharing of values and loyalties, and caring, that human loving of another without demanding anything in return.

Years ago the old-fashioned boarding-house supplied many psychologically disabled with a ready-made social matrix. You had your own room but you shared a living-room and two meals a day with others and you could interact with them to the extent that you wished; a social group was always there. This boarding-house is no more. In Vermont we have recreated two of them for long-term psychiatric patients. Such a boarding-house functions best for patients who are able to work but need a social matrix to sustain them during the non-working hours of the week. In the boarding-house situation, a social matrix is provided in which one guest caring for another can occur, and most of this caring goes on between different guests of the boarding-home. The director of the home supplies the setting in which caring can occur. The social matrix is there even during times when the individual guest may not be able to play his part in maintaining it. As long as the matrix is provided, the guest can participate and survive. This matrix would not sustain itself from the participation of its members. A planned outside effort is essential for this social support system to survive.

Providing such caring is a strenuous task. First, these caring relationships are not controlled by appointments or eight-hour shifts. Caring does not go off duty. Let us look at the same dilemma in another field and different country. The original communist plan in Russia for child-rearing proposed that 80 per cent of all children be raised in state-run homes which could see to it that the children received the scientifically correct physical, cognitive and emotional stimulation at the appropriate times. Maximum development would be guaranteed. The correct teaching of the values of socialism and patriotism would be assured. This programme was abandoned. They were unable to supply an adequate substitute for parental caring, especially maternal caring. The limitless commitment of mother to her child cannot be duplicated by a series of 40-hour-a-week workers.

Caring requires constant interaction between the provider and the person for whom he is caring. So a caring relationship is the complement of a professional relationship. One of the hallmarks of professionalisation is that it limits the interaction between therapist and patient. The therapist administers treatment, be it for five minutes or for an hour. Good therapists are kind and considerate, but their professional relationship does not go outside the professional part of their lives. We do not bring our patients home to dinner. The caring relationship differs from the professional relationship also because caring involves taking risks. The family aspect of a caring relationship centres around the willingness to take risks. If misfortune occurs, the social network provides crisis intervention, without trying to measure and determine who should receive how much caring. But the very purpose of the professional relationship is to protect the therapist from such responsibility. And so, although mental health literature is filled with attempts to find professionalised ways of providing caring, I am convinced that this is a dream not to be. The professional role in this situation is, first, to make the decision that such a setting is needed and, second, to see to it that it has stability over time. Caring cannot be institutionalised, but we can create institutions in which caring can occur.

The caring itself depends on non-professionals who utilise human qualities given to all of us. Our third-party payers pressure us to take these caring individuals and train them in some way to professionalise them so that they can justify paying for their services, to make them part of the treatment team. But the more we professionalise them, the less they can provide the very caring for which we originally added them to the staff. Caring for the chronically ill is an exhausting business because one must continually give and only occasionally receive. The reason the professional has to limit his relationship is that he wants to live his own private life and must build protective walls against the encroachment of his treatment responsibilities into his private life.

In the ideal setting, a professional would decide what was needed, an administrator would provide the continuity of the setting, but the non-professional would provide the caring. There is another important reason for having non-professionals provide caring. While the patient relates to the professional as a parent-figure, most commonly it is in the client's parental relationships that there have been the most long-standing unresolved problems. But if the person providing caring is a non-professional, the guest can relate to this non-professional more on a peer basis, and our experience indicates that chronic psychiatric patients can make better progress in peer relationships than they can in relationships with parent substitutes. Again, the non-professional can help the patient in a way not open to the professional.

At Spring Lake Ranch in Cuttingsville, Vermont, we have learned to utilise college student volunteers who come for three to twelve-month periods to provide this kind of caring. Knowing that the commitment is time-limited, they can afford the kind of total involvement demanded of them. They can forego many personal freedoms for limited periods of time if they value the purpose. These students are not therapists, and their caring is not treatment. These young people learn a great deal about themselves and mental illness, but they do not become professionals. We give neither courses nor award diplomas.

If we are to have an extensive system of halfway houses, who will do the caring? And who will pay for caring? Material care and professional treatment can be financed because they are susceptible to measurement and thus to quality control in some form.

Any chronic psychiatric patient needs basic physical care which can be standardised and supplied according to routine formulae. This kind of basic care is measurable; one can train inspectors to visit the facilities where it is supplied and check on the quality of the housing, the quality of the food, the safety precautions and the cleanliness. The measurable aspect of treatment is found in the professional qualifications of the therapist. As long as treatment is supplied by individuals with acceptable qualifications, whether they be as psychiatrist, social worker, psychiatric nurse, occupational therapy worker, recreational worker, dance therapist, art therapist and many others, financing is obtainable.

The level of payment is related to the length and intensity of the training. The assumption is that all professionals use the 'correct' treatment and that all treatment will have beneficial effects. With basic care, measurable physical conditions are checked for quality control, while with treatment, the professional qualifications of the therapist are checked: I believe we must learn to describe clearly what any halfway house provides; we must convince third-party payers that this caring is an essential ingredient in dealing with psychiatric illnesses, and that it must be provided by non-professionals even though this reduces the ability to provide quality control. We might start this process by clearly defining different kinds of halfway houses.

The term 'halfway house' is used in a very general way today and describes many different facilities. Many varieties of halfway houses are needed. We need community care homes which take care of chronic patients of whom we have no expectations for improvement, but for whom we would like to provide the best life possible. We already have other community care homes which deal with patients who we hope may gradually improve further and perhaps someday leave the home. Obviously, these two homes require different methods of treatment and caring. The first is interested in stability over time, preventing undue stress and pressure on its guests, enriching their lives to whatever degree is possible. The second kind of home must continually try to push the guest beyond his previous plateau of adjustment, to challenge him with opportunities for higher levels of functioning, and to support him strongly when he makes any move forward. In supporting these forward moves, the homes take risks with their guests, like a family with children. So far we have not differentiated these two types of community homes, but I believe that the chronic patient put into a home which expects him to improve will have an unduly difficult time, while the patient who has the potential to improve, if placed into a chronic care home, is unlikely to realise his potential. There are homes that specialise in vocational rehabilitation, the teaching of social skills, easing the transition from hospital to community etc.

Institutionalising caring raises the problem of financing the houses that provide caring, and financing raises the problem of quality control. Third-party payers are interested in quality control. Unfortunately, caring is something that is not measurable. Usually quality control becomes equated with control of the physical environment and professional treatment, the number of square feet per guest, the number of hours of professional time per day, the quality of records. This is the kind of thing an inspector can verify.

We must find ways to prevent valid quality control from rewarding only material care and professional treatment, to the constant detriment of caring. In Vermont we are exploring the possibility of establishing new kinds of quality control standards. Under this system, community care homes beyond meeting minimum physical standards, would be asked to describe the programme that they propose to carry on for their guests, and when inspected, the inspector would try to see whether the programme described by the home itself was in fact being carried out. In other words the community care home would be measured against its own standards. Initially, the home would present its proposed programme for approval by the licensing authority.

Since true caring is as impossible to purchase as love, in the long run I do not believe that any insurance plan, however generous, will be able to supply the needed caring by making money available. At best, money can allow the creation of settings in which caring might occur. It would be difficult to involve an insurance plan in providing caring itself because, as we have already mentioned, caring involves taking risks which entail legal liability. Third-party payers wish to minimise risk, and consequently do not want those providing caring to take chances. But a facility that supplies caring will by definition be taking risks, and risks which are probably uninsurable at that. To a certain extent, of course, the nature of a halfway house is itself a form of protection because the caring environment tries to simulate the family, and one hopes that family members do not sue each other. In the final analysis, however, just as caring itself cannot be bought, neither can its failures be absolutely insured against, and this fact together with the necessity to have caring provided by non-professionals, makes it hard to finance caring as part of a health insurance plan.

Caring is needed in many areas of our society. In the long run, I cannot see how we can meet our needs for caring unless we institute some type of generalised required work service for all of our young people where they would contribute one or two years to do those jobs which no one will do for money, whether they be working in areas of social isolation or in community care homes, in psychiatric hospitals, in hospitals for the chronically and terminally ill, with the poor and unfortunate of all types in our society and the drudgery of most routine military duty. The Peace Corps and Vista were attempts to provide caring by people who were willing to give a time out of their life for this purpose without the consideration of financial reward. Only by combining our care and treatment programme with this type of service programme, can we add the caring element on any long-term basis to our programme for the psychiatrically disabled.

Disability pensions are a part of our care and social support system. Our present system of disability pensions ends up penalising the disabled person who tries again and again. A client of mine was recently turned down for social security disability pension because her earnings were too extensive. These earnings had been produced with a fabulous support system supplied by many different individuals. The client would repeatedly get acutely paranoid at work and would have to call a member of the support system up and maybe spend half an hour being reassured and, so to speak, talked down. No one was financing this support system, but without it she would not have amassed the earnings which denied her her social security pension. As long as she is not receiving disability pension, she also cannot obtain Medicaid. So she can afford to buy the medication which she needs only with financial help from her mother, but her mother is in her 70s and will not be able to do this for long.

This client is an example of two flaws in our current system of health care financing. First, she is able to function only by virtue of a social matrix and support system which our current system will not pay for. The matrix which this client is using is voluntary, and there are limits to the extent of voluntary assistance. As a professional who must earn his living, I can only allow myself to start caring for a small number of my patients. The second flaw in our health care financing system, illustrated by this example, is her inability to get a pension. The purpose of the treatment was to allow her to work normally. As soon as she succeeded in working, she was disqualified for the support which allowed her to continue working. In recent years that has been called 'Catch-22'. This client is an example of a voluntarily provided social matrix and social support system which allows this client to function, but which our present programme, which only deals with treatment and physical care, will not finance. I believe we must find some system which would allow a person to go on a disability pension, be allowed to earn to the extent that they were able, paying back some of their pension whenever they were earning well. But these people can earn only enough money to pay for their physical care, and they cannot pay for the needed supportive social matrix which makes it possible for them to earn the money for their basic care. We must have a system which makes it possible to supply the supportive social matrix which in turn allows these people to work at simple jobs. Community mental health was to supply much of this social matrix, but it has gone the route of professionalisation, so it cannot supply caring. The early indigenous workers were non-professionals; they provided caring for ghetto clients. They were quickly turned into paraprofessionals, who are low-priced professionals.

Of course, one of the saddest experiences is to work with a chronic psychiatric patient to the point where they could handle some simple job, only to find that the unemployment situation is such that it is totally unrealistic to expect an employer to give a job to our handicapped individual. Perhaps it is time that we in the US passed a law similar to the one in Great Britain which requires all employers of more than a certain number of employees to always have amongst these employees a certain percentage of the severely handicapped. Further, some of our clients cannot work a 40-hour week, but two or three of them between them could maybe handle a job. In Canada some factories have started to allow women with children to share jobs between them. The two women promise to cover the job completely and then divide the hours up between them to their convenience. This kind of arrangement would allow our clients who occasionally cannot deal with ordinary stress to take some time off without losing their job.

What is the size of our problem? In Vermont at the present time we have 2,000 psychiatrically disabled people in community care. This covers both the chronic psychiatric patient and the mentally retarded. Most of these are in small private community care homes. The population of the State of Vermont is 440,000, and an extrapolation from these figures for the country at large would tell us that we need to provide community care throughout the US for approximately 500,000 people.

How should this be done? A caring environment tries to come as close to the model of a well-functioning family as possible. A home staffed by three shifts and relief personnel obviously cannot do this. Most of our homes in Vermont are private, run by people who make our clients members of their extended family. The people who run these homes are not professionals; they have had no special training, but the caring I observe as I provide the aftercare for these clients is heartwarming. Vermont is a rural state, and perhaps what we are doing is feasible in a rural area where distance from others, privacy and opportunities for simple outdoor activities are easily available. In many of these homes one member of the family carries on with an outside job or perhaps the family runs a farm. Since the community care homes are only paid for physical care and not for caring, the enrichment provided by social and recreational activities must be provided from other sources, and is for this reason at the moment provided by payments for treatment by a variety of professionals. The community care homes should be supplemented by an enriching social support system supplied by the area community mental health center. This social support system provides recreational and social activities. The caring itself is provided gratis by the operators of the homes. The private community care home keeps costs at a very low level since the primary operators do not work on a 40-hour week and have such a small number of clients that they can truly know them, can be caring, and can individualise their programming. The community mental health center also continually monitors the community care homes, arranges for vocational training or job placement when indicated. It also helps clients change homes if they are dissatisfied or mismatched.

Using the support of community mental health centers, the isolation of a chronically ill psychiatric patient in a community care home can be offset. Given that this possible isolation is offset, the opportunity for caring provided by the small care home makes it a good alternative to hospitalisation.

For a community care home to function as we have suggested, it must obviously be able to control its admissions. It must be allowed to specify the kind of client it can best work with and to see to it that those are the clients it receives. It is tempting sometimes with community care homes to do the same thing that welfare departments do with unusually good foster homes. They gradually load them with more and more problem cases until the foster home or the community care home completely collapses or deteriorates and must be closed down. We ask them for caring beyond their capabilities. Our capacity for caring is limited, so ways must be found to prevent the pressures of the moment to lead to overloading.

The common splitting of the financial responsibility for physical care and professional treatment leads to a complication. Although the agency responsible for treatment would like to prevent re-hospitalisation and would be willing to make some extra effort to achieve this when a client decompensates, the physical care home receives no extra rewards for taking care of someone during an acute episode of disturbance, and therefore feels put upon if it is asked to do so, and feels that when someone decompensates they should be allowed to send this client back to the hospital. Perhaps this problem could be handled by having the community mental health center provide some staff support to the community care home while it is dealing with a decompensated patient.

In summary, the halfway house now covers a great variety of facilities from a boarding-home at one extreme to a small chronic care facility at the other, from family homes with two or three guests to mini-institutions under public auspices. Unfortunately the pressure of third-party payers has brought about a professionalisation of staff as the halfway houses try to receive adequate financial compensation. Money is certainly absolutely necessary to provide the social systems in which caring can take place. But as we have tried to indicate, one of the most important contributions the halfway house can make to the care of the chronic psychiatric patient is to provide a setting in which caring can occur, and caring itself, as distinct from the physical surroundings and the social system in which it occurs, cannot be bought and cannot be professionalised. So the current third-party payment system is working to remove the element of caring from the very halfway houses designed to allow it.

Whether caring on a massive scale for the 500,000 individuals for whom we must provide community care can ever be provided without a national work service, I am not prepared to say. In the fields of nursing and of social work we have seen the same kind of pressure to professionalise. Florence Nightingale started nursing to add caring to the treatment of battle casualties. And while nursing consisted mostly of personal sacrifice, the nurse used to be truly wedded to her job. She has now become highly professionalised and one of a large group of therapists. Nuns and monks provided caring through a lifetime of service. We keep adding new non-professionals to the treatment team to provide the caring, while economic necessity soon teaches them to professionalise themselves in some way to improve their pay, leaving the patient again without anyone who can concentrate on just caring. No one will tackle a lifetime of caring. The job can only be done if everyone gives a period of their life over to caring.

The small private community care home can provide physical care and caring at a very low price. As soon as the community care home becomes an institution with a 40-hour work week, its costs will begin to equal those of most hospitals and the caring will again disappear. We must learn to distinguish many different types of community care homes, and we must not let quality control end up as an overemphasis on the measurable aspects of the physical setting and professional treatment, again making caring the neglected stepchild of our programmes.

Our goal should be to provide social settings in which each client will experience at least one caring relationship. We will need research to help us with this task.

Insurers pay for much social support in the guise of treatment, even though Dr May's studies indicate that only basic social support like help in finding housing and jobs affects long-term outcome. They pay for questionable treatments because they are professionally standardised. There are many aftercare programmes where third-party payers finance social, recreational and occupational programmes without even asking the question of how much is needed. We demonstrated sixteen years ago that minimal social support and enrichment can reduce recidivism for chronic psychiatric patients as much as the fancy programmes of today. Could we dream of using the money now expended on unwarranted enrichment to make possible the provision of caring?

References

Clark, A.W. and Yoemans, N.T., *Fraser House: Theory, Practice and Evaluation of a Therapeutic Community* (Springer, New York, 1969).

Glasscote, R.M., Gudeman, J.E. and Elpers, R., *Halfway Houses for the Mentally Ill* (Joint Information Service of the American Psychiatric Association and the National Association for Mental Health, Washington, DC, 1971).

Huessy, H.R., 'Spring Lake Ranch – The Pioneer Halfway House', in Huessy (ed.), *Mental Health with Limited Resources* (Grune and Stratton, New York, 1966). See also other published articles by Huessy.

25 THE ROLE OF THE HALFWAY HOUSE IN COMMUNITY MENTAL HEALTH PROGRAMMES IN THE UNITED KINGDOM AND AMERICA

Elly Jansen

Both in the United Kingdom (1959) and in the United States (1963) a major step in the direction of community mental health was taken by passing a law that made provisions for various measures to counteract the former isolation of the mental patient. It might be expected that among such measures the halfway house would take a prominent place, especially in view of the existing gulf between recommendations for care in and by the community and the unreadiness of the public to implement this. For a start, the relatives of the mentally ill are rarely the appropriate people to accept such responsibility. Whatever causes the onset of emotional or mental illness, the repercussions on family life in terms of feelings of guilt, inadequacy, anger and frustration are such that unless considerable work can be done with the whole family the home is usually not the most beneficial setting for aftercare. Nor can one expect, after a tradition of over a century of separating the mad from the sane, that society as a whole is going to accept, without appropriate education, such a 'dangerous' mixing, in which confusion can arise about what is sanity and who possesses it.

If institutionalising patients may be seen as the consequence of an attitude on the part of society, then the halfway house should be seen not just as a stepping stone for the ex-mental patient, but also as a learning situation for the neighbourhood community – a place of confrontation where the community can recognise its likeness to the disturbed rather than its unlikeness, and take back some of the projections that isolated the patient and impoverished the community previously. In reclaiming its rejects, society could not only rescue individuals but also gain extended awareness of itself and reduce its need to victimise.

In view of the considerable contribution that halfway houses could make to the community mental health programme by undertaking this dual task, it might be expected that the new laws would make ample provision for setting them up. Both laws, however, instead of making halfway houses an essential part of the programme, made them optional on the part of the local or state authorities. This could well reflect lack of confidence in this particular area – and with some reason, since the halfway house concept was, and still is, largely unexplored. It may be commendable that governments wait for the voluntary society to gauge the temperature and take the plunge, but unless funds are available to do just this the provision of halfway houses becomes a hazardous undertaking financially, and indeed is discouraged.

Some Current Projects and Their Philosophies

In spite of financial risks, many isolated attempts to establish these houses are made, especially in America, with the result that there is a kaleidoscope of rational and not-so-rational theories and practices. In their interesting book, *The Halfway House Movement: A Search for Sanity*, Raush and Raush[1] discuss various approaches, accounts of which were written by the directors of the houses concerned. But on visiting such houses I was struck by the discrepancies between write-ups and actual practices. This may well be caused by the complexity of community living where the real transactions are hard to put one's finger on. Some descriptions glorify the halfway house, conveying the impression of a sedate community where disturbances just do not arise, and noticeably pasting over the deep cracks that one glimpses during a visit; while others do not do justice to what appears to be very effective work. There is a dearth of descriptions that deal realistically with the problems and the role conflicts that such a situation must necessarily carry.

From observation it appears that the common denominator in a majority of halfway houses both in England and America is the underestimation of the resident's capacity to take responsibility and of the corresponding need for staff to assume a parental role. This emphasis is slowly shifting to one in which higher expectations are made of residents and in which greater respect is shown. However, the basic 'unlike us' assumption is still prevalent, not only – and appropriately – where the staff role is concerned but also in the usually unconscious valuation of the other as unequal. There are often strong elements of patronage: 'see how well my monkeys can perform tricks', or the kind of pride parents display in the child who begins to walk and talk. Another subtle manifestation of pseudo-equality is the praise and blame, and sometimes overt reward and punishment, that in some houses are accorded by staff to recommendations or decisions made by the residents as a group.

The management principles in the halfway house movement tend to adopt one of two distinct positions:

1. There is still a number of authoritarian houses where the phrase 'management of the patient' is totally relevant: these are impersonal, repressive settings where there is a minimum of conflict because the environment does not permit the luxury of emotional expression. Many of the old-established houses, in spite of their benevolence, carry the stamp of their age. In his survey of halfway houses in England, Robert Apte[2] indicates the disregard of goals and the failure to rehabilitate and to return residents to the community by many houses run on traditional lines, including some recently set up by the local authorities.
2. In contrast, many of the newer houses, particularly those run by voluntary bodies, place an increasing emphasis on self-government and on the contribution each person in the community can make to the recovery of its members. The approach is at times carried to an extreme, when it is considered that whatever happens is therapeutic; some communities as a result of this conviction allow themselves to be at the mercy of the most disturbed members and to go through crisis after crisis, suffering useless pain unaccompanied by proportionate learning.

The virtues of the self-government approach are particularly professed by some of the addiction units which are often called staffless; in reality they are led by ex-patients who have adopted staff roles, without monetary remuneration but sometimes with considerable other gains. Many of these communities feel that the only people who can be of any use are those who have been addicted themselves and who 'see through' the lies and manipulations. The philosophy is often one of salvation by being put through the mill and undergoing humiliation; by the proper response to and acceptance of the punitive treatment, people can progress to an elevated position, e.g. from cleaning the lavatories to lording it over the newcomers. These ideas are well portrayed in the play *The Concept* and in a film on Synanon. One would like to see honesty of confrontation applied, without the indoctrination and punitive aspects that are thought to be essential for success.

In many of the addiction programmes, as well as in some other halfway houses, there is a strong anti-professionalism, a conviction that professionals are a 'dead loss'. Psychotherapy is felt to be a waste of time and money, and it is held that community members can provide all that is needed in this respect. This is often associated with the moral therapy approach, which provides the residents with a firm work programme to counteract the atrophy of their working habits. In the absence of skilled help from other disciplines, the training of staff specifically for this work would seem all the more indicated, but this is considered heretical and a waste of time. (In one house on the east coast the idea of wanting to change people at all is denigrated, but the actual programme of the house happily (I think) shows this to be a false appraisal. The desire to see people progress, as well as opportunities provided for this to occur, are manifest.)

The Richmond Fellowship Experiment

My own ideas have developed from the halfway house experiment which I conducted in Richmond, London, in 1959. It began with few preconceived ideas apart from the firm belief that people's behaviour makes sense, and that the clue to the reconciliation and integration of the 'sick' individual with society lies neither in the authentication of extreme 'sickness' nor in identification with 'sane' society and its demands, but in establishing contact with and between the two.

At the age of 18, while studying psychology, I looked after a group of autistic and other problem children and later, maladjusted youngsters. Being more unaware than most people of what constitutes normal behaviour, my very innocence stood me in good stead. It allowed me to understand eccentric behaviour partly because I expected little in the way of conformity; at the same time it led me to have high expectations in terms of talents, mutual concern and fulfilling obligations because I had no reason not to have them. After ten years of study and training, the experiment at Richmond that led to the formation of the Richmond Fellowship was still largely based on that earlier experience.

During the first six months at Richmond, much anxiety had to be endured – partly the pain of trial and error. To start with, I was on my own, a foreign student in England and without financial, psychiatric or moral support. I had engaged in an experiment for which no guidelines had yet been formulated. The members of the community were a highly intelligent and manipulative group; they did not let up in their efforts to change me so that they need not change, or to press me into parental, nursing or servant roles; they ganged up to test to the utmost whether I was sincere and consistent, and whether I had the wits and willpower to hold firm and realise my concept. It was at times with private despair that I persevered, but eventually my efforts were rewarded by the community's settling down and adopting some of the functions that they had been pressing on me.

Nevertheless, some of my initial notions did not stand the test of the experiment; for example, I soon had to drop the idea of a totally egalitarian community. I was there with a different purpose from the others, motivated for some reason to provide what the others had come there to seek, and whether I liked it or not my role was different: I had to exercise leadership and carry the final responsibility. This did not mean that much was not delegated; it was. But the staffless house proved illusory, and I think that wherever a community of over five or six people exists, even if all members are ex-patients, a leader will be chosen. That leader will be called upon to provide what he, by virtue of his position, can no longer look to others for – leadership, security and, when things go wrong, a scapegoat (in the form of himself unless he can find another). In relinquishing the amateur position, I acknowledged the complexity of the task and the external assistance required to meet the residents' needs, including not just the support of the neighbourhood, but also the initial referral and continued supervision by the psychiatrist.

But where community life was concerned a *modus vivendi* had to be worked out with the residents themselves. It took several months before we were able to agree on our goals in living together – to provide a realistic situation in which the members could be helped and could help one another to understand themselves more fully, and to find legitimate satisfactions through relationships and the re-learning of social skills and work disciplines. *We defined the task as working toward the eventual independence of each member and his reintegration into society.*

The structure we developed had little in it that would not be expected in family or other communal life; but apart from the normal courtesies, it required all members to take responsibility for the common life and its activities, including contact with the locality, the running of the household, and the welfare of the individuals in it. It made attendance at the weekly group meeting obligatory for everyone so that problems could be faced and worked through and practical steps taken with the involvement of each person concerned.

We became less idealistic and more practical about household chores, and members began to confront one another and demand a fair contribution from each, rather than leaving this to 'the staff'. As it was important to establish good working patterns, people who did not have outside employment were required to maintain the house and garden and to start work at 9.00 a.m. Incidentally, this rule rendered the prospect of employment more attractive!

Organisational Expansion and Implications for Staffing

The experiment drew some attention, and within a few months the applications outnumbered the places available, thus indicating the need for further halfway houses. But the problems encountered made it plain that it would be impracticable to duplicate this project *per se*. Each halfway house would, if isolated, have to cope with the maximum odds, and suffer excessive insecurity both in financial and in psychological terms. It became obvious that if halfway houses were to fulfil a major role they would need to join forces, learn from one another, and undertake certain tasks together. For these reasons an organisation was formed, with the task of purchasing properties, raising the necessary funds, negotiating overall financial terms with state and other authorities jointly for all houses, recruiting and training staff, formulating professional standards, acting as a clearing house for providing both staff and residents with the most appropriate placement, and conducting research to explore the comparative effectiveness and merits of various methods.

This organisational approach proved effective. The second house was established by staff and residents from the first house with greater ease and experience, and with greater financial stability and public support. The expansion, at first slow, accelerated. While each house differs according to its purpose and the personality of staff and residents, the basic structure has been found applicable to all, and staff find that they share the same problems. It is in and through the exploration of their common task and the sharing of experiences that the staff members become equipped for this difficult work.[3] From the very beginning emphasis has been given to training the staff and others concerned with community mental health. This has developed into a full-scale college with in-service and full-time courses in group work and human relations.[4]

The quality of the halfway house programme stands or falls with the calibre of staff members, who need a great deal of support and supervision if they are to see the issues and maintain a firm and consistent position, especially when their self-esteem and popularity are at stake. The exercising of responsibility, which the patient has given up by virtue of his breakdown, is the very issue over which the main fights will be fought, often by manipulative acts that corner and threaten staff and make life uncomfortable. The challenge to staff is to treat the individual consistently as a grown-up, with respect for him as a person, and to mobilise the group's resources to recognise and resolve its difficulties. The role of the staff member is a particularly difficult one in that, by virtue of his job, he is both the social worker and part of the everyday environment through which the resident needs to come to terms with his problems; the staff member is the person to whom and about whom many of the residents' complaints are made. He lives on the job and is expected to do without the traditional barriers, yet he needs to maintain a necessary distance and to insist on his own rights and needs.

The Case for the Organisational Approach

The major problem of the halfway house programme is recruiting the right kind of staff and providing appropriate training and supervision. For this reason, many local authorities continue to turn a blind eye to the need for halfway house facilities, and no central government grant has yet been given to promote this work nationally. Many patients therefore are obliged to enter or stay in mental hospitals for no other reason than that the state pays for the hospital services but not for preventive care and aftercare. A similar problem is prevalent in America, where insurance carriers are paying large sums for hospitalisation but not the lesser fees of the halfway house, and where the government pays the often high cost of hospital beds but makes no general allocation of funds for aftercare, thus 'spoiling the ship for a halfpence of tar'. In England this problem is to a considerable extent counteracted by the pressure that an organisation such as the Fellowship can exercise; but in America the lack of a joint representation is very evident, witnessed not only by the financial struggle but also by the scarcity of staff. Halfway houses are few and far between, and sharing of experience is too often merely on the basis of defending the status quo of each house. On this basis it is hardly reasonable to expect firm government support, but it appears that, even if a superlative case can be made for support, the government administration (in America even more complex than in England) will defeat any but the most indefatigable demand for subsidy.

It is clear that through lack of co-ordination, much learning and experience are wasted, too little comparison takes place, and too many staff members and ventures fail, with a wastage of energy, goodwill, courage and money. If the halfway house movement is going to cope, and cope effectively, with the many patients in need of help and with its educational task, it is necessary not only to co-ordinate efforts but also to explore and research the various approaches.

Intra- and Inter-Organisational Problems

Yet this is not to say that an organisation does not present difficulties too. There are the obvious mutual phantasies between the branches and the centre, which exist in every organisation and which are intensified in this insecure and potentially explosive field. Instead of having to cope with an outright and external reality, e.g. having to find the necessary funds, staff members have a tendency to abdicate responsibility, to lose sight of financial realities, and to become antagonistic about restrictions on spending. The problems with which the staff in the houses have to cope are often such that they in turn wish to act out, and attach their feelings to inappropriate issues, especially in relation to the parent body. This then appears to be a depriving object, withholding material and emotional food and failing to protect staff from crises in which their self-respect, adequacy and general personality are under fire. Under strain, staff often act out by ignoring routine administrative requirements – a manoeuvre that distracts from the original problem but solves nothing. To recognise the issues and make straightforward and appropriate representation is an essential part of staff maturation, not only as an organisational necessity but also because the residents identify with the staff and use them as models.

In estranging the parent body (i.e. the very people who are most needed to give support), alternative support is looked for, at times in the form of the psychiatric consultant or the local house committee, who are invited to support the house director and if possible are split off. Because of their proximity to the house and their desire to assist, or at times to take over, the psychiatrist or the committee can easily collude, unwittingly support irrational demands, and increase the tension. Sooner or later the situation, driven to its logical conclusion, becomes clear to the committee; they reverse their verdict, and suddenly the house director finds he stands alone and understandably feels deserted. It requires education and regular contact to ensure that the centre works together with the house committee as well as the staff, and to give the staff the maximum and businesslike support with appropriate expectations, flexibility, and demands.

Relationships with other organisations in this field are usually complex and understandably give rise to some problems. There is, for example, the potential rivalry and ambivalence between organisations that have some of their tasks in common. This presents as lack of co-operation or as definite obstruction, or as reluctance on the part of mental hospitals to let go of the charges who have traditionally been in their custody. This problem was highlighted by Dr Temple Phillips in an article in *The Medical Officer*.[5] A survey carried out by the Fellowship on discharge procedures of mental hospitals in the UK revealed that of the 25 per cent that returned the questionnaire less than 50 per cent had a procedure for systematic consideration of aftercare for patients. Frequently the patients referred are not those with whom the most can be achieved but those who have become a management or disposal problem for the hospital. Some hospitals do not refer because they feel the problem is too great to tackle it at all; the financial battles involved in getting adequate grant aid make for the all too easy solution of keeping the more integrated patient in the hospital, where he makes a welcome addition to the acute and chronic patients to whom the community mental health programme would inevitably restrict the hospital population. Understandably, because of its diminished role, the hospital staff may wish to take part in the new developments. Consequently some hospitals take a halfway house under their wing, thereby creating hospital wards in the community instead of encouraging the separate functioning of the halfway house as a social (as distinct from a medical) agency, to which the psychiatrist could act as consultant.

Conclusion

I have pointed out the contribution that halfway houses can and should make to the community mental health programme, and argued the case for an organisational approach; obviously the effectiveness of any social work organisation will depend on the quality of thought and work it can engender on all levels, and the right combination of flexibility with maintenance of standards. Major obstacles to the organisational approach always lie in the threat of constraints and in the question of what degree of independence may have to be surrendered in return for the benefits afforded – a question that assumes that similar constraints do not operate in isolation. In conclusion, and with recognition of my bias, I wish to submit the proposition that if halfway houses grow up independently from each other, the movement cannot but be condemned to insignificance, amateurism and instability. If the halfway houses are to fulfil their potential within the community mental health programme and to meet the great demand, they will need to join forces, to use hospital and community resources to the full, and to receive the requisite financial aid from the government with assistance from foundations and many sectors of the community.

Notes

1. J.L. Raush and C.L. Raush, *The Halfway House Movement: A Search for Sanity* (Appleton-Century-Crofts, New York, 1968).
2. R. Apte, 'The Transitional Hostel in the Rehabilitation of the Mentally Ill' in G. McLachlan (ed.), *Problems and Progress in Medical Care* (Oxford University Press, London, 1966).
3. A. Julia, 'A Hostel for the Mentally Ill as a Stepping Stone in the Community', in *New Thinking about Institutional Care* (Association of Social Workers, London, 1967), pp. 68–75.
4. E. Jansen, 'The Therapeutic Community and its Implications for Training' unpublished paper read at a conference for Medical Officers of Health, London, April 1968; E. Jansen and D.A. Pond, 'The Richmond Fellowship', *British Journal of Psychiatry* (April 1968).
5. H.T. Phillips, 'Hostels for the Mentally Disordered', *The Medical Officer* (February 1966).

LIST OF CONTRIBUTORS

Thomas F. Barton was a Counsellor at Overing Apartments, Soundview, Throgsneck CMHC, Bronx, New York. Now, Executive Director, Gateway Communities, Inc., Stamford, Connecticut, USA.

Joseph H. Berke, Co-Director Arbours Association, Ex-Resident of Kingsley Hall.

Anthony Bloom at the time of writing was Archbishop of Western Europe of the Russian Orthodox Church. Now, Metropolitan of Sourozh.

Theodore Cooper was then Assistant Secretary of Health. Now, Dean of New York University Medical School, USA.

David F. Crompton was then Director of Social Services, London Borough of Havering. Now deceased.

Norman Fowler MP was then Conservative Shadow Minister for Health and Social Services. Now, Minister of Transport.

Pierre Gauthier, Director of the School of Psycho-Education, University of Montreal, and Lecturer in Psycho-Education, Richmond Fellowship College, London.

Sue Harris at the time of writing was Supervising Psychologist at East New York Mental Health Center, and Researcher, Community Alternatives for Schizophrenics.

Peter Hawkins was then Warden/Tutor; now, Supervisor/Training Officer, Richmond Fellowship, London.

Howard A. Hoffman, Associate Medical Director and Director of Education, The Psychiatric Institute, Washington DC, USA.

Hans R. Huessy, Director Outpatient Psychiatry Service, Medical Center Hospital of Vermont, USA.

Elly Jansen, Founder and Director of The Richmond Fellowship UK and International.

Michael Kelly, Supervisor, The Richmond Fellowship, London.

Thomas Main, Chairman, Medical Executive Committee, The Cassel Hospital, Ham Common, Ham, Surrey.

Frank M. Ochberg was then Director, Division of Mental Health Service Programmes, National Institute of Mental Health, USA. Now, Commissioner of Mental Health, State of Michigan, USA.

Maryann C. Phillips was then lecturer at Brunel University. Now, part-time Lecturer at the Richmond Fellowship College, London.

M.A.J. Romme, Professor of Psychiatry, University of Maastricht, and Chief Adviser to the Dutch Mental Health Inspectorate.

Mitchell Rosenthal, President, Phoenix House Foundation, New York, USA.

Harley C. Shands, Director of the Psychiatric Service at the Roosevelt Hospital, New York, USA.

Elisabeth Shoenberg was then Consultant Psychiatrist, Claybury Hospital and WHO. Now, Visiting Consultant to Australia on mental health for Aborigines.

Michael H. Wells, Director, Spring Lake Ranch, Inc., Cuttingsville, Vermont, USA.

INDEX

For Product Safety Concerns and Information please contact our EU
representative GPSR@taylorandfrancis.com
Taylor & Francis Verlag GmbH, Kaufingerstraße 24, 80331 München, Germany

www.ingramcontent.com/pod-product-compliance
Ingram Content Group UK Ltd.
Pitfield, Milton Keynes, MK11 3LW, UK
UKHW022024061126
477531UK00002B/15

* 9 7 8 1 0 4 1 4 3 8 8 5 4 *